Crisis Communications

Now in its sixth edition, this book provides engaging, practice-oriented case studies analyzing communication professionals' crisis preparation and responses, illustrating key considerations for communicating with both internal and external stakeholders during and after a crisis.

This edition continues its strength as a student-friendly text that demonstrates how to craft, target, and deliver messages during crises in order to mitigate further controversy and distress. Classic cases lay the foundation, while contemporary cases shed light on cutting-edge practices in use today. Many cases from previous editions have been updated and new cases added, including the COVID-19 crisis and U.S. vaccination campaign; Starbucks and racial discrimination at a Philadelphia branch; Will Smith and the Academy Awards slap; the role of Gander, Newfoundland in supporting stranded tourists after the attacks of September 11, 2001; and a look at how schools can prepare communication responses to school shootings. Each case pays particular attention to the actual and ideal use of social media in the crisis and there is a new section on the important issues of misinformation and disinformation.

Crisis Communications, 6th Edition is intended for courses in crisis communication, crisis management, disaster response, corporate communications, and public relations.

Student and instructor online support materials feature selected previous editions' case studies no longer in this edition, as well as an Instructor's Manual with suggested activities, discussion questions, and sample quizzes: www.routledge.com/9780367894450.

Kathleen Fearn-Banks is a tenured professor with emeritus status in the Department of Communication at the University of Washington, USA.

Kevin Kawamoto is a former associate professor at the University of Hawaii at Manoa, USA.

Routledge Communication Series
Jennings Bryant/Dolf Zillmann, Series Editors

For a full list of titles please visit: www.routledge.com/Routledge-Communication-
Series/book-series/RCS.

Crisis Communications

A Casebook Approach

Sixth Edition

Kathleen Fearn-Banks with Kevin Kawamoto

Routledge
Taylor & Francis Group

NEW YORK AND LONDON

Designed cover image: RichLegg/© Getty Images

Sixth edition published 2024
by Routledge
605 Third Avenue, New York, NY 10158

and by Routledge
4 Park Square, Milton Park, Abingdon, Oxon, OX14 LGB 4RN

Routledge is an imprint of the Taylor & Francis Group, an informa business

First edition published by Routledge 2011

Fifth edition published by Routledge 2017

Library of Congress Cataloging-in-Publication Data
Names: Fearn-Banks, Kathleen, author. | Kawamoto, Kevin, author.
Title: Crisis communications : a casebook approach / Kathleen
    Fearn-Banks with Kevin Kawamoto.
Description: Sixth edition. | New York, NY : Routledge, 2024. |
    Revised edition of Crisis communications, 2017. | Includes
    bibliographical references and index.
Identifiers: LCCN 2023059110 (print) | LCCN 2023059111 (ebook) |
    ISBN 9780367894566 (hardback) | ISBN 9780367894450
    (paperback) | ISBN 9781003019282 (ebook)
Subjects: LCSH: Public relations—Case studies. | Crisis
    management—Case studies. | Advertising—Case studies.
Classification: LCC HD59 .F37 2024 (print) | LCC HD59 (ebook) |
    DDC 659.2—dc23/eng/20240223
LC record available at https://lccn.loc.gov/2023059110
LC ebook record available at https://lccn.loc.gov/2023059111

ISBN: 978-0-367-89456-6 (hbk)
ISBN: 978-0-367-89445-0 (pbk)
ISBN: 978-1-003-01928-2 (ebk)

DOI: 10.4324/9781003019282

Typeset in Sabon
by Apex CoVantage, LLC

Brief Contents

Contents

Preface

The world is fraught with crises, and the United States is not an exception. The environment and climate change affect the entire globe; the people are the causes of the crises (flooding, wildfires, the melting of glaciers) as well as the victims. Pandemics, epidemics, and syndemics continue to adversely affect life. HIV/AIDS (human immunodeficiency virus and acquired immune deficiency syndrome) began their damage worldwide in the 1970s. There are treatments and preventions but the disease remains. COVID-19 started its deadly spread in 2020; preventions and treatments were developed but the disease remains. Gun violence is rampant in the United States more than other countries. There are no promises of relief. There has been, in recent years, a rise in being unkind. It is like people were given permission to be mean, hateful, and eager to harm others.

Ignorance is the great similarity that ties all these crises together. Crisis communications cannot solve all the world's crises, but it can be used to educate, inform, persuade, and convince. The right words must be delivered by the best methods to the right people who will act.

This, the sixth edition of *Crisis Communications: A Casebook Approach*, features case studies in crisis communications achieving some measure of success to solve or ease crises. Lessons can be learned if you, the professional, want to institute tactics and strategies by understanding what others have done successfully.

Chapter 1 **Crisis Communications Today** centers on the status of the field, including journalism and other information gathering and presentations of that information. It introduces a section "Disinformation and Misinformation," terms that describe many communications in recent years.

Chapter 2 **Crisis Communications Theory** centers on suggested theories academic research has developed. It presents crisis communications vocabulary. It concludes with a new case study "Will Smith and the Academy Awards Slap," a discussion of a well-known illustration of the apologia theory.

Chapter 3 **The "Textbook Crises"** are "Exxon and the *Valdez* Oil Spill" and "Johnson & Johnson and the Tylenol Murders," so named because they gave birth to crisis communications as a field of study and a profession. Each case study has an update.

Chapter 4 **History-Making Crises** was added as a chapter because the included crises, marked by numerous deaths, are frequently revisited by the news media and crisis communicators when similar crises occur. "Thinking Outside the Box" centers on the COVID-19 crisis in the United States and the national campaign to get people to get vaccinated. It set the tone for the health battle to lower death rates. "Gander, Newfoundland and 9/11" goes back to September 11, 2011 when Canadians in Gander, a town of only 10,000 people, hosted for several days 6,700 European tourists whose flights were diverted when U.S. airspace was closed after the 9/11 attacks. "Columbine High School and the Shooting Tragedy" was not the first, but it is like the grandfather of school shootings. When school massacres occur, they are inevitably compared to this 1999 shooting in Littleton, Colorado. Added is a new update/case study "Hoping for the Best, Anticipating the Worst," on how crisis communications for schools might prepare for a shooter since they seem to be likely. In 2023, they averaged more than one a month. "Hurricane Katrina and New Orleans" has turned out to be the grandmother of hurricane crises, the one by which others are compared. The update/case study (longer than an update but shorter than a case study), "Hurricane Katrina, New Orleans, and Brad Pitt," is an account of how one solution to the 2005 hurricane backfired.

Chapter 5 **Communications to Prevent Crisis** is a slightly revised chapter addressing communications to various targeted publics.

Chapter 6 **Communications When the Crisis Strikes** considers coping with the news media and lawyers during a crisis. A new case study, "At Starbucks, Lawyers Can Prevent Crises," features a Starbucks corporate lawyer and how her work and the work of the Starbucks crisis communications team softened a racial disturbance.

Chapter 7 **Social Media and Crisis Communications** is a revised chapter with new observations by professionals.

Chapter 8 **Culture Crises** looks at the case of AIDS in Africa, revised and updated, featuring the following countries: Botswana, Zambia, Uganda, South Africa, Zimbabwe, and Eswatini (formerly Swaziland). Added is an update/case study "HIV/AIDS Plus COVID-19, a Syndemic," a look at how both diseases impacted the countries studied. "Nut Rage and Korean Airlines" is a case study following the Cho family heading Korean Airlines, a chaebol family which thinks of itself as royalty, a chasm between the haves and the have nots. "Yuhan-Kimberly and Baby Wet Wipes" is from the previous editions with an added update which relates to another aspect of Korean culture. "Saginaw Valley State University and the Theater

Controversy" is repeated from other editions and centers on how a university president dealt with a student play centered on sexual preference.

Chapter 9 **Transportation Crises**. "Holland America Line and Cruise Crises" is a repeat of the crisis in previous editions but adds an update/case study on how cruise companies battled COVID-19. "US Airways and 'The Miracle on the Hudson'" is the original case study still worth discussing even though the airline no longer exists. The commercial flight struck by birds made a successful emergency landing manned by a skillful pilot. The communications were still a difficult job.

Chapter 10 **Truth and Privacy**. "Wendy's and the Finger-in-the-Chili Hoax" is a repeat of how Wendy's crisis communicator quietly fought a woman who falsely charged that she found a finger in her cup of chili. "Mini-Case: Dominos Pizza" presents a brief treatment of how employees betrayed Dominos and what the company did in response.

Chapter 11 **The Crisis Communications Plan** presents a step-by-step plan on how to develop the crisis communications plan.

This edition includes five completely new case studies, four update/case studies associated with the chapters they follow, one new section to the introductory chapter, numerous updates, and a mini-case study followed by instructions on how to develop a crisis communications plan, a sample crisis communications plan for a non-profit, a crisis communications plan for a small business, and a new plan for after a cyberattack.

Acknowledgments

All the people I shall mention here were very valuable to me in producing this sixth edition of *Crisis Communications: A Casebook Approach* and I thank them and honor them.

My editorial team is first. Kevin Kawamoto joined me this time as co-author. Writing a book during a pandemic was demanding. Fortunately, Kevin and I have, for many years, regularly exchanged emails and dissected nearly every crisis in the news. What crises could be avoided? Which were handled poorly? Which had interesting conflicts? His knowledge and abilities are admirable. Joining us as editor and contributor was April Peterson. Both of them have earned Ph.D. degrees in communication from the University of Washington where I was a professor for 30 years until I earned emeritus status in 2020. Both of them have professional experience in mass communications and university teaching. Kevin, April, and I live on three different U.S. coasts, three different time zones—April on the East Coast, Kevin on the Hawaiian coast, and I on the West Coast. This communication would not have been possible several years ago. Darius Presley, a recent UW graduate, was technical advisor.

Also very special to us was the team from Routledge/Taylor & Francis: Felisa Salvago-Keyes, Sean Daly, and Emma Brown. Understanding, helpful, persistent, and cooperative are words to describe them. Contributing writers were communications professionals Kim Hunter, Elodie Fichet, and Susan West. Anthony Hill's assistance was especially valuable.

Simona Simmons was an excellent research assistant. Zabrina Jenkins at Starbucks was a great interview, as well as a speaker in my crisis communications course. Valuable data came from Peter Kahle and Lani Jacobsen, and also from Mark Canlis and his assistant, Abby Lewis, at the Seattle fine dining restaurant Canlis. Artist Gina Arnold has contributed drawings for all editions. In this volume, she provided drawings of a phone booth in Gander, Canada and picket signs at Starbucks. Tina Wilson, Jeremy Fearn, and Erik Elvejord provided photos for figures. Professional Copy & Print provided copies and electronic transmissions.

Undergraduate student researchers in the Crisis Communications course were Mikal Bailey, Savanna Ellis, Navin Fernandes, Kathrine Guzik, Saif Kelawala, Mikaela Lobe, Justin Lowe, Patricia Madij, Tyler Nixon, Isabella Qiao, Ida Roennow, Beverly Shane, Chandler Stein, Adrianne Stowe, Claudia Yaw, and others.

Chapter 1

Crisis Communications Today

The most devastating crisis in the United States and the rest of the world since the last edition of this textbook was published (2017) is undoubtedly the Coronavirus-19, commonly called COVID-19, and its variants. The death toll passed one million in the United States in mid-2022 (Johnson, 2022). The global death toll was nearly 7 million by the end of 2023 (World Health Organization, 2023).

Also devastating were the statistics of mass shootings. The U.S. totals are higher than in any other country. According to *Education Week*, 188 school shootings took place between 2018 and 2023 in which at least one person was killed or injured (2023). It is likely that more occurred after this volume went to press because they occur so frequently—so frequently that those with low numbers of deaths often are not reported by national newscasts.

There were numerous airline crises. Fortunately, these crises were not commercial crashes. Travelers reached their destinations and when they returned home, their luggage didn't. Prior to this edition of this book, the last fatal crash in the United States was 13 years previously. But there was extreme cruelty and rudeness to a greater degree than any time in the history of flight travel. During the COVID-19 pandemic, travelers were violent and rude to flight attendants and other airline personnel, and to other passengers. Much of this was related to a refusal to follow government and airline rules about masking. Before the pandemic, news releases from the airlines seemed laughable until one considered how serious they were. Passengers were trouble in many ways other than violence. They brought with them their "emotional support" cat, peacock, miniature horse, diapered duck, hamster, rodent, a smelly pig whose owner wanted it to have a seat, a cello whose owner wanted it to have its own seat, a flying squirrel, an aggressive pit bull, and a French bulldog not as aggressive because it died in the overhead bin. The passengers also charged the airlines with unforgiveable conditions—toilets that did not work; a man was trapped in a restroom with a faulty door; a woman said she had to sit for 11 hours on a urine-soaked seat; flight attendants made fun of a child named "Abcde."

DOI: 10.4324/9781003019282-1

Then in 2022, the airlines could not keep enough staff and crew to keep schedules on time, so thousands of flights were canceled (Figure 1.1). During year-end holidays, so many people never got to their intended destinations and celebrations and in many cases, did not return home easily.

Attacks by racists and homophobes raged. A Black man in Minnesota, George Floyd, was killed when a policeman stepped on his neck while passersby videoed the crime on their cell phones for the world to see. A Black woman in Kentucky, Breonna Taylor, asleep in her bed, was shot to death by police who were in the wrong residence seeking a criminal. Attacks of people of Asian descent for no apparent reason other than they were Asian took place on city streets. Peaceful demonstrations turned into riots. People were killed; businesses in Los Angeles, Seattle, and other cities were destroyed and looted.

Acts of God are usually not held against people, but that is often not the case today. There was excessive flooding, greater wildfires, extreme heat, record snowfall, and hurricanes late in the year when hurricane season is generally over. God didn't do it but much of the population has not learned some climate change crises are caused by humans. So often, nothing is done.

Crisis communicators cannot solve all crises—but often, communications can be part of the management of a crisis. For example, the January 6, 2021, attack on the U.S. Capitol by a violent mob was a series of crimes, not crises. The legal system solves crimes. A crisis communications team could be hired to clear up the name and reputation of the former U.S. Capitol Police Chief Steven Sund, who resigned the day after the insurrection because, as he said, his "men and women were not adequately warned."

Figure 1.1 In 2022, airlines had so many canceled flights that many passengers, eager to travel after the wearying pandemic, never made it to their end-of-year holiday destinations. If they had scheduled connected flights, often they made the initial flight but the connection was canceled and they were stuck away from home.

Source: Eviart/Shutterstock.com

There are crises than can be helped and even solved by effective communications, but not all crises. For example, apologies can ease poor relations between individuals or groups. Communications was used to persuade people to get vaccinated for COVID-19 and also to wear masks. Scientists developed vaccines to treat the virus; crisis communicators developed campaigns to get people to accept the treatment. Cruise ship companies lost tens of billions of dollars due to the COVID-19 pandemic (Hines, 2020). For a while it seemed cruising was doomed, but then the marketing departments made deals that were too good to refuse. Public relations (PR) departments—crisis communicators—went on social media, print media, and electronic media persuading future and past travelers that the ships and the crews were pristine and ready for travelers. Soon, the cruise ships were seeing their goal of "butts in beds."

Some crises are solved by non-communications management methods, some by lawyers, and some by government agencies. Lobbyists use communications to prevent or settle crises experienced by their clients. Crisis communications can clear confusion, inform answers to problems, correct false information, or suggest solutions and many tasks, but they all involve communications through many channels.

The crisis communicator's job is more difficult today because many—if not most—crises are compounded with other crises. Political instability is added to the issues of mass shootings and gun control. Is the crisis at the southern border (Figure 1.2) just immigration, or is it also political instability? Political instability enters the picture when one questions the spread of COVID-19, when one asks why climate change is mostly ignored.

Figure 1.2 Immigrants seeking asylum in the United States have appeared in great numbers at the Mexican border. This is a crisis not near settlement as this book went to press. These hopefuls were at Yuma, Arizona in 2021.

Source: Ringo Chiu/Shutterstock.com

When it comes to crisis communications, the most dire issue is that all of these crises have been affected by misinformation and disinformation. Crisis communicators, like journalists, are bound by truth. Crisis communicators can originate true information or false information. Journalists and crisis communicators know that a half truth is a whole lie, and they can pass true information through mass media and social media, so it is imperative to make the commitment to truth first.

This chapter explains misinformation and disinformation after first explaining basic crisis communications terms and tools.

Crisis communications demands that one use the best crafted truthful message (fact) delivered by the most effective method to the precise public (audience). This has not changed. What has changed is the fact that social media make it possible for faster communication than traditional methods and to a very precise, often chosen, public. The message still needs to be carefully written—mistakes on social media can live forever—but social media encourage rapid and frequent two-way communication between an organization and its segmented publics, without a gatekeeper. Social media can build positive or negative relationships with these publics.

So what the new technology has done is present new methods of communicating faster and possibly better. It has not eliminated the need for traditional methods, and it has not changed the facts of human behavior—ethical and professional standards, the basic tenets of crisis communications.

What Is a Crisis, and What Is Crisis Communications?

A *crisis* is a major occurrence with a potentially negative outcome affecting the organization, company, or industry, as well as its publics, products, services, or good name. A crisis interrupts normal business transactions and can sometimes threaten the existence of the organization. A crisis can be a strike, terrorism, a fire, a boycott, product tampering, product failure, or numerous other events (see the list in Chapter 11, p. 322, Table 11.1). The size of the organization is irrelevant. It can be a multinational corporation, a one-person business, or even an individual.

Public relations professionals often say, "I have a crisis every day." This is an exaggeration, of course. The term *crisis* denotes something more serious than a "problem." Public relations people deal with problems—solving them or avoiding them. By definition, however, a crisis interrupts the normal flow of business, so a crisis cannot be a normal part of this flow. Many professionals use the term strategic communications to mean public relations, but public relations is preferred because it stresses that the field is about relationships more than strategy. On the other hand, a crisis is not necessarily so catastrophic that the life of the organization is destroyed. Exxon suffered the crisis of crises after its oil spill in 1989. It still suffers from a bad image, but it continues to thrive in business. (See the Exxon case in Chapter 3.)

This book advises you to plan for the worst that can happen, whether it be a crisis or a problem, and it brings us to another expression: "Be prepared." This book shows you how to prepare yourself and your organization to cope with crises that may occur. It deals with preparations made far in advance, as well as with strategies and tactics to be used during a crisis. It examines the experiences of public relations professionals in crises, describing what they did, what they wished they had done, and what hampered their progress. You can learn from their successes and failures.

In a crisis—in contrast to a problem—emotions are on edge, brains are not fully functioning, and events are occurring so rapidly that drafting a plan during a crisis is unthinkable. Simply following one is difficult.

Crisis management is a process of strategic planning for a crisis or negative turning point, a process that removes some of the risk and uncertainty from the negative occurrence and thereby allows the organization to be in greater control of its own destiny.

Crisis communications is the dialogue between the organization and its public(s) prior to, during, and after the negative occurrence. The dialogue details strategies and tactics designed to minimize damage to the image of the organization.

Effective crisis management includes crisis communications that not only can alleviate or eliminate the crisis but also can sometimes bring the organization a more positive reputation than it had before the crisis.

Public relations deals with publics. *Publics* are the specific audiences targeted by programs. People frequently use the term "general public," but public relations professionals are usually more specific in their targeting. Examples of corporate publics include groups such as employees, customers, stockholders, community members, board members, unions, and retirees.

Proactive public relations programs can be used to build relationships with certain publics. They can prevent crises; they can also make these publics supportive when there is a crisis. Trust is at the heart of each type of public relations.

These programs might be the following.

- *Media relations:* Building a positive relationship with the news media so they know you are reliable, professional, accurate, and ethical. Tactics for the news media would include not only news releases but also pitch letters, backgrounders, media advisories, media tours, news conferences, and others.

- *Community relations:* Building a positive relationship with community leaders, organizations, families, and individuals. Tactics may include advisory boards, open houses, speakers' bureaus, public service announcements, CSR (corporate social responsibility) activities, exhibits, and scholarships.
- *Employee/internal relations:* Building a bond with employees even if there are only one or two, making employees feel a part of the organization. These would be volunteers in non-profit organizations. Tactics would be the use of an intranet, newsletters, and other house organs, closed-circuit television (CCTV), email and other social media, contests, awards, and gifts.
- *Consumer relations:* Building a mutual bond between the company and its customers. A returns policy, tours, sales advantages, brochures, posters/flyers, open houses, educational material, and a complaint system are possibilities.

There can also be programs for government relations, labor relations, international relations, investor relations, and others. An organization depends on these publics for survival because they have some stake in the organization.

Public relations is concerned with reputation. It exists to avoid a negative image and to create or enhance a positive reputation. It is largely the fear of a negative image that causes organizations to develop public relations departments, hire public relations agencies, or both. Too often, an organization does not consider utilizing public relations until it is in a crisis. Then it wants a speedy recovery.

Research shows that companies with ongoing two-way communications often avoid crises or endure crises of shorter duration or of lesser magnitude (see Chapter 2, "Crisis Communications Theory"). Research also shows that companies with a crisis management and/or crisis communications plan come out of a crisis with a more positive image than companies without such a plan.

Whether an organization is a large multinational company or a small business, a *crisis communications plan* is needed. A crisis communications plan is preferably a part of a company-wide *crisis management plan* that includes sections on evacuation, work sites, equipment, and so on. If a company does not have a crisis management plan, a crisis communications plan is still advisable—even urgent.

The media to which you have tried unsuccessfully to pitch ideas for news stories, the media that toss "perfect" news releases in the trash, the media that never return phone calls—those media will call on you in a crisis. They will probably not telephone in advance. They will show up on your premises "in your face." The media, seeing themselves as advocates for the people, can be the principal adversaries in a crisis.

This is a time when public relations takes front and center—in a very crucial way. This is not to say that public relations will operate independently—that might be a greater disaster. It is a time, however, when the CEO (chief executive officer) may listen to the PR pro whose name he can never remember.

Sometimes, even in a crisis, the head of the company or organization does not listen because business schools often teach CEOs to make their own decisions. There are many documented cases of disasters during which CEOs acted independently. The Exxon crisis is an example. Exxon's CEO, Laurence Rawl, did not respond as the media and environmentalists would have preferred. He did not accept responsibility as rapidly as critics felt he should have. He did not fly to Valdez to express concern. All the moves the public relations experts would advise, Rawl ignored. Rawl is not alone among corporate heads in his response, but the number of bad responses is declining as organizations learn the effects of public opinion.

In a crisis, when everyone else is in a state of panic, public relations practitioners must offer a calming presence: "This is not as bad as it seems" or "This could be worse. We cannot turn crises into catastrophes. This is what we do."

The Five Stages of a Crisis

A crisis has five stages:

1. detection;
2. prevention/preparation;
3. containment;
4. recovery;
5. learning.

Detection

The detection phase may begin with noting warning signs, or what Barton (1993) referred to as *prodromes* or the *prodromal stage*. Some crises have no noticeable prodromes, but many do.

When an organization in the same business as yours suffers a crisis, it is a warning to your organization. The 1982 Tylenol tampering case was a prodrome to other manufacturers of over-the-counter drugs. Most companies heeded that warning and now use tamper-proof containers. Imagine how many crises were avoided by noticing that what happened to Tylenol could happen to other companies.

On the other hand, Johnson & Johnson itself had little warning before it was hit with this crisis. No one had ever before poisoned an over-the-counter painkiller; it was not a crisis which Johnson & Johnson had anticipated. The only warning the company had was a phone call from a journalist from the *Chicago Tribune*, taken by a Johnson & Johnson public relations staff member. The journalist asked questions about the company's holdings, the spelling of names, and so forth. The employee reported the call to supervisors, who called the newspaper and found out that there were deaths attributed to Tylenol (see Chapter 3, "Johnson & Johnson and the Tylenol Murders").

The *Exxon Valdez* oil spill was a prodrome to other companies as well as Exxon itself. Oil companies now know better how to prevent spills, how to clean up spills, and how to react to the public after spills.

There are other less obvious prodromes. Employee discontent over any issue is a sign of a brewing crisis. Perhaps there is an increase in complaints about work hours, work conditions, or unreasonable supervisors. Any one of these and many more issues can be an early sign of a work stoppage. The same prodromes can be early signs of workplace violence.

An organization should watch for prodromes and make attempts to stop a crisis at this stage, before it develops into a full-blown crisis. To detect these early signs, organizations form employee committees that function like lighthouse keepers watching for vessels at sea, watchdogs, or whistle-blowers. These whistle-blowers report warning signs to organization officials who can implement plans to avoid the impending crisis or at least have time to prepare to address the media or other publics.

Crisis detection also refers to a system within the organization in which key personnel are immediately notified of a crisis. An organization has a considerable advantage if it knows about a crisis before its publics do, especially before the news media get the tip. This gives the organization time to draft a statement, make preparations for a news conference, notify the crisis team, and call in spokespersons. As mentioned earlier, the phone call from a *Chicago Tribune* journalist gave Johnson & Johnson some lead time before the public knew about the Tylenol murders.

Crisis Prevention

Ongoing public relations programs and regular two-way communications build relationships with key publics and thereby prevent crises, lessen the blows of crises, or limit the duration of crises.

The establishment of a corporate culture conducive to the positive and open interaction of members also minimizes crises, as does including crisis management in the strategic planning process (see Chapter 2, "Crisis Communications Theory").

There are other specific tactics and actions that an organization may adopt to prevent crises. These tactics must be communicated to appropriate publics. A company must not only do what is right. *It also must tell its publics that it is taking appropriate action.* This may appear to be bragging, but if the company does not reveal ethical and professional business practices, publics will never know. Crisis prevention tactics include the following.

1. fostering the continued development of organizational policies that allow for updates and changes based on variances of publics and mission;
2. reducing the use of hazardous material and processes;
3. initiating safety training and providing rewards for employees with stellar safety records;
4. allowing the free flow of information from employees to management, with no punishment of employees who deliver bad news;
5. following up on past crises or problems;
6. attending community meetings;
7. developing a community board with key outside members who are public opinion leaders;
8. circulating a newsletter to frequent consumers;
9. offering scholarships to employees and their children, as well as to other children in the community;
10. hosting community or employee picnics;
11. sponsoring community activities, such as Little League teams and charities.

In communications, diligence can sometimes prevent crises. A public relations executive in the Midwest tells of a telephone call from a West Coast journalist at 5 p.m., just as she was leaving for the weekend. She could easily have refused the call, but she decided to take it. The reporter was preparing to write a story for a big city newspaper about the failure of a product manufactured by the PR executive's company. The story was one that could have sparked a full-scale crisis. The PR person took the time to locate information that proved the information to be baseless. The reporter was satisfied and the crisis that could have been was averted.

If all members of the management staff are trained to be media savvy, numerous crises can be prevented. Using the preceding story, the PR executive could have consulted a respected expert on the issue to refute the charges and nip them in the bud. Public relations personnel and key organizational leaders should always be aware of who these experts are and of how to reach them in emergencies. Prompt responses to media inquiries are also a plus.

Crisis Preparation

Crisis preparation is necessary for dealing with crises that cannot be prevented. Pepsi had no way of anticipating the scare in which hypodermic syringes were found in cans of Diet Pepsi. The presence of these syringes in the cans cried "AIDS"—acquired immune deficiency syndrome—and fear of the illness and death far surpassed brand loyalty.

The crisis communications plan is the primary tool of preparedness (see Chapter 11, "The Basic Crisis Communications Plan"). This plan tells each key person on the crisis team what his or her role is, whom to notify, how to reach people, what to say, and so on. The crisis communications plan provides a functioning collective brain for all persons involved in a crisis, persons who may not operate at normal capacity due to the shock or emotions of the crisis event.

Containment

Containment refers to the effort to limit the duration of the crisis or to keep it from spreading to other areas affecting the organization.

Pepsi used an advertisement to end its crisis. After several hoaxes had been exposed without the discovery of one documented case of a syringe in a can after the original incident, the company decided the crisis was over and told the world so. And it was.

Foodmaker, Inc., parent company of the fast-food chain Jack in the Box, was charged by PR critics with delaying the resolution of an *E. coli* crisis that killed several children and one adult in 1993 because the company did not take responsibility for the tainted meat soon enough. However, as long as people—especially children—were sick and dying, there was no way Foodmaker could curtail the crisis. It was contained to the Pacific Northwest and did not affect all outlets of the chain, and Jack in the Box communicated to consumers that other food products in the restaurants were not contaminated.

Recovery

Recovery involves efforts to return the company to business as usual. Organizations want to leave the crisis behind and restore normalcy as soon as possible. Recovery may also mean restoring the confidence of key publics, which means communicating a return to normal business.

Snapps, a fast-food restaurant in Fort Pierce, Florida, suffered from a rumor that one of its managers had AIDS and had infected hamburgers. To implement recovery, health department officials participated in a news conference telling the public that all managers had been tested, that none had the AIDS virus, and that the virus could not be transmitted through hamburgers.

Exxon attempted to recover from the *Valdez* oil spill by making efforts to persuade tourists that Alaska was still a beautiful place to visit. It is particularly interesting that Exxon looked beyond its own recovery to the way its crisis had affected the tourism industry.

Learning

The learning phase is a process of examining the crisis and determining what was lost, what was gained, and how the organization performed in the crisis. It is an evaluative procedure designed to make the crisis a prodrome for the future.

One might think that this is like closing the barn door after the cows have escaped. Any farmer will tell you that once the cows are back in the barn, they will escape again unless you close the door this time. The fact that a company has suffered one crisis is no indication that it will not happen again. Johnson & Johnson, after its second tampering crisis, learned its lesson by selling over-the-counter medications in tamper-proof containers. Other companies followed suit. Public relations personnel set about the task of telling the public about the new safety containers.

Another example of the learning phase is illustrated by the case of the U.S. airlines that were plagued with hijackings during the 1960s and 1970s. The airlines set up metal detectors at airports for persons boarding planes. The procedure was extended to cover employees after an irate employee boarded a plane with a gun, shot a supervisor, and caused a fatal crash. The airlines' public relations personnel informed passengers of the new safety procedures.

The learning phase brings about change that helps prevent future crises.

Public Opinion

In a crisis, the public perceives truth to be whatever public opinion says. An organization in crisis must prove to its publics—and often to the general public—that the prevailing negative opinion is not factual. In contrast to a U.S. court of law, where a person is innocent until proven guilty, in the court of public opinion, a person or organization is guilty until proven innocent.

Public opinion is difficult to define, but it is based on individuals' attitudes toward specific issues. These attitudes are based on age, educational level, religion, country, state, city, neighborhood, family background and traditions, social class, racial background, etc. All of these help to form each individual's attitudes, and a predominance of similar attitudes makes up public opinion.

On any given issue, people are in favor, against, neutral, or so disinterested that they could not care less. Most people, unfortunately, fall into the last category. Public relations aims to reinforce positive attitudes, change negative attitudes, and provide information in a way that causes the unopinionated and neutral to form the opinion most conducive to the organization's function.

An organization has no choice in accepting a crisis. A crisis is forced on it, and the organization must cope with it. Organizations can ignore a crisis and hope it will go away. Occasionally, it does. More often, it does not. A crisis ignored is an organization failing.

The essential role of crisis communications is to affect the public opinion process and to be instrumental in establishing and communicating proof that the prevailing "truth" is not factual or not wholly factual. Then explanations of how much is true must follow. If the organization is actually at fault, owning up to it is usually the best policy. The public is forgiving if measures are taken to prevent recurrence.

The news media are prime tools for changing public opinion. The media can reach the masses in a short period of time because most Americans utilize some form of the news media, primarily social media and television (TV). Radio is popular during prime traffic hours. Public relations experts are trained in knowing how to reach the media, when and how to call a news conference, when and how to conduct one-on-one interviews, and when and how to disseminate written material.

Crisis communications, like public relations, is not merely the distribution of news releases. Nor is it only media relations. Frequently, community relations, consumer relations, employee relations, investor relations, government relations, and many other kinds of public relations are involved.

Disinformation and Misinformation

The furor over where former U.S. President Barack Obama was born was nicknamed "birtherism" and was a warning sign of what was to come in the area of disinformation and misinformation. He said the circulation of charges that he was not born in the United States began as early as when he began to campaign for the U.S. Senate seat he won in 1996 and accelerated in his second term (Figure 1.3). Obama called the growth of disinformation on social media "the demand for crazy on the Internet" (Merica & O'Sullivan, 2022).

The novel Coronavirus-19 took the attention of the world during the first three months of 2020. At the time, research by the World Health Organization (WHO) estimated that about 800 persons in the United States were deceased or dying mostly because they believed misinformation, had not been told facts, or were not heeding the facts (WHO, 2021). Hospitals were overcrowded and healthcare workers were quickly overworked worldwide. Not only did they run out of beds and ventilators but also personal protective equipment (PPE) like masks and gowns. There was not enough space in morgues to store bodies. Persons diagnosed with the virus and near death

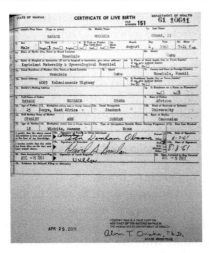

Figure 1.3 Most people point to "birtherism," the misguided belief that former U.S. President Barack Obama was not born in the United States, as the beginning of a current wave of misinformation/disinformation. The birth certificate was always available for all to see, a basic requirement that Obama's campaign leaders would not have missed.

Source: Brendan Smialowski / Stringer via Getty Images

still did not believe experts who advised them they were suffering from it. People high in political positions told them differently as did trusted friends. Therefore, WHO termed the pandemic an "infodemic."

The Institute for Public Relations in its *Third Annual Disinformation in Society Report* in 2022 defines disinformation as "the deliberate spread of misleading or biased information" (McCorkindale & Henry, 2022).

This includes outright lies, exaggeration, embellishment, sensationalism, and half-truths which are violations of all the codes of ethics in journalism and public relations fields. It also includes what was true yesterday but is no longer true today, what may or may not become true tomorrow but is no longer true today, and what may or may not become true tomorrow. These statements are intended to divide people and urge them to take actions—to make moves to satisfy the liar's purposes.

Outrageous disinformation during the pandemic included the following.

1. The COVID-19 vaccine causes infertility.
2. People can ingest the drug hydroxychloroquine to cure the COVID-19 virus.
3. The government-approved vaccine can infect a person with the virus.
4. Vaccines were overly rushed to the public without tests for effectiveness and safety.

5. There are microchips in the vaccine that can track you.
6. The Obamas had purchased a home in Dubai.

All were untrue. Number 6 is said to have originated from a website admitting to being fiction, then it spread as if it was truth because spreaders did not check the facts and thought it was true.

The sender may not always intend to send harmful information. This is often careless unprofessionalism. Both misinformation and disinformation are to be avoided. Both are part of the "war on truth" or "truth decay." Both are spread easily and quickly and are difficult to delete as written and impossible to delete from people's minds.

Persons eager to spread information designed to achieve their goals often are not concerned if the information is accurate or not. The goal dictates the hand they play. If it achieves the goal, to them it is news. For example, if they reveal that a product will cure headaches, any seemingly convincing data to support that goal suffices, no matter the source of the data.

By June 2020, the BBC (British Broadcasting Company) and the UK (United Kingdom) government started a "Stop the Spread" campaign to warn the news-seeking public that before acting on advice, check facts before passing them on to others. That simple effort can save problems, save reputations, and sometimes save lives.

A few months later, another campaign called "Reporting Information" urged people to report falsehoods to social media platforms and publications. This campaign reached participants in several countries where English, Spanish, French, Russian and Arabic are spoken.

Misinformation and disinformation go beyond the pandemic and politics. They pervade communications—the exchange of information. They can exist in any field, in any subject, and publication or mode of communication. When a person shares a story with another person, there is often a tendency to change facts ever so slightly to make it more interesting. This occurs frequently and is one cause of misinformation. No responsible journalist would do this, but they are often under pressure to deliver interesting stories. Traditional newspapers have editors who seek out these "interesting, if true" batches of information and take measure to find the truth or omit the falsehoods from their publications (Coddington & Lewis, 2021). Any experienced reporter can tell a story about arguing with an editor until one of them determined that a point of information was proven. Usually the editor wins—it is his or her job to know—but not always, and the results often enlighten both sides.

Kathleen Hall Jamison, University of Pennsylvania and founder of FactCheck.org, summed the issue as follows.

Humans are always subject to error. Institutions are as well. We've got to come back to a middle ground where we've got places where we can anchor knowledge with custodians of knowledge we trust. Journalism used to be one of those. But now you have a public that looks at journalism and says, "I'm going to divide it into whether it fits my ideology or not."

(Stanton, 2021)

Americans believe that Facebook and politicians were at least somewhat responsible for spreading disinformation to the public, according to the previously mentioned *Disinformation in Society Report* (subtitled *How Americans Perceive Intentionally Misleading News or Information*), which was conducted by the Institute of Public Relations and polled 2,200 Americans in November 2021. The report uses the term "disinformation" and not "fake news" because fake news can have various meanings. First, fake news is an oxymoron. It is a meaningless term. If information is news, it's not fake and if it's fake, it's not news. The same is true of "alternative facts." There is no alternative to truth.

Also, some information in television newscasts is not intended to be news but commentary or features. Both CNN and MSNBC concentrate on panels, usually three experts or persons experienced in coping with a given issue (Figure 1.4). These panelists offer commentary—their opinions or viewpoints or interpretations of something said or done. They explain to you the news so you can form your own opinion.

Features might be non-news, something interesting or heartwarming like a celebrity who has a new pet. National opinion shows include "The Rachel Maddow Show," "Anderson Cooper 360," and Laura Ingraham's

Figure 1.4 Anderson Cooper and other anchors on 24-hour hour national cable news networks MSNBC and CNN often feature panels of 2–3 experts and their views of current news events and issues. This is commentary and is not intended to be news. Some persons from opposing political sides call such commentary "fake news."

Source: World History Archive / Alamy Stock Photo

"The Ingraham Angle." In traditional newspapers, the editorial page is the opinion of the editors of the publication. The op-ed page refers to the page physically opposite the editorial page and it includes letters to the editors from readers. Editors often choose letters because they are well-written and they express diverse opinions of newsworthy issues. These readers also express their opinions on issues much like the panelists on CNN and MSNBC. Then, there are columns written by notable persons. These columnists may write regularly or as guests of the publication.

Who Do You Trust?

Social media like Google, Facebook, Twitter (now known formally as X but still referred to by many using its former name), Snapchat, and TikTok say they are working to separate themselves from disinformation and misinformation and those who would originate or spread false information. They want to be the organizations to trust, the authorities to seek when one wants the accurate data.

The State of Journalism Muck Rack Survey 2022 reveals that reporters find the following most valuable to their work (percentage of journalists):

Twitter (77%)
Facebook (39%)
LinkedIn (24%)
Instagram (18%)
YouTube (16%)
Reddit (9%)
TikTok (4%)
Snapchat (1%)

(Schneider, 2021)

Since the survey of 2022, there has been a rapid growth of TikTok. An article in the *Washington Post* online said, in November, 2022, "If you have not used Tik Tok, you are rapidly becoming the global exception." It continued,

In five years, the app, once written off as a silly dance-video fad, has become one of the most prominent, discussed, distrusted, technically sophisticated, and geopolitically complicated juggernauts of the internet . . . Its dominance is hard to overstate. TikTok's website was visited last year (2021) more often than Google. No app has grown faster past a billion users, and more than 100 million of them are in the United States.

(Hartwell, 2022)

Despite TikTok's popularity, especially with younger users, lawmakers in the United States and in other countries have deliberated about whether this social media platform should be more strictly regulated due to concerns related to the protection of used data and the platforms of Chinese ownership. Congress has advanced legislation allowing U.S. President Joe Biden to ban TikTok from all networks nationwide. Some state governments have banned the app from government computers. In May, 2023, the state of Montana was the first to ban TikTok from operation in that state effective Jan. 1, 2024. As this textbook went to press, the legislation is being challenged on First Amendment grounds.

The dissemination of news has grown rapidly with more news media services, more methods of communication, faster communication, more individuals supposedly "in the know," more groups affecting decisions and outcomes, and fewer guidelines and rules.

How does trust enter the picture? Reputable publications earn trust through years of responsible journalism. They have shown they are working toward delivering accurate information. They confirm and verify facts with authorities. They correct inaccuracies immediately and admit them immediately. An aspiring professional journalist, public relations professional, or crisis communicator also becomes trusted after being accurate and timely over an extended period.

It might be a good idea if all high school and college students be required to take at least one journalism course—a course based on recognizing the struggle to be accurate and truthful. This course would not be for prospective reporters but for people planning to live in this world—people who need to discern truth in order to handle life's challenges. They would learn how facts become facts; how they are confirmed; how reputable organizations, publications, and professionals share data; and how mistakes can develop and become cancers if not corrected.

Dr. Jelani Cobb, dean of the Columbia Journalism School, agrees. He feels that since we live in a world of mistrust in the news media, journalists can renew the public trust if the public is taught how the job is done. He said, "It will allow people to know how information they're consuming came to be in front of them. Even restaurants have to be transparent about that now. Locally sourced! This is how we got the food in front of you. Journalists have to do the same" (Choiniere, 2022).

Crisis communicators face the necessity for trust and truth just as journalists. The public demands it. They may spread misinformation and disinformation. Or even worse, they may originate the false information and pass it on to journalists who pass it on to the news public. This would mean all communications, but most particularly in news releases, reports, white papers, annual reports, social media posts, and even pitches. Remember that false information spread without sinister intentions is extremely unprofessional. It is much easier to keep a good reputation than to recover from a bad one, so being vigilant is important.

The following national/international news sites and sources, among others, over the years, have earned a measure of trust. That does not mean they never err but they are known for being accurate and known to concentrate on getting the facts.

New York Times
Washington Post
Associated Press
Reuters
National Public Radio (NPR)
British Broadcasting Company (BBC)
Public Broadcasting System (PBS)
Agence France-Presse (AFP)

In an era of pervasive misinformation and disinformation circulating as "news," how can the average news consumer evaluate which news sources are trustworthy? A non-profit organization called The Trust Project has some recommendations. According to its website (https://thetrustproject.org), the Trust Project's mission is "To amplify journalism's commitment to transparency, accuracy, inclusion and fairness so that the public can make informed news choices." It is an international consortium of news organizations that strive to provide truthful, verified news and information in a context that gives them meaning, according to the organization's website. The Trust Project has come up with eight "Trust Indicators" that news and information consumers can use to identify reliable, ethical journalism. When confronted with what appears to be news content, consumers should ask themselves about the following.

- *Best Practices*: Is the reporting independent, accurate, honest, and trustworthy?
- *Journalist Expertise*: For investigative, in-depth, or controversial stories, does the journalist provide sources for each claim? Do they give details so we can check the sources ourselves? Do other sources back up what is being said?
- *Labels*: Is the story impartial, or does it have a clear opinion? Is it highly partisan, sponsored, or advertising something? Is the purpose clearly shown?
- *References*: For investigative, in-depth or controversial stories, does the journalist provide sources for each claim? Do they give details so we can check the sources ourselves? Do other sources back up what is being said?

- *Methods*: How much reporting was done? What methods were used? Who else was involved in the process?
- *Locally Sourced*: Was the reporting done with deep knowledge about the local situation or community? Was the journalist on the scene? Did the journalist make an effort to listen to members of the community?
- *Diverse Voices*: Does the newsroom commit to bringing in diverse perspectives? Is there evidence that the journalist pays attention to diversity? Are some communities included only in stereotypical ways, or completely missing?
- *Actionable Feedback*: Does the news site invite the public to participate? Do they ask for feedback? Do they correct errors quickly, clearly and prominently?

The Trust Project's mission has attracted the support of many media and technology organizations, including Microsoft, which created ads that raised online awareness of the Trust Indicators and directed consumers to The Trust Project's website.

Professional ethical journalists pursue truth and confirm it. But what about other people? How do they discover false information? Who do they trust?

The Institute of Public Relations in the *Third Annual Disinformation in Society Report* polled 2,200 Americans in 2021 (McCorkindale & Henry, 2022). The study determined, among other information, tendencies that are bad indications of consumer habits.

Most disturbing is that Americans view their families and friends as the most trustworthy sources for accurate news or information and the least likely to spread disinformation. The critical point here is that people trust family and friends because they love them, not because they are adept at discerning truth or researching to confirm facts.

Another finding was that fewer people check statements to determine they are factual. The report states that four in five Americans think they can recognize disinformation when they see it, and four in ten Americans say they avoid watching TV news because of disinformation. Do they check to see if it's disinformation or do they simply ignore the information, whatever it may be? Are these people your family and friends whom you trust?

Two-thirds of people polled believe misinformation and disinformation are major problems in society and that number is growing.

Using Reliable Sources

Check your sources. Are the persons who originated the information known to be reliable and factual? What are their credentials? Are they known experts? Are they members of an organization, company, or group known to have bias? Does the source's information have a purpose? Is the source selling an idea or convincing people to take a stand for a cause? Is the information intended to manipulate? Why was the information written? Does the purpose clash with your beliefs?

Confirm the data with other sources whom you know to be honest.

If your source's data is especially interesting, hot, there's a chance it's not true. People tend to embellish facts. Check it out.

Proven facts are better than opinion.

There are fact-checking organizations and websites which fight misinformation battles. Some of them are the following.

FactCheck.org
Washington Post Fact Checker
Annenberg Public Policy Center
Google News Initiative
Poynter.com
Snopes.com
PolitiFact.com
Ballotpedia.org
Duke Reporting Lab
Teen Fact-Checking Network
France's Science Feedback
India's Factly
Africa Check

Careful Factual Writing

Well-meaning professionals can pass on misinformation and disinformation easily just by writing that first news release with false information, unverified information, or "facts" which are expected to be news later.

Many professionals and many companies have lost good reputations because of using "facts-to-be" to get their news out first and in advance of competitors. Most of the following advice is useful in all news releases; some of the warnings are taught in elementary, basic news release writing. If you write using facts to persuade, as in public relations writing, remember *confirmation bias*. Many people, when reading crucial data in the midst of a crisis, read only until they find information that supports their own beliefs while ignoring information that might make them consider changing beliefs. For example, read the following news story:

The Centers for Disease Control and Prevention (CDC) announced that children under five years of age may safely receive either the Pfizer or Moderna vaccines. More than 1200 children of that age have died of the COVID-19 virus and many more have been hospitalized. Children will no longer have to miss preschool, sports activities, birthday parties and other events due to the lack of access to the vaccines older people have been given. The vaccine for children, 18 months to 5 years, is now available.

Though the CDC says there is no danger, some parents fear side effects. Only an estimated 18 percent of parents plan to get their children vaccinated.

To get vaccinations, check . . . .

If the story's purpose it to convince parents to get children vaccinated, confirmation bias tells us that the purpose fails on reading the final sentence even though the story may continue with additional advice about the vaccination. If parents have basic hesitation, many will discount all the data in the first paragraph and focus on that final sentence which satisfies their opinion because it says 82 percent of parents agree with their hesitation and will not get their children vaccinated.

Another frequently used sentence that encourages readers to stop reading is "There's not widespread agreement on this matter."

Also the final sentence in the story begins with "only," which makes the 18 percent even less significant and makes the persuasion less effective. Further persuasion will be needed to change minds.

Ann Wylie, in *PR Say: The Voice of Public Relations* (Wylie, 2022), advises that writers should aim to make sure that readers begin to get your main point after reading only a few words, maybe just the headline or the subject line in an email. She advises that writers paraphrase rather than try to use a lot of direct quotes—unless the quote will communicate opinion, emotion, or controversy. Also, she suggests that you make sure that after reading a story or news release, make sure the reader recalls the main point, the intended purpose. She uses specific words because details are colorful and memorable and therefore stronger.

The following warnings are simple journalistic rules but if you violate one, readers will question everything you've written.

Make sure all supporting information—photos, captions, drawings, maps, headlines, subheads, links—all relate to the main idea.
Be sure the facts are accurate in the first drafts. Making corrections later is problematic. Nevertheless, a late correction is better than none.
Make sure websites used are true websites and not satirical.
Avoid warnings like "This is not a hoax."
In trying to be interesting, don't use shock terms; it is so easy to exaggerate, and exaggerations are lies.
Do not use cute emojis.

Be brief—only use the word or words that work exactly.

Do not use all capital letters. That's visual noise.

Do not use excessive punctuation.

Make sure there are no misspellings. People taught to recognize misinformation and disinformation are told that a misspelling is a warning sign. The same is true with grammar errors.

Quotes must be stated correctly.

Do not assume that the head of a company or business is a CEO or president. Get the title exact, just like the name.

Many new communication writers think that of the "Five Ws and H" (who, where, what, why, when, and how), the "when" is the least important. Don't believe it. When did it happen? Readers can believe it was a month ago. Even "yesterday" may need definition.

Watch superlatives. Writers love to use "the most," "the first," "the best," etc. You may think you know. Be sure.

Conclusion and Going Forward

Kurlansky, in his 2022 book *Big Lies: From Socrates to Social Media* and in his op-ed in the *Los Angeles Times*, "A History of the Big Lie from Plato to TikTok," says of Plato, who believed that societies needed "a grand lie" to create an impressive national myth, that Plato lied in the then-new written word in 375 BC. In an 1806 bio of George Washington by Mason Locke Weems, the author claimed young George said to his dad, "I cannot tell a lie"—and that parable was a lie. George never said it. In newspapers, during World War I, a *London Times* reporter wrote that a German soldier chopped off the arms of a French baby. That was investigated and never confirmed. In radio, Catholic priest Father Charles Coughlin, who pioneered talk radio, told antisemitic lies on the air. As criticism rages about lies on the Internet, particularly Facebook, Twitter, and TikTok, as if lies are a new problem, Kurlansky said, "There are differences now. Social media celebrates amateurism. Any idiot can weigh in" (Kurlansky, 2022).

Twitter and TikTok, as mentioned earlier, are two of the most popular social media platforms. However, magnate Elon Musk purchased Twitter for $44 billion and many followers began to be distrustful of the network, thinking that Musk's politics would spoil the platform they have known and trusted. TikTok, a growing platform, became questionable when it was revealed that its Chinese parent company might give users' personal data to the Chinese government. So, the futures of both Twitter and TikTok are not certain. Actually, no social media is certain. Just prior to printing, Meta (formerly Facebook) developed Threads, a competitor to Twitter; it was immediately popular. What is certain is that there will be social media and users must choose the right one for their needs.

In recent months, the communications world encountered a subject called artificial intelligence (AI), which simulates human intelligence through computers and other machines. It can be used for good or for nefarious reasons. The great fear is that it will be used for the latter reason, and that humans are not intelligent enough or diligent enough to determine the difference. Early forms of AI are the familiar, helpful, and appreciated Alexa from Amazon, Siri from Apple, and Cortana from Microsoft. A problematic form of AI was apparent when in March, 2023, a news photo circulated of Pope Francis dressed in a large white puffer jacket (Figure 1.5). The pontiff never wore such a jacket. It was a fake photo generated by AI.

Recent news stories about an AI tool called ChatGPT has evoked differing opinions about the persuasive power of AI to spread false information and what should be done about it. In short, questions asked of ChatGPT are answered in conversational form using information quickly harvested from the Internet. It is a dynamic, evolving technology that can result in detailed answers that may appear at face value to be true and accurate but is actually false because it is based on false information found on the Internet. It can be difficult for the average user to distinguish between truth and falsity because the natural language that AI uses in ChatGPT is so convincing.

Despite concerns about AI, it is likely to become more integrated into people's lives over time and even evolve in ways that we haven't yet

Figure 1.5 Artificial intelligence (AI) was founded and has grown considerably. Controlled by computers, it instantly began to challenge truth. Actors on strike during much of 2023 feared that their voices and visual appearances may be used without their permission. This image of Pope Francis, for example, circulated in 2023 and depicts the pontiff in a white puffer coat. He never wore one.

imagined. An enduring question at the public policy level is whether and how to regulate it. There are good arguments for and against regulation. One solution is to offer AI literacy in schools that begins as early as when students begin learning about computers and other communication and information technologies. It would be similar to media literacy or news literacy classes in the schools. The learning goal would be to raise awareness about AI—what it is, and how it can be helpful or fun to use, as well as harmful and dangerous in spreading misinformation and disinformation. As with media literacy, students need to be taught how to be critical evaluators of AI content and to develop a healthy skepticism about the technology, just as they should be taught healthy skepticism about advertising claims or about partisan news shows that engage more in opinions than facts. If AI literacy appears ineffective, lawmakers may advocate for more restrictive measures, a process that requires a careful balancing act between the free flow of information and communication regulation.

Mini-Case: White Star Line's *Titanic* Sinks

To illustrate terms, let's examine a well-known crisis: the sinking of the *Titanic* in 1912.

Titanic was one of several ships of the White Star Line, which had a primary rival, the Cunard Line. The Cunard Line had two famously fast ships—the *Lusitania* and the *Mauritania*. White Star decided not to compete with Cunard on speed but to surpass it, as far as public opinion was concerned, in size, elegance, sumptuousness, and safety.

The White Star Line planned to launch three ships—the *Olympic*, the *Titanic*, and the *Gigantic*, in that order. In the area of media relations, advance publicity praised the immensely luxurious ships. Postcards went out claiming the *Titanic* was "the largest moving object in the world." A promotional brochure claimed the *Olympic* and the *Titanic* were "designed to be unsinkable" (Ziakas, 1999, p. 109). The trade journal *The Shipbuilder* bragged about the *Titanic*'s opulence—its grand staircase, its elevators, its Turkish baths, and, of course, its "unsinkable" construction.

Titanic personnel were chosen to appeal to a celebrated and wealthy clientele, the targeted public. Captain E. J. Smith, called the "millionaire's captain," was the highest-paid captain on the seas and a celebrity in his own right. The musicians were the top in their field and could play a wide range of music. White Star felt that it had thought of everything and had attained the highest form of customer relations.

Crisis management plans and crisis communications plans were believed to be unnecessary. After all, if the ship couldn't sink, what could happen? There were medical facilities on board should any passengers suffer a heart attack or some other unforeseen illness. The ship had state-of-the-art communications equipment; if help was needed, personnel could radio other ships.

We've learned that it was always possible, though unlikely, that the ship would sink. A long gash in the hull was the worst-case scenario, and that is exactly what happened. So, the non-planners were shortsighted. What about fires? Certainly the ship could burn. An adequate number of lifeboats would still be needed. In fact, a fire out of control on a ship could have been a worse disaster.

A crisis management plan would have detailed what would be done in the event of fire and other tragedies—how evacuation would take place, how practice drills would be conducted for the crew and possibly for passengers, who would lower the lifeboats, who would ensure that passengers were guided safely to the closest lifeboats and ships, who would contact persons ashore by radio, when crew members would save themselves, and so on. A crisis management plan would also have included making sure effective insurance policies were in place. In today's crises, one must be sure that payrolls can be met; special insurances may be necessary to cover computers.

The crisis management plan would have included the crisis communications plan. The crisis communications plan would have included notification of the home office, where personnel acting as public relations professionals would, in turn, notify the press, White Star Line executives and employees, and passengers' relatives. These were also key publics. (The term *public relations* was not used at the time, although that management function has always been important to the success of any company or organization.)

The crisis communications plan would have also included details about who would be the spokesperson once the passengers were brought to safety. If Captain Smith had survived, he would have been the best spokesperson. As it was, Smith went down with the ship. However, the managing director of White Star, J. Bruce Ismay, was aboard, survived, and was rescued from a lifeboat sent from the *Carpathia*. Many felt he should have given his place on the lifeboat to a passenger. However, because he survived, he should have been the spokesperson. Instead, he hid in the luxurious quarters of the *Carpathia*'s physician until the ship docked in New York, hoping to avoid the other survivors who huddled on floors and under tables.

There were two persons connected to White Star who participated in the media communications. Harold Bride, a radio operator on the *Titanic* who worked for Marconi Wireless Telegraph Company, was among the passengers picked up by the *Carpathia*. He wrote a first-person account of the tragedy that he sent to the *New York Times* by wire from the rescue ship. Phillip A. S. Franklin, who had been hired to head White Star's New York office, called together a kind of crisis communications team. This came after David Sarnoff, also a Marconi employee, heard the signal from the *Olympic* that the *Titanic* had run into an iceberg and was sinking fast; Sarnoff gave his story to the Associated Press. Franklin attempted to stop the Associated Press from running the story, saying that even though the ship had run into an iceberg, he had "absolute confidence in the *Titanic* . . . . We are not worried about the ship but we are sorry for the inconvenience of the passengers" (Ziakia, 1999, p. 116).

The morning before the sinking, the *New York Times* ran a story announcing that the "The New Giantess *Titanic*" would soon arrive in New York. The story was a PR person's dream, a proactive story aimed primarily at a public of potential passengers and at educating and informing the general public, thereby assuring that when asked, "What is the biggest, most elegant ship afloat?" anyone would say, "The *Titanic*." The *Times* story described the ship's impressive size, luxury, and illustrious passengers aboard its maiden voyage.

On April 15, White Star was in a reactive mode, as is almost always the case in a crisis. Presented with information from the Bride and Sarnoff stories, the *New York Times* ran a story with this headline:

NEW-LINER *TITANIC* HITS AN ICEBERG;
SINKING BY THE BOW AT MIDNIGHT;
WOMEN PUT OFF IN LIFEBOATS;
LAST WIRELESS AT 12:27 A.M. BLURRED

A later *New York Times* headline read as follows:

TITANIC SINKS FOUR HOURS AFTER HITTING ICEBERG;
866 RESCUED BY *CARPATHIA*, PROBABLY 1250 PERISH;
ISMAY SAFE, MRS. ASTOR MAYBE, NOTED NAMES MISSING

Other newspapers' April 15 headlines indicated that the editors were much less aware of accurate details of the story. The *New York Sun*'s headline was "All Saved from *Titanic* after Collision." The *Washington Post* apparently chose to believe the spokesperson for White Star, Franklin. The *Post* headline was the following:

TITANIC'S 1470 PASSENGERS ARE NOW BEING
TRANSFERRED IN LIFEBOATS TO CUNARD LINE
Twenty Boat Loads have Already
been Transferred to the *Catania*,
of the Cunard Line . . . No Loss of
Life is Feared . . . Officials Confident
throughout Long Period of Suspense . . . Halifax
Hears that *Titanic* is on Her Way to That Port.

(Note that newspapers made estimates of the numbers of passengers rescued and deceased in early coverage. Also, the *Washington Post* thought the rescue ship was the *Catania*, not the *Carpathia*.)

The *Manchester Guardian*, on April 16, wrote about the miscommunications of White Star. Newspapers love to write about corporate mistakes; it's the stuff of which interesting articles are made. Under the headline "The Day's Strange Reports in America," the story was a timeline of every arrogant message from White Star's Franklin and from other reports. One message from the Government Marine Agency in Halifax said that the *Titanic* was sinking, whereas a message from Franklin said that "all passengers are saved, and the *Virginian* is towing the *Titanic* toward Halifax" (Ziakas, 1999, p. 117).

Franklin finally received a telegram confirming that the ship had sunk, and he later described his reactions:

> it was such a terrible shock that it took us a few minutes to get ourselves together. Then at once I telephoned, myself; two of our directors, Mr. Steele and Mr. Morgan, Jr. and at the same time went downstairs to the reporters. I got off the first line and a half where it said: "The *Titanic* sank at two o'clock a.m." and there was not a reporter left in the room—they were so anxious to get out and telephone the news.
>
> (Ziakas, 1999, p. 117)

At Pier 54 in New York harbor, the surviving passengers came ashore and were regarded as celebrities from that point on. An embarrassed and tearful Franklin went aboard the *Carpathia* to meet with Ismay, who was in a state of mental and physical collapse. Ismay and Franklin drafted White Star's official reaction to the disaster and came ashore long after the passengers had left. Ismay and Franklin also were present at a stressful media availability event and later issued a formal statement (Figure 1.6).

The surviving passengers issued their own statement, which read in part:

> We, the undersigned surviving passengers from the steamship *Titanic*, in order to forestall any sensational or exaggerated statements, deem it our duty to give the press a statement of facts that have come to our knowledge and that we believe to be true . . . . We feel it is our duty to call the attention of the public to what we consider the inadequate supply of life-saving appliances provided for on modern passenger steamships, and recommend that immediate steps be taken to compel passenger steamers to carry sufficient boats to accommodate the maximum number of people carried on board.
>
> (Ziakas, 1999, pp. 120–121)

In the presence and under the shadow of a catastrophe so over-whelming my feelings are too deep for expression in words. I can only say that the White Star Line, its offices and employees will do everything humanly possible to alleviate the suffering and sorrow of the survivors and of the relatives and friends of those who perished.

The Titanic was the last word in shipbuilding. Every regulation prescribed by the British Board of Trade had been strictly complied with, the master, officers, and the crew were the most experienced and skilful in the British service.

I am informed that a committee of the United States had been appointed to investigate the circumstances of the accident. I heartily welcome the most complete and exhaustive inquiry, and any aid that I or my associates or our builders or navigators can render is at the service of the public and the governments of both the United States and Great Britain. Under the circumstances I must respectfully defer making any further statement at this time.

Figure 1.6 Formal statement made by J. Bruce Ismay, managing director of White Star, following the sinking of the **Titanic**. Ismay was aboard the doomed ship and issued this statement after consultation with Phillip A. S. Franklin, who headed White Star's New York office (Ziakas, 1999, p. 120).

The survivors were viewed as heroes, as was Captain Smith, who went down with the ship. Ismay was cleared of any wrongdoing by both British and U.S. inquiries, but his reputation never recovered. In motion pictures about the *Titanic*, Ismay was portrayed as a villain. The denotation of *Titanic* was "huge, colossal," whereas its connotation was "doom." White Star Line became synonymous with bad management. It suffered financial problems during the European Depression and, in the 1930s, merged with Cunard, with Cunard holding 62 percent of the shares. Both flags were flown on the ships until 1957, when the White Star flag was withdrawn. White Star liquidated its ships, and Cunard bought the remaining shares. By 1958, White Star no longer existed. Cunard went on to produce the *Queen Mary*, the *Queen Elizabeth*, and the *Queen Elizabeth II*. The *Queen Elizabeth II* still makes transatlantic crossings.

Prodromes for the *Titanic* tragedy were ships that had sunk previously. White Star thought it had made, in the construction of the ship, all the necessary adjustments in response to warning signs. The company concentrated on the positives rather than the negatives. It did not examine the worst-case scenario: "What if this doesn't work?" That question was apparently never asked or heeded.

Prevention and preparation would have included making sure there were enough lifeboats and developing crisis management and crisis communications plans. Containment would have meant recognizing the danger as soon as the iceberg was sighted and putting into effect the crisis management and crisis communications plans. However, much arrogance ("This ship is unsinkable") existed. Although there were a limited number of lifeboats, many went unfilled because of poor crisis management. There was apparently time—if there had been a plan to be carried out—to save many more passengers.

Total recovery was not likely in this crisis. The reputation of White Star remained damaged after nearly a century had passed. If the company had done anything right in the pre-launching, the sinking, or the post-sinking, there might have been a possibility of the recovery of their reputation.

In some cases, a company in crisis can seem to be a victim of crises, but this was not true in the sinking of the *Titanic*. The company was guilty of its own negligence and arrogance.

Bibliography

Barton, L. (1993). *Crisis in organizations*. Cincinnati, OH: South-Western.

Cherenson, M. (2021, May 4). To serve the public good, PR pros can help stop spread of vaccine misinformation. *PR say: The voice of public relations*. Retrieved April 22, 2022, from http://prsay.prsa.org.

Choiniere, A. (2022, October 13). Dr. Jelani Cobb and his mission to reshape journalism. *Editor and publisher*. Retrieved November 1, 2022, from editorandpublisher.com.

Coddington, M. & Lewis, S. (2021, October 6). Interesting if true. *Nieman lab*. Retrieved April 22, 2022, from www.niemanlab.com.

Education Week. (2021, March 23; updated 2023, June 15). School shootings over time: Incidents, injuries, and deaths. *Education Week*. Retrieved January 31, 2024, from https://www.edweek.org/leadership/school-shootings-over-time-incidents-injuries-and-deaths.

Fake news. (2022, February 16). *Library guides*. Retrieved April 22, 2022, from https:libguides.uwf.edu.

Hartwell, D. (2022, October 14). How Tik Tok ate the Internet. *Washington Post*. Retrieved January 31, 2024, from https://www.washingtonpost.com/technology/interactive/2022/tiktok-popularity/.

Hines, M. (2020, November 19). 'Devastating impact': Cruise industry says 254,000 American jobs, $32 billion in economic activity lost. *USA TODAY*. Retrieved January 31, 2024, from https://www.usatoday.com/story/travel/cruises/2020/11/19/cruising-faces-254000-american-jobs-32-billion-lost-pandemic/3776982001/.

Johnson, C. K. (2022, May 22). US deaths from Covid hit 1 million, less than 2 1/2 years in. *Associated Press*. Retrieved January 31, 2024, from https://apnews.com/article/us-covid-death-toll-one-million-7cefbd8c3185fd970fd073386e442317#:~:text=The%20U.S.%20death%20toll%20from%20COVID%2D19%20hit%201%20million,every%20day%20for%20336%20days.

Kurlansky, M. (2022, September 11). A history of the big lie from Plato to TikTok. *Los Angeles Times*. Retrieved September 11, 2022, from losangelestimes.com/article33.

Maheshwari, S. & Holpuch, A. (2023, May 23). Why countries are trying to ban TikTok. *The New York Times*. Retrieved May 25, 2023, from www.nytimes.com/article/tiktok.

McCorkindale, T. & Henry, A. (2022, March). *Third annual disinformation in society report: How Americans perceive intentionally misleading news or information*. Retrieved April 22, 2022, from https://instituteforpr.org.

Merica, D. & O'Sullivan, D. (2022, April 10). Birtherism to the big lie: Inside Obama's fight to counter disinformation. *CNN politics*. Retrieved April 22, 2022, from cnn.com.

Schneider, M. (2021, April 19). *New muck rack survey: The state of journalism 2021*. Retrieved April 11, 2022, from https/info.muckrack.com.

Sinclair, H. (2021, April 19). 7 ways to avoid becoming a misinformation superspreader. *How to be a better human series*. Retrieved April 22, 2022, from ideas.ted.com.

Stanton, Z. (2021, March 11). Our era's defining battle: Facts vs. information. *Politico*. Retrieved April 22, 2022, from www.politico.com.

Witze, A. (2021, May 6). How to detect, resist and counter the flood of fake news. *Science news*. Retrieved April 22, 2022, from www.sciencenews.org.

World Health Organization (WHO). (2021, April 21). Fighting misinformation in the time of COVID-19, one click at a time. Retrieved February 7, 2024, from https://www.who.int/news-room/feature-stories/detail/fighting-misinformation-in-the-time-of-covid-19-one-click-at-a-time.

World Health Organization (WHO). (2023, December 22). Covid-19 epidemiological update: 22 December 2023. Retrieved January 31, 2024, from https://www.who.int/publications/m/item/covid-19-epidemiological-update---22-december-2023.

Wylie, A. (2022, January 4). Top 8 writing tips for 2022. *PR say: The voice of public relations*. Retrieved February 2, 2022, from PRSay.prsa.org.

Ziakas, T. (1999). Titanic and public relations: A case study. *Journal of Public Relations Research*, 11, 105–124.

Chapter 2

Crisis Communications Theory

Academic researchers study the methods and procedures of professional communicators and develop theories of what is and what is not effective. Professionals rarely study theory but many have "tried and true" methods of practice that are, in effect, theory. Often, these practices of professionals are the same theories that academicians have studied and named.

A *theory* is used to explain what will work, what decisions should be made and how, what actions are likely to result and how, and how things relate. It is a prediction based on what has happened before. Theory-based practice is preferable because, in most aspects of life, we learn from our previous experiences and the experiences of others. Theorists have examined the actions of numerous practitioners and culled their findings into succinct theories.

Theories exist in various fields. Crisis communicators can benefit from many theories in the social sciences. The relatively new fields of crisis communications and public relations are developing their own theories, but theories applied to crisis communications are often theories in communications (including persuasion and rhetoric), sociology, and psychology.

Theories also tend to change, so it is necessary to regularly test them. Variables and relationships and conditions change, and results are sometimes vastly different in subsequent tests. Also, theories build on previous theories. Often, in using a theory, the researcher recognizes a missing element that does not necessarily find fault with the original theory but is deemed worthy of a new or more multifaceted theory.

Some theories are described in this chapter. They are followed by the predominant public relations/crisis communications theory called the *excellence theory*, proposed by James E. Grunig and Todd Hunt in 1984 and continued by Larissa Grunig (Figure 2.1).

Apologia Theory

When an organization has been accused of a misdeed, its reaction to its publics is often called *apologia*. It is, as one would assume, an effort to

DOI: 10.4324/9781003019282-2

Figure 2.1 James Grunig is founder of the excellence theory based on four models noting excellence in the practices of public relations and crisis communications. In the models, two-way communications and truth are key. Larissa Grunig, his wife, has been prominent in the research. The Grunigs are professors emeritus in the Department of Communications, University of Maryland, College Park.

Source: Permission by James and Larissa Grunig

defend reputation and protect image. But it is not necessarily an apology. The organization's effort may deny, explain, or apologize for the action through communication discourse.

If a soft drink manufacturer, for example, is accused of using inferior ingredients in its products, the apologia might contradict the charges by explaining what ingredients were actually used. The aim is to counteract a negative or damaging charge. Publics—the news media, consumers, employees, and key opinion leaders—may express disappointment with the company and expect some explanation, if not a full apology.

The organization may insist that the charges are false and totally deny them, or the organization may communicate to its public(s) that it did not "intend" to commit the misdeed. This is called *redefinition*. Publics tend to forgive if the organization's policies are above reproach and somehow, someway, something unforeseen happened. One individual, whose employment may subsequently be terminated, might be blamed. However, the public's forgiveness is not guaranteed. If the organization can show how it has taken steps to prevent the occurrence or the recurrence of the misdeed, all *may* be forgiven.

Apologia strategy may also include informing publics that the organization might *seem to have* committed a misdeed but actually has not. This is called *dissociation*. Facts explaining should follow. In the preceding example, if the soft drink's color has changed slightly, the manufacturer might explain that the ingredients have not changed but the food coloring is different; all ingredients are still pure and perfect. The organization, if faced with a large number of complaints, might also explain that it is returning to the former food coloring. That would be using dissociation and explanation.

A third strategy might be the actual apology: "We are guilty. We are sorry. Please forgive us." This is called *conciliation.*

Muslims in Turkey, Iraq, and the Palestine territories wanted Pope Benedict to make a conciliation in 2006 when he cited a medieval text that characterized some of the teachings of the Prophet Muhammad as "evil and inhuman," particularly "his command to spread by the word the faith he preached." The Pope said he was "deeply sorry," but the complainers from the Muslim countries felt the apology was insincere and made merely to protect his public image. The pontiff said the comments were those he cited from an old source, not his opinion (Associated Press, 2006).

A man in the state of Washington was frustrated because his wife was missing. He called 911, and an employee of the county sheriff told him his missing wife didn't "meet the criteria for a search" and that he should "check the jails and hospitals." The man threatened to get the news media involved—and did. As the public's concern grew, a tracking was done after two days using cell phone technology. The woman's car had gone over an embankment where no one from the street could see it in foliage; she was trapped in the car but alive. The sheriff, representing her department, apologized "for not doing a better job of explaining the process" to the man. This was redefinition. The sheriff did not admit that her department and employee had any culpability in the man's crisis or that "the criteria" would change. She said the process should have been explained better (Castro, 2007).

Image Restoration Theory

This theory builds on the apologia theory. In this theory, the organization determines what is threatening reputation or image and also determines which publics must be addressed and persuaded in order to maintain and restore positive image.

Organizations sometimes take the attitude "Don't bring me bad news!" They may refuse to read or watch negative news coverage in specific publications or they may close their eyes to consumers or other publics. In refusing to know what some people think of them, they cannot possibly know how to respond. Organizations should seek to read bad news just as much as they keep positive news clippings, and read them carefully.

When it comes to publics, the organization must know which publics have negative impressions and what the extent of their knowledge is. Does the public know all the facts, some of the facts, half-truths, or lies? One must know where these publics stand before they can be targeted for communication. In most public relations campaigns, the first step is research. The same holds true for crisis communications.

On the other hand, one must determine if the publics know anything at all that might damage reputation. Sometimes it is better to remain silent on the issue. At other times, it is best to tell your own bad news. This is a judgment call but a crucial judgment call determined by carefully researching one's publics continually.

An example of image restoration took place when Walmart realized in 2009 that it was getting bad press. Apparently many people felt that the huge company had a serious case of corporate greed and that it would do anything to earn money.

To build its customers' trust, executives decided the company should have an open information policy, one in which customers would know the origins of the products sold in the stores. The policy was part of a sustainability agenda that also included requiring suppliers in China, the United States, and the UK to comply with environmental laws. It also included having stronger audits, offering awards to energy-efficient suppliers, and urging the suppliers to come up with quality merchandise with no returns due to defects.

Decision Theory

Decision theory is concerned with counseling management and other leaders to make the most effective decision. Decision theory may be applied to all areas of management, but it is useful in public relations management and crisis communications. The theory is especially applicable to issues management and the effort to prevent a crisis.

Decisions are made under various conditions. The outcome may be certain, vague, ambiguous, or risky. The theory suggests that the decision maker should consider the possible benefit of each alternative; this is called *maximizing*. How useful is one alternative compared to others?

The best decision possible garners the greatest benefit—the greatest utility for the organization. Often, decision theorists note that decision makers do not opt for the greatest benefit but settle for the decision that will satisfy minimum requirements, usually because they do not have adequate data with which to formulate decisions. This practice is called *satisficing*.

Obviously, it is better when trying to build longstanding relationships to maximize rather than to satisfice. When satisficing, a public or publics may not be happy with the decision, or the decision may be temporary, a Band-Aid solution to a cancer in the organization.

Diffusion Theory

Also called *diffusion of innovations theory*, this theory examines how new procedures, practices, and objects are adopted and accepted by companies and individuals.

Diffusion theory has a five-step process: awareness (the body is exposed to the idea), interest (the body develops interest in the idea), evaluation (pros and cons are determined and considered), trial (the idea is implemented, perhaps temporarily to determine its effectiveness), and adoption or failure to adopt (acceptance or rejection of the idea, change, or innovation).

Whether something is adopted or not depends on the following three variables.

1. *The Past*: What has happened previously? What are past problems and needs? Basically, you must know where you are before you make decisions to make changes and to go forward.
2. *The Decision Makers*: What are the characteristics of the decision-making body that make it open to or closed to change? Are there closed-minded persons with great influence over others? How do experience, age, education, and other socioeconomic variables impact the decision-making process? Is the body made up of all leaders and no followers?
3. *The Innovation/Change*: Does the innovation show more obvious advantages and few disadvantages over present practice or procedure? Does the innovation call for drastic change, or can it be easily assimilated into current practice?

The *change agents*, often communicators or public relations professionals, try to move the body forward toward adoption. They often use the mass media during the awareness and interest stages. During evaluation and trial, personal contacts are valuable.

An example of *diffusion theory* in crisis communications might be a theater with an aging clientele suffering from poor single ticket sales and declining subscriptions. The plays have, for years, been the classics. Theater management wants to offer more contemporary plays to attract a younger audience, but they also want to keep the faithful clientele. Communicators might make announcements through the news media of this effort showing reasons in the *awareness stage*. In the *interest stage*, they might hold focus groups of persons from Generation X and seniors.

In the *evaluation stage*, the focus groups are studied, and comments are offered by members of the executive and community boards. In the *trial stage*, one contemporary cutting-edge play is produced with careful publicity, interaction, and communications, with leaders of both groups attending to help them understand. Follow-up interviews are conducted. The same effort is made to get the younger group to understand and appreciate a chosen classic.

The *adoption stage* results if most efforts succeed; during the following season, perhaps two contemporary plays may be offered.

Excellence Theory

Most recent public relations research builds on the *excellence theory* developed by J. Grunig and Hunt (1984) and later expanded by J. Grunig and L. Grunig (1992). The excellence theory is based on types of public relations practices called "models." The four models defined by J. Grunig and Hunt provide a way of classifying the types of public relations that individuals and organizations may practice.

In a spectrum of excellence of public relations programs, Model 1 would be the least desirable. Model 4 would be the most desirable, or could be said to be the "most excellent." Model 2 and Model 3 fall between these two extremes.

Model 1—Press Agentry/Publicity Model

In this model, public relations practitioners are interested in making their organizations or products known. They may or may not use truthful statements. Falsehoods, half-truths, and incomplete facts are all permissible. The practitioners' abiding slogan "All publicity is good publicity" indicates a one-way transfer of information from the organization to the publics. Little or no research is required. There is no feedback.

J. Grunig and Hunt (1984) revealed that this model was used by 15 percent of public relations practitioners. Later, J. Grunig and L. Grunig (1992) found the earlier data to be inaccurate and reported that most public relations practitioners, unfortunately, still fall into this category.

As practitioners become more knowledgeable and as the profession of public relations grows in respect, the number of practitioners using this model is expected to decrease.

Model 2—Public Information Model

This model is characterized by the desire to report information journalistically. It is different from Model 1 in that truth is essential. Most public relations practice in government agencies today falls into this category. Companies that simply distribute news releases are examples of this model. The practitioner is often called a flack.

This model also involves a one-way transfer of information from the organization to the publics. Little or no research is required. There may be some type of evaluation, such as readership surveys or the counting of news clips. Model 2 is most common in corporations.

Model 3—Two-Way Asymmetric Model

In this model, also called the *scientific persuasion model*, the public relations practitioner uses social science theory and research, such as surveys and polls, to help persuade publics to accept the organization's point of view. There is some feedback, but the organization does not change as a result of communications management. In asymmetric public relations programs of this type, the organization rules. It always knows best. Its attitude is that publics should adhere to the organization's viewpoints. An example of asymmetric action is a letter informing a public of a new policy or a recorded telephone message with no technology available for returning messages.

Model 4—Two-Way Symmetric Model

The public relations practitioner in this model, also called the *mutual understanding model*, is an intermediary between the organization and its publics. The practitioner tries to achieve a dialogue, not a monologue as in the other models. Either management or the publics may make changes in behavior as a result of the communications program.

Research and social science theory are used not to persuade but to communicate. Effective public relations programs based on this model are said to be "excellent" programs.

Symmetrical public relations programs negotiate, compromise, bargain, listen, and engage in dialogue. The organization knows what the publics want and need; the publics, in turn, understand the organization's needs and desires. An example is talking to consumers by telephone or at a public meeting in which the consumers can talk back and changes result.

In crises, organizations are frequently forced, by circumstances, to practice symmetrical communications with adversarial publics. Although most organizations practice Model 1 and Model 2, research by J. Grunig and L. Grunig (1992) revealed that PR practitioners would prefer to practice Model 4 if they had the expertise to do so and if their organizations were receptive to that practice.

The preceding classifications are not precise. For example, an organization may practice Model 2 and Model 4. If the organization practices Model 2 more than Model 4, it is considered a Model 2 public relations operation.

The new social media networks are a boon to the possibilities of two-way symmetrical practice. An organization can, if it desires, listen to its publics and make changes in its programs on the basis of those communications. It can also use them to explain its policies to these publics. After listeria-tainted meat had killed several people, the Canadian company concerned—Maple Leaf Foods—responded to a consumer on the corporate blog, explaining the precautions the company had instituted to ensure that this would not occur again. When it responded to that one irate blogger, other consumers read it.

If a company uses social media to count kudos from its publics and not to carefully consider change for mutual benefit, the social media interchange is Model 3.

Grunig and Repper on the Excellence Theory

J. Grunig and Repper (1992) identified theories on strategic management, publics, and issues as having two primary propositions. Both are conducive to a study of crisis communications programs.

1. Public relations is most likely to be excellent (contribute to organizational effectiveness) when it is an integral part of an organization's strategic management process and when public relations is managed strategically.
2. Public relations is managed strategically when it identifies stakeholders (separates active publics from stakeholder categories) and resolves issues created by the interaction of organization and publics through symmetrical communications programs early in the development of issues.

These propositions mean that excellent public relations programs, as well as excellent crisis communications programs, have the following characteristics.

1. The public relations head is an important part of the top management of the organization.
2. Programs are designed to build relationships with all key stakeholders of an organization or company.
3. Public relations, through research, identifies who the organization's key stakeholders are and ranks them in order of importance. They may be customers, the media, employees, competitors, unions, special interest groups, vendors, suppliers, environmental groups, consumer advocates, and critics, to name a few.
4. An ongoing public relations plan is developed for each key stakeholder. This necessarily goes beyond media relations into a Model 4 program (two-way symmetrical program). These programs can sometimes prevent crises. At other times, they can help lessen the severity of crises.
5. In segmentation, public relations breaks down large publics into smaller subpublics with which they can communicate more effectively about

issues or problems. These publics are usually, but not always, active rather than passive. Active publics seek out information and are more likely than passive publics to act on an issue. For example, if an organization wants to gear a program to all public schoolchildren, it might direct its program to the National Education Association or the American Federation of Teachers, organizations consisting of members who are educators and who can reach all public schoolchildren. Organizations that do not segment their stakeholders might send a news release to metropolitan newspapers, hoping that teachers will read the resulting article and communicate its contents to the children in their classes.

6. Issues management is part of a two-way symmetrical program that is best handled by the public relations department. (Although issues management is, in many cases, handled by public affairs or corporate communications departments, which are separate and apart from public relations departments that handle only media relations, Grunig and Repper's theory does not advise this separation.) A public makes an issue when it perceives that a problem is brewing or already exists. In issues management, the public relations department anticipates the issues that are potential crises and ranks them in order of possible damage to the organization, then strategies and tactics are developed and implemented to lessen the likelihood of crises. The crucial element here is early identification of potential crises, like treating a sniffle before it becomes the flu. The treatment might involve making allies with potential adversaries or meeting with community activists to explain a procedure that might be construed as damaging to consumers. Consequently, the odds are enhanced that an issue can benefit the organization rather than hamper it.

Marra and the Excellence Theory

Marra (1992), in an attempt to build on and validate a model of excellent crisis public relations, suggested that organizations develop a theoretically based crisis public relations model that would allow practitioners to identify which variables could be adjusted to make a crisis communications plan work and which variables, if not adjusted, would cause it to fail. Marra argued that this knowledge could allow public relations practitioners to know before a crisis what would or would not work. He identified the following strategies and techniques common to excellent responses to crises with the following hypotheses.

1. An organization having strong and well-developed relationships with its key publics prior to a crisis will suffer less financial, emotional, or perceptual damage than an organization with weak and poorly developed relationships with its key publics prior to a crisis. Key publics

would not only be the media but also employees, customers, community members, and so forth.

2. Organizations with weak pre-crisis relationships are those with asymmetrical practices; that is, they are Model 1, Model 2, or Model 3 organizations. Therefore, an organization that uses two-way symmetrical crisis communications procedures will suffer less financial, emotional, or perceptual damage than the Model 1, Model 2, or Model 3 organization or the organization that uses silence as a crisis response.

3. An organization that establishes and puts into effect continuing risk communications activities and prepares crisis communications plans prior to crises will have stronger relationships with key publics, use two-way symmetrical crisis public relations practices, and as a result suffer less financial, emotional, and perceptual damage than the organization that does not.

4. An organization with communication ideologies that encourage, support, and champion crisis management preparations, crisis communications plans and actions, and two-way symmetrical communications practices will suffer less financial, emotional, and perceptual damage than the organization that does not (Figure 2.2).

Fearn-Banks and the Excellence Theory

Two additional characteristics are suggested (Fearn-Banks, 1996):

1. An organization that anticipates, through crisis inventory (see Chapter 11), the precise type of crisis will suffer less financial, emotional, and perceptual damage than the organization that does not.

2. An organization that maintains the reputation of having an overall "open and honest" policy with stakeholders and the news media will suffer less financial, emotional, and perceptual damage than the organization that does not. (This is a specific area covered broadly in Marra's fourth characteristic.)

The "Five Ws" of Public Apology for Celebrities and Businesses

Of all the crisis communications theories, apology is the one most applied to life in the 21st century. Perhaps this is true more in the United States than other countries, but as businesses become more global, public apologies seem to be part of the routine. Google the word "apology" and you will get a lot more than you want to know—from athletes, politicians, celebrities, business spokespersons.

As public apologies are so overused, they are often not trusted. Offenders know the right words; their publicists write them. They are actors, either by profession or by ability, so they exude sincerity, Academy Award performances—the public often does not believe there is true regret.

CRISIS COMMUNICATIONS VOCABULARY

Strategy: An approach on how one handles a problem.

Stakeholders: People who are linked to an organization or who have an interest in an organization and are affected by the decisions made by that organization. Examples of company stakeholders are employees, stockholders, communities, and government officials.

Strategic publics: Stakeholders who are crucial to an organization. The organization cannot function without them. Examples are boards of directors, investors, and unions.

Strategically managed public relations: Communications programs designed to build relationships with strategic publics, the crucial stakeholders of an organization.

Segmentation: The division of a market, population, or a large public into groups whose members are bound by mutual interests, concerns, and characteristics.

Risk communications: An ongoing program of informing and educating various publics (usually external publics) about issues that can affect, negatively or positively, an organization's success. The program builds solid relationships between an organization and its key publics, the publics on which an organization's survival depends. These relationships must be established prior to a crisis. It is too late after a crisis erupts.

Organizational ideology: An organization's philosophy, its working climate, its corporate culture. Each person's experience with the organization—no matter how small or large—puts him or her in contact with that organization's ideology, or corporate culture. The elements of that culture (such as norms of dress, formal rules, informal codes of conduct, taboos, jokes, language, etc.) make up an invisible, internalized whip that cracks and tells people what they can do, what they cannot do, what they can say, and what they cannot say in their dealings with the organization. It is inescapable that the culture determines to some degree how people within the organization behave. Popular examples of organizational ideology include "Look busy whether you are or not" and "The boss is always right." Johnson & Johnson relied on its organizational ideology in 1982 when, without a crisis management or communications plan, it followed its credo after several people died from poisoned Tylenol capsules.

Communications ideology: The organization's philosophy and attitudes of behavior in communicating with publics. Again, Johnson & Johnson's public relations program during the tampering case is an example. The company's basic rule in coping with the media, and thereby with the consuming public, was "open and honest information." It is difficult for a public relations department of a major corporation to have a communications ideology different from the organizational ideology. A productive public relations operation necessarily suffers from an unproductive organizational ideology and vice versa. (This is further examined in Chapter 3, "Exxon and the *Valdez* Oil Spill.")

Figure 2.2 To comprehend crisis communications theory, certain terms must first be understood.

Why Apologize?

Given that one may not be believed anyway, determine whether a public apology is needed. Might the public appearance make you look worse? Can a private apology work if there are few people offended? Who will know? Who cares? Is an apology needed at all?

Apologies are intended to help restore or repair relationships, retain loyal customers, fans, or constituents. Will critics believe the apology is just an attempt to benefit financially? If the offender—a politician, an athlete, an entertainer, a business owner—is honest, financial gain is often the core reason. Even if one is truly sorry, the positive response to the apology is ultimately some financial gain. Be honest with yourself and know that convincing the public of true regret is difficult and not easily faked.

What Constitutes an Apology?

Benoit suggested that if a company or individual in public life has committed an offensive act or made an offensive statement—or if the public perceives that an offensive act has been made—steps must be taken to restore image (Benoit, 1995, 1997). There may be denial, evasion of responsibility, reduction of offensiveness, or corrective action.

The corrective action may take place before the apology or after, depending on how long a correction may be required. Nevertheless, the apology includes a confession, a plea for forgiveness, and a promise to make corrections. Others suggest that an explanation also be included.

The apology also takes into consideration fault, humility, dignity, and validation. There is no one magic formula for an apology. Sincerity is the key.

Who Should Apologize?

Sometimes the public will easily forgive if the offense is explainable and believable. That was the case when Krispy Kreme, in Hull, England, had a promotion titled Krispy Kreme Klub. Obviously, managements of the franchise liked alliteration; if they had let the last word begin with a "C" as it does, there would have been no crisis.

However, Krispy Kreme Klub, for a special event, became "KKK Wednesday." That might have been appropriate in Hull alone, except it was posted on the UK Krispy Kreme Facebook page. It was seen all over the world. Little did the owners/managers realize that KKK is commonly known to stand for Ku Klux Klan, the white supremacist organization, primarily in the United States. There was great outrage against Krispy Kreme, so a PR representative for the brand sent an email to international news media saying, "We are truly sorry for any inconvenience or offense this misstep may have caused our fans."

The representative acknowledged that it was not intentional; that was believable. She also indicated the franchise had removed the offensive material both online and in the shops, and apologized locally. A simple apology and explanation from PR was all that was needed. If the material had been used repeatedly, there would have been a different story and outcome. If a U.S. franchise had made the same mistake, it would not have been so easily forgiven. Doughnut lovers were satisfied and were happy that they did not have to boycott Krispy Kreme.

It was a greater issue and a more difficult problem to solve when 22 Canadians died from listeria resulting from eating processed meats from the company Maple Leaf Foods, Inc., based in Toronto. No PR person could apologize effectively. When deaths have occurred, the spokesperson must be the person at the top. That's exactly what happened.

Often in these dire times, CEOs consult lawyers first; PR must wait. CEO Michael McCain admitted publicly that his company was at fault as soon as he recognized the origin of the bacteria was the company's slicing machines.

McCain was on television and on YouTube admitting that the buck stopped with Maple Leaf and he was Maple Leaf. He said, "There are two advisers I've paid no attention to. The first are the lawyers and the second are the accountants. It's not about money or legal liability" (Interview with Maple Leaf). It was not time for the PR representative to speak, although PR delivered the apologetic messages to print media. McCain expressed concern for families with lost loved ones and to those who were ill. The gist of the messages was, "It's our fault. We'll fix it so it won't happen again." There was no ducking and dodging. The blame was totally on his company.

He could have placed the blame on the makers of the slicing machines or on employees who were supposed to check. But even if those things entered into the picture, it was still Maple Leaf, people had died, and others were battling for their lives.

An apology from the CEO is what Exxon needed in its 1989 oil spill in Alaska. Had the CEO come forward to meet the news media gathered at Valdez, picked up a dead bird covered in oil, and cried, history would have been different (see Chapter 3).

Where Do You Apologize?

Sometimes an apology is needed to make peace with one person and only one person. The offending statement or deed may have affected only one group of people. If the conversation is limited to one social medium, for example, don't broadcast it. When two employees of Domino's Pizza performed disgusting acts on YouTube, the company president created a YouTube response (see Chapter 10) in which he apologized to customers assuring them the acts were not condoned by the company and that the employees had been fired. His apology basically said he was sorry the company made a mistake in hiring the offenders. Owing to his tone and his words, customer publics believed the apology was heartfelt and that Domino's was a victim of this misdeed.

YouTube was particularly effective because it is visual and viewers could see his body language, the disgust in his face when he said, "It sickens me." You knew it did. He said, "These actions impact 125,000 men and women who work for Domino's in 60 countries" and "We're examining our hiring practices to make sure people like this don't make it into our stores." The sincerity came through.

Sometimes, with today's rapid media, if a celebrity makes an apology in one medium, other media will pick it up. A social media apology can be picked up by television news, for example, or the reverse can occur. Each medium monitors other media. One doesn't know if the public is driving the apology or if the news media or social media are determining the acceptance or lack of acceptance of the apology.

That was the case with celebrity chef Paula Deen. She admitted, in 2013, that 30–40 years ago, she used the "N" word. She apologized, but to whom was the apology directed? She was certainly not directing the peace-making "I'm not a racist" to African-Americans who remember life 30–40 years ago. No one would be surprised. Born in the 1940s and having lived in Georgia all her life, it is possible she used the "N" word and so did her family, friends, and neighbors. It would be unbelievable if she said she never did. It was a different time. The term was never a nice word, but niceties were not expected at the time. If she used that offensive term, in recent years, it would be a sign of racism.

But racism is not limited to a word; it's how one treats minority groups today. A person who never used the "N" word can still be racist. Maybe Deen did something else that can be called racism but the news media stuck to the "N" word story. Although she apologized on the *Today Show*, she lost her TV series. Did anyone explain history to the public? What about all the minority people who dined in her Savannah restaurants and were treated well for so many years? Did that matter?

When to Make an Apology?

Most apology experts advise that individuals and companies should apologize immediately even if one doesn't have the entire picture. You can still regret that the offense related to you or your company occurred. Sandra Fathi of Affect said, "Apologizing immediately shows that you acknowledge that something wrong has occurred. It does not equate to admitting any wrongdoing" (Fathi, 2013).

This is the strategy Johnson & Johnson adopted back in 1982 when seven people died from cyanide poisoning after ingesting laced Tylenol capsules (see Chapter 3). James Burke, the CEO then, was certain the capsules were not poisoned on their premises, but Johnson & Johnson would have to prove that (they did later). So, he apologized to all affected and asked consumers not to take the capsules in their possession; he recalled all those on the stores' shelves. "Our first responsibility is to our customers," he said. By coming forward immediately, he could have saved lives.

On some occasions, the apology is not acceptable because of the nature of the offense. It may be unforgivable. In those cases, if one cannot find perfect words, it may be best not to make an apology at all. If the apology is likely to be misinterpreted or will be exposed to more people than the original offense, it may be better not to apologize.

The communications director for Congressman Steve Fincher (R—Tenn.), Elizabeth Lauten, criticized the attire of President Obama's daughters, Sasha and Malia, at the annual turkey pardoning at Thanksgiving at the White House (see Chapter 7). Lauten said on Facebook that they "should show more class" (Durando, 2014). The girls were dressed like typical teenagers, no flashy or revealing clothing; actually, they were dressed rather conservatively.

There was great outrage. Some said Lauten must not have teenage daughters—but most of the complaints were that she chose to complain about children. If she intended a typical Republican complaint against a Democrat, children are considered off-limits. Their mother can and has been criticized about attire, but most reactions to the message were that Lauten had crossed the line.

The apology was:

After many hours of prayer, talking to my parents, and re-reading my words online, I can see more clearly how hurtful my words were. Please know that these judgmental feelings truly have no place in my heart. Furthermore, I'd like to apologize to all of those who I have hurt and offended with my words, and pledge to learn and grow (and I assure you I have) from this experience.

(Durando, 2014)

There's nothing in the apology that expresses real sorrow. She should have talked to God and her parents before making the comments. She never mentioned the Obama girls in the apology, who were the ones she would have hurt, if they ever heard about the criticism. The overall feeling was she regretted getting payback. She had to resign her job. Twitter conversation called her "bitch," "tramp," and "criminal," especially after it was revealed that when she was a teenager, she was caught shoplifting.

Case Study: Will Smith and the Academy Awards Slap

For many years, businesses, organizations, and well-known persons who publicly disrespect, accuse, embarrass, or harm others have been expected to issue a public apology. Public disdain usually subsides if that apology is made sincerely and swiftly. No one seemed to care what words were spoken or written, just an apology. There are lists of words and phrases used in apologies; as long as those words are used, one can usually make peace.

Here is a list of frequent apology words: sorry; so sorry; I should have known better; I regret; forgive me; excuse me; oops; mistake; my behavior was not acceptable; I was wrong; never again; remorse; I take responsibility; atone; vindication; it was inexcusable; it was unforgiveable

Writers of apologies often pick and choose words in a reasonable arrangement. That has usually sufficed. Just get the apology out, like a parent saying to a mischievous child, "Johnny, did you apologize to Joey?" Then, Johnny says to Joey, "Sorry, Joey." And that's the end of it. Today, after more than 70 years of apologies on national television and years of social media apologies, sincerity is not accepted so readily. It's not a matter of using the key words so much as a demand to be more personal, more heartfelt.

This was apparent after the 2021 Academy Awards of the Academy of Motion Picture Arts and Sciences—also called "The Oscars"—on March 23, 2022 when actor/rapper Will Smith slapped comedian/actor Chris Rock on live TV; the annual broadcast was seen all over the world. Both men were previously liked and praised for their talents and they were not associated with Hollywood's "bad boys."

Smith and his actress wife, Jada Pinkett Smith, were seated on couches near the stage of the Dolby Theatre in Hollywood. He was on the precipice of winning the award for Best Actor for playing the title character in the film *King Richard* (the story of the father of tennis superstars Venus and Serena Williams). It was one of those years when everyone was sure who would win.

Smith had been nominated twice before for the Best Actor award—for *Ali* in 2002 and *The Pursuit of Happyness* in 2006. The award is supposed to be for a single film that year but sometimes it seems the Academy votes to do what people will most appreciate. Before the 2016 ceremony (celebrating 2015 films), Jada led a demonstration to make note that there was a lack of racial diversity in nominees. Will was not nominated that year, but he did star in a film, *Focus*. Rock, the host, turned that into a joke: "How can she boycott something she wasn't invited to?" (Nahas et al., 2022, pp. 35–37). Some say that was the origin of Will's contempt for Rock, but that is not certain.

The insult joke Rock made at the 2016 Oscars was typical of jokes made by hosts and other entertainers at all Oscar ceremonies since icon Bob Hope started hosting in 1940 and continued for 19 years. The use of insult humor is also called "roasting." Not very many years ago, there were televised roasts where the guest of honor was roasted by all celebrities present. It was an honor. At the Oscars, Johnny Carson used insult humor for five Oscar ceremonies. Billy Crystal did it for nine Oscar broadcasts. It is standard fare.

As anyone would likely be, Jada said she was crushed when her hair fell out in the shower in 2018. She learned it was alopecia and as time passed, she turned lemons into lemonade and found a way to handle it. Most determined actresses wouldn't let a thing like hair stop them. So after steroid injections, she found a short hairstyle she liked. Just two weeks before the Oscars, she was televised saying she loved her hair.

At the pre-Oscar broadcast on the red carpet, she was resplendent as she pranced around for all to see her billowy green gown and her pixie hairdo. She knew she was gorgeous.

Those present at the rehearsal for the 2022 broadcast show said Rock did not include the joke about Jada's hair in his monologue. It is possible that he saw her with her short hairdo on the monitor in his dressing room and then conceptualized the joke. He knew where she would be seated because at rehearsal the names and photos of nominees and other celebrities attending are displayed on giant cards in the seats up front so camera people as well as performers will know how to find them. Seeing those cards may also have encouraged him to do the joke.

In the broadcast, the first joke aimed at the Smiths was made by Regina Hall, one of three women hosts. Her joke referred to the rumor abounding in Hollywood about the Smiths having an "open marriage." Many TV viewers not aware of Hollywood gossip had no idea what it was about. The Smiths certainly were familiar with it, but the joke didn't seem to bother them.

It was a different reaction when Rock delivered his monologue and said, "Jada, I love ya. *G.I. Jane 2* can't wait to see ya" (Nahas, 2022, pp. 35–37). *G.I. Jane* was a 1997 film starring Demi Moore in the title role. She sported a shaved head like the other military recruits to show that she could do and be whatever they could do and be. She was equal to the men. At first Will laughed, then he looked at his wife and jumped on the stage—which was easier to access than in previous years—and smacked Rock in the face (Figure 2.3). At first, viewers in the audience and at home thought it was a stunt, but it was not.

The joke was not the funniest Rock had ever told but it really was not an insult. To say she would be a great G.I. Jane is praise. Some film studio should consider it. Rock said he never knew of the alopecia and if he knew, he would not have made the joke. If she looked pitiful, he would not shame her, but she was great-looking. Short hairdos are popular. It is likely that if women see Jada in any hairdo, they are likely to imitate. That's what royalty does and when you are a queen, you don't need hair to wear a crown.

Figure 2.3 More than a year after actor Will Smith slapped comedian Chris Rock at the Academy Awards broadcast social media and TV personalities continued to bring up the subject. It was never revealed if Smith had been under the influence of anything that might affect his judgment.

Source: Neilson Barnard / Staff via Getty Images

The late Sidney Poitier, the first African-American actor to win the Best Actor Oscar, was respected by all actors not only for his talent but because he was a true gentleman, a class act when it came to behavior. Denzel Washington and Jamie Foxx won the award in later years and have spoken about the sage advice Poitier gave them to respect and honor the award. Foxx, doing a spot-on imitation of Poitier, said in a Bahamian accent, "You must have responsibility."

It would be expected that Washington would pass Poitier's sage advice to Smith but perhaps it was too late. Washington said he told Smith, before the incident, "At your highest moment, be careful; that's when the devil comes for you" (Nahas, 2022, pp. 32–37).

Those who knew about Poitier's advice said they were pleased Poitier, who had passed away two months earlier, didn't have to see the smack.

Minutes seemed to pass in seconds until Smith was announced, as expected, the winner of the top male actor. Crisis communications and apology students said they held their breaths as Smith accepted the award hoping that he would apologize to the Academy, the viewers, and Rock. It was the most appropriate time for the apology. But no such luck. He apologized to the Academy saying, "Art imitates life. I look like the crazy father. Just like they said about Richard Williams. But love will make you do crazy things" (Associated Press, 2022).

Would he be arrested? Surely something would happen.

Rock did not want to press charges. At the end of the show, he and the Smith family went to various after-parties. There was no interaction between them. The TV viewers were numb at what they witnessed. Most people don't even know who won the awards following the slap incident. It's not every day that you see actors in a violent confrontation. Most people who thought Smith was not wrong did not see the show or did not know the nature of the Academy Awards.

As punishment for his violent behavior at the awards show, the Academy banned Smith from membership for ten years. At the same time, he resigned. Then, the day after the incident, Smith sent an apology via Instagram. It read:

Violence in all of its forms is poisonous and destructive. My behavior at last night's Academy Awards was unacceptable and inexcusable. Jokes at my expense are a part of the job, but a joke about Jada's medical condition was too much to hear and I reacted emotionally. I would like to publicly apologize to you, Chris. I was out of line and I was wrong.
(Nordyke, HWR.com, March 28, 2022)

Television, print news, radio, other social media picked it up and circulated it. It was appropriate for Smith to send it to his Instagram followers because he had more than 62 million, but some believed he should have made the apology first over television because that's where the infraction occurred. Instagram and television audiences are not necessarily the same people, but both groups were important.

Rock's mother, Rose Rock, said her son deserved a more genuine apology. Rose, an author and family advocate, said "His people wrote up a piece and said, 'I apologize to Chris Rock,' but something like that is personal. You reach out" (Wang, 2022). Rock's brother, Tony Rock, complained that Smith's apology sounded like the work of a publicist. TV viewers on call-in shows agreed with them. In social media, there was a viral agreement that the apology was not good enough. A poll by *The Week* (2022, April 8) revealed that 61 percent of Americans said Smith was wrong compared to 21 percent who said Smith was justified.

There was no suggestion that Smith may have imbibed a bit on backstage liquid refreshments. Actress Jessica Chastain, who won the Best Actress Oscar for *The Eyes of Tammy Faye*, said on Kelly Ripa's post-Oscar show that before she won, she was so nervous that she sought a drink backstage to steady her nerves. Was Will doing the same? Would Rock and the world have accepted an immediate face-to-face apology like this: "Man, I'm so sorry! There I was either about to receive the greatest honor of my life or I was going to have to act like I was OK about not winning again. I didn't know if I was up to it. I needed help so I had a couple of drinks. I was crazy before the drinks and crazy afterwards but I never ever thought I would do that!!!"? The apology wouldn't be an excuse, but it would be an explanation. Frequently the public forgives people with admitted human frailties like they may have. Also an immediate and verbal apology is more believable and sincere.

Developing apologies is a key task in the publicist's job description. Unlike years ago, an apology with the key words was not enough. They could not see the sincerity. The standard apology did not convince.

The social media posts and the talk shows stayed with the issue for weeks; it was daily fare. People wanted a better apology. It wasn't that they wanted him canceled. His fans, according to his number of Instagram followers, increased. It was not a dislike for Smith but mostly a determination that it was just wrong to attack another person on a TV show seen globally. It is wrong and a crime to attack a person for any reason. The attack was wrong, even if Rock did know about Jada's alopecia.

In July, an apology was presented that seemed to be acceptable. It was a five-minute video apology on YouTube that was picked up by newscasts, Hollywood gossip TV shows, and talk shows. *People* talked about it, as did *Variety*, *The Week*, *The Independent*, and numerous daily newspapers. Read Will Smith's third apology in Figure 2.4.

When watching the apology on video, one saw Smith's face and body language. It was a perfectly phrased and professional apology. It was perfectly phrased because it sounded natural, unpolished, without needless repetition, human—like he was pouring out his heart. It didn't seem to be on cue cards. Of course, it still could have been prepared by a publicist and delivered by the newly named Best Actor. If so, they worked on it, and that's the future of apologies. Whether Rock accepted it was not immediately known, but the social media enthusiasts and talk show personalities dropped the daily controversy.

The lesson learned here is to write apologies to be believable. As the public and its expectations mature, so must communications. Also, remember that no one is obligated to accept an apology, no matter how heartfelt or seemingly sincere.

> **An interviewer asked why he didn't apologize to Rock on Oscar night. The response:**
>
> "I was fogged out by that point. It is all fuzzy. I've reached out to Chris and the message that came back is that he's not ready to talk. When he is, I will reach out. I will say to you, Chris, I apologize to you. My behavior was inacceptable and I am here whenever you are ready to talk.I want to apologize to Chris's mother. I saw an interview, and that was one of the things I didn't realize—I wasn't thinking—but how many people got hurt in that moment. I want to apologize to Chris's mother.
>
> I want to apologize to Chris's family, specifically Tony Rock.We had a great relationship.Tony Rock was my man.This is probably irreparable.
>
> I spent the last three months replaying and understanding the nuance and complexity of what happened in that moment. I'm not going to try to unpack all of that right now, but I can say to all of you, there is no part of me that thinks that was the right way to behave in that moment.No part of me thinks that is the optimal way to handle a feeling of disrespect or insult."
>
> **Asked about whether he reacted to Jada, his response was the following:**
>
> "No. It's like, I made a choice on my own, from my history with Chris. Jada had nothing to do with it. I'm sorry, babe. I say sorry to my kids and my family for the heat that I brought on all of us.To my fellow nominees, this is a community. I won because you voted for me."

Figure 2.4 After two public apologies, Will Smith made a third apology. The first two were not accepted by social media communicators and TV fans; they did not seem sincere. However, this the third apology was widely accepted. After that, the public concern of the issue seemed to fade. It was expected to be compassion fatigue when people reach their limits of emotional support.

Bibliography

Crisis Communications Theory

Associated Press. (2006, September 16). *MSNBC.COM.* Retrieved December 28, 2009, from www.msnbc.com.

Barton, L. (1993). *Crisis in organizations.* Cincinnati, OH: South-Western.

Benoit, W. L. (1995). *Accounts, excuses, apologies: A theory of image restoration strategies.* Albany, NY: University of New York Press.

Benoit, W. L. (1997). Image restoration discourse and crisis communication. *Public Relations Review, 23,* 177–186.

Biswas, T. (1997). *Decision-making under uncertainty.* New York: St. Martins.

Castro, H. (2007, October 5). Sheriff apologizes but defends policy. *Seattle Post-Intelligencer,* A1.

Fearn-Banks, K. (1996). Crisis communications theory and ten businesses hit by news-making crises. In G. Amin & S. Fullerton (Eds.), *Global business trends: Contemporary readings* (pp. 847–851). Cumberland, MD: Academy of Business Administration.

Grunig, J. E. & Grunig, L. A. (1992). Models of public relations and communications. In J. E. Grunig (Ed.), *Excellence in public relations and communication management* (pp. 85–326). Hillsdale, NJ: Lawrence Erlbaum Associates.

Grunig, J. E. & Hunt, T. (1984). *Managing public relations*. New York: Holt.
Grunig, J. E. & Repper, F. C. (1992). Strategic management, publics, and issues. In J. E. Grunig (Ed.), *Excellence in public relations and communication management* (pp. 117–157). Hillsdale, NJ: Lawrence Erlbaum Associates.
Hearit, K. M. (2001). Corporate apologia: When the organization speaks in defense of itself. In R. L. Heath (Ed.), *Handbook of public relations* (pp. 501–512). Thousand Oaks, CA: Sage.
Marra, F. J. (1992). *Crisis public relations: A theoretical model*. Unpublished doctoral dissertation, University of Maryland, College Park.
Rogers, E. M. (2003). *The diffusion of innovations* (5th ed.). New York: Free Press.
Schick, F. (1997). *Making choices: A recasting of decision theory*. New York: Cambridge University Press.
Ware, B. L. & Linkugel, W. A. (1973). They spoke in defense of themselves: On the generic criticism of apologia. *Quarterly Journal of Speech*, 59, 273–283.

The "Five Ws" of Public Apology for Celebrities and Businesses

Arends, B. (2014, December 2). When apologizing makes no sense. *Fortune.com*. Retrieved March 5, 2015, from http://fortune.com.
Axia Public Relations. (2014, December 22). *When should a company apologize on social media?* Retrieved March 6, 2015, from www.axiapr.com.
Breckenridge, D. (2013, March 20). The anatomy of an apology. *Ragan.com*. Retrieved March 5, 2015, from www.ragan.com.
Durando, J. (2014, December 1). GOP aide resigns after comments on Obama girls. *USA Today network*. Retrieved March 5, 2015, from www.usatoday.com.
Fathi, S. (2013, October 3). PR insider: The executive apology, avoid making it worse once you've already screwed up. *PR news online*. Retrieved March 2, 2015, from www.prnewsonline.com.
Grisham, L. (2015, February 17). Krispy Kreme apologizes for "KKK" doughnut club. *USA Today network*. Retrieved February 17, 2015, from www.usatoday.com.
Little, K. (2015, February 17). Oops: Krispy Kreme sparks outrage for "KKK" event. *CNBC.com*. Retrieved February 17, 2015, from www.cnbc.com.
Wilson, T. (2012, September 10). The best legal advice is often an apology. *The globe and mail online*. Retrieved February 10, 2015, from www.theglobeandmail.co.

Case Study: Will Smith and the Academy Awards Slap

Anderson, E. (2022, August 15). Will Smith's new apology, Chris Rock's next moves. *People*, 13–14.
Associated Press. (2022, April 8). Actor Will Smith gets 10-year Oscars ban over Chris Rock slap. *Associated Press Newswire*. Retrieved October 5, 2022.
Nahas, A., Chiu, M., Leonard, E., Brody, L., Morse, L. & McNeal, L. (2022, April 11). Will, Jada, & Chris; what just happened. *People*, 32–37.
Nordyke, K. (2022, March 28). Will Smith apologizes to Chris Rock in Instagram post, calls behavior unacceptable and inexcusable. *Hollywood Reporter Online, HWR.com*.
Sharf, Z. (2022, May 1). Chris Rock's brother slams Will Smith's slap apology. *Variety.com*. Retrieved October 5, 2022, from https://variety.com/2022/film/news.

Strohm, E. (2022: April 18). What's next for Chris Rock? *People*, 17–18.

The Week. (2022, April 8). The Oscars: What Smith's smack revealed. *The Week*, 17.

Wang, J. (2022). Chris Rock's mother doesn't consider Will Smith's Oscar ban punishment: He slapped all of us. *Entertainment Weekly*. Retrieved October 5, 2022, from https:www.msn.com/en-us/tv/recaps/chris-rocks-mother.

Whiting, A. (2022: July). Will Smith's Oscar dinner's video apology to Chris Rock transcribed in full. *Independent*. Retrieved October 5, 2022, from www.independent.co.uk/arts-entertainment.

Chapter 3

"Textbook" Crises

The Johnson & Johnson Tylenol case and the *Exxon Valdez* oil spill case, both in the 1980s, set the stage for the development of the field of crisis communications. Up to and including these landmark cases, organizations and companies, for the most part, handled their crises as best they could, without crisis management or crisis communications plans.

These crises made the organizations realize that there should be plans, and provided the key examples of what to do and what not to do. Johnson & Johnson was reputed to be the stellar company and Exxon to be the prime example of what was bad in communications and public relations. Actually, the case studies reveal that Johnson & Johnson made a mistake in its handling of the crisis, although it was honest about the mistake. And Exxon, though still blamed for the tragic, widespread oil spill, was not solely responsible and made some positive moves to help the state of Alaska recover.

Case Study: Johnson & Johnson and the Tylenol Murders

Before September 30, 1982, manufacturers felt that if they made a good product and dealt fairly with consumers, retailers, employees, and other publics, they could maintain a positive image and be considered consumer-friendly and a good company with which to do business.

Johnson & Johnson was one of those companies. It was an old and trusted company. Consisting of 165 companies in 53 countries throughout the world, it made baby products, baby powder, lotions, shampoos, cotton swabs, adhesive bandages, surgical instruments, Reach toothbrushes, Ortho-Novum birth control pills, and pharmaceuticals on the WHO list of essential drugs. Johnson & Johnson was a household name.

The corporation also had a positive image among its employees. It was listed as one of the 100 best places to work. The company credo was written by the son of the company's founder in the 1940s. The credo said that the company

DOI: 10.4324/9781003019282-3

had four responsibilities in the following order of priority: to the consumer, to the employees, to the communities, and to the stockholders (Figure 3.1).

The company also had continually good relationships with the media. Little did it realize just how crucial those relationships would become.

September 30 began like any other workday at the headquarters in New Brunswick, New Jersey. Then a fateful telephone call came in.

A reporter from the *Chicago Sun-Times* telephoned a public relations staff member asking such questions as "How long has Tylenol been on the market?" and "What is Tylenol's share of the market?"

The reporter did not know why he had been asked to prepare background information on Tylenol. Someone else was writing the story. An editor had merely assigned him to do background research to use in the main story. The Johnson & Johnson staffer, who then alerted most of the department, thought the call was a bit strange and reported it to Public Relations Director Robert Kniffin. Kniffin called Arthur Quilty, an executive committee member who had responsibility for McNeil Consumer Products Corporation, a subsidiary. Quilty alerted James Burke, CEO. The reporter later called back and explained there had been reported deaths from the intake of Extra Strength Tylenol.

Corporate Vice President Lawrence Foster, who was on vacation, called in, as was his daily practice, and when he learned what had happened, he immediately returned to the office and took charge of the public relations activities.

The corporation had no specific crisis communications plan—few companies did at the time. It did have an emergency plan and a call list for incidents such as plant fires. The first step was to notify the chain of command.

There was an immediate meeting in Burke's office with top executives, including Lawrence Foster, head of public relations; David Clare, president and chairman of Johnson & Johnson's executive committee; Joseph Chiesea, president of McNeil Consumer Products Company; and David Collins, chairman of McNeil.

At that meeting, Foster dispatched Kniffin to McNeil's headquarters nearby. Collins, who had been president of McNeil Pharmaceuticals and knew the subsidiary well, was sent to McNeil by Burke. This would actually have been the next step in a crisis communications plan—had there been such a plan.

The executives all said that it was a period of great fear. There were no warnings, no prodromes. Nothing like this had ever happened to them or any other company that provided products for human consumption. What was going on? Was there a psychopathic murderer in the plant?

When the story ran in the media, the public also was afraid. The very idea that a person could take a capsule for a headache and die was terrorizing. People were saying, "I have a terrible headache, but I'm alive." Even consumers outside the Chicago area were afraid of Tylenol capsules, if not also afraid of all over-the-counter pain medications.

Our Credo

We believe our first responsibility is to the doctors, nurses and patients,
to mothers and fathers and all others who use our products and services.
In meeting their needs everything we do must be of high quality.
We must constantly strive to reduce our costs
in order to maintain reasonable prices.
Customers' orders must be serviced promptly and accurately.
Our suppliers and distributors must have an opportunity
to make a fair profit.

We are responsible to our employees,
the men and women who work with us throughout the world.
Everyone must be considered as an individual.
We must respect their dignity and recognize their merit.
They must have a sense of security in their jobs.
Compensation must be fair and adequate,
and working conditions clean, orderly and safe.
We must be mindful of ways to help our employees fulfill
their family responsibilities.
Employees must feel free to make suggestions and complaints.
There must be equal opportunity for employment, development
and advancement for those qualified.
We must provide competent management,
and their actions must be just and ethical.

We are responsible to the communities in which we live and work
and to the world community as well.
We must be good citizens — support good works and charities
and bear our fair share of taxes.
We must encourage civic improvements and better health and education.
We must maintain in good order
the property we are privileged to use,
protecting the environment and natural resources.

Our final responsibility is to our stockholders.
Business must make a sound profit.
We must experiment with new ideas.
Research must be carried on, innovative programs developed
and mistakes paid for.
New equipment must be purchased, new facilities provided
and new products launched.
Reserves must be created to provide for adverse times.
When we operate according to these principles,
the stockholders should realize a fair return.

Johnson & Johnson

Figure 3.1 The Johnson & Johnson credo that guided the company's crisis team through the ordeal of saving the company's image, even as news accounts reported that the company's Tylenol product was killing consumers. Reprinted by permission of Johnson & Johnson.

Johnson & Johnson, with headquarters in New Brunswick, New Jersey, is frequently cited as a favorite place to work and a trusted manufacturer in the
pharmaceutical world, according to the annual Fortune 500 lists.

Source: Photo by Tina Wilson

Collins immediately set up a seven-member crisis team. The team's first
task was to find out what sickness it was actually facing. Then it would
determine how to go about the healing process. The crisis team handled
decisions in the area of communications and was in charge of all strategies
and tactics. With Burke's approval, the team decided to recall all Tylenol
capsules from stores in the Chicago area.

Cyanide turned out to be the cause of the deaths. The recalled batch was
tested and two additional cyanide-laced capsules were discovered. Still,
the team and company were uncertain of how the cyanide got into the
capsules. It indeed hoped that the criminality was not in the company, but
there was no certainty.

Johnson & Johnson had one overriding priority: Warn the public. The
company did just that by being completely open and cooperative with the
media in getting the news out.

Foster said he believed that three points marked the reason why Johnson & Johnson was successful in coping with the crisis:

1. The company was open to the media.
2. It was willing to recall the product, no matter what that meant to the
   company.
3. It appealed to the American sense of fair play and asked for the public's
   trust.

Foster was responsible for the communications aspect of the crisis team's work. The team was concerned with aiding police and the Federal Bureau of Investigation (FBI) in finding the responsible party and in dealing with the Food and Drug Administration (FDA).

First, the crisis team identified its key publics:

1. consumers (through the media);
2. the medical profession;
3. employees and other internal groups;
4. the FDA.

All publics were notified initially, and the team kept in touch with them throughout the crisis.

The first story appeared in the morning edition of the *Chicago Sun-Times* on October 1. The *Chicago Tribune* ran a story that same afternoon under a banner headline:

5 DEATHS TIED TO PILLS: FEAR KILLER PUT CYANIDE IN TYLENOL

A study of the *Tribune*'s coverage revealed that the newspaper was as supportive of Johnson & Johnson as it could have been in telling the bad news. Its support is especially noteworthy compared to later newspapers and television broadcasts, which basically attacked companies in crisis. The opening pages of two *Tribune* stories are shown in Figure 3.2 and Figure 3.3. The company's executives, the police, the FBI, and the newspapers knew from the start that the tampering could possibly have happened at the plant. Nevertheless, there was no insinuation of this in the *Tribune*'s coverage.

The name Johnson & Johnson was not mentioned on Page 1. In the continuation of the story on Page 2, nearly buried in the middle of 12 column inches of copy, was the following statement:

A spokesperson for Johnson & Johnson, parent firm of the company that makes Tylenol, said Thursday evening his firm "launched an investigation this morning to track down the capsules."

The spokesman, Robert Andrews, and two other Johnson & Johnson officials met for an hour and a half with Elk Grove Village detectives and evidence technicians.

He said his firm is "collectively shocked."

(Houston & Griffin, 1982, p. 2)

There were four *Tribune* stories about the Tylenol crisis on that one issue. Other than in the preceding quote, all other mentions of the company were of McNeil Consumer Products Company, not as familiar a name to consumers as Johnson & Johnson.

OTHER REMEDY MAY BE SAFE, BUT CUSTOMERS DON'T BUY IT

CHICAGO TRIBUNE

DUST IS COLLECTING on some drugstore shelves in the Chicago area, and people apparently are learning to live with headaches in the wake of last week's tragedy involving Extra Strength Tylenol laced with cyanide.

An informal survey of drugstores throughout the Chicago area showed that sales of most acetaminophen products have dropped while sales of aspirin have increased slightly. Acetaminophen is the nonaspirin substance used in Tylenol and other pain relievers.

"In general acetominophen products are not selling. Point blank. Done in. Dead. Aspirin products are picking up a bit, but the scare seems to have spread through the shelves," said pharmacist Paul Bablak of the Hinsdale Medical Center Pharmacy. "We're collecting a lot of dust on our shelves. People are scared, and you really can't blame them."

If the fear of cyanide poisoning can be measured by the stillpacked medication shelves at drugstores, then the fever is spreading through the metropolitan area, several other pharmacists said.

"I think everybody's walking around with headaches," said Jerry Denny, a pharmacist at Family Pharmacy in west suburban La Grange. "All the acetaminophen products are just sitting on the shelves. Even generic acetaminophen is moving slowly."

The slow sales were found not only in smaller, private drugstores but also in chain stores. Jane Armstrong, director of consumer affairs for the Jewel Foods Co., which operates almost 200 Jewel grocery stores and Osco drugstores in the Chicago area, said, "It's too early to tell what's happening to other acetaminophen products. We have noticed an increase in aspirin sales, although it's not a groundswell at this point."

The results have been the same for major drug wholesalers in the area. Drug buyers from several large wholesalers said they expect orders to increase for aspirin and the substitute acetaminophen products once fear subsides, but they added that it is too soon to accurately measure the effect of the tragedy on drug sales.

Figure 3.2 One of four news stories appearing in the Chicago Tribune on October 1, 1982, the first day of news coverage of the Tylenol crisis. Note that the story did not mention Johnson & Johnson. Chicago Tribune Company. Reproduced by permission.

STORES AROUND NATION
PULL TYLENOL CAPSULES

By BARBARA MAHANEY,
CHICAGO TRIBUNE

STORES NATIONWIDE quickly ordered personnel Thursday to strip their shelves of Extra Strength Tylenol capsules and hospital spokesmen reported rashes of phone calls after cyanide-tainted capsules were linked in three deaths and possibly two others in suburban Chicago.

The nation's largest grocery chain, Safeway, in Oakland, Calif., ordered all stores to remove bottles of the over-the-counter pain killer in the 96,000-bottle lot-MC 3000, which was recalled by McNeil Consumer Products Co., of Fort Washington, PA.

All 1,000 Revco Discount Drug Centers and 400 CVS pharmacies in New England pulled every bottle of Extra Strength Tylenol. "We have pulled it off our shelves completely," said Bernie Thomas of Perry Drug Stores, Inc., which operated 124 stores in five states, including 98 in Michigan.

Meanwhile, poison centers and hospitals were reported swamped with thousands of calls from worried consumers, many of whom said they took Tylenol capsules from the recalled lot, but apparently suffered no ill effects.

"We've had questions ranging from 'Do you know anything about Tylenol being contaminated' to 'Oh my God, I just took Extra Strength Tylenol, am I going to die?'" said Cathy Piccillo of the Indiana Poison Center, which received 50 phone calls.

Figure 3.3 Another of the four stories appearing in the *Chicago Tribune* on the first day of coverage of the Tylenol crisis. Again, there was no mention of Johnson & Johnson. Chicago Tribune Company. Reprinted by permission.

The captions for the related photographs on Page 1 and Page 2 of the *Tribune* also did not mention the company. The caption on Page 2 indicated that medical examiners believed "the capsules were tampered with after leaving the manufacturer's plant in Pennsylvania" (Shanker & Grady, 1982, p. 2).

On Saturday, October 2, the headline in the *Chicago Tribune* was "Stewardess is 7th Capsule Poison Victim." The Page 1 headline was not the dominant headline on the page. A bomb explosion that had killed hundreds of people in Tehran, Iran, took that honor. There were two other stories about the Tylenol crisis—one about the efforts to track the source of the poison, and another about funeral services for the victims.

On Sunday, October 3, the Tribune's front-page banner headline, "Shoplifter is Sought in Poisoning Probe," referred to a story about a man who had been arrested a couple of months before for stealing Tylenol. The story continued on Page 4 with excerpts referring to the Johnson & Johnson plants. The first excerpt read as follows:

> Consumers nationwide were urged to stop using Extra Strength Tylenol capsules. Johnson & Johnson, parent company of the painkiller's manufacturer, announced it is recalling all Extra Strength Tylenol in the Chicago area.
>
> (Shanker & Grady, 1982, p. 4)

The second excerpt took the following form:

> Investigators have been unable to determine how and where the cyanide capsules were placed in any of the suspect containers—whether the killer infiltrated the drug company's sophisticated manufacturing and distribution system at some point between plants in Pennsylvania and Texas and warehouses elsewhere or whether the killer removed and replaced containers once they had been placed on the shelves of local stores.
>
> Stein said he could not rule out "factory error" because of the reported disclosure by Lawrence Foster, a spokesman for Johnson & Johnson.
>
> Foster said potassium cyanide is used in chemical tests at some of McNeil's laboratories, but not in the manufacturing process. The labs are remote from the manufacturing areas and cyanide would be detected even if someone tried to introduce it during manufacturing, he said.
>
> (Shanker & Grady, 1982, p. 4)

There was another front-page story in the October 3 *Tribune*, this one about a 12-year-old who had died from the poison four days before.

Johnson & Johnson installed 33 telephones to communicate with publics during the crisis (Interview with J & J PR). Pre-taped statements were placed on special toll-free telephone lines to expedite news gathering. The messages were regularly updated. A full-page advertisement was placed in major Chicago newspapers offering consumers an exchange of Tylenol capsules for Tylenol tablets.

During the first week of the crisis, Kniffin handled the media from McNeil, whereas Foster was in charge at headquarters. Approximately

180,000 news stories ran in newspapers nationally. The story was at the top of television and radio newscasts.

About 2,000 telephone calls were taken from the media, and 30,000 calls from consumers came in during the first months following the deaths.

Still, there were glitches.

During the first three days, as the *Chicago Tribune* articles showed, Foster issued a statement to reporters that there was no cyanide in the manufacturing plants. A few days later, the Associated Press heard that there was cyanide in the manufacturing plants and called Foster to confirm the report. After checking again, Foster discovered that indeed a small amount of cyanide was used in the manufacturing plant for quality-assurance testing of some kind. However, the cyanide was kept in a completely separate facility from the production line. Also, none of it was missing. There was no way that it could have got into the capsules accidentally. Even if it had, it would have been so dispersed as to be harmless.

Foster called the Associated Press and told the truth. He had a reputation for being honest, fair, and ethical. He could not afford a cover-up. When he told the wire service that there was no way the cyanide could have got into the capsules, the reporters believed him and agreed not to run the story—unless some other news outlet got the information, too.

Sure enough, the *Newark Star-Ledger* of New Jersey got word of the information, called Johnson & Johnson for confirmation, and again Foster said, "Trust me." The reporter agreed.

Keeping his promise to the Associated Press, Foster called and told the wire service that the *Star-Ledger* had the information but had also agreed not to run it. The Associated Press agreed once more not to run the story unless still another newspaper or TV station got the information. After all, the *Star-Ledger* was basically a neighbor to the company.

However, when the *New York Times* got the information, Foster decided to give up. He called both the Associated Press and the *Star-Ledger* and asked them to use discretion in running the story. The resulting stories had very little impact. They were run in insignificant places in the Sunday newspapers, and the facts were not blown out of proportion (as had happened with other crises). The newspapers merely reported the information as Foster had revealed it.

With this, Foster realized that his positive dealings with the media over the years had paid off. The story could have made front-page headlines everywhere, but it did not because the media trusted the public relations professional from their past dealings with him.

The FBI and the FDA never found any evidence of tampering at the two Johnson & Johnson plants. They found that the contaminated capsules had come from both plants—one in Texas, the other in Pennsylvania. This was proof that no person at Johnson & Johnson had ever been in contact with all the capsules. It was not an inside job. The finger now pointed to some external, malicious psychopath who bought the Tylenol, laced it with cyanide, and placed it back in the containers and on the shelves of stores.

After the crisis team discovered what had transpired, its members were relieved to be assured that the contamination could not have occurred in the plants. The task of the team now turned to saving Tylenol and restoring sales. Because of the company's diversified product line, the team was not worried that Johnson & Johnson would go under. Sales were not down for other Johnson & Johnson products. There was no boycott against the company. However, there was a fear of Tylenol capsules. The future of Tylenol was at stake.

To reach the employees who were concerned about their company's future, CEO Burke spoke to an assembly at McNeil and promised that Extra Strength Tylenol was coming back. Employees wore "We're Coming Back" buttons. Those employees who had been manufacturing Tylenol were given other, temporary jobs. Videotaped reports of activities were shown to employees explaining what was going on with the crisis.

Information packages were sent electronically—by fax, telegram, and other methods—to major distributors, who, in a short time, notified half a million retailers and medical professionals.

Up to this point, there was a debate over whether to recall the product. The FBI and the FDA advised against a recall because it would mean giving in to the criminals.

The decision not to recall would have worked if it had not been for a copy-cat crime that took place in northern California on October 5. The company decided then that removing the product from all stores was the only way to show the public that it was concerned about the welfare of its customers. On October 5, all Tylenol products were removed from stores nationwide.

Later, there were approximately 250 copycat reports, all of which were found to be groundless.

During the recovery period, a decision was made to repackage the product. A 60-second television commercial featuring the medical director at Mc-Neil notifying consumers of the upcoming return of Tylenol aired in October and November to an estimated 85 percent of U.S. television households.

The triple-seal safety package devised for the product was announced at a November 11 news conference transmitted by satellite to 29 different sites where reporters were gathered. Burke also announced the availability of coupons that could be used toward the purchase of any Tylenol product and a special toll-free telephone number through which consumers could learn about the special promotion. More than 200,000 calls came in to the toll-free information number. Coverage of the press conference in the now-defunct *Kansas City Times* applauded Burke and the company for their efforts and described the new Tylenol safety package as having "glued flaps . . . that must be forcibly opened. Inside, a tight plastic seal surrounds the cap and an inner foil seal wraps over the mouth of the bottle" (Goodman, 1982, p. A3). Johnson & Johnson could not have paid for better news coverage.

Johnson & Johnson executives did interviews with network television shows, such as *Donahue*, *60 Minutes*, and *Nightline*, as well as with major newspapers and magazines, such as the *Wall Street Journal* and *Fortune*.

As a result of the crisis, all Tylenol capsules were discontinued, as were capsules of other brand names. Tamper-proof, triple-sealed safety containers were swiftly placed on the shelves of retailers 10 weeks after the withdrawal. Other manufacturers followed suit.

The crisis cost the company more than $100 million. Tylenol regained 100 percent of the market share it had before the crisis. Seven people died. Other lives were saved by the company's decision to recall all the capsules in the Chicago area. The Tylenol murderer was never found. A $100,000 reward offered by Johnson & Johnson still remains unclaimed.

An October 11, 1982 *Washington Post* front-page article praised Johnson & Johnson's crisis response:

> Johnson & Johnson has effectively demonstrated how a major business ought to handle a disaster . . . what executives have done is communicate the message that the company is candid, contrite and compassionate, committed to solving the murders and protecting the public.
>
> (Knight, 1982, p. 1)

Johnson & Johnson has expanded and also acquired numerous other companies in the United States and abroad since the tampering incident. Fifty-eight mergers and acquisitions were made in the decade spanning 1994–2004. This added more than 50 companies and product lines to the Johnson & Johnson name. International affiliates of the company were founded in China (Xi'an, 1985; Shanghai, 1990), Hungary (1990), Poland (1990), Russia (1990), and the Czech Republic (1991).

In 2004, the company had more than 110,000 employees worldwide. When *Fortune* ranked its "10 Most Admired Companies" in 2002, Johnson & Johnson was No. 7. Harris Interactive ranks companies according to its National Corporate Reputation Survey, and Johnson & Johnson ranked first for six consecutive years (1998–2004).

Johnson & Johnson was named "The Most Respected Company" in 2009 in a *Barron's* magazine online survey. It was "One of the Best Places to Work" according to the Human Rights Commission, was ranked #1 by *DiversityInc* magazine, and has been one of the "Top 100 Companies for Working Mothers" since *Working Mother* magazine began its annual list in 1975.

In November, 2009, Johnson & Johnson issued a voluntary recall of five product lots of Tylenol Arthritis Pain formula caplets because consumers complained of a moldy smell, nausea, stomach pain, and diarrhea. In December, the company recalled all lots of the painkiller with the red "EZ-Open Cap." The moldy smell apparently resulted from the presence of trace amounts of a chemical called 2,4,6-tribromoanisole used to treat the wooden pallets that transport and store packaging materials. The same chemical can give wine a corky, musty smell. The side effects were said to be "temporary and non-serious."

In January 2010, Johnson & Johnson issued a third and even more extensive recall of batches of Tylenol, and also of Motrin and St. Joseph's aspirin—all because of the sickening moldy smell.

As late as January 2010, the FBI was still investigating the 1982 Tylenol crime. The prime suspect, James Lewis, provided DNA samples on the orders of a Massachusetts judge. Lewis resided then in Boston. Shortly after the murders, he was convicted of extortion for demanding $1 million to "stop the killing." He served 12 years in prison and was released in 1995. Lewis told a Massachusetts TV show he is innocent of murder. Lewis died in July 2023 in Cambridge.

In 2014, Johnson & Johnson kept a promise made in 2013 and removed two potentially harmful chemicals from its baby products—formaldehyde and 1,4-dioxane. This is a first step toward removing ingredients that have become increasingly unpopular. The danger was not great; a person's exposure to formaldehyde in an apple is greater than it is in baby shampoo. Levels of 1,4-dioxane were also low. Other companies did the same. (See "Yuhan-Kimberly and the Baby Wet Wipes" in Chapter 8.)

In 2016, two juries had ordered Johnson & Johnson to pay millions of dollars over claims that its talcum powder caused ovarian cancer in two women who used it for hygiene purposes. Carol Goodrich, a spokesperson for the company, said the company stands by the talc used in all "global products" and they are evaluating their legal options. She continued, "The recent verdict goes against decades of sound science proving the safety of talc as a cosmetic ingredient in multiple products, and while we sympathize with the family of the plaintiff, we strongly disagree with the outcome" (Interview with Goodrich).

Johnson & Johnson has had some bad press in recent years on numerous lawsuits charging that its baby powder contained asbestos and caused ovarian cancer in more women than the 2016 charges. The charges did not extend to babies, the intended target for the product.

Still, Johnson & Johnson ranked first on the "Pharmaceutical List" of companies in the Fortune 500. It was also listed in the "World's Most Admired Companies" and was named in the 2023 inaugural list of the most innovative companies. The company's mission is still in its credo, developed in 1886.

What Could Have Been Done If Social Media Had Existed

- The team could keep constant updates of the news on the crisis on the J & J website, as well as create a special Facebook page keeping all concerned parties well informed, providing pertinent instructions to the public (e.g., If a consumer took Tylenol, what should they do?). Through Twitter, health officials could provide consumers with timely information about cyanide poisoning, symptoms, and steps to take in an emergency.
- Thanks to YouTube and the array of social media platforms, after broadcasting pertinent statements from key J & J parties, everyone would have access to view or listen to those statements for future reference.
- Through social media, the public would have a voice, and J & J would have an opportunity to hear it. They could immediately respond to comments from various publics, address fears and concerns, dispel myths, and quickly answer questions.
- J & J's key publics (consumers, medical professionals, employees, and the FDA) could be addressed with fast, strategic, tailored messages (e.g., J & J employees, through internal social media platforms created just for them, could be updated on the crisis as well as their role as employees). Those key publics could in turn deliver messages through their own social media vehicles.
- J & J recalled all Tylenol capsules from stores in the Chicago area. Through the omnipresent force of social media, news of the crisis would have spread within seconds of transmission. Word of mouth would then follow, in addition to retweets, and comments on top of comments on social media. An aftereffect of social media is that with crisis comes immediate public reaction and response. Through social media vehicles, which can be far-reaching, methodical and strategic, carriers of Tylenol products could have taken action and quickly responded to the crisis, alerting the public and hence, creating a mini-reactive campaign on their own.
- Additional possibilities:
  - use of effective social media may have actually played a role in preventing deaths because consumers would have more quickly received the news of the contamination;
  - social media has many eyes and ears, and could have played a role in identifying the person who contaminated the bottles.

Natalie Ryder Redcross, Ph.D., assistant professor, public relations, Iona College, New Rochelle, N.Y.

Case Study: Exxon and the *Valdez* Oil Spill

In the late 1980s, Exxon was one of the five largest companies in the United States, with sales of $80 billion. Exxon CEO Lawrence G. Rawl had been employed at Exxon for 37 years before getting the top job in 1986. He was considered a strong leader who disliked publicity and the media.

The *Valdez* oil spill crisis started shortly after midnight on Friday, March 24, 1989. The *Exxon Valdez*, a 987-foot oil tanker, was headed for Long Beach, California, from Prince William Sound off the coast of Alaska. A reporter later described the ship as "longer than three football fields, [and] loaded to the top with enough oil to fill the Rose Bowl almost halfway to the top" (Turning Point, 1994).

The weather was calm. The water was beautiful. During daylight hours, an abundance of sea life could be seen. It was the time of the migration that brings to the area the largest concentration of migratory fowl in the entire world. Sea otters, seals, whales, salmon, herring, and halibut inhabited the sound.

Just before midnight, the local pilot, who had guided the tanker out of the harbor, went off duty. Captain Joseph Hazelwood, in command, put the supertanker on autopilot and headed straight for Bligh Reef, one of several well-known hazardous areas in Prince William Sound. Hazelwood had sailed the route more than 100 times. Some said he could do it nearly blindfolded. He had been with Exxon for 21 years, ten of them as captain.

On this night, Hazelwood left his post at the bridge and put Third Mate Gregory Cousins in charge, telling him to keep the tanker on course for three minutes, then turn right, thus avoiding the reef. Although Cousins was qualified to take command during normal times, government investigators later said that he was not qualified to take command at that critical period when the ship had to be steered in a very precise maneuver.

Cousins waited too long before ordering the turn, and the *Exxon Valdez* headed for the submerged rocks. He told Captain Hazelwood, "I think we're in serious trouble." Hazelwood radioed the Coast Guard with the message, "We've fetched up hard aground . . . . Evidently, we're leaking some oil" (Smith, 1992, p. 84). Cousins and Hazelwood had just made the two understatements of 1989.

The tanker had run aground on the rocks of Bligh Reef, ripping open a hole in the hull nearly as long as the ship itself. Over the next hours and days, 11 million gallons of crude oil poured out into Prince William Sound. The oil spread relentlessly. Some said the oil slick was 10 feet wide and 4 miles long—the worst oil spill ever in American waters.

Obviously, the beautiful waters were no longer beautiful, but more importantly, sea life perished. It was estimated that one million migratory fowl and one-third of the sea otter population—about 2,500—died. Seals and sea lions also fell victim to the slick. Some sources revealed that two million animals died as a result of the oil, although this did not include halibut, pink salmon, herring, clams, and worms that remained uncounted. Some scientists claimed that wildlife may still remain poisoned by the oil years later. Others later said Prince William Sound totally recovered from the spill.

The weekend news reports came from local media and through the three major television networks. By Monday, media people from all over the world began to pour into the town of Valdez. The media frenzy had begun. (Examples of the news coverage are shown in Figure 3.4.) In addition, hundreds of environmentalists arrived in Valdez to help save the animals, the beaches, and the water. Concern was rampant.

Don Cornet, who later became Exxon's Public Relations Manager, was Alaska coordinator for Exxon at that time; he reported to the head of public affairs and rushed to the scene as soon as he got word of the accident. The company's immediate strategy was to focus on the cleanup effort. Exxon's theory was that the initial spill was regrettable, but that at this point the most crucial task was to clean it up as swiftly as possible and restore normalcy to the area.

Frank Iarossi, then president of Exxon Shipping (the grounded tanker came from its shipyards), was Exxon's main representative at the Valdez site. CEO Lawrence Rawl was nowhere to be found. Iarossi dealt with the logistics of the spill response. Early on, he pointed a finger at Captain Hazelwood. Years later, there was still some confusion over whether Hazelwood had been drinking that night, but it was a fact that his driver's license had been revoked for drunken driving and that he had once been hospitalized for alcohol treatment. He denies he was drunk and no court has ever proven he was. At any rate, Hazelwood was fired. Third Mate Cousins blamed the crisis on "poor seamanship" (The Big Spill, 1990).

Some Exxon employees placed the blame on Exxon's corporate culture. They said that to save money the company had cut crews, and that the short-staffed crews worked long hours and got little sleep. They felt that human fatigue was responsible for the accident. Moving the oil was a cardinal rule, they said, and employees who did not work fast and long enough feared losing their jobs.

Smith (1992) said that in 1986, the *Exxon Valdez* was designed for a crew of 33. Yet on the fateful night of the spill, the crew numbered only 19.

According to requirements of the State of Alaska, the Alyeska Pipeline Service Company—a consortium of several companies working on Alaska's North Slope—was responsible for the initial response to the spill. Exxon, Atlantic Richfield (ARCO), British Petroleum (BP), and five other companies initially participated in the response. Exxon soon after took over the cleanup efforts from the other companies.

At the start of the crisis, Cornet set up a media center in Valdez, a remote town with limited facilities, equipment, and accommodation. Critics charged that the media center should have been in New York or Chicago,

CRUDE OIL FOULS SOUND

Oil Officials React Slowly to Disaster

BY LARRY CAMPBELL
DAILY NEWS REPORTER

VALDEZ—As the largest oil spill in the history of the United States entered its second day, only a feeble containment effort has been mounted and a crowd of state, federal and oil company officials remained undecided about how to clean up the mess.

A 32-square-mile, multi-hued sheen continued to float and spread atop the waters of Prince William Sound. The Sound is surrounded by land on three sides. Two large islands, Hinchinbrook and Montague, lie across its open, southern end. That means that unless the spilled oil can be dealt with, it is a near certainty that it will wash ashore somewhere in the Sound.

Valdez residents grew increasingly critical Friday of what seemed to be sluggish movement by Alyeska Pipeline Service Co., which operates the oil terminal here, and Exxon Shipping Co. in dealing with the spill. Nearly 24 hours after the Exxon Valdez ran aground on Bligh Reef about 25 miles southwest of here, officials had done little to contain the spill or clean up what was beyond containment.

Oil keeps spreading in Sound State says

Alyeska's cleanup effort inadequate, slow

BY LARRY CAMPBELL
DAILY NEWS REPORTER

VALDEZ—State, federal and oil company officials ended Saturday as they had begun it, no closer to a solution to the problems posed by more than 11 million gallons of North Slope crude oil washing around the fish-and-wildlife-rich, enclosed waters of Prince William Sound.

But while the oil of the nation's largest spill was left mostly unmolested, the chief of the state Department of Environmental Conservation assailed the Alyeska Pipeline Service Co. for its failure to respond quickly to the disaster.

Figure 3.4 Excerpts from front-page news stories appearing in the *Anchorage Daily News* on March 25, 1989, the day after the oil spill from the *Exxon Valdez.*

cities that could better accommodate such a large gathering of reporters and photographers. Others insisted that it had to be at the site, regardless of the difficulties. The media said that photographs and videos of the spill, citizens of Alaska, and government officials were all necessary to the stories communicated to the public.

Contradictory statements about the seriousness of the crisis were issued from various news sources. One statement said the damage was minimal. Another said the damage was substantial.

Four days after the spill, local fishermen in the village of Cordova were angry because cleanup efforts had not worked. They and the media were not happy about the response. Iarossi held a press conference without first being briefed by public relations personnel; he was verbally slaughtered. Brian Dunphy, another spokesperson for Exxon Shipping, said that he would not verify the extent of the damage or what was being done about it, a statement that was not well received.

CEO Rawl still declined to go to the site. He said that he felt "technologically obsolete." The media, the fishermen, the environmentalists, and the public were irate. Customers began to cancel their Exxon credit cards. The media continued to attack more vociferously. Exxon had not anticipated the intensity of the public's concern about the environmental crisis, nor had it anticipated such a large spill or the difficulties with cleanup and communications.

Exxon's Concern for Alaska

In 1989, George Mason, APR (Accreditation in Public Relations), was vice president of Bradley/McAfee Public Relations, Alaska's largest public relations firm. The firm was part of Bradley Advertising, the state's largest advertising agency. (The company's name was later changed to Bradley/Reid Communications.)

"Alyeska Pipeline Service Company was our largest account, and we'd held it for 14 years," said Mason, who was not personally responsible for the account but had, on occasion, handled crisis communications for the client (Interview with George Mason).

When the *Exxon Valdez* ran aground on the night of March 24, 1989, Mason contacted Alyeska's public relations director, John Rattermann, to offer assistance. "What is often forgotten in the news stories," he said, "is that Alyeska was responsible for [the] initial response in the event of a spill."

The day after the angry public meeting, Mason flew to Valdez to meet with Cornet. "In my opinion," said Mason, "Mr. Cornet had already grasped the futility of the situation as far as the degree of damage Exxon's image had suffered. He seemed to accept this and had begun to look ahead to the long-term future."

Cornet asked Mason to develop and implement strategies for three areas that he expected would be of future concern: (a) the tourism industry, Alaska's third-largest industry; (b) the animal rescue centers Exxon had already begun to set up in Valdez; and (c) the seafood industry, Alaska's second-largest industry behind oil.

Mason agreed to handle the first two and referred the third to a public relations agency in Anchorage that handled the state's seafood account.

Exxon's Animal Rescue Centers

Mason went to one of the animal rescue centers, where there was additional mayhem. Teams of wildlife professionals and their equipment had been flown into Valdez. They were trying to set up the center to help rescue some of the animals.

"Reporters and interested community people were given free access to the facility, again in an effort to cooperate," recalled Mason. "However, the result was impossible. On more than one occasion, eager reporters, mostly freelancers trying to make a buck, were in the way, and in some instances had stepped on injured birds being treated."

Again, Mason, in agreement with the head of the animal rescue center, put security guards to work. This time, it was the media and others not connected with the rescue effort who were kept out. The facility was roped off. Then media tours were arranged and guidelines were constructed to guarantee the protection of the animals.

Mason subcontracted a staff member to do the same work with a second animal rescue center in Seward, Alaska. He subcontracted others to act as community liaisons in other communities. "The purpose here," said Mason, "was to ensure credible connection between Exxon and the community."

Exxon's Success at Restoring Tourism

Mason headed the tourism campaign himself. He already knew, from previous research, that the greatest concern was that the spill had occurred in spring, the peak time of year when tourists make plans for vacations. "We suspected," he said, "that the televised reports of thick oil and dead animals would seriously impact decisions of tourists contemplating travel in Alaska. An early survey of vendors statewide confirmed our fears."

Mason said that the tourism industry telephoned from all over Alaska. The fear was that American tourists would think that the spill had marred all of Alaska. Cancellations were also rampant. Some callers asked, "How deep is the oil in Fairbanks?" Fairbanks is an inland city nowhere near the oil spill.

Mason designed a crisis plan that was further developed and fine-tuned by a team of experts, including public relations heads of Westours and Princess cruise lines. The plan was quickly funded by Exxon and approved by the Alaska Tourism Marketing Council, a combined state and industry group.

The crisis plan involved bringing travel writers to Alaska to witness the conditions and encouraging them to travel within the state to report what destinations were and were not affected by the spill. A telephone hotline was also instituted for travel editors to get information swiftly.

News conferences were held in New York, Los Angeles, San Francisco, and Seattle with feeds to major television network programs. The news conferences in San Francisco and Los Angeles were organized by Ketchum Public Relations offices in those cities. Erik V. Peterson, APR, who was formerly Mason's boss in Alaska, did the groundwork for the Seattle news conference. The agency Padilla, Speer, Beardsley set up the New York press conference. Alaska Gov. Steve Cowper participated in the news conferences in Seattle and San Francisco and was a very credible participant because he had been so publicly critical of the spill. When he said, "Alaska is beautiful," people believed him.

At the same time, Exxon funded an advertising campaign developed jointly by Mason's agency and McCann-Erickson of Seattle. The public relations campaign reached an estimated 50 million Americans. The advertising campaign reached even more. Both were successful in defusing negative travel publicity.

That season, Alaska's tourism set a new record. It was 5 percent higher than it had been the year before the spill. The public relations campaign won a Silver Anvil Commendation from the Public Relations Society of America, as well as numerous other national and regional awards.

"None of it [the tourism and the animal rescue efforts] would have been possible were it not for the cooperation and support of Exxon," said Mason, who continued:

> The lesson I learned from that crisis and have since applied to other crises is that once the crisis begins and the public hysteria begins, it is too late to worry about your PR. All you can really do is hang on, get on with the work, and continue to do what you think is best and most honest.

After the Crisis

Rawl eventually issued a statement via television telling the public what chemicals would be used to clean up the spill. He made no apologies to the fishermen whose livelihoods had been affected. He showed no emotion over the impact of the disaster.

Ten days after the spill, Exxon released full-page ads expressing concern and vowing to clean up the spill. Still, the company did not accept responsibility for the damage. Three weeks after the spill, the CEO went to Alaska, apparently no longer feeling "technologically obsolete."

All oil companies operating in Alaskan waters now have crisis plans approved by the state. In 1989, Alyeska Pipeline Service Company's plan anticipated a much smaller oil spill and allotted only five hours for containment. A primary response in these plans was the use of dispersants as well as in situ burning for cleanup. The Coast Guard and the Alaska state government could not decide on the use of dispersants for the *Exxon Valdez* spill, and this debate prolonged the cleanup. A dispersant test was attempted on the Monday following the Friday night spill, but harsh weather prevented its completion. In addition, the spill was so massive that there were not enough dispersants in Alaska to deal with the problem.

A month after the spill, Exxon finally had the equipment for a full-scale cleanup, which was not completed until 1992. Some Alaskans said there was still evidence of the oil in Prince William Sound. In 1994, Exxon issued information to the media showing that predictions of long-term damage resulting from the spill were exaggerated, and that there was oil from other sources in Prince William Sound. Independent scientific studies seemed to confirm this, but oil from these sources was minuscule compared to that from the *Exxon Valdez*.

Although various controversies about the Exxon spill remained, one thing was certain: The *Exxon Valdez* was a warning sign, a prodrome for other oil companies. Later, BP suffered an oil spill in the Pacific Ocean off the coast of Huntington Beach, south of Los Angeles. BP reacted with haste, even getting underwater photographers to capture images of the hole in the ship for the media.

In a few days, the BP accident was no longer news. This spill, however, was in no way as massive or as difficult as the Exxon spill. It should also be noted that Exxon sent personnel and equipment to help work on the cleanup of this BP spill.

Rawl resigned in 1993 and Lee Raymond became Exxon's chairman. In 1989, the position of Public Relations Manager did not exist at the company. In organizational restructuring under Raymond, Cornet took this position. In this new organizational hierarchy, there were fewer layers between the CEO and the public relations department. Cornet reported to the head of public affairs, who reported directly to Raymond.

Although Hazelwood was acquitted of operating the tanker while intoxicated, he was convicted of negligent discharge of oil (a misdemeanor), fined $50,000, and ordered to perform community service. After eight years of appeals, the Alaska Court of Appeals in 1998 upheld Hazelwood's sentence of 1,000 hours of community work (Sentence Upheld Over Oil Spill, 1998). After being fired from Exxon and sued, he was unable to find work as a ship's captain, though his credentials and skills were highly praised. He worked for a time in New York as a claims adjuster for his lawyers. In 1999, at 52, he began to do his community service and was scheduled to complete 200 hours a year for five years (Exxon Valdez Captain Finally Will Do Community Service, 1999). Although he resents being fired by Exxon and sees himself as a victim, Hazelwood said, "I felt terrible about my involvement . . . as any normal human being would" (Serving Time, 1999).

What Could Have Been Done If Social Media Had Existed

In 1989, when the *Exxon Valdez* spilled 11 million gallons of oil into the Prince William Sound, there was no #SaveTheSound hashtag trending on Twitter. There was no footage taken from cell phone cameras uploaded to YouTube and subsequently aired on the 5 o'clock news. The public relied on TV and newspapers for news on this catastrophic event.

Social media would have been an important tool in achieving many goals, namely preserving Exxon's reputation, sharing information of the disaster to an interested public, and requesting help in the form of volunteers and financial resources.

One example of how it could have been used to achieve these goals is if a prominent environmental rights organization, such as Greenpeace, had played a role in sharing the impact of the spill through photos and messages distributed through Facebook, Twitter, and Instagram. Greenpeace could have championed a "text to give" campaign (in the same way the American Red Cross did with earthquake relief in Haiti). This would have raised critical funds to support the effort and created some momentum around a huge community united by a cause.

Additionally, Exxon could have used social media to pulse out CEO updates (provided he overcame the challenges of being "technologically obsolete") via video on Exxon's Twitter account. The Exxon communications team could use Twitter to provide constant and unbiased updates on cleanup efforts with behind the scenes shots, interviews with animal rescue workers, volunteers, and environmental experts all of which would go a long way to demonstrating their willingness to share information and do what's right—focus on cleanup efforts.

Kelly Bray, Communications Manager, Lifelong

Cousins, the third mate who was left by Hazelwood with the responsibility of steering the ship away from Bligh Reef, continued on his ladder of success to become a second mate on a U.S.-flagged bulk ship (Nalder, 1999).

Ten years after the *Exxon Valdez* oil spill, the largest marine disaster in U.S. history, scientists announced that Alaska's Prince William Sound was recovering, although full ecological recovery had not been achieved. According to scientists, humans could not do much more to hurry the recovery. Only two of the 28 types of herring were declared recovered. Although sea otters were recovering, it could take decades to make a full comeback in some of the area's most heavily oiled bays (Watson, 1999).

Exxon was ordered by a federal court to pay $5 billion to fishermen and others damaged by the oil spill. Although saying it "deeply regrets" the spill, Exxon argued that there were limits to its deep pockets. It cited the $2.1 billion in cleanup expenses and another $1 billion in fines, criminal restitution, and civil settlements to state and federal governments as sufficient punishment for the damage, saying that a greater amount would send a "perverse message" after all the company had done to mitigate the accident's effects (Connelly, 1999).

Environmental organizations—particularly Greenpeace, MoveOn.org, the Alaska Coalition, and the Sierra Club—still demonstrate against Exxon because of the spill and also with regard to issues such as global warming. John Passacantando, director of Greenpeace, said while demonstrating in 90-degree weather at a Washington, DC, gas station, "It's going to get hotter thanks to ExxonMobil, thanks to them more than any other company on the planet." The manager of the gas station said he had noticed no impact in business at the pumps. Exxon says it is investing in new technologies to reduce greenhouse-gas emissions and produce cleaner fuels (Ruskin, 2005).

Exxon and Mobil merged to be ExxonMobil in 1999. The company was number 3 on the Fortune 500 list of largest companies by annual revenue in 2023.

Bibliography

Case Study: Johnson & Johnson and the Tylenol Murders

Goodman, H. (1982, November 12). PR effort launches new Tylenol packages. *Kansas City Times*, p. A3.

Houston, J. & Griffin, L. J. (1982, October 1). 5 deaths tied to pills: Fear killer put cyanide in Tylenol. *Chicago Tribune*, pp. 1–2.

Knight, J. (1982, October 11). Tylenol's maker shows how to respond to a crisis. *The Washington Post*, p. 1.

Peachman, R. R. (2023, October 10). World's best employers. *Forbes*. Retrieved January 31, 2024, from https://www.forbes.com/lists/worlds-best-employers/?sh=3f52ef21e0ca.

Shanker, T. & Grady, B. (1982, October 3). Shoplifter is sought in poisoning probe: Reportedly stole Tylenol. *Chicago Tribune*, pp. 1, 4.

Thomas, K. (2014, January 17). The "no more tears" shampoo, now with no formaldehyde. *The New York Times*. Retrieved January 18, 2014, from www.nytimes.com.

Case Study: Exxon and the Valdez Oil Spill

Connelly, J. (1999, May 4). Exxon says it has paid enough for Valdez spill. *Seattle Post-Intelligencer*, p. A1.

Exxon Valdez captain finally will do community service. (1999, February 17). *Seattle Post-Intelligencer*, p. A3.

Nalder, E. (1999, March 14). Exxon Valdez captain: Was he the villain or the victim? *Seattle Times*, p. A1.

Richest merger of all time. (1998, December 1). *Seattle Times*, p. A13.

Ruskin, L. (2005, July 13). Protestors: Exxon still owes debt to Alaskans. *Anchorage Daily News*, p. F1.

Sentence upheld over oil spill. (1998, July 5). *Seattle Times*, p. B3.

Serving time. (1999, July 12). *People*, p. 62.

Smith, C. (1992). *Media and apocalypse*. Westport, CT: Greenwood.

The big spill. (1990, February 27). *Broadcast*. Boston: WGBH.

The Fortune 500. (2023, April). *Fortune*, p. F1.

Turning Point. (1994, June 15). *Transcript of Telecast of News Magazine*, p. 1.

Watson, T. (1999, February 11). Wildlife recovering from Exxon spill. *USA Today*, p. 3A.

Chapter 4

History-Making Crises

The case studies in this chapter, called history-making crises, are so called because each crisis made history in a big way. When similar crises occur, they are usually compared to these crises. And in the same way, the handling of the crises can also have similarities. "Thinking Outside the Box" tells us steps people made to conquer the COVID-19 pandemic, the largest pandemic in our lifetimes. "Gander, Newfoundland and 9/11" centers on the deadliest attack on U.S. land. "Columbine High School and the Shooting Tragedy" is not the deadliest school shooting. Choosing one is impossible. But it is the school shooting the news media always compares to new incidents; it woke us up to what is going on. "Hurricane Katrina and New Orleans" is the grandparent of natural disasters.

So we examine these not just to look back—but to look ahead.

Case Study: Thinking Outside the Box

The Coronavirus that began to spread throughout the world in early 2020 was commonly called COVID-19, as it first emerged in December, 2019. There were more deaths in the United States than any other tragedy in the memory of every person alive. More than the Spanish Flu of the 20th century. More than any natural disaster. More than both world wars. More than the 9/11 attacks. More than the HIV (human immunodeficiency virus)/AIDS pandemic.

The death toll of one million was reached and surpassed in May, 2022 and was still climbing as this book went to press. One million deaths is shocking. Contemplate seven 100,000-plus seating capacity college football stadiums. Imagine Michigan, Penn State, Tennessee, Ohio State, Texas A&M, Alabama, and Texas, plus slightly smaller stadiums USC and LSU. Visualize them with no empty seats. The total number of fans gathered does not surpass the U.S. death toll from COVID-19, not to mention the rest of the world.

DOI: 10.4324/9781003019282-4

Each one of those people was a heartfelt story. Many of their relatives had to say goodbye virtually because of the fear of spreading the infection. Many people who were not personally affected saw those deaths as numbers or dots on an aerial view of the football stadiums.

Joe Biden was elected the 46th President of the United States in November, 2020. On January 20, 2021, he took office. In between those two dates, two things happened. The first person vaccinated against COVID-19 in the United States, a nurse named Sandra Lindsay, got the shot on December 14.

And the President and his team developed the National Strategy for the COVID-19 Response and Pandemic Preparedness (White House, 2021). The 200-page strategy was released and announced on the day after Biden's inauguration, letting the world know how important the fight against the virus would be. At that point, the death toll was 400,000.

The document urged people to work together to reduce vaccine hesitancy. "Friends and neighbors need to continue looking out for one another." He promised a "safe, effective, comprehensive vaccination campaign" (p. 4).

The long range and lofty goal at the time was *herd immunity*. In herd immunity, a large majority of the public would need to be vaccinated. The estimated goal then was 75–80 percent of the total population. If that goal was achieved, it would lower the number of persons who could possibly be infected and the virus would die.

Dr. Anthony Fauci (Figure 4.1), director of the National Institute of Allergy and Infectious Diseases in Washington, D.C., said herd immunity would be difficult to achieve but possible. He offered a timeline for ending the pandemic (Powell, 2020). Dr. Rochelle Walensky, who had been nominated by Biden in December 2020 to head the U.S. Centers for Disease Prevention and Control (CDC), took office on January 21, 2021, again the day after the inauguration, made appearances on several news and interview TV shows and urged people to **think outside the box** to encourage others to get vaccinated.

Thinking outside the box or brainstorming is—and should be—a frequent practice of crisis communicators and public relations professionals, even in non-crises. Facts don't always do the job. Even well-written, strong news releases and pitches to the news media cannot always satisfy objectives. Something stronger than logic and reason was necessary. In a way, it was an effort to trick people into living.

When a communications team charges its members to come up with something creative or original, they are advised to dream something perhaps ridiculous, something that might be overly expensive, something somebody in another profession did, something foolish, something far-fetched. Some resulting idea may still not work but the thinking process

Figure 4.1 Anthony Fauci, as director of the National Institute of Allergy and Infectious Diseases (1984–2022), was prominent in the U.S. battles against HIV/AIDS and COVID-19. He was chief medical advisor to President Biden for 2021 and 2022 and warned of the possibilities of COVID-19 spread. He was the top infectious disease expert in the United States during the terms of six presidents. He retired in 2022 and joined the faculty of Georgetown University as a distinguished professor.

Source: AUL LOEB / AFP via Getty Images

helps people adjust to realizing they can make changes. They begin to see possibilities.

What Is "Thinking Outside the Box?"

Following are two examples of thinking outside the box.

Mark Canlis is co-owner with his brother Brian of Canlis, a popular fine-dining restaurant in Seattle on the shores of Lake Union with a view of the Cascade Mountains. Canlis was built by their grandfather in 1950. The restaurant won three James Beard awards and was nominated for 15 others. In early 2020, friends in China informed him about the rapidly approaching COVID-19 virus. Knowing he would likely be required to close, Mark called upon his executive team to think outside the box and develop ideas to keep his 108 employees working despite the pandemic.

Their first effort was to open a burger stand in the parking lot. It was successful and employed 50. "We kept reinventing ourselves," he said, "to get and keep everyone employed and to inspire Seattle to stay encouraged". So, another idea was to start selling breakfast bagels—and then, 12 more people were working. Then came delivery of meals to customers, which added the rest of the employees. They also set up a Jerk Village in the parking lot. They continued like that for 471 days until July 2021, when they returned to fine dining. "The year after the pandemic, 2022, was the best year in our history," said Mark. The staff also raised $250,000 for charity.

Another example was also in Seattle and centered on one of the city's most famous tourist spots, the Pike Place Market; the main attraction of the market, in addition to great restaurants, stores, open-air produce, crafts, poultry, is the flying fish. The Pike Place Fish Market opened in 1930 and John Yokoyama took it over in 1965. In 1986, the market was near bankruptcy, and a consultant was brought in to help put them in the black. The consultant asked the fishmongers to think outside the box for ideas that might push sales. The always energetic and outgoing guys took the assignment to heart and one of them said, "We want to take a stand and become world famous."

So, they came up with a plan that made them world famous. When a customer selects a whole fish (they are huge), the fishmonger yells out the order so loud that most people in the big market can hear it. The other fishmongers follow by repeating the order in a kind of chant, and then, as the crowds gather around, the fish is thrown into the air in a high arc and lands in the arms of the wrapper. This usually encourages other people to buy another fish to see it again. The market has had as many as 10,000 visitors a day.

Some companies do contests where the employee or team member with the best idea wins a prize. In this case, the thinking is an individual process. More often, it is a team of people who can challenge others and be challenged, support and be supported and also debate. Many agencies and groups find that organizational or corporate retreats are a good convenient occasion to think outside the box. There still needs to be a definite goal but creative thinking might result from everyone being in a relaxing atmosphere.

Young professionals sometime seem to be more capable of developing creative ideas than their older or more experienced colleagues. They will not be discouraged by comments like, "We tried that five years ago and it didn't work" or "Our competitor already did that." Things tried before and by others should at least be in the mix to determine if they just might work now.

Younger professionals also are not as affected by theories of what will and will not occur. Consequently, teams might be wise to include interns and recent grads in such think sessions.

If possible, retreats should be held away from the office or usual location/workplace. Even if the regular offices are luxurious, find another luxurious place, at least a different and peaceful spot. Don't include things that will divert the attention of the participants. One committee held a retreat in a fabulous aquarium, one that most members had not visited and wanted to see. The participants were so attracted to the sea life that they did not concentrate on the purpose of the retreat. Most importantly, make sure there are no disturbing computers, telephones (even cell phones and tablets), bells, and people not related to the task at hand.

Andy Slavitt and President Biden

In January 2021, Andy Slavitt (Figure 4.2) was named senior pandemic advisor to President Biden's COVID-19 Response Team. Slavitt's background is in healthcare and business. He had been praised for his efforts to work with both political parties. During the previous president's administration, he had effective communications with the offices of governors.

His job with Biden's team he described as "in charge of public communication." This was not his background but he had a history with communicating with the states, so he was the crisis communicator to help get the country vaccinated. His aim was to move toward herd immunity, though valuable time had been lost. Slavitt advised state representatives that the White House encouraged them to use creativity to influence people to be vaccinated. "We are nothing if not responsive to good ideas," he said. "We encourage states to use their creativity to draw attention to vaccines and get their states and the country back to normal as quickly as possible" (Groppe, 2021).

Figure 4.2 Andy Slavitt was on President Joe Biden's COVID-19 Response Team. A businessman and healthcare advisor under former President Barack Obama, he became a crisis communicator to help get the U.S. population vaccinated. At the time, he was trying to achieve "herd immunity" by encouraging the states to be creative and come up with ways of encouraging people to accept the vaccine. Dr. Fauci realized that herd immunity might not be possible—and he was right.

Source: Star Tribune via Getty Images

The Biden team also offered ideas for employees to use to persuade the constituents to get vaccinated and that included lotteries and incentives. Slavitt followed President Biden's mission of establishing more trust in the government and government scientists and each other. So he hosted briefings on television every Monday, Wednesday, and Friday with Fauci and Walensky.

He had never faced news cameras and reporters. He said he was encouraged when his wife, Lana, said that all the viewers needed was "competence" (Groppe, 2021). His focus was "clear, consistent public health messages; honest scientific analyses . . . and accountability for what we promised to deliver." He also delivered messages via Twitter.

Each state and each company were challenged to think outside the box and get others to accept vaccinations in the spirit of neighbors helping neighbors. Many states took the charge seriously and they came up with incentives that seemed never-ending. When reading the incentives, evaluate whether they seem results of thinking outside of the box or was the incentive just "to do something—anything"? Were any incentives likely to improve the relationship between the state and its citizens? Was the incentive likely to result in more vaccinations? Were any of the incentives partisan or anti-Biden? What about your state?

The sweetest offer was a national one. Krispy Kreme made people fatter. It offered a free glazed doughnut every day to any customer in its 1,400 stores who could show proof of vaccination (Figure 4.3). There were complaints that the offer was not an incentive. The customer getting the free doughnut was already vaccinated. Did anyone think a person would get

Figure 4.3 Probably the sweetest incentive to encourage Americans to get vaccinated came from the doughnut manufacturer Krispy Kreme. It offered a free glazed doughnut to any customer who could show proof of vaccination. This offer was good in all of 1,400 stores and was offered daily.

Source: EWY Media/Shutterstock.com

vaccinated so they could get a free doughnut? Hopefully not. The doughnut was like the lollipop a child gets for behaving at the doctor's office. The free doughnuts were marketing tools, but who cared what it was? It promoted the vaccinations. Anyway, Krispy Kreme took the offer further. Employees were offered up to four hours of paid time to get vaccinated. The doughnut company also delivered free treats to vaccination centers for healthcare workers.

If anyone did get the shot merely to get a free doughnut, who cares? The numbers of people vaccinated still rises. Maybe it's tricking people into living longer. Krispy Kreme still supported the move to vaccinate and promoted its products at the same time.

Anheuser-Busch offered free Budweiser beers to people over 21 after Biden's goal of 70 percent was reached. In this incentive, people had to not only get vaccinated but encourage others.

McDonald's cooperated with Biden by promoting the "We Can Do This" campaign on its Times Square billboard and on coffee cups. White Castle offered a free dessert-on-a-stick to anyone who could prove they had the vaccine. No purchase was necessary.

Doughnuts and beer helped, but research by the COVID-19 Health and Politics Projects of UCLA found that a third of unvaccinated people would be more influenced by cash than anything else. Sandra Crouse Quinn, professor of family science at the University of Maryland and senior associate director of the Maryland Center for Health Equity, said, "in order to motivate people to change their behavior, the incentive has to be something they value—like cash" (Will, 2021).

A study by the Society for Human Resource Management found that 25 percent of employed Americans who said they probably or definitely will not get vaccinated said they could be convinced if offered a cash bonus. Another study by Blackhawk Network indicated that the amount of a cash bonus needed to change minds ranged from $10 to $1000.

Cigna Medical Plan in Connecticut offered a $200 award for employees who got the vaccination. Awarding employees is a more manageable arrangement than making such offers to customers because it can be budgeted. The company knows the maximum expenditure before making the offer. It must be considered that these businesses had probably already suffered financial losses from the pandemic, so companies had to be clever and careful.

Next to cash, money-based offers like scholarships, gift cards, and freebies worked. Kroger gave employees $100 in store credit plus $100 cash. Publix Super Markets gave employees a $125 gift card after doses of the vaccine. Other employers such as Instacart, Target, Trader Joe's, Petco, and McDonald's offered time off and amounts of money. The offer from Cleveland's Chagrin Cinemas was free popcorn to those with a vax card.

How Did the States Comply??

The states followed with their own methods of cooperation. The following are descriptions of some of the incentives in some states.

Ohio: Governor Mike DeWine, Republican, spoke to his staff about thinking outside the box. "How many people will die if we don't do this?" was his guiding question. He had a brainstorming session with his staff and asked, "What else can we do?' A woman made a suggestion that became the Vax-a Million Lottery, a campaign which offered fully vaccinated Ohioans an opportunity to win a $1 million lottery. When she made the suggestions, she prefaced it with "This is a kind of wacky idea." DeWine said, "But it worked. When the vaccine is readily available to anyone who wants it, the real waste is when a life is lost to COVID-19." Ohio also offered five full-ride scholarships to an Ohio college or university. His team was the first to offer incentives, and other states began to ask him for advice.

Maryland: A Baltimore pizza chain offered a free eight-inch pizza to Marylanders who had their first shot by June 30. All vaccinated residents 18 and older were automatically entered into a $40,000 daily lottery.

Minnesota: The first 100,000 citizens to get first vaccinations beginning on Memorial Day got free passes to attractions like fairs, sporting events, state parks, etc.

New York: People vaxxed at walk-in subway stations got a free seven-day Metro card. Those who got shots at city-operated sites got a ten-ride pass on the New York ferry system. Students 12–17 years old could benefit from a raffle for a full scholarship to a state university after showing they had the first dose of the Pfizer vaccine. Shake Shack and Mayor Bill de Blasio offered New Yorkers free crinkle cut fries with the purchase of a burger or chicken sandwich.

Oregon offered all adults who got one dose by a specific date eligible to choose from entry in a drawing of $1 million or one of $10,000 prizes in each county.

New Mexico residents with one proven shot could win $250,000 in weekly drawings.

West Virginia distributed $100 savings bonds to all citizens ages 16–35 in the state's effort to encourage young people. Five hunting rifles, five hunting shotguns, two trucks, and hunting licenses were offered in a lottery for those vaccinated.

Georgia: Atlanta and Fulton County school districts raffled off stays at tropical resorts and gift cards from Delta Airlines. Teachers with shots received special T-shirts they could wear to school with jeans, a departure from the normal dress code.

Michigan: Detroit Public Schools teachers and school employees received a $500 bonus and 16 hours of sick leave.

Washington, D.C.: The World Central Kitchen gave persons who dine in its local restaurants $50 gift cards if they show proof of vaccination. Uber and Lyft offered free rides to and from vaccination sites.

Washington (state): Microsoft opened its campus park as a vaccination center. Amazon offered President Biden its help in getting 100 million people to agree to the vaccination within 100 days. In "Joints for Jabs," adults 21 and older could claim a free marijuana joint courtesy of local legal pot shops.

Indiana: Residents got one free box of Girl Scout cookies with a vaccination.

Illinois offered 50,000 free tickets to Six Flags Great America to persons who got their shots in the Six Flags parking lot vax center.

Maine offered 5,000 fishing licenses and 5,000 hunting licenses to vaccinated persons.

Arkansas: Vaccinated people received a $20 discount on hunting or fishing licenses.

Andy Slavitt resigned in June 2021 to write a book (Slavitt, 2021). Herd immunity was never reached. Dr. Fauci and other experts, from the beginning, said it was possible, not likely. Still, the nationwide effort was worthwhile because it saved lives and prevented hospital stays of many thousands of people whether they listened to scientific experts or really wanted a free doughnut. As for Slavitt, we can determine how he felt about the projects by merely taking note of the title of his book, *Preventable: The Inside Story of How Leadership, Politics and Selfishness doomed the U.S. Coronavirus Response*.

Case Study: Gander, Newfoundland and 9/11

The terrorist attacks commonly called "9/11" happened in 2001 before most students were born. No one who remembers wants to relive those memories, yet there is one crisis story that should be told. This story is about as nice as a crisis communications story can be about the worst attack on American soil in all our lifetimes.

The townspeople of Gander, Newfoundland, Canada are not professional crisis communicators. They would never have dreamed they would be called on to settle such a big crisis with social interaction and communications. So, there was no crisis plan. The handling of the crisis came naturally and probably could not have been handled better. The world needed something to go right—and in Gander, it did.

This story has already been told in theater, film, documentary, and radio. Now, it's told in crisis communications terms. This study comes primarily from two books: *The Day the World Came to Town* by Jim DeFede (2002) and *Flown Into the Arms of Angels* by Mac Moss (2021).

On September 11, 2001, four large commercial airliners departed from U.S. airports, were hijacked by Islamic terrorists and were crashed—two into the Twin Towers of the World Trade Center (WTC) in New York City, one into the Pentagon near Washington, D.C., and one into an open field in Pennsylvania. By the end of the day, the 9/11 attacks, as they are usually called, had killed 2,996 people, injured more than 6,000 others, and cost trillions of dollars in damages. Victims were on the planes, in the buildings, on the ground, and included rescue workers.

The United States made a wise move right away when airspace was shut down completely. The planes hijacked originated from airports on the East Coast. Word was that the Islamic terrorists, following Osama bin Laden's lead, planned to hijack planes on the West Coast with targets like Los Angeles, San Francisco and Seattle. But due to time zone differences, the earliest Midwest and West Coast flights were canceled.

The first crash off the WTC's North Tower occurred at 8:45 a.m. New York time. All planes in the air were ordered to land immediately or be shot down. Pilots were not told why. The 2004 Michael Moore documentary *Fahrenheit 9/11* tells the story of planes that did not immediately land, but that's another story, another concern. Flights already in the air from other countries close enough to their original departure sites were told to return.

All domestic planes had to land at the nearest airport. About 300 planes were in Canadian airspace, and the fear in Canada was that there would be crashes as pilots had to change directions and altitudes to land at their assigned sites, but each plane landed safely.

Sometimes the Best Communication Is No Communication

Some pilots in Canadian airspace learned about the attacks from other pilots; others did not. They were told there was a crisis in the United States and airspace was closed. The pilots were told if they knew more, they should not discuss details with passengers. There was still a concern that terrorists might be on the planes with plans for additional attacks. When the pilots heard "You are *instructed* to land in Vancouver," they knew that was an order, not a request. One corporate jet pilot maintained that his prestigious passengers must be an exception. He and others who argued were told if they entered U.S. airspace, they would be shot down.

Imaginations were running wild among passengers but no assistance came from the pilots as they began to land at unplanned destinations in Canada. Most probably some were annoyed thinking it was another airport snafu that would delay their arrival. They had no idea how late their arrival would be, but the passengers on planes that landed at Gander International Airport began to understand when they saw 37 other planes land there. It was undoubtedly more than a snafu.

There were 226 planes with passengers who thought they were headed to various U.S. destinations. Passengers went to 17 airports in Canada and were treated well in all of them. The story of Gander is special because it is a little town with a big airport which embraced more passengers (6,132) and more planes (38) than any other of the 16 sites except Halifax. And Halifax, the capital of the province of Nova Scotia, took in 47 planes and 8,000 passengers but it also had a population of 400,000. Gander had about 10,000 residents and a few hotels.

Eventually the 38 planes with 6,132 passengers and 500 crewmembers landed and parked at Gander. Why Gander? Gander, Newfoundland, on the northeast tip of Canada, was the home of NAV Canada Area Control Center, the organization in charge of getting planes assigned to airports. Also, Gander Airport (Figure 4.4) had been built in 1936 and until the 1970s was a staging point for commercial and military planes to refuel before or after crossing the Atlantic. At one time, it was the largest airport in the world serving the United States, Canada, and England. It was Newfoundland's only international airport and at one time the largest gas station in the world. It could park as many as 50 planes and had four huge runways covering a mile in length.

The town of Gander in the province of Newfoundland grew up around the airport. In land area, it is a little more than 40 square miles and is in the northeast corner of North America. Private and corporate jets often stop there; they like the unusually long runway. Some of the pilots have been Brad Pitt, John Travolta, and Tom Cruise. Every pilot who flies over the Atlantic knows where it is. If a passenger gets sick or goes crazy en route, it's the place to stop when en route to or from Europe. The town has a few big stores like a Walmart, a couple of malls, and parks, nothing special— and the locals like it that way.

What few people know about Newfoundland is that it has a time zone of its own. It is one hour and 30 minutes ahead of U.S. Eastern time. When it is 9 a.m. in New York, the time is 6 a.m. in Los Angeles. But the time in Newfoundland is 10:30 a.m. No other country or province in the world is in the same time zone.

There's a famous observation of the people of Newfoundland. It says that they are the people in heaven who want to go home. They love life there and each other.

Passengers, told at first that there was an emergency in the United States, were not content with that explanation. Experienced travelers knew this had never happened before, so there was a lot of buzzing on the planes. What could it be? Cell phones were not plentiful at the time, and neither

Figure 4.4   The airport in Gander, Newfoundland, Canada is and has been since World War II a fueling stop for military and business aircraft en route to and from Europe. Gander is only a dot on the map of Canada, a dot on the northeastern border, the last possible place to stop before a flight over the Atlantic or a flight returning from the Atlantic. It was an easy choice parking commercial jets en route to the United States when airspace was closed.

Source: Peter Hermes Furian/Shutterstock.com

cell phones nor the sky phones could get connections at first. One passenger, a New York state trooper, had three telephones—a regular cell phone and two world phones issued by the government. The sky phones also didn't work. None of them worked.

A local telephone operator answered a cell phone and told the caller that the only calls he could assist were to toll-free numbers.

As the planes sat on the tarmac, there was gradual and temporary clearance to use cell phones and passengers shared with others trying to find if relatives were safe, telling them they were safe and getting information on what had happened. Passengers were getting information which in many cases was *misinformation*. (see Chapter 1: "Disinformation and

Misinformation," pp. 12–16) They were often told that seven planes had been hijacked (False: there were four), that the WTC towers had been attacked and collapsed (True). The White House was hit (False). Ten thousand people were killed (False).

A radio junkie on board persuaded his pilot to try to get New York commercial radio station, 770 AM WABC, which had a strong signal. So he and the pilots and crew gathered in the cockpit and were eventually successful. They were able to listen to President Bush's address to the nation. Teary-eyed passengers on that flight now knew the truth. But that was just one plane. There was no socializing with passengers from other planes. There were varying stories about how the other planes got the information and some never did while aboard. Some passengers had trouble believing the true or the false information, especially that the WTC towers had collapsed.

The planes remained on the tarmac for hours. As hours passed, the travelers learned the basics of the attacks. They learned it all from the phone calls as more and more calls were made but they still had lots of questions. One family was most concerned because one of its members was a New York City firefighter and was missing. His mother was not satisfied when she was told he was found and OK. She felt they said it just to save her from reality while going through her own misadventure.

Other than camping out for hours on a plane, there was an eating problem and a smoking problem on all the planes. After the snacks were gone, fast-food businesses KFC and Subway, as well as pizza places in Gander, sent food to the planes. Some pilots opened the doors and permitted smokers to stand at the doors and blow smoke outside. Pharmacists in the town sent smoking patches to help the smokers. There was no camaraderie between planes. It was not one large tourist group. They didn't know each other—and don't let it be forgotten that some planes might carry terrorists planning additional attacks. The diverse body of visitors was not only international—it was multiracial, multigenerational, and multicultural.

Of the 38 planes, they originated in Milan, Budapest, Brussels, Amsterdam, Rome, Paris, and numerous flights from the UK and Germany. London and Frankfurt are major hubs connecting flights to the United States from all over the world.

The officials in Gander began to make plans to bring the passengers into the city. They were taking in 6700 people (including crew), a higher number than half its total population. They decided to deboard planes from Europe first. The first planes landing would not be the first planes deboarded. One plane, boarded in Paris, was parked in Gander for 24 hours before it was deboarded. Another plane's passengers had been onboard for 29 hours.

It was also decided that passengers would not stay in hotels. The number of hotels was limited and reserved for pilots, flight attendants and other crewmembers who are required to have rest before flights, and it was not known when they would depart.

Community Relations and International Relations

The Canadian Red Cross (CRC) and the Salvation Army were the community relations organizations in Gander. They were the people trained and with experience in taking care of people in emergencies, according to author DeFede. They led the planning by contacting churches, a summer camp, an Air Force base, the Lions Club, the Royal Canadian Legion Hall, schools, halls, and lodges to provide sleeping spaces for the passengers. The only media relations needed for this operation was easily taken care of when the CRC went over television and radio with public service announcements asking citizens to donate clothes, food items, towels, blankets, cots, and pillows. Within minutes, a caravan of cars two miles long headed to the designated community center to offer help.

Bus drivers on strike put down their picket signs and went to assist. Local stores made significant donations. Ham and cheese and other sandwiches were made and brought for the arrivals.

No Communications Again

The CRC headed the registration of passengers. Its first task was to eliminate communications. The passengers by then knew basically what happened in the United States, but they wanted more details. The CRC knew that if all the people started making calls from the bank of pay phones in the airport, registration of so many people would take a week. They had to know who was in their country, where they were headed, what plane they were on, where they were from and where they were being sent in Gander and environs. So, the Red Cross officials placed "out of service" signs on the phones (Figure 4.5). They unplugged all the televisions in the area for the same reason. They would see the unforgettable drama soon enough.

Passengers had to remain on planes as each was emptied, one by one. As they entered the airport, they saw a large map on the wall of the terminal to show passengers where they were since most of them had never heard of Gander. What they didn't do was separate people by what sections of the plane they were seated in. First class and coach passengers were the same. Those who had achieved some measure of achievement or celebrity were not identified. Everyone was equally welcome.

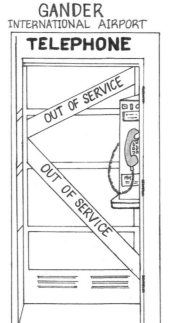

Figure 4.5 Officials at Gander International Airport, charged with registering and finding housing for stranded passengers, had to stop the passengers from taking time to use pay phones by placing "out of service" signs on all of them.

Source: Drawing by Gina Arnold

So as people were registered, they boarded big yellow school buses and were taken to various locations. Some of them were driven to nearby towns, like Appleton, Gambo, Lewisporte, and Norris Arm.

Wherever they were placed, most raced to televisions to find the real story. Wherever there was a TV, there was a group of silent viewers, eyes glued to the TV, some in tears, some with mouths open in disbelief, some with heads in hands.

People to People

The people of Gander continued to show the people who they were. Townspeople took plane people on tours of their town and the countryside. Many invited them to their homes to take showers and some invited them to spend the night.

Newtel (now Bel Aliant), Newfoundland's telephone company, set up a bank of phones so the plane people could make long-distance calls. They also set up computers with Internet access.

People took turns using phones to make long-distance calls. In four days, the visitors called more than 30 countries: Pakistan, Iran, Syria, Israel, Egypt, Russia, every country in Western Europe, and North America including Mexico. One school's phone bill was usually 2–3 pages, but this one was 67 pages. The Salvation Army paid its bill.

The Red Cross developed a toll-free phone number so that the U.S. public could call Gander and ask questions. Volunteers manned the phones 24 hours each day providing answers to questions of whether their relatives and friends were there.

Rogers Communications, a cable TV service, provided each church and shelter housing travelers with Cable News Network (CNN) service so passengers could keep up to date on the news.

Passengers were not able to claim checked luggage so they were without important medicines. Pharmacists contacted hometown druggists to get prescriptions at no cost. This was a very difficult task because medicines have different names in different countries. On this first day, more than 1,000 prescriptions were filled at no cost. The druggists also provided toiletries and 4,000 toothbrushes.

The golf course opened to all the passengers; regular customers were asked to lend their golf clubs. Everyone who was called agreed.

The Canadian Tire Store employees in Gander were asked to think outside the box (see "Case Study: Thinking Outside the Box" on pp. 77–85) and determine what the plane people might need. The bosses instructed, "Anything the passengers need that we can provide, please do it." They gathered sleeping bags, cots, air mattresses, pillows, bottles of water, and toys. The store didn't have toys at that time of year but they drove to a store in another town which did. There were toys for every child. The store made rounds to every lodge, every school, every site where passengers were living making sure the children had dolls, stuffed animals, computer games with batteries, trucks and cars, but no war toys.

A woman who was the manager of the town's only animal shelter and had once worked for the local chapter of the Society for the Prevention of Cruelty to Animals (SPCA) was worried as time passed, the planes sat, and the passengers moved into the town. There probably were animals on the planes in the cargo hold with the luggage. Had anybody given them a thought? A day had passed. She made it her business to find out.

In cages in cargo were nine dogs, ten cats, and two monkeys, but no food or water. She arranged to load a truck with water, food, and cleaning supplies, and she and her friends headed to the airport. There was still the fear of terrorists perhaps hiding among the luggage. The cages were filthy and the smell was breathtaking. They couldn't take the animals out because of the fear of spreading diseases, so they crawled carefully around to reach each pet, cleaned the cages, and gave them food and water. If the animals had names on their cages, they were careful to address the animals by name. In one cage, they found a pill attached that indicated the cat needed to take it in a timely manner. The local vet was away treating a cow but he returned to supervise the animals' move to an empty hangar where they were tended for the balance of the stay.

Schools offered the passengers the use of their facilities. A man and a woman passenger asked a principal if they could use the computer lab. The man said, "We have a small business to run" (DeFede, 2002, p. 168). The principal agreed and the pair went to work on the archaic computers which were still better than no computers. As they left, they handed the principal their business cards and she discovered that the small business they ran was The Rockefeller Foundation, one of the largest philanthropic organizations in the world. When the executives returned to the United States, they arranged to replace the outdated computer lab. The principal felt she should not accept gifts from the unexpected visitors, but she was told, in response, "This is something we want to do and we'll do it whether you want it or not" (DeFede, 2002, p. 168). The lab was accepted with grace and appreciation.

Another school helped people send faxes to family and friends who could not be reached by phone. The school employee said she sent so many faxes that her index finger was swollen.

There had not been any categorizing of passengers by status, by who was in first class and who was in coach. They came from numerous countries and were of various races. Gander is 91 percent white. Its people prefer being called Irish rather than the nickname Newfies. All diverted passengers were welcome.

Leaving Gander

As notices arrived about leaving Gander, some flight crews, fearing hijackers, were afraid to fly if certain Middle Eastern passengers were onboard. The Royal Canadian Mounted Police assured them that there was no threat.

There was no great system for leaving Gander. Some passengers wanted to continue with their trip as previously planned. Others wanted to return home where they started. Airspace was not open everywhere in the entire United States, so continuing was not always possible. Passengers said returning would mean having to make new arrangements and even more delays. It meant two additional flights across the ocean. People on vacation had limited time and had already spent three days in Gander. People near home in the United States wanted to stay in Gander until airspace was open. Some wanted to take ground transportation across the border to the United States and then make arrangements. Nothing was easy, but by the fourth day, all the uninvited visitors had left Gander.

One wealthy German made arrangements for a private jet to pick him up, then he thought about it, called his assistants and told them to cancel the jet. He said wherever his fellow passengers went, that would be when, where, and how he would go. However long it took them to get home, that's how long he would be gone. He said it would be an act of betrayal if everything they had been through—sleeping on Army cots with hundreds of others for 72 hours—to leave them (DeFede, 2002, p. 194). To quote author DeFede, "Given everything that was wrong in the world, it was re-assuring to see that right now, right here, in one small corner of the planet, something had gone right" (DeFede, 2002, p. 194).

When it came to time spent in Gander, 126 hours passed between the time the first plane landed on Tuesday and the last plane left on Sunday. As people reached their homes all over the globe, they sent numerous cards and letters, photos, gifts, and donations to schools and charities, express-ing their appreciation to the whole town and individuals. Some of them made intentional return trips. The mother of the New York City firefighter sadly discovered that her son had perished in the collapse of the WTC. But in a strange way, the family was a bit fortunate in their misfortune. The son's body was discovered intact under a stairway. Most families of vic-tims had nothing more than a finger or a piece of jewelry returned to them.

Come From Away, the musical of this heartwarming true story by Irene Sankoff and David Hein, has been seen on numerous stages and made it to Broadway in 2017 where it won a Tony Award for best direction as well as numerous other nominations. The BBC radio play *The Day the Planes Came* by Caroline and David Stafford was heard first in 2008. A Canadian Broadcasting Company TV film *Diverted* aired in 2009.

Case Study: Columbine High School and the Shooting Tragedy

To Rick J. Kaufman, APR, executive director of Jefferson County Public Schools in Colorado, April 20, 1999, began like many other workdays. On this day, there was a special community event. He and most of the district's administrative team attended a county-wide celebration of individuals and community groups for their outstanding contributions to Jefferson County.

When he returned to the office around 11 a.m., there was a call from a radio station. The station had heard on a police scanner that there had been a shooting at a school in the south part of the school district. Media calls of this nature were not an everyday occurrence, but it was not overly alarming, either. Kids do have guns occasionally.

He and Barb Monseu, an assistant superintendent who oversaw the region of the county that included Columbine High School, immediately left for the school. Kaufman, who had been in that position only seven months, was not yet familiar with all 145 schools in the district. He only knew that Columbine was one of the high schools in the south area of the county and recalls:

> We believed that a student had fired off a gun in the parking lot, or that there had been some sort of altercation. This was a school that, up to that time, we just did not believe something as tragic as the shooting would happen (Interview with Kaufman).

Columbine High School, one of the sprawling school district's top-performing schools, and had been rated among the top high schools in both academics and athletics in the state of Colorado. Its students came from upper middle-class families and it had a reputation as a "community-centered school" with a lot of parent involvement. It didn't fit the perception of an inner city or rural school where violence could occur.

"Columbine High School is a 30-minute drive from the district's educational services center (central office). We made it to the school in 15–20 minutes," said Kaufman. "We topped speeds of 100 miles per hour en route. All the way, we were trying to establish contact with the principal or someone at the school to determine what was taking place."

They had no idea why they couldn't reach anyone. They soon learned why. Columbine High School sits on a portion of Clement Park, a large community park and open space bordered by a residential area to the south, Pierce Street to the east, and Bowles Avenue—a six-lane highway—to the north. There were so many emergency responders—fire, police, paramedics, emergency helicopters to transport victims, and police helicopters trying to find the location of the shooters—that Kaufman and Monseu couldn't get close enough to the school, so they parked on Bowles Avenue and ran toward the school. "We heard what sounded like gun shots and explosions as we neared the building, though we didn't know if that was coming from police or someone from within the school," said Kaufman. "It was a very unsettling, and yet surreal experience."

Parents, who by now had heard media reports of shots fired at Columbine High School, were racing to the school as well, leaving parked vehicles on the two highways bordering the school and park. Students and school employees were fleeing out of the school in every direction throughout the park, having either witnessed or heard shooting. At this point, police did not have a perimeter secured around the school as they were trying to locate where the shooter or shooters were and tending to wounded students who had escaped the building. So Kaufman, a former emergency medical technician who had trained to be a paramedic, went to the aid of a student who had been shot multiple times, and remembers:

> I checked his vitals, and when we couldn't get a pulse or response from this young man, with the help of two other first responders we basically dragged him and put him in a rescue vehicle. The rescue guys asked me if I wanted to ride along to the hospital, but there was nothing more I could do, so I said, "No." I did check his wallet for a student ID so I could write his name and address down, in case we would need to contact his parents. I truly thought he had perished but as it turns out, thankfully, he did survive after being shot seven times, including a shotgun blast to the face.

Eventually, responding law enforcement personnel from multiple agencies established a safe perimeter around the building to keep parents, bystanders, and media out of harm's way. Students and school staff continued to escape on their own, or were aided by police who had entered the building. Columbine High School principal, Frank DeAngelis, was able to escape, but not before encountering one of the shooters and then helping a number of students escape. Kaufman states:

> With Mr. DeAngelis' help, we were working with law enforcement drawing up a schematic layout of the school to be relayed to police who were inside of the building looking for the shooters and freeing students and staff who were trapped. We also started identifying potential students who might be responsible for the shooting, based on eyewitness accounts from those who had safely fled.

Kaufman also communicated information back to his office, where a crisis command center had been established by the district's communications team and superintendent. In the immediate hours after the shooting began, Kaufman served as the liaison between school personnel and law enforcement at the crisis site and the district's command center.

Asked if he had a crisis communications plan or a crisis management plan, Kaufman replied:

> The district certainly had a crisis plan in place and I had written a number of crisis plans for other school districts, but as the events unfolded, we didn't take the opportunity to pull out the plan and follow it to the letter.

Kaufman did call on lessons learned from a mock crisis drill he had developed while working for a school district in Wisconsin prior to moving to Colorado in 1998.

> I had developed the first mock crisis drill of an attack on a school with the help of a local technical college and representatives from law enforcement, fire and hospital. We created a full-scale mock shooting on a school to determine the effectiveness of our newly written crisis plan. We wanted to make sure the plan was sound. I learned a tremendous amount from that drill, and I called on what I had learned throughout our work and response to the Columbine tragedy.
>
> What was most problematic at the time was that I was not in the district long enough to have conversations with law enforcement and public information officers to determine, in advance, what would be done when multiple agencies needed to respond to a crisis or emergency at one of our schools. We did not have the opportunity to determine, who does what, where, and when before the shooting.

Kaufman said that as the afternoon wore on, attempts to communicate with the district's command center or other responders via cell phone were nearly futile because of the sheer volume of cell phone traffic in the area.

> Whenever we were able to establish a connection, there were times when we would be cut off in midsentence. Often, it took repeated calls to give or receive information from the command center, or request assistance. That was one of the most frustrating aspects of our work that day—the lack of the ability to communicate information as well as access to things we needed.

Kaufman said he knew early on that the news media's focus would be on events as they unfolded and that the criminal aspect would require law enforcement personnel to respond initially. The news media, after such a violent incident, were interested in what was happening, who was killed, who was injured, and who was responsible. From the school district's perspective, media needed only the basics, such as the size and layout of the school, the number of students attending, the staff who worked in the building, and names of students who might have been injured or killed.

Said Kaufman, "I knew early on that we would not be media's primary focus. It was really the police, the public information officers who would take the lead in disseminating the initial information because this was a major crime scene."

Kaufman, and later Marilyn Saltzman (Figure 4.6), a staff member of the district's communications department, were the initial district spokespersons.

Figure 4.6 Marilyn Saltzman was part of the crisis communications team following the Columbine High School shooting in Littleton, Colorado. She
was PR manager for Jefferson County Schools for 20 years. In 2006,
her crisis communications skills were useful again when a student in
Colorado's Platte Canyon School District was killed by an intruder.

Source: JEFF HAYNES / AFP via Getty Images

Saltzman, manager of communications, worked with the news media that
had sent teams of reporters and photographers to the site, while Kaufman
continued to assist law enforcement at the school: "We established a location near the school, but outside the police perimeter, for media to gather
and receive updates from both law enforcement and district personnel."

At the district's Educational Services Center, communications department staffers—with help from school public relations professionals from
other Denver metropolitan area school districts—established a volunteer
phone bank to handle the hundreds of calls that were coming into the district asking for information and offering help.

Superintendent of Schools Jane Hammond had also pulled together an
emergency response team of school board members, principals, and central
office administrators who worked to calm the fears of other school personnel and parents throughout the district. Early on, a rumor had circulated
that the Columbine shooting was a coordinated attack and that others
might have planned similar attacks at multiple school sites throughout the
district. Kaufman pointed out:

> Remember, this was before the 9/11 attacks so there were certainly no
> thoughts that this was a terrorist attack. But rumors were quick to be

formed and shared because of the awful news coming out of what was happening at Columbine High School. Those rumors had to be refuted at the other schools as well as to the mass public.

The attack on Columbine High School garnered national and international media attention, as well as round-the-clock coverage in Colorado. Kaufman said:

> It was one of those seminal events that dominated media attention 24/7. It was crucial to dispel any erroneous information before it got out. We weren't necessarily successful, but we worked very hard to ensure that whatever information the school district shared publicly was corroborated and not based on hearsay.

Parent relocation sites were set up at a nearby elementary school and a public library. Students who were able to flee the school were reconnected with their parents at these two sites. At the same time, Kaufman and others were attempting to account for all students and staff.

> It wasn't until early evening, 5 or 6 p.m. [Mountain Standard Time], that we received word there were multiple fatalities. It wasn't until much later in the evening that we were able to account for those who had made it out safely.

However, school district leaders still did not know the condition of those hospitalized, or even how many had been transported to medical facilities, so the information was still incomplete.

It was also that night that the district learned the names of the alleged shooters. There was still concern, however, that there might be others involved, and that information was not easy to reveal. Kaufman said:

> We had pretty good knowledge based on law enforcement sources that [Dylan] Klebold and [Eric] Harris [both seniors attending Columbine High School] were the alleged shooters because they had committed suicide in the library. Law enforcement didn't feel comfortable confirming this information because this was still a very active crime scene and, after all the shooting had stopped, the investigation was just getting underway.

Later that evening, Kaufman returned to the district's command center, where he briefed the superintendent and the assembled district emergency response team on the day's events from the school. He also coordinated the development of initial information that would be disseminated to parents, the community, and the news media the next day. The reporters and photographers who responded to the shooting were—for the most part—local media or national news bureaus based in Denver who fed other national affiliates with the stories and pictures. But Kaufman said that on Day 2, the morning after the shootings:

> The nationals were already setting up in the park adjacent to the school when I arrived at 3 a.m. We were getting a lot of requests to do interviews or to arrange to have students and staff go on these national morning news shows. We refrained from doing that because we were still in the mode of collecting information and trying to determine what happened. We didn't have a complete account. We were not going to provide information that could have been perceived as speculative still at that point. It would not have served us well to do that, so we limited our access to interviews, and those we did, were very brief factual statements.

On Day 2, a joint press conference was held with the Jefferson County Sheriff's Office, the lead law enforcement agency; the Jefferson County District Attorney's office; and the school district. Kaufman said:

> It was our first opportunity to express our condolences to the families of those murdered and our concern for those students and staff who were injured, to put a human face to the sadness we were feeling and experiencing. We used the opportunity to share some information about what we knew had happened, but more importantly how we were responding to students and staff needs. We wanted to be up front with as much information as we could as it became available, and when we could corroborate it and substantiate it, and that's what we shared.

On the third day after the shooting, the weather turned to dark skies and heavy snow. "The weather was a reflection of what we were feeling. Our hearts were very heavy for the victims and the community, and we knew we were entering into some very difficult days ahead with the funerals," said Kaufman. It was also at this time that Kaufman realized he didn't have enough staff trained in crisis response to adequately manage the crisis. He turned to his friend and colleague, Rich Bagin, the executive director of the National School Public Relations Association based in Rockville, Maryland, to help coordinate school public relations professionals from across the country who would commit their time and expertise to aiding Kaufman's crisis response team.

Superintendent Hammond created two emergency response teams. One, headed up by Kaufman, concentrated on all the media relations and communications, and worked directly with schools, parents, community, religious organizations, and others. The second response team, headed up by Assistant Superintendent Monseu, coordinated the mental health and grief counseling for students and staff, and worked to arrange for Columbine students to return to a neighboring school for the remainder of the school year.

The following is Kaufman's report of the campaign and is reproduced with Rick Kaufman's permission.

The Columbine Tragedy: Managing the Unthinkable— Project Summary

Assessment

The tragic shooting of 12 students and a beloved teacher at Columbine High School on April 20, 1999, created unforgettable experiences for the thousands of students, staff, and community residents of Jefferson County, Colorado. The tragic events of that day and subsequent weeks thrust the Jefferson County Public Schools' Communications Team into the spotlight as the core communicators for a community and organization in crisis. While managing speculation and rumor perpetuated by more than 750 media outlets from across the world, this team of public relations professionals helped to restore calm and confidence to their organization and healing to the community during what history may label as the defining tragedy of our time.

The Jefferson County Public Schools' Communications Services team developed a crisis communications structure that established key duties and protocols in a crisis. This plan was adapted as a result of the nature and magnitude of the Columbine High School tragedy and continues to be revised to reflect lessons learned from this tragedy and its aftermath.

The Jefferson County Public Schools' Communications Team consisted of six professionals and support staff when the tragedy struck, but received volunteer assistance from members of the Colorado and National School public relations associations.

Communication Objectives

The overall public relations objective throughout the crisis was to quickly adjust the school district and community's position from one of response and reaction to one of proactive control, enabling the team to aid in school and community healing. To attain this objective, the Jefferson County Public Schools' Communications Team did the following.

- provided on-site guidance and leadership to students and staff;
- developed key communication vehicles to reassure parents and the community;

- strengthened proven strategies to propel those affected beyond the crisis to learn and grow stronger;
- communicated the school and district's point of view with professional grace and insight;
- reinforced the healing process, while aiding in return-to-education objectives;
- cultivated a semblance of triumph in the face of tragedy.

While juggling demands from the news media at an unimaginable rate, the driving force behind every decision and event remained the motivation to help students and staff heal and return to the learning process as quickly as possible.

Another objective was to demonstrate and emphasize the school district's commitment to the emotional and physical needs of affected faculty, staff, students, and the families of the murdered and injured students and teacher.

Planning

- Assisted, prior to the tragedy, in the development of a district crisis management plan, including an emergency response checklist of steps for the first 24–48-hour period after a crisis.
- Consulted with school administrative and PR officials from each of the prior school shooting sites, and with the National School Public Relations Association, the National Organization of Victims Assistance, and the Crisis Prevention Institute to identify strategies of crisis response and management.
- Organized briefings with district management team, school board officials, employee association representatives, and community leaders to review responsibilities outlined in the crisis management plan, including the establishment of two command centers—an on-site communications center (near Columbine) and a central operations center.
- Participated in daily briefings with law enforcement, state and federal emergency management agencies, and governmental groups to coordinate the ongoing crisis response and management.
- Created a database of media outlets that contacted the district for information and interviews, and used this list to distribute updates on the district's response to the tragedy and its efforts to help the community heal and return to normal. The media list was used frequently to distribute information on how the school's students and staff, and the community were healing and moving forward.

- Analyzed media coverage daily throughout the crisis to evaluate how Jefferson County Public Schools' messages were received and to assess changes in media attitude and public perception.

Target Audiences: Parents, students, faculty and staff, media, state and federal legislators, the Jefferson County community, and the residents of Colorado.

Project Summary Continued From

Strategies

- Implemented a Crisis Communications Command Structure. The structure designated primary functions for managing the crisis, including strategic communication counsel, internal and external communication, media management, research and media monitoring, event management, and coordinating volunteers.
- Created several methods for communicating with parents, students, employees, business and community leaders, political and governmental officials, and the public, and continually updated those methods for efficacy.
- Responded promptly and honestly to requests for information and interviews from the media, and anticipated changes in news cycles and demands.
- Apprised daily all staff throughout the 89,000-student district of the status of the investigation and recovery milestones. Spoke with "one clear voice" and "stayed on message" as determined by the district's management team and developed by the district's communications team.

Techniques/Activities

- Responded to more than 1,000 inquiries a day from local, national, and international media outlets for the first four weeks after the tragedy, and continued to maintain contacts to update media about recovery efforts. Coordinated the media efforts for the special first day back to school event in August 1999, and planned all events to mark the first-through fifth-year anniversaries.
- Managed all communications, including twice-daily press conferences and daily fact sheets and news releases, distributed throughout the state and nation. Drafted daily talking points for district spokespersons.
- Established one-on-one opportunities with local reporters to interview key district personnel involved in the recovery efforts, and to strengthen

TIMELINE OF COLUMBINE TRAGEDY AND ITS AFTERMATH

The attack on Columbine High School on April 20, 1999, left 12 students and a teacher dead, and 23 others wounded. Some liken the attack to an "earthquake" because of its devastation on individuals, families, and a community. As the days, weeks, and months following the tragedy came and went, so too did the "aftershocks" that have impeded the students, staff and community's ability to heal and return to normal.

To follow is a timeline of highs and lows in the year after the tragedy.

April 20, 1999
Two students attack Columbine High School killing 12 fellow classmates, a teacher, and wounding 23 others in the worst school shooting in U.S. history.

April 25, 1999
Statewide memorial service pays tribute to the fallen students and teacher with then-Vice President Al Gore and other state and national dignitaries. Over 75,000 people attend the event.

May 2, 1999
Jeffco Public Schools holds special remembrance memorial for the victims of the Columbine tragedy at Red Rocks Amphitheater. Several hundred students, staff, and community members attend the solemn event.

May 3, 1999
Columbine High School students and staff return to classes at sister school Chatfield Senior High.

May 20, 1999
On the one-month anniversary, President Bill Clinton and First Lady Hillary Clinton visit the Columbine victims' families in a private meeting, then pay tribute to the victims and survivors at a special memorial.

August 17, 1999
Columbine High School students and staff return to "Take Back Our School" for the start of the 1999/2000 school year.

September 24, 1999
CBS News airs portion of cafeteria surveillance videotape it obtained from an Albuquerque, NM television station that captured the chaotic scenes of students fleeing the school. The videotape was being used as part of a law enforcement training exercise.

October 20, 1999
Columbine High School marks the six-month anniversary with news that a student who was a friend of the killers has been arrested for allegedly making a threat at the school.

Figure 4.7 This was the timeline of the work of Rick Kaufman and his communications staff at the Jefferson County School District in Colorado for the first year after the tragedy that resulted in the deaths of several students and a teacher and the injuries of others. Courtesy of Jefferson County School District.

October 22, 1999
The mother of critically injured student Anne Marie Hochhalter commits suicide at an area store.

December 4, 1999
Columbine High School captures 5A high school football championship, capping season dedicated to Matt Kechter, one of the slain students and a member of the football team.

December 13, 1999
Time magazine cover story carries excerpts from videotapes made by murderers outlining attack on Columbine High School, including cover photo of perpetrators in the cafeteria. Article surprised community, and students and staff, who were caught off-guard by the release of the information. Neither Jeffco Public Schools nor Columbine High School had been given advance warning of the contents of the article.

December 15, 1999
Student receives Internet threat that claims to "finish the job begun" on April 20, 1999. District cancels classes at Columbine High School for next two days, sending students and staff to an earlier than expected holiday break.

February 14, 2000
Two Columbine students found murdered in Subway Sandwich Shop located near the high school. Students informed by teachers of identity of the murdered students during second period class, prompting many students to leave the school or seek counseling. No arrests made to date.

April 20, 2000
Columbine High School and community mark 1-year anniversary with private and public events. Many students choose to stay away from public events because of the intense media coverage.

April 27, 2000
Jefferson County district attorney makes available to public (for $25) a videotape of Littleton Fire Department "training" video that depicts graphic scenes from the library and other parts of the school and video footage from a news helicopter. Columbine High School staff is shown the tape and a warning is issued to parents of the impending public release.

May 4, 2000
Popular student-athlete commits suicide at his home.

May 15, 2000
The Jefferson County Sheriff's Office releases its long-awaited report—by court order—on the tragic events of April 20, 1999. The report is issued on a CD-ROM because of its extensive notes and information, including videotape footage, excerpts from 911 calls, and law enforcement traffic and audio recordings.

Figure 4.7 (Continued)

the relationships with local journalists who remained long after national and international media left.

- Created weekly talking points for administrative staff at 143 other district schools to share with staff and parents.
- Met daily with legal and administrative management teams to formulate key messages and address emerging issues.
- Created a community hotline designated to accept offers of monetary contributions, donations of materials, and services from around the world. In the first three weeks after the crisis, the crisis command center received over 1,000 phone calls a day.
- Assisted in the development of a Columbine Tribute website, and created a videotape showing the positive images of recovery to replace the negative images that were repeatedly aired on local and national media.
- Coordinated special events, including two large memorial services, separate visits by then-President Bill Clinton and Vice President Al Gore, tours of the reconstructed school, and the "Take Back Our School" first day of school assembly.
- Developed a presentation—*The Columbine Crisis: Managing the Unthinkable*—for school district officials, emergency responders, and law enforcement officers.

Evaluation

The school district's communications and management team personnel did their solemn, professional best in a difficult situation and emotional environment. In the ongoing efforts, the team focused on the district's mission to help students, staff, and the community heal and recover, and share the story of our efforts with all key audiences. Further examples of how we achieved our objectives:

- We always kept the feelings of the victims' families in the forefront. Today many of our district leaders have personal relationships with families of the murdered and injured students and teachers based on our work with them.
- Target audiences read or saw Jefferson County Public Schools' messages in more than 1,550 print stories (primarily local and large national publications) and 450 broadcast stories. A database of all the media coverage was created and exceeds 700 pages.
- Public perception both locally and nationally was positive and supportive of the district's crisis response, based on letters from former President Bill Clinton, private organizations, national media, and community sentiment.

- A strong working relationship was developed with the Jefferson County Sheriff's Office, the Jefferson Center for Mental Health, the Jefferson County and federal emergency management agencies, and the FBI.
- Hundreds of requests have been received from organizations for crisis management training. Members of the district's communications and management teams have presented nearly 100 seminars and training sessions since August 1999. Organizations requesting presentations/training include the FBI, Los Angeles County law enforcement agencies and school districts, state emergency and educational associations, and the U.S. Department of Education.
- A special "Welcome Back to School" event and picnic for all staff was developed to celebrate the accomplishments of recovery. Over 2,000 staff attended the event, which included the planting of a tree and placement of a commemorative plaque on a large boulder in memory of Dave Sanders, the only teacher killed in the April 1999 tragedy.

The tragedy was very emotional for everyone connected. No one on Kaufman's staff had family at Columbine, but that didn't eliminate the emotional impact. Kaufman said one of his staff members had to be put on a medical leave of absence for a brief time because the heart-wrenching concern for others had impacted on him personally. Grief counselors helped employees deal with their emotions throughout the response effort.

Kaufman himself said he ran on adrenaline, like most crisis communicators. He said:

I didn't sleep for the first four days. I mean, I literally did not lay my head down to sleep for four days. In hindsight, that was dumb, because when you start coming down off that adrenaline, you're going to crash and make mistakes in your work and decision-making. I was responsible for so many people that we started to work in shifts. I forced people, including myself, to start rotating work on and off times. Often we would only get three–four hours of sleep, but it was enough to keep us going. We needed to take care of ourselves because it was apparent that this tragedy had legs far beyond anything we had ever experienced.

The media calls continued long after the students returned to school. Marilyn Saltzman had a friendly wager with a friend in the media: The day that the district's communications team did not receive a call or request for information about the Columbine shooting would be the day she and her friend would go to lunch. It was June 2000, a year and two months after the incident, that the communications team went a whole day without a single inquiry about the tragedy.

Today, the inquiries continue. "I receive, on average, at least one to two Columbine-related calls or emails each week," said Kaufman, who continued:

> It might be a parent asking if we can help them because they learned a student in their school had a hit list, or a teacher or emergency responder that wants to know what we did, or what policies we have put in place to prevent another tragedy. I feel a sense of responsibility to never turn away a request for information. We aren't experts at crisis management and communication, but we learned enough about it to help others. If nothing else, callers have told me it is comforting to them to know that we endured and we survived.

And then every year, the news media does their anniversary stories.

Update: Subsequent Commentary

Dave Cullen (2009), author of *Columbine* and a journalist who covered the massacre, followed his original coverage with nine years of research including hundreds of interviews, 25,000 pages of police evidence, video and audio tapes, and numerous articles and reports by other journalists.

Cullen praised much of the news coverage; many, he felt, were deserving of the numerous awards won by journalists and photographers. However, he writes also of the media errors. He said the most accurate story was the first story in the now-defunct *Rocky Mountain News*. The special edition of the newspaper covered the incident on day one before the bodies had been found.

Often, the first news story after a crisis is full of "holes." Facts have not yet been determined, and assumptions, observations, and often opinions of police and other experts are used to put together the most reasonable story possible. The story is chock full of "he said" and "according to" phrases. In the Columbine massacre coverage, Cullen believes the opposite was true. That first story was accurate; then the errors began.

In later news stories, the two shooters were called members of the Trench Coat Mafia (TCM), a band of gay Goths with heavy makeup who were school misfits. This was discovered later to be untrue. There was a TCM presence at the school, and since the shooters wore trench coats, a few students assumed they were part of the group. The news media repeated the claim. Then more students "knew" it was true because the news media said so. The error was repeated so often that most people all over the world still believe the killers were members of the TCM.

There were other media mistakes. The killers did not target jocks, people wearing white hats, or minorities. One emotional survivor had said that, but what she apparently meant was they were shooting randomly, that among those shot were athletes, hat wearers, and minorities. In this situation, the survivor speaking was a non-expert expert. Non-expert experts are people who speak as if they are knowledgeable and have authority when actually their appeal is based on emotions and excitement (see Chapter 9). She was widely believed because people wanted facts and because she had been in the midst of the massacre and survived.

When Columbine High School was scheduled to reopen, the school community planned a ceremony to be titled "Take Back Our School." The students felt the school was synonymous with "mass murder" and that they had been termed bullies or pompous rich kids. In the ceremony of "Take Back Our School," they had to take back the school from an enemy. The news media was chosen as that adversary. Cullen said, "The news media had made their lives hell." The coverage was never-ending, both local and national. "How do you feel?" was asked over and over. However, when reporters converged this time, a shield of parents and community members blocked reporters from the event.

Kaufman bluntly told reporters that the human chain was there to shield students from the news media. Reporters were, of course, angry. Eventually, a compromise was made and students who wished to were permitted to approach reporters; reporters agreed not to approach students. Cullen and Kaufman said the school felt victorious.

When Dylan Klebold and Eric Harris opened fire at students at Columbine High School in 1999, the World Wide Web was years away from being a household term and social media like Facebook and Twitter were still in the far distant future. Even text messaging was just getting off the ground. Were social media around during Columbine, they could have been used in different ways. For example, Klebold and Harris may have had Facebook pages or Twitter accounts whose contents could have raised red flags that indicated they were hatching a plan that would endanger their fellow students. Someone, perhaps another student, could have seen that content and told a parent, and that parent could have informed the authorities.

What Could Have Been Done If Social Media Had Existed

If the shooters had gone forward with the killings, the students in the school who had access to the web via their smartphones or on-site computers could have sent messages via social media describing what was going on within the walls of the school, information that would be crucial to law enforcement, school officials, and loved ones.

Once the shootings were over and the students were safe but still sequestered, they could have used social media to send reports to alleviate their loved ones' fears: "Mom (or Dad) I'm scared but alive. Gotta go." Those few words could mean the world to a petrified parent waiting for news.

Social media could also be used for official communication—the school, school district, and law enforcement communicating with parents, for example, to supplement other communication channels. And given the rapid-fire speed at which messages get transmitted and retransmitted via online technologies, information would get around fast. One major caveat is the possibility—if not likelihood—that misinformation could also circulate quickly, so it is especially important for those who have authoritative information to get that out quickly and clearly to counter any harmful rumors.

Social media could be used in the process of community recovery and healing, as well as continuing proactive control and support. Although the site of a school shooting may not fully return to "normal"—especially as anniversaries or case studies remind the public and families of what occurred there at one time—social media can help move the school from tragedy, to remembrance, to healing, and then to refocusing again on the mission of educating students for a promising future.

Kevin Kawamoto, Ph.D., media and communication scholar

Update/Case Study: Hoping for the Best, Anticipating the Worst: Preparing for a School Shooting

School shootings occur with alarming frequency in the United States compared to other countries in the world. According to *Education Week*, there were 51 school shootings that resulted in injuries or death in 2022, which is the highest number since the publication began tracking school shootings in 2018. In fact, school shootings more than doubled in 2022 compared to 2018 and 2019, respectively (Education Week, 2022).

Unless it has already happened, no school would like to believe that a school shooting could take place on its campus. But the sad reality these days is that it is not outside the realm of possibility. For that reason, school spokespersons should be prepared for the worst, even while hoping that they never have to face frantic parents, frightened students, concerned teachers, vigilant law enforcement, a shaken community—and, of course, the inquisitive news media that want to know the who, what, when, where, why, and how of any crisis involving gun violence and children, and they want to know *now* so they can report the news to their reading and viewing audiences as soon as possible. Timeliness is a news value, and this compels most journalists to seek immediate answers for their breaking news stories and in the follow-up stories that air or get published in the days following a traumatic event of significant public interest.

If the school shooting affects a large number of people—such as the shooting that occurred in an Uvalde, Texas, elementary school in which 19 students and two teachers were killed by an 18-year-old man with a military-style rifle on May 24, 2022—the media interest will be swift and the questions unrelenting. Expect that reporters from across the nation will travel to the location where the shooting occurred and demand answers from law enforcement, school officials, and others in positions of accountability or who have information needed to put the story into context.

The News Media Will Be Prepared—Will You?

As such, schools need to be prepared for immediate media contacts following a school shooting and have a crisis communication plan in place. Some of the questions that reporters will ask are predictable, and those are the ones that should be prepared for ahead of time. For example, reporters will want to know something about the school itself: What are the grade levels at the school? How long has the school been in existence? How many students are currently enrolled at the school? How many teachers work at the school? Does the school have its own security force? What kinds of training has the school done for an active shooter incident? What is the name and title of the person considered to be the head of the school? Is the school a public or private institution? If the school is public, what government jurisdiction does it fall under? Who is the superintendent? Who is the spokesperson from the superintendent's office? If it is a private school, is it independent or is it part of a system, such as a religious organization's educational system? Has the school had mock drills to prepare for an active shooter incident, and if so, how recently?

These are just a handful of questions that the news media will ask. They are questions that you can prepare for by keeping such information updated. You may even want to have a fact sheet prepared, and updated as needed, so that the fact sheet can be distributed to reporters. The information might also be posted on a website or on social media and reporters referred there to avoid having to answer the same questions in person over and over again. Local reporters may already know the answers to most of these questions, but out-of-town reporters may be clueless.

Who will be the spokesperson for the school when the news media converge on location after a school shooting? This should be decided ahead of time as part of crisis communication planning. Who does the spokesperson have to consult before releasing information to the public? Consider, as well, publics in addition to the news media that are urgently seeking answers. These would include, first and foremost, the parents of the schoolchildren, especially if their children are still in lockdown and the parents don't know how their children are doing or whether they are still alive. You can imagine the desperation and terror that these parents must feel, and the heightened emotions that they may display if they are not getting the answers that they need.

Make a list of questions that you anticipate journalists, parents, and others will be asking after a school shooting, and answer those questions in advance in-house as much as possible, perhaps as a role-play exercise. It will be one less thing to be scrambling over in the chaos of a hectic and rapidly evolving crisis situation. When needed, pull the questions out and update as necessary. The spokesperson for the school should not appear ignorant about basic information such as number of students enrolled in the school and number of teachers employed, and so forth. That would make the spokesperson look foolish when cameras and microphones are aimed at the spokesperson for all the nation and possibly the world to witness.

There are some questions that cannot be prepared for ahead of time because of the details of the crisis have yet to happen. It should go without saying that the school's spokesperson must convey deep concern for the safety of the children and of all the school's personnel right off the bat, regardless of whether the status of the shooter, the students, and the school staff is known. In the panic triggered by the situation, it may be easy to unintentionally forget to convey that concern before jumping into the known details of the crisis, but not immediately conveying concern for the victims and families may come across as callous. If information a spokesperson can share is sparse, it is also important to explain that the situation is evolving and that more details will be forthcoming as soon as they become available. If pressed by the news media, it may be necessary to remind reporters that as this is an active shooter situation, and thus it may not be safe for students and others trapped inside the school building to have law enforcement operations discussed publicly at this time. The school spokesperson should be flanked by others in a position to answer those kinds of questions, such as a law enforcement spokespersons, and should not be the only person responsible for answering all of the news media's questions.

Remember that a school spokesperson does not have to answer every question that is posed by a reporter if the information is unavailable or if it inadvisable to share the information at that particular time due to security or other reasons. A school spokesperson can always defer to another official or defer providing details until more information becomes available. However, the spokesperson may be able to answer questions such as what counseling services the school has available for students affected by the shooting, how the school is communicating with parents, how the school is communicating with other publics, who to contact if reporters have additional questions after the press conference is over, and what other message the school would like to convey to the general public via the news media.

Politicians and other public figures may decide to visit the site of the school shooting to make a public appearance in a show of support and concern. School officials may need to decide whether and how to be involved in those visits. The public figures may request a meeting with the school principal or other key personnel. The news media and possibly even the public figures' own public relations representatives will likely be in tow. Again, consider the school's public response in such a situation. It may involve thanking the public figure for reaching out at such a traumatic and distressing time and reinforcing the school's support for affected students, family members, and the community.

Keep in mind that reporter questions may continue for days, weeks, and even months. One year after the Uvalde, Texas, shooting, there were still news stories being written about the tragedy (Depart, 2023). Indeed, "anniversaries" of tragedies often present an opportunity to revisit the precipitating event. School shootings almost always give rise to renewed calls for gun control legislation, as well as for opposing views from gun rights advocates. This controversy co-evolves with the primary focus of the story, which is the specific school shooting incident in question.

Be Prepared Exercise

To prepare for media inquiries after a school shooting, here is a two-part exercise to do beforehand.

Part One: Imagine the worst. In other words, imagine that a school shooting has just occurred at your school and that the incident resulted in deaths and injuries. Now put yourself into the role of a news reporter, a parent, a community member, law enforcement, other government officials with jurisdiction over your school district, and others with a relevant interest in the crisis. What questions would you want to know the answer to? What information would you need to get a sense for what happened and to capture the sentiments of those most affected? In these various roles you are role-playing, what emotions are you experiencing while you wait for information?

Part Two: Look up actual stories involving school shootings in which students were killed or injured. Unfortunately, there are plenty of examples that can be found by doing a Google search. Read the stories and watch video segments of news coverage. Find press conferences that have been recorded and posted on YouTube. Pay close attention to the details. What details appear in the stories that were most likely the result of reporters asking questions of school officials? If a school official or officials appear at a press conference, listen closely to reporters' questions to them. Most likely those will be similar questions asked of you should your school experience the tragic aftermath of an active shooter.

What are people saying about the shooting on social media? Decide whether part of the school's crisis communication activities should be to monitor social media for misinformation (unintentionally incorrect information) and disinformation (intentionally incorrect information) so that inaccurate and potentially harmful information can be addressed publicly and corrected. School spokespersons need to use their own professional judgment about such matters.

There *may* be instances in which it is better to ignore the lies, rumors, and conspiracy theories on social media rather than call more attention to them. In other cases, it may be prudent to issue a prepared statement acknowledging the existence of false information circulating on social media, and then officially correcting that information. The media environment today is far different than what existed on April 20, 1999 when there was a mass shooting at Columbine High School in Littleton, Colorado. Today there are many more channels of information, misinformation, and disinformation to monitor. What is similar, however, is that both truth and falsity often co-mingle during and after a public crisis. That was certainly true at Columbine, when various types of information were circulated that later turned out to be false (Brockell, 2019).

Finally, reporters will not only want information about the victims of the school shootings but also about the shooter. If the shooter is another student currently or formerly enrolled at the school, the news media will likely seek as much information as they can get from as many different sources about the shooter. Schools should be prepared for those kinds of questions, as well, and consult with legal advisors about what can or should be shared with the news media about current or former students.

The takeaway lessons here: Always hope for the best, and anticipate the worst. Learn from the past. Prepare as best as possible to be an effective public communicator during times of crisis, confusion, and calls for immediate answers to sensitive questions.

Case Study: Hurricane Katrina and New Orleans

In a study of crisis communications, natural disasters are a key component because even though organizations cannot be blamed for starting them, organizations are blamed if a state of normalcy is not achieved swiftly. They almost always make news, especially if there are deaths.

No matter where people live on planet earth, no matter how ideal the setting, how depressed the surroundings, natural disasters may strike. In the United States, the southeastern states, the Gulf Coast, and the East Coast are subject to hurricanes. The West Coast (as well as numerous other places) is earthquake-prone. Tornadoes, floods, wildfires, and severe snowstorms do their damage on most of the rest of the country.

Hurricane Katrina, in 2005, was a natural disaster that directly affected thousands of people in New Orleans. After hitting Florida first, Hurricane Katrina made landfall on August 29 and caused death and destruction in Alabama, Mississippi, Louisiana, and Florida. The stories are tragic in all the states, but in a study of crisis communications and crisis management, New Orleans stands out. The crisis touched everyone in the state in some way but specifically every person and every business and organization in New Orleans.

There was death and suffering in Florida, Mississippi, and Alabama, but death and suffering were more visible in New Orleans because of the news media coverage. There were bodies floating in the flooded streets, people screaming to be rescued from their rooftops, and thousands of people trapped in unlivable shelters—and it was hot, sizzling hot—exciting news, especially for television and newspaper photography. In addition to the excitement, there was miscommunication and controversy, elements that were not so apparent in the other cities and states where nature did its damage and exited.

There were evacuation plans, but the plans obviously did not consider certain segments of the New Orleans public: (a) people who were too ill to evacuate, even with help from neighbors (some were mute or blind); (b) people with pets who could not bear to leave them (some would volunteer to die rather than leave their pets, which were not admitted to the primary shelters); (c) people who did not have cars or money for gas to evacuate, or places to go if they had gas (U.S. Census statistics reveal that 112,000 residents did not own cars); and (d) a great number of people who decided to sit out the storm because they had heard warnings to evacuate so many times before and each time before it had been unnecessary. The plans did not include what would be done with these publics, probably because the actual crisis was worse than the worst-case scenario imagined by the person or persons who devised the plan.

We know from Chapter 1 that the first stage of a crisis is the prodromal stage, a point before a crisis when warning signs are analyzed and heeded. Crisis management and crisis communications plans are developed based on these warnings and an effort is made to avoid the worst-case scenario. That does not mean we ever ignore the worst-case scenario. The worst-case scenario is the absolute worst tragedy that *can* occur. We make crisis communications and crisis management plans based on likelihood and degree of devastation but we should always consider what will be done if the worst happens.

Let's begin with this fictional narrative:

It was a broiling August afternoon in New Orleans, Louisiana, the Big Easy, the City That Care Forgot. Those who ventured outside moved as if they were swimming in tupelo honey. Those inside paid silent homage to the man who invented air conditioning as they watched TV "storm teams" warn of a hurricane in the Gulf of Mexico. Nothing surprising there . . . .

But the next day, the storm gathered steam and drew a bead on the city. As the whirling maelstrom approached the coast, more than a million people evacuated to higher ground. Some 200,000 remained, however—the car-less, the homeless, the aged and infirm, and those die-hard New Orleanians who look for any excuse to throw a party.

The storm hit Breton Sound with the fury of a nuclear warhead. Pushing a deadly storm surge into Lake Pontchartrain, the water crept to the top of the massive berm that holds back the lake and then spilled over.

Nearly 80 percent of New Orleans lies below sea level . . . so the water poured in. Thousands drowned in the murky brew that was soon contaminated with sewage and industrial waste. Thousands more who survived the flood later perished from dehydration and disease as they waited to be rescued. It took two months to pump the city dry, and by then the Big Easy was buried under a blanket of putrid sediment, a million people were homeless, and 50,000 were dead. It was the worst natural disaster in the history of the United States.

(Bourne, 2004)

The narrative continues with "When did this calamity happen? It hasn't—yet." This piece was written by Joel K. Bourne, Jr. and published by *National Geographic* magazine in October 2004, nearly a year before most of his predictions actually happened. Bourne, not a psychic or a seer, merely predicted the mass destruction.

This mass destruction had been predicted by geologists for years. The state lost more than a million acres of coastal wetlands in the past 70 years or so. The soil has destabilized for various reasons, including industrial plants, offshore gas and oil particularly (which actually made the disaster at least partly man-made and not a natural disaster at all). With the eroding ecosystem, the Gulf of Mexico gets closer to New Orleans all the time. In the Gulf, hurricanes are nursed until they make landfall. They grow stronger over water and weaker once they hit land, so the land closer to the coastline stands to suffer stronger hits.

In addition, many experts say global warming had helped the likelihood of a devastating hurricane in New Orleans. Some disbelieve global warming is of any great significance, but those who do say the deep extensive pool of warmer water in the Gulf charged the hurricane.

Levees and floodwalls were built to protect the city from floodwaters from the Mississippi. The levees would work against 95 percent of all hurricanes. The levees would withstand up to, perhaps, a Category 3 hurricane. If that rare 5 percent of storms—Category 4 or Category 5 hurricanes—were to hit New Orleans, engineers warned, the strong storm surge would either pour over the levees or destroy them.

Protecting the city from those strong hurricanes would cost hundreds of millions of dollars. The state could not afford it, and apparently it was not a priority for the federal government.

So the crisis planning went awry in the first stage. Planners just assumed—hoped—that what had never happened would not happen. This is not an unusual occurrence in developing plans. People on the San Andreas Fault in California are not prepared for the earthquake called the Big One. There were no detection or warning devices in the Asian countries hit by the 2004 tsunami, even though it was always possible. People build homes and communities under Mt. Rainier, a sleeping volcano in the state of Washington that could erupt at any time. However, organizations and individuals should learn a lesson from Katrina and make plans. One should plan for the worst catastrophe—it is easier to adjust down if a lesser one occurs than to adjust up.

This case study deals primarily with the first week of the expectation of Hurricane Katrina and its aftermath (Figure 4.8). It is concerned primarily with the people of New Orleans and secondarily with observers of the unfolding crisis. We might call it the prodromal and containment stages, but this is a difficult label because the crisis and the crises it spawned will perhaps last for years. When the Asian tsunami hit on December 26, 2004, and when terrorists attacked on September 11, 2001, the attacks were swift, and immediately afterward there was the containment stage. This was also true in the other states struck by Katrina.

NEW ORLEANS KATRINA: TIMELINE

Friday, August 26:

- Gov. Kathleen Blanco declares a state of emergency in Louisiana.

Saturday, August 27:

- In a letter, Gov. Blanco asks President Bush to declare a federal state of emergency.
- The White House announces a federal emergency is declared and DHS and FEMA are given authority to respond.

Sunday, August 28:

- Mayor Ray Nagin orders mandatory evacuation.
- The *St. Petersburg Times* says George W. Bush, Michael Brown, and Michael Chertoff were warned of levee failure by the National Hurricane Center.
- The *Times-Picayune* reports that water has toppled over a levee.
- The *Times-Picayune* says about 30,000 are in the Superdome with 36 hours' worth of food.
- The *Boston Globe* reports that the Louisiana National Guard has requested 700 buses for evacuations.

Monday, August 29:

- Katrina makes landfall as a Category 4 hurricane.
- On NBC's *Today* Mayor Nagin announces that water is flowing over the levee and that a pumping station is not operating in the lower Ninth Ward.
- FEMA Director Brown requests that DHS dispatch 1,000 employees to Katrina-torn areas. AP says the request lacked urgent language, the employees had 2 days to arrive.
- The *Times-Picayune* reports a Bucktown levee is breached.
- Gov. Blanco again requests assistance from President Bush. News week reports she said "We need everything you've got."
- 5,700 National Guard members are called up.

Tuesday, August 30:

- Water continues to rise; eventually 80% of New Orleans is underwater.
- TV's *Meet the Press* later interviewed Chertoff who said this was the day he became aware that the levee had failed.
- WWL-TV reports that the Pentagon claimed there were enough National Guard in the region to handle hurricane needs.
- The Associated Press says President Bush was playing guitar with country singer Mark Wills.

Figure 4.8 This is a timeline of major events and actions during the first two weeks of the Hurricane Katrina disaster.

Wednesday, August 31:

- The *Boston Globe* reports that National Guard troops had arrived. WWL-TV showed a local emergency director advising that the food and water supply was nearly gone.
- Reuters reports that former mayor Sidney Barthelmy estimated that 80,000 people were trapped in the flooded city.
- The *Times-Picayune* reports that 3,000 are stranded at the Convention Center without food or water.
- On CNN, FEMA Director Brown says, "I must say this storm is much bigger than anyone expected," and "You can tell them, you've talked with the FEMA director and it's going to happen."

Thursday, September 1:

- The *Washington Post* quotes President Bush as saying, "I don't think any body anticipated the breach of the levees."
- Mayor Nagin blasts Bush and Blanco saying, "Get off your asses . . ."

Friday, September 2:

- Newsweek reveals that President Bush's staff made up a DVD so Bush could see "horrific reports coming out of New Orleans as he flew down to the Gulf Coast the next morning on *Air Force One*."
- Bush praises Brown with "Brownie, you're doing a heck of a job."
- National Guard arrives in force and brings food and water.
- Commercial airplanes begin flying evacuees to sites all over the United States. Some had no idea where they were going until they were en route.

Saturday, September 3:

- President Bush blames state and local officials for the New Orleans slow response.
- The *Wall Street Journal* says FEMA finalizes a request for 1,335 buses.

Sunday, September 4:

- The Superdome is completely evacuated.

Monday, September 5:

- A breach is closed and water begins to be pumped out of the city.

Tuesday, September 6:

- Mayor Nagin orders forced evacuation because the city is not safe.

Friday, September 9:

- FEMA Director Brown is removed from the Katrina relief efforts.

Monday, September 12:

- Brown resigns as Director of FEMA.

Figure 4.8 (Continued)

However, in New Orleans, the discovery of the extent of the tragedy seemed endless.

The Governor Contacts President Bush

Governor Kathleen Blanco wrote a letter to U.S. President George W. Bush on August 27, before Katrina made landfall. The letter was sent through the Federal Emergency Management Agency (FEMA). The opening, in part, read:

> I request that you declare an emergency for the State of Louisiana due to Hurricane Katrina for the time period beginning August 26, 2005, and continuing. The affected areas are all the southeastern parishes including the New Orleans Metropolitan area and the midstate Interstate I-49 corridor and northern parishes along the I-20 corridor that are accepting the thousands of citizens evacuating areas expecting to be flooded as a result of Hurricane Katrina.
>
> (Blanco's State of Emergency letter, 2005)

A section read, "I have determined that this incident is of such severity and magnitude that effective response is beyond the capabilities of the state and affected local governments, and that supplementary assistance is necessary to save lives" (Blanco's State of Emergency letter, 2005).

The letter went on to cover various specifics and estimates and what the state could and would do.

The Mayor's Communication Problems

Also on Saturday, August 27, Mayor Ray Nagin and his team set up a command center in the Hyatt Hotel because it was only a block from City Hall and it had a backup generator for power and food. Much of his staff had been evacuated safely out of town. Only a skeleton team remained in New Orleans.

On that team was Sally Forman, the mayor's director of communications. Forman said there was a crisis communications/management plan. However, she said:

> We had never considered there would not be a way to communicate. All of our resources were wiped out. We could occasionally call out on a landline in the power company's command center. I got a few SOS messages to someone on my staff and those messages were released to the news media.
>
> Another call was to a local AM radio station. I was only able to form a Joint Information Bureau (JIB) once the military arrived and provided support. [The military apparently had the only satellite phone in the city.]

On that same day, Nagin, in a joint news conference with Governor Blanco, told those of his constituents who hadn't left town already to evacuate, saying, "This is not a test. This is the real deal. Things could change, but as of right now, New Orleans is definitely the target for this hurricane."

As winds began to grow in strength, he said, "We want you to take this a little more seriously and start moving—right now, as a matter of fact." He told them that the stadium then known as the Louisiana Superdome (now called Caesars Superdome) would be a shelter of last resort for evacuees with special needs and advised people seeking refuge there to bring their own food and drinks for 3–4 days and comforts such as folding chairs, as if going camping.

He said, "Looters will be dealt with severely and harshly and prosecuted to the full extent of the law." This was necessary to ease the minds of evacuees that their homes would be safe if they left.

On Sunday, August 28, according to a New Orleanian who evacuated and later wrote a blog, "It was 8 o'clock in the morning and Mayor Nagin's concerned face looked directly into the television camera as he pleaded with the citizens to please leave as soon as they could." That blogger did as the mayor asked, but many felt as some of her family members: "They were certain that this was another Ivan" (a previous hurricane that bypassed the city). A writer for the *Times-Picayune* said:

> I don't always defend the mayor, but considering the number of hurricane threats we've had, he might have had to put people on buses 3 times each year. How can a city do that? How many times will people cooperate after so many false alarms? Also, how many times can you ask people on high ground to keep 10 extra people in their houses? The concern on the mayor's face was real because maybe this storm was the big one, but maybe it was not. People are using hindsight when they say what he should have done.

Also on that Sunday, Nagin ordered a 6 p.m. curfew and said that emergency services would be provided until winds exceeded 45 mph. He dispatched firefighters and police to use sirens and bullhorns to urge people to leave.

Meanwhile, both landline telephones and cell phone towers were out and there was no way the mayor's team could communicate to the outside world. Mayor Nagin said:

> All communications broke down. I got cell phones as high up as the White House that did not work. My BlackBerry pin-to-pin was the only thing that worked. I saw the military struggle with this, too. No one had communications worth a damn.

Greg Meffert, the mayor's right-hand man and chief technology officer, said the emergency communications plan basically depended on phone service—at least cell phone service—being functional. The mayor and his staff were able to learn what was going on from police radios. Looters were raiding the hotel while they occupied it.

On Monday, August 29, Katrina made landfall. Winds had already taken away one side of the hotel. Both the Superdome and the Ernest N. Morial Convention Center were filled beyond capacity with those who could not or would not evacuate. Thousands of others were still in their homes. After the hurricane passed, they thought everything would return to normal and power would be restored. That was not to be the case.

On Tuesday, August 30, the levees broke and water began to flood the city, even around the Hyatt.

On August 31, the mayor's team was finally able to make a call outside from an Internet phone account set up recently by technology team member Scott Domke and linked to his laptop. They used an Internet connection at the Hyatt and eventually linked eight lines through a single Vonage Internet phone account. Meffert, realizing he needed more lines and more phones, went out with others to a nearby Office Depot where, with the aid of Chief of Police Eddie Compass, they "officially looted" the store for the supplies.

President Bush had flown over the New Orleans scene and seen some of the disaster. The president telephoned that night and Nagin said he told him that "flying over New Orleans in Air Force One did not do the crisis justice."

In an interview with radio station WWL on September 1, the mayor lost his patience and said of President Bush and Governor Blanco, "Don't tell me 40,000 people are coming here. They're not here. It's too doggone late. Now get off your asses and do something, and let's fix the biggest goddam crisis in the history of our country." Forman said CNN picked up the local piece and broadcast it all over the world.

Also on September 1, the team moved to a higher floor to evade some 200 gang members they heard were en route. They took with them some cordless phones that had a range of only 300 feet—sometimes they had to lean over a balcony toward the inside of the building to use the phones. Meffert said, "It felt like the Alamo—we were surrounded and had only short bursts of communication."

Meffert told the *Wall Street Journal* that the city was unable to spend more on emergency communications because of its budget crisis and also because of cuts in federal assistance. Still, improvements had been made since Nagin had taken office two years before. Crime, though still high, was down. The city's website reportedly ranked first out of 70 major cities. The site stayed up throughout the hurricane and its aftermath because Domke shifted it to a Dallas server.

Forman said if she could do it over, she would have had bullhorns and satellite phones. Forman said she is developing a new plan. She says the office should have its own generator to power up a copy machine and should explore some type of alert system during evacuations. She said:

> Cities are not prepared for great disaster; if you are hit in more than one place, you are up a creek. Plans must include alternate locations outside of the city that may be in crisis. A lot of people compared our situation with Mayor [Rudy] Giuliani in New York. This is an unfair comparison; as tragic as the September 11 attack was, Mayor Giuliani could go to his office and work.

Warnings by the News Media

The *Times-Picayune* is the metropolitan newspaper in the Big Easy. People who actually read the newspaper in the days leading up to the hurricane were aware of just how big the threat was. Those who merely glanced at the newspaper may not have been persuaded because the headlines and front-page stories were not alarming. It must be emphasized that even though it was possible that the destruction would be as bad as it was, it was by no means certain that the levees would be breached and the city would flood. It was also not known, at first, how many people had remained in their homes. It is possible, even likely, that persons who chose not to evacuate had not read the newspaper.

On Saturday, August 27, Katrina had hit Florida and was headed toward Louisiana and, if it continued in the same direction, the eye of the storm would hit New Orleans. The headline on Page A1, occupying two-thirds of the page above the fold, read:

KATRINA
PUTS END
TO LULL
STORM'S WESTERN PATH PUTS N.O. ON EDGE
Hurricane lashes south Florida, leaves six people dead

There was a map showing the storm's path but nothing alarming on Page A1. However, in the "jump" of the story on Page A10, there was a map showing evacuation routes to Interstate 10 to Baton Rouge, and halfway through the story that occupied nearly half of the six-column page lengthwise, there was a paragraph that said that "if" the storm hit the city, it would be a Category 4 with a storm surge of 18–22 feet, several feet more of waves, and winds greater than 131 mph.

In the story, Mayor Nagin was paraphrased as saying he was alarmed about the potential path and the lack of time to prepare fully. "This storm really scares me," he said. The story added that city officials would make a decision about mandatory evacuations later that day. Because the city had escaped hurricanes earlier in the season and some people had evacuated without cause, Nagin wanted to be sure that it was necessary.

The newspaper that day had a story about the six people killed by Katrina in South Florida. There was a story saying Gov. Blanco, expected to be named chair of the Southern Governors Association in Atlanta, might not be able to make the trip for the swearing-in ceremony because of the coming storm. Interestingly, the front page of the local section had a story about Mayor Nagin, indicating he would not seek a race for a possible open seat in Congress despite the suggestion by political handicappers that he would be a contender due to his "pro-business stance."

August 28 edition. The banner headline (in 1½-inch-high bold letters) and subheads on Page A1 were the following:

KATRINA TAKES AIM

AN EXTREME STORM	**GET ON THE ROAD**	**WALL OF WATER**
Monday landfall likely to be as strong Category 4	Officials strongly urging residents to leave area	Levees could be topped in the entire metro area

These were the three foremost warnings: (a) the storm is huge; (b) evacuate; and (c) there may be great flooding. The lede indicated the storm would make landfall on Monday. The hurricane was, at the time, a Category 4 that "could build to a top of the chart Category 5 with winds of 155 mph or higher." Below the fold was a second story with the headline:

Katrina Bulks up to Become a Perfect Storm

The lead indicated the storm surge could "flood much of eastern N.O." The National Hurricane Center Director said, "I don't remember seeing conditions as favorable as this for a strengthening hurricane for a long time." A color photo occupying much of the front page showed cars evacuating to the west in the normally eastbound lanes of I-10, a contraflow. Page A15 had a full-page ad from Entergy, the power company, urging residents to be prepared for long power outages and advising them of how to be safe when lines and poles are down.

The jump stories from Page A1 had a banner headline in 1½-inch-high bold letters reading:

PREPARING FOR THE WORST

It included the mayor's warning, "This is the real deal," made the evening before. The coming hurricane was called "a threat of first magnitude." The mayor's spokeswoman, Tami Frazier, was quoted as saying that people should not plan to retreat to the Superdome, but should evacuate the city. The Superdome was to be "a special needs shelter of last resort" for persons who absolutely could not evacuate the city. Ten buses with lifts for disabled people in wheelchairs were sent to take prequalified people to the Dome. The regular city bus system would pick up people at 12 locations and take them to the Dome. Another story on the same page revealed that oil rigs in the Gulf would be closed because the storm is "coming right on top of us."

A half-page color map on Page A21 showed a projected aerial view of what might happen if the wall of water surged against the levees and the city flooded. On Page A23, next to the final page of the section, there was a warning from hurricane researcher Ivor van Heerden: "The bottom line is this is a worst case scenario and everybody needs to recognize it. You can always rebuild your house, but you can never regain your life" ("Katrina Takes Aim," 2006, p. A23).

In the sports section, the headline story was that the New Orleans Saints would evacuate that day and head to Oakland, California, where they had a preseason game the following weekend. Tulane University's football team was to evacuate to Jackson, Mississippi.

The Sunday paper also urged readers to email their hurricane experiences to the newspaper at talkback@timespicayune.com. Many people, when safely evacuated, did that, and NOLA.com, the online paper, carried their poignant blogs later. On Monday, August 29, the day Katrina made landfall, the newspaper was out. The large banner headline, in 2-inch-high bold uppercase letters read:

GROUND ZERO
SUPERDOME BECOMES LAST RESORT
FOR THOUSANDS UNABLE TO LEAVE
NEW ORLEANS BRACES FOR NIGHTMARE
OF THE BIG ONE

A large photo taken the day before showed lines of New Orleanians filing into the Superdome—people carrying plastic bags, cases of bottled water, and hand luggage. The estimate then was 10,000 people; eventually 25,000 people took refuge there. A smaller photo showed an empty highway after evacuees had left. The city was awaiting the storm. Most people expected to be in the Dome for a few hours, not days. Even on that first day, some complained to reporters that no food or water was being provided. One person brought food only because she expected the lines to the concession stands would be long, but warnings from the mayor by television and newspaper had urged people to bring food, water, and clothing—that none would be provided.

Page A3's major headline spanned four-fifths of the page and dominated the middle of the page under a photo of a mother and baby who had found safety in a Red Cross shelter:

Surge Likely to Top
N.O. Levee System

The story, a jump from Page A1, made it clear that the worst-case scenario that was about to occur was no surprise. A story occupying the entire left column indicated that the utilities already knew there would be no electricity or landline phone service "for weeks, or even months" if flooding and damage hampered repair crews. The Convention Center, where thousands more were gathered, was not mentioned as a shelter, but the mayor had said that additional buildings and boats would be commandeered for shelter.

The other stories on Pages A4–A5 were about the success of the contraflow of traffic out of the city, the downtown hotels housing only stranded tourists, and a Carnival Cruise ship that had been diverted to Galveston, Texas.

The flooding began that day, and the newspaper's circulation was immediately and perhaps permanently changed. The staff were forced out of the newspaper's building because it was taking on water. There could be no home delivery, no hawking at newsstands. Instead, the newspaper communicated in a way it could not have if the disaster had occurred just a few years earlier. It also set a precedent for other cities that may suffer similar tragedies. The newspaper already had an online version, NOLA.com. After Katrina, it had only the online paper until Thursday, September 1. The web-published paper provided regular updates of news events much more regularly than a printed newspaper could do. Fortunately, NOLA.com's headquarters are in New Jersey, so it was not affected by the flooding when other websites were down; it had more bandwidth.

In addition, not only did the regular readers who had evacuated have access to information but also the hundreds of thousands of people all over the world who wanted to know what was going on in New Orleans from New Orleanians.

In addition to news, NOLA.com had photographs, details of housing available, and forums on topics such as tracing missing persons—this forum was titled, "Tell Them You're OK."

Frances Spencer was an external web producer for NOLA.com during the disaster. She and others were taking urgent phone calls from people saying things such as "Help my grandmother in the Ninth Ward," or "An insulin-dependent man is still in his house." Spencer said, "We would get word through to emergency response teams to find these people."

Then, she saw an email from a woman in Illinois whose 6-year-old daughter had just died after a trauma-filled life. She had been shaken by her father as a nine-week-old infant and was thereafter blind, brain-damaged, and bed-ridden. The father had been given a 25-year prison sentence. Just a few days before Katrina hit, the child had died—according to the mother, due to an injury caused by a careless healthcare worker. The mother had sent the child's body to a New Orleans funeral home/cemetery for burial in a family crypt. The family was to gather for a funeral and burial in a few days. When Katrina and the flooding occurred, the mother could not reach the funeral home. She did not know if it was underwater and whether her child's coffin might be floating in the New Orleans muck.

Spencer wanted to put the message on the NOLA.com blog page, but a temporary editor thought the story was so outrageous it had to be an urban legend. So Spencer researched the incidents of the child's life and found news stories in Illinois and Missouri from when the child was injured six years earlier, then found stories about the child's death a few days earlier, and the missing coffin more recently.

Armed with these stories, she brought them to the attention of NOLA.com editor John Donley who permitted the blog to run the piece. Bloggers began to respond and offer assistance. Soon, the funeral home responded to the mother, saying the coffin had been sent to Lutcher, Louisiana before the hurricane and that it was intact.

Ashton Phelps, Jr., publisher of the *Times-Picayune*, said some of the journalists on the staff had lost their homes and had only the clothes on their backs. They were determined to continue to work, to deliver information to the public. They evacuated the building, and some set up shop at the *Houma Courier's* offices while others worked from Baton Rouge on the campus of Louisiana State University.

From their temporary digs, the staff members produced a newspaper circulated in areas where readers gradually returned home after the flood water was pumped out. The paper also was distributed to displaced New Orleanians in Baton Rouge.

The September 2 edition declared, in red letters over the name of the newspaper, "Katrina: The Storm We've Always Feared." This tribute of sorts ran for weeks, at least, because the city would not soon recover from the crisis, if ever. The headline taking up nearly a third of Page A1, quoted a desperate woman pictured, in another third of the page, on her knees at the Convention Center, praying:

HELP US, PLEASE

The emphasis of articles was the need for assistance with the efforts to rescue people from the Superdome, the Convention Center, and homes all over the city. Buses and planes had begun to transport people to Houston and other cities, but the move was slow. National Guard troops were needed to assist Louisiana Guardsmen and local police to combat looting and violence. Prominent in the paper were full-page ads from insurance companies promising to be there to help.

On September 3, the newspaper concentrated on President Bush finally recognizing the conditions and promising support and relief. Photos of troops were seen arriving. Numerous ads ran from companies seeking employees and offering assistance.

The September 4–5 newspapers centered on more evacuations and the uncertainty of recovery. There was no potable running water and no power; the streets were still flooded with a gumbo of sewage, vermin, dead bodies, gasoline, and oil. The mayor was calling for total evacuation, which was not to be, as some people began to return to their homes even when there was nothing for them to retrieve.

The disaster was not a surprise to the staff of the *Times-Picayune*. It had run a story warning city, state, and federal government of the likelihood of the tragedy three years before in an award-winning series of articles. The articles read, "Eventually a major hurricane will hit New Orleans head on . . . . It's a matter of when, not if."

The *Times-Picayune*, in a crippled advertising economy with a diminished subscriber base, as of early 2006, kept most of its staff members on salary, and continued to put out the newspaper, an online edition, and a blog page.

TV News Warnings

Dave Walker, a TV columnist for the *Times-Picayune*, on the evening of Friday, August 26, was attending a taping of the syndicated game show *Wheel of Fortune* in the Ernest N. Morial Convention Center. When he arrived home, he learned Katrina was headed toward New Orleans.

He would evacuate later, but his immediate action was to monitor TV news broadcasts of three local stations—WWL Channel 4 (CBS), WDSU Channel 6 (NBC), and WGNO Channel 26 (ABC). Walker has high praise for the newscasters, who, despite having to cope with the disaster as it impacted their own families, struggled to serve their viewers. WVUE was off the air for about two weeks, but its meteorologist, Bob Breck, broadcast from Dallas. Throughout the critical period of the crisis, the other stations were able to broadcast by moving their operations to other sites.

On the Saturday morning, Margaret Orr, from WDSU, told viewers, "Dallas is looking good at this time"; Walter Maestri, a local disaster specialist, talking about the hurricane, said, "This is a bad lady"; WWL anchor Eric Paulsen interrupted meteorologist John Gumm and asked viewers, "Would you go ahead and leave now?"

Later that day, Breck at WVUE suggested the viewers take their kids' cell phones to free up airspace for crucial calls. By Saturday evening, Walker said, "CNN was airing a prepared piece spelling out the well-known worst-case scenario for poor New Orleans and its even poorer below–sea-level citizens." At the end of the piece, the CNN anchor said, "That'll make you sit up and take notice, won't it?" Walker replied, "If you're in charge of FEMA, evidently not."

As the cable networks arrived to cover the crisis, Walker's family evacuated. He stayed as long as he could to monitor coverage.

On Sunday morning, WDSU's Ed Reams warned, "What you love about New Orleans may not exist 24 hours from now." Reams then covered the Superdome where Walker said everything was already "coming apart at the seams." By late Sunday, Walker evacuated himself to Baton Rouge. He said his notes changed from "New Orleans pounded" to "New Orleans dodges bullet" to "New Orleans swamped."

He saw the first of many boat rescues that day on WWL. WBRZ's helicopter toured the flooded city at dusk. Meteorologist Bruce Katz, narrating the live tour of the city, realized on air that his own home was flooded. Katz also narrated the sight of early looting and expressed outrage.

Walker found the debate over the word *refugee* trivial in describing people like himself. He said he was "more concerned with words like 'de-watering' meaning removing the water from my street and 'civil unrest' meaning civilians pillaging a defenseless city."

Walker's house had some flooding, and he and his family lived on the second floor of the house for months while the ground floor was being restored. He said, "It's the worst thing that's ever happened to us, but we're the luckiest people we know."

Wheel of Fortune cast and crew Pat Sajak and Vanna White, along with the big wheel and letter board, escaped the Convention Center just in time. The show had planned to do a series of ten episodes but cut it short and made nine. About 100 staff stayed over Saturday night, and their Sunday flights were canceled, so they were bused to Texas, then flown back to Los Angeles. The week of shows aired in November showing New Orleans landmarks before flood damage.

Radio station WWL managed to stay on the air throughout the crucial periods of the disaster. Many New Orleanians had battery-powered radios, and those who did not evacuate found this their only source of news. This was also true of people in nearby cities and towns, such as Baton Rouge, which also lost power. The wind caused some damage there, but many people talk of visiting neighbors with generators to watch newscasts.

The New Orleans Culture

The culture of the residents of New Orleans is not that of the French Quarter. New Orleanians like jazz and creole music but rarely do they go to the Quarter unless they are entertainers. They like their "second-line dancing," but they only do it in the Quarter if they are entertaining for events such as Mardi Gras. They do not eat at Emeril's. This is partly because many cannot afford French Quarter prices, but they also like to prepare their own gumbo and shrimp creole and pralines. They have their own recipes, their own combination of ingredients and spices, and when they do venture out to eat, it would be to neighborhood spots such as Barrow's Catfish Restaurant, a New Orleans eatery for generations.

The French Quarter is for tourists who come in and out of New Orleans and never see where the people in the city live; the only New Orleanians they see are maids in the hotels, employees in the restaurants, taxi drivers, and musicians in the clubs and on the streets. Many people who visited New Orleans had never heard of the Lower Ninth Ward, the poorest neighborhood, until it was flooded and its people were homeless or dead.

Louisiana has the largest percentage of native-born residents of any state in the union. Many family lines, Black and white, date back to French settlers who founded the city in 1718. New Orleans was 67 percent African-American when Katrina hit, and their culture is different from African-American culture in other U.S. states. They not only have roots in West Africa but also in France, Spain, and Italy. They have names such as Thibodeaux, Rousseau, and Etienne. For many years, they clung to their European heritage. They were mulatto (half-Black), quadroons (one-quarter Black), octaroons (one-eighth Black), and the children and grandchildren of mulattoes, quadroons, and octaroons. They understood and cherished this heritage and would explain their ancestry to anyone who would listen. Then they developed more Black American pride during the Black Power Movement of the 1960s and 1970s. According to Lolis Elie, a columnist for the *Times-Picayune* and a lifelong New Orleanian, there has been a resurgence in creole culture to embrace both the European and African heritages. This cultural difference separates Black New Orleanians from white residents, though the two groups share some love for music and cuisine.

The Lower Ninth Ward was once swampland, and houses were built usually with stilt-like foundations and high porches in case of moderate flooding. According to Elie, 30 years ago the working poor—longshoremen, teachers, factory workers—were able to purchase homes in the ward. This is how 45 percent of the homes in the ward were owned. In the poorest neighborhoods of most U.S. cities, nearly all of the residents are renters. However, the children and grandchildren of N.O. homeowners have not had the skills or employment to keep up the houses. They also have not had the financial ability to purchase hurricane insurance, not to mention flood insurance. Property taxes are non-existent or very low. New Orleans has one of the highest unemployment rates in the United States. When unemployment is high, crime rates are usually high.

All these statistics and facts explain why a number of residents did not want to leave their precious homes, the homes they or their families have owned for years. They wanted to protect them from looters; looters were thought to be more likely to take over a house than a flood. There were problems with getting police protection, even in the best of times. The New Orleans Police Department had been suspected of corruption for years and that suspicion continued through the Katrina aftermath when police officers did not show up for work to protect and serve the people.

Also, New Orleanians were evacuation-weary. They had been warned numerous times to evacuate, and each time, the storm had blown in another direction. Some recalled Hurricane Betsy in 1965, which had caused some flooding, and said, "I lived through Betsy so I'm not leaving."

Stranded New Orleanians Communicate

Approximately 50,000 New Orleanians who, for various reasons, stayed in their homes rather than evacuate, realized that the flood waters were not going to go away soon and they later wanted to be rescued. Many had battery-powered radios, a staple in a city prone to storms and power outages, and were told the water level would not soon subside and would probably increase. Some called 911 as the water seeped or poured into their homes and were told it was too dangerous for emergency workers to attempt the rescue. One blogger wrote "The 911 operator told me, 'You should have listened when you were told to evacuate.'"

The 911 operators working downtown had a dilemma they will never forget. Realizing it was impossible to rescue people as the hurricane-force winds roared and the water rose, they took calls from frantic, desperate, doomed people. They tried to calmly give good advice such as, "Go to your attic," and the caller would say, "I'm already on the roof and the water is rising." One caller said she had a handicapped girl and a baby on a pump machine and said, "We're on the bed and the water is coming up."

They promised to help as soon as possible, knowing there was no one to send. The 120 operators said they could only handle calls for 15 minutes at a time, then they had to take a break to recover composure. Eventually, they had to evacuate as their center flooded—and as they left, the phones were still ringing.

As flood levels grew, it was not possible to use most landline phones, but a few continued to work, especially those that did not require electricity. In some areas, pay phones worked longer than home phones. Cell phones worked for a while, but cell towers were soon down and cell phones went dead. In other areas, especially the Lower Ninth Ward, the houses were nearly submerged except for roofs. Sadly, more than 1,000 people died. Some swam to safety on a highway overpass or at the Convention Center or the Superdome.

Survivors retreated to their attics and, in many cases, broke through to their roofs. News helicopters captured shots of stranded people with signs large enough to be seen by pilots. Many later said they wondered why the news helicopters did not attempt to save them, but these choppers are not equipped for rescues. Many news cameramen in the helicopters did say they told rescue people where to find people. It is interesting that people would have had supplies for signs in their homes, even more surprising in their attics. These were people who did not expect a great flood, so it seems they would not have anticipated rescue by helicopter. After the flooding that was swift, there was no time to search for paintbrushes, posterboard or cardboard, and paint, so these supplies had to be readily available. Some people painted signs directly on their roofs.

Communicating With Persons in New Orleans

People who had fled from New Orleans knew from the news media that the city was flooding. But they were as frantic about finding news of relatives and friends as they had been to find safe shelter and food. Many wondered if they would have been less stressed out if they had stayed home and weathered the storm with loved ones who could not or did not evacuate.

At the same time, families and friends who lived in other parts of the United States and the world were stressed because of the lack of communications. For a while, they managed to get through on cell phones, but service was intermittent. They might connect, but the connection would die before a conversation could be made or completed.

Ham radio (amateur radio) operators revealed that people dialed random numbers on their cell phones hoping to reach anyone who could send word to help trapped people. A man in Oklahoma got word by cell phone that his New Orleans relatives were trapped on the second floor of their home and their cell phone had died. The man called the Red Cross, which was instrumental in contacting an organization of ham operators who specialize in emergencies. The organization was unable to reach ham operators in New Orleans. However, one of them was able to connect with another operator in Utah who was able to reach operators in Louisiana. Subsequently, emergency personnel rescued the Oklahoma man's aunt and about a dozen others.

Mobile phone providers urged consumers to use text messages instead of voice calls because they are sent in packets of data that use less bandwidth to get through overloaded lines. However, text messaging is so impersonal when lives are being lost. It was necessary to actually hear a person's voice, to not only know the words that were being said but to ascertain frame of mind, mood, and fear from voice tone.

One man in Washington, D.C., said he was comforted when he finally heard the voice of his stubborn aunt who had refused to leave her apartment until the levees broke. His calls had not been getting through; he had tried postings on the Internet, which did work for some people, but no one had responded to him.

Many people outside the hurricane-stricken area were irritated with the news media for its concentration on looting and the blame game when there were still people camping out on highway overpasses and on their roofs, not to mention the thousands of people in the nightmare that was the Superdome and the Convention Center (Figure 4.9).

Figure 4.9 The news media were not welcome at many places in the New Orleans area during the aftermath of Hurricane Katrina. New Orleanians felt their plight was personal. As bodies piled up at this morgue in St. Gabriel, signs barred curiosity seekers.

Source: OMAR TORRES / AFP via Getty Images

Lack of Communications in the Superdome and Convention Center

The Superdome and the Convention Center are the two places in New Orleans that will hold the most people. Many locals who could not afford to evacuate went there before the storm. Others retreated there after the floods began to overtake the city. Estimates are that 25,000 were in the Superdome and the Convention Center.

Even though Mayor Nagin asked people to bring food, water, and comforts for 3–4 days, many people felt that they would only be there for a few hours, the storm would pass, and they would return home—so there was no food and no water. There was great shock when they found out that most of the city was underwater. Apparently there was no official announcement of what would happen to them. No one was in charge.

With no air conditioning, the heat was unbearable. There were no bathing facilities. The toilets, which often backed up during sports events, were useless. Sickly people died and were just covered in sheets and blankets, but their deteriorating bodies remained among the living. There was crime—stealing for sure, and some reported murders and rapes.

There were no television monitors giving people information. A few—too few—members of the Louisiana National Guard, patrolling the buildings, told the persons they encountered that buses would "soon" come and take them away. They didn't know when "soon" would be.

Evacuees housed in the Superdome and Convention Center were eventually taken to Baton Rouge and Houston by buses. Many were taken by plane and bus to cities all over the United States, where many still reside. Courtney Scott, a mass communications student at Louisiana's Southern University who had family members housed in the Convention Center, said some buses left passengers standing on I-10 to wait for other buses to rescue them—buses that never came.

Scott also said, "National Guardsmen 'protected' the evacuees from harm but some also took bribes to provide food and other amenities and to load certain passengers on buses first."

Cell phones were out. Pay phones did not work. The primary source of communications was rumor. People did not know they would be rescued until they actually were. It would seem that there should have been someone in authority who could have utilized low-technology tools, such as a bullhorn, to inform the people.

One rumor greatly exaggerated was the number of deaths in the Superdome and the Convention Center. Many people who took shelter in these places spoke about seeing murder and rape, and one estimate was that there were as many as 200 bodies either from natural causes or murder or suicide.

When the buildings were emptied, the Louisiana National Guard brought in a refrigerated 18-wheel truck to transport the bodies. They reported finding only ten at the Superdome, and four of those were found in the street nearby. Four persons died of natural causes, one overdosed, and there was one suicide. The number of atrocities reported by the news media and some evacuees turned out to be false. An officer who played a key role in the security at the Superdome said that "99 percent of the people were very well-behaved."

At the Convention Center, four bodies were discovered, and one was apparently slain, according to law, military, and health officials. The crime rate in New Orleans was high before the disaster; in 2003, the murder rate was eight times the national average and 52 more per 100,000 citizens than in New York. There were 5,000 murders in 2003, and all this happened in a city plagued by charges of police corruption. So, in a pressure-cooker situation such as that in the Superdome and the Convention Center, some crime would be expected.

World News Coverage

While the people of New Orleans were suffering in a kind of fishbowl, the whole world was watching round the clock, helplessly. All the world's viewers knew more about the disaster than the people trapped in New Orleans. Viewership was up 371 percent on CNN, 165 percent on Fox News, and 191 percent on MSNBC. The networks broadcast news bulletins often and had pre-empted regular programming with special news broadcasts in the evening.

At first, the TV news reporters and anchors seemed to blame the people for not evacuating; then, apparently, they learned that some actually were incapable of evacuating. Reporters on the scene waded through the gumbo of flooded streets, taking some risks themselves to tell the stories. Word was that there were rats and snakes swimming through the toxic muck, along with bodies and sewage. One report said a shark was sighted. The stories were very poignant until it became apparent that the federal government had not taken steps to rescue the people in the Superdome or the Convention Center. Then the coverage turned to the blame game, and it was the main storyline until the people were transported to Houston and other cities and even afterward.

Looting and crime were reported widely (Figure 4.10), and as mentioned in the previous section, much of the reporting of crime was overblown. There were reports of shooting, and speculation was that this might have been why President Bush did not fly to the site immediately, but instead flew over it. There were shots of looters taking items such as television sets, and reporters wondered aloud what they could do with them in a city with no power, no people, and few homes. Information also came from blogs and websites in New Orleans and later sprang up from all over. Again, this information was accessible to the world but not to the people struggling to fulfill their basic needs.

Figure 4.10 Opportunists often took advantage of business owners during the disaster. This rug shop owner put up a sign to communicate with anyone who might loot his store. He warned he was protected by "a big dog, an ugly woman, two shotguns, and a claw hammer." He and his store survived.

Source: Steven Clevenger / Con derechos gestionados via Getty Images

Crises of Words

Mini-crises within the crisis erupted over comments made and words used by both news reporters and newsmakers. Bloggers on various sites, including Yahoo.com (August 31) and Boingboing.net (August 30), complained that the news media, particularly the print media, were racist in photo captions. A Black man hauling food through the flood waters was called a "looter." However, a white man and woman who were doing the exact same thing were "finding" food. There were no stores visible in the photos, and all were carrying food products. The photo of the Black man was an Associated Press photo and the other was shot by AFP/Getty Images.

Rapper Kanye West, now known as Ye, was one of several celebrities who appeared on an NBC special fundraiser for Katrina victims on September 2. West was supposed to read a script prepared by the show's producers about the impact of Katrina on the Gulf states. Instead, he complained about Black families being called "looters" by the news media. He did urge viewers to make donations. But then he said, "George Bush doesn't care about Black people." This also was not in the script, and, at this point, the director cut him off and went to another celebrity. The show was live, so it was seen by East Coast viewers with a disclaimer from the network say-ing, "Kanye West departed from the scripted comments that were prepared for him, and his opinions in no way represent the views of the network." The rapper's comments were cut entirely from the West Coast broadcast. This made news nationwide. Some columnists and editorials, especially in African-American newspapers, praised him, whereas others criticized him.

What some critics of the news media did not understand is that journal-ists are not one body working together to label people. If one reporter or one newspaper were to categorize Black people taking food as "looters" and whites as "surviving," it would indeed be cause for concern and claims of racism would be understandable. However, if the two photos and cap-tions on the sites are the only photos in question and they originated from different sources, the racist claim is unfounded.

Considering the situation in New Orleans with no stores being open, it is likely that all the people pictured did not purchase the food, so they are all technically looters. Eventually news media and TV viewers came to comprehend the dire circumstances and realized that stealing food was necessary for survival, so we have "understandable looters."

Other comments were termed insensitive. President Bush was caught by a television crew engaged in small talk. He mentioned that Sen. Trent Lott of Mississippi had lost "one of his homes" but that it would be replaced with a "fantastic house—and I'm looking forward to sitting on the porch." This made the President seem oblivious to the thousands of people who would never recover from the tragedy as easily as did Lott.

The President's mother, according to John Kass of the *Chicago Tribune*, put her "silver foot" in her mouth, too. Barbara Bush, after touring the Houston Astrodome where thousands of evacuees had to live, said to a TV news reporter, "And so many in the arena here, you know, were under-privileged anyway, so this is working well for them."

Probably the most interesting faux pas in the spoken/written lan-guage of Hurricane Katrina was the word *refugee* used to describe the displaced persons. The *Random House Dictionary of the English Lan-guage* defines refugee as "a person who flees for shelter or protection from danger or trouble, like a storm." Then it adds "especially to a foreign country."

Critics argued that the word *refugee* was condescending and negative, and that its connotation signals second-class citizens, not Americans who had lived in the United States all their lives and paid taxes. Most news or-ganizations stopped using *refugee* and started using *evacuee* because argu-ing over the use of a word would be counterproductive to their purpose as news disseminators. It just was not worth it.

The furor over the word is reminiscent of the incident in 1999 when a staff member of then-Washington, D.C. Mayor Anthony Williams used the word *niggardly* in a meeting with other staff members. The word means "miserly," and the staff member used it correctly, but the others were not familiar with it and felt it was a racial slur. It became a concern of which the news media became aware, and it turned into an international incident when the staff member resigned under the pressure and the mayor accepted his resignation. People were furious that the man would be losing his job when he had used the word correctly. So the mayor urged him to return and he did. Nevertheless, many who argued on behalf of the staff member agreed that *niggardly* is a word one can easily omit from conversation if there is a chance that it will be misunderstood.

Images and Sound Bites

The images of the disaster, seen over and over on television and the print media, were of rescues by helicopter and boat, people on their rooftops waving to news helicopters not knowing they could not make rescues, President Bush hugging two young Black sisters, President Bush looking at the flooded city from a window on Air Force One, dead bodies floating in the toxic flooded water, a parking lot full of school buses that ostensibly could have been used to evacuate people, helicopters dropping MREs (meals ready to eat) and water and victims scrambling to catch them, a woman sitting on the ground next to the body of her husband wrapped in a sheet, a dead person in a wheelchair.

A memorable sound bite was President Bush congratulating FEMA head Michael Brown, saying, "You're doing a great job, Brownie," when the whole world knew Brownie was not doing such a good job. He would later be demoted, and he then resigned from FEMA altogether.

News anchor Ted Koppel on ABC's *Nightline* said to Brown, who didn't know about the thousands of people seeking shelter at the Convention Center, "Don't you guys watch television?"

Mayor Nagin peppered some of his emotional comments with expletives such as, "I don't want to see anybody do any goddam press conferences. No press conferences until we get some supplies down here." He later said, "The president told me he appreciated my frankness and bluntness and I told him I was sorry if anything I said had been disrespectful."

Communications to Locate People

As people were evacuated from the Superdome by bus, desperate parents passed their children overhead to assure them places in the bus and did not make the buses themselves. In other cases, helicopters and boats rescued children first from rooftops and homes and promised to come back for parents but did not. Some people did not know to what cities they were being transported until they were en route. So in these cases, children sometimes ended up in different places, even different cities than their parents. The same was true for various other family members.

Mayor Nagin said:

> I saw stuff that I never thought I would see in my lifetime. People wanting to die. People trying to give me their babies . . . . It was a helpless, helpless feeling. There was a lady waiting in line for a bus who had a miscarriage. She was cleaning herself off so she wouldn't lose her place in line. There were old people saying, "Just let me lie down and die." It's unbelievable that this would happen in America.

The American Red Cross (ARC), the Salvation Army, and organizations such as Craigslist, the National Next of Kin Registry, the National Center for Missing and Exploited Children, as well as TV cable stations and networks, helped connect families. All had websites, but some actually talked face-to-face with missing family members and used photos to help find loved ones. Many complained that the news media spent too much time with the blame game and looting rather than being instrumental in locating people.

A website, tattoo.about.com, catered to the tattoo community. One blog was about a man with a crown tattoo who had apparently had a stroke and could not communicate. The site sought the artist who created the tattoo in hopes that he might know him and might be able to notify his family where he was. Other messages offered jobs to displaced tattoo artists.

A site, www.katrina.com, was the business site for a web designer named Katrina who lent it to the cause because she was getting hits anyway. She provided links to various help organizations and agencies and a message board.

When evacuees settled in Houston, organizations there helped locate and relocate people. They also helped provide information to help people decide whether to return or not.

FEMA Emails

After much national and international criticism of the federal government's handling of the crisis in New Orleans, FEMA head Michael Brown was removed from the leadership position of the Katrina relief effort on September 9. Then, on September 12, he resigned from his position as Director of FEMA.

In October, the Senate Homeland Security and Governmental Affairs Committee made public 19 pages of email communications between a

FEMA official on duty in New Orleans and Brown and his staff. Marty Ba-hamonde, a public affairs officer from Boston, was the first FEMA official to survey the crisis developing in New Orleans. He sent the first message on August 28, the day before the hurricane hit. The messages support crit-ics of the government and its failure to be concerned about the plight of the victims.

On August 28, Bahamonde wrote on his BlackBerry, "Everyone is soaked. This is going to get ugly fast." On August 31, in a message directly to Brown, he wrote:

> Sir, I know that you know the situation is past critical. Here are some things you might not know. Hotels are kicking people out, thousands gathering the streets with no food or water, hundreds still being rescued from homes . . . . Estimates are many will die within hours.

Brown's press secretary, on the same day, wrote to Bahamonde, "it is very important that time is allowed for Mr. Brown to eat dinner . . . . He needs much more than 20–30 minutes." She went on to talk about the woes of dining in a busy restaurant. Indignant, Bahamonde's response to other FEMA staff was the following: "I just ate an MRE and crapped in the hallway of the Superdome along with 30,000 other close friends, so I understand his concern about busy restaurants." Later news vindicated Brown to an extent, showing he sought aid earlier.

Companies and Organizations in Crises

It would be hard to even imagine a company, business, or organization in New Orleans that was not affected by the hurricane or its aftermath. The following are some of these businesses and organizations, and what they did to communicate.

CHARITY HOSPITAL

Charity Hospital was a Level I trauma center that treated people despite their inability to pay. After the hurricane blew through the city, the hos-pital was without electricity to operate monitors and ventilators and air conditioning. The temperature was 100 degrees. There were no working toilets and no elevators.

After the water began to rise, the medical personnel carried 50 patients up a flight of stairs. They tried to call FEMA and the Louisiana National Guard, to no avail. One doctor said they were promised FEMA would rescue them, but two days later, he said, "We've been forgotten . . . we've disappeared from the radar screen for five days. It's unbelievable."

They put a sign hanging outside a high window reading, "God of Abraham, Help Us O God." In desperation, they went to the news media and the news media got help to get the medical personnel and patients evacuated.

AARP

The American Association of Retired Persons (AARP) was planning a convention in New Orleans beginning September 29. Actually, it was more like a party for 20,000 people of retirement age. Most people had already paid for the three-day bash, had airline tickets, and were beginning to pack their bags when Katrina changed their plans.

AARP staff members stopped the news releases promoting the event and its highlights: a concert, a lecture by Maya Angelou, a swamp tour, great meals in French Quarter restaurants, pigging out on beignets at Café du Monde. An announcement was posted on the AARP website telling members they could get refunds. The organization threw away some pamphlets and other promotional items that were relevant only to 2005 and New Orleans and saved other materials that could be adapted to future conventions. Trinkets being trucked to Louisiana were halted. New Orleans T-shirts, beads, and hurricane glasses (a Louisiana souvenir for many years) had been loaded into souvenir packages. The shirts were retrieved and were sent to clothing drives in Louisiana. The enameled logo pins were sent to registrants with a letter of explanation.

On a positive note, hundreds of registrants sent emails refusing the refund and asking AARP to forward their fees to relief efforts instead.

OTHER ORGANIZATIONS THAT HELPED ALLEVIATE THE CRISIS

Numerous employers engaged in employee relations and/or community relations programs.

Wal-Mart (which rebranded as Walmart in 2008), often under fire itself for employee problems, was the first major company to step forward and offer jobs to its displaced employees wherever they might be. Also, Wal-Mart employees whose stores were closed due to the storm received their salaries for three days whether they were scheduled to work or not. After three days, they were offered temporary work at other Wal-Mart or Sam's Club stores. Financial assistance was offered for lodging and food; $250 cash was available from store managers for food and clothing.

Harrah's Entertainment, which operated casinos in New Orleans, Biloxi, and Gulfport (which were all closed after the hurricane), offered employees emergency supplies and money. Employees were paid for up to 90 days.

Prior to the hurricane, museums in New Orleans sent email messages to institutions further inland requesting space to store valuable art objects.

The pieces were transported to these places safely so that most museums could return to normalcy sooner than many city attractions could.

Mortgage lending institutions Freddie Mac and Fannie Mae urged lenders to excuse late payments. The Internal Revenue Service (IRS) offered extensions to taxpayers who requested more time to file returns or pay taxes. Telecommunications provider BellSouth (which was later acquired by AT&T in 2006) set up mobile units in Louisiana and Mississippi so that affected employees could rest and do laundry, and their families could eat three meals a day.

In Houston, before evacuees arrived there in great numbers, an organization called NOAH (New Orleans and Houston) was formed to secure gigs for transplanted musicians. The organization's founder developed a website (www.noahleans.com) with a database linking New Orleans musicians to professional Houston players. He also urged music store owners to offer free rentals of musical instruments because most musicians lost their instruments in the flood. The founder said, "Just think of the music of New Orleans on the streets of Houston."

Habitat for Humanity deployed teams to check and repair homes the organization had built. Many were lost, and the organization hopes to build more.

When evacuees settled in Houston, the newspapers, particularly the *Houston Chronicle* and the *Houston Defender*, ran stories of what was going on in New Orleans. They helped locate people but they also told stories of rebuilding and recovery, stories that helped displaced persons know whether or not to return, whom to contact about jobs, insurance, housing, and so on.

Fundraising Scams

The list of organizations raising funds for Katrina victims ranged from single individuals to the ARC, the agency that led the relief effort and raised nearly $2 billion.

Most of the fund collections were run by concerned, honest citizens, but the news media urged people to donate to the ARC or the Salvation Army because there were numerous scams. The FBI said 60 percent of the 2,000 sites it reviewed were registered to persons outside the United States and were expected to be fraudulent.

Scam artists were primarily persons or organizations purporting to be raising funds for Katrina victims; they reached people in person, by mail, and online. However, *PC World* also warned against the sale of flood-damaged cars from Louisiana being sold as if they were in pristine condition.

There were many websites with Katrina names, such as katrinahelp. com, katrinadonations.com, and katrinarelief.com, and many were scams.

Florida's attorney general took action to shut down the sites and filed a civil action against the webmasters. There was a phishing scam in which donors divulged their credit card numbers or PayPal accounts, not knowing the donation was being made directly into the webmaster's private PayPal account.

Also, some sites were set up to look like news reports, but clicking on "read more" led to being linked to sites that secretly installed Trojan horse software that give hackers control over computers. There was another scam, promoted through faxes and email, urging investing in post-Katrina stocks. The fax stated, "Any company that gets a tiny slice—even 1 percent—of this business could add a minimum of $260 million to its bottom line."

Crisis Begets Crises

At the end of 2005, the disaster that was New Orleans was still at crisis point and had spawned other numerous crises with no end in sight (Figure 4.11). There was uncertainty that all bodies had been recovered from once-flooded homes. There was great uncertainty over the reconstruction of the levees. Some members of the U.S. Congress felt rebuilding the city would be useless if the levees were not rebuilt to withstand Category 5 hurricanes—and there seemed not to be funds for such a restructuring.

The people of New Orleans were displaced and living, permanently or temporarily, in all 50 states. Some had not located their families and loved ones at the end of the year. Out of 200,000 homes, 120,000 were damaged by flood waters. Approximately 80,000 homes had no insurance at all. Most with hurricane insurance were told by insurance companies they were not covered for flooding.

FEMA's assistance to displaced New Orleanians was sporadic and slow. The people were encouraged to find work and housing. Some did; some did not, for various reasons. President Bush's approval rating dipped considerably because of his and the government's failure to respond adequately and swiftly, and partly because of the public attitude toward the war in Iraq.

In December 2005, the president of the ARC, Martha Evans, resigned after the organization drew criticism for its internal conflict, for moving too slowly in response to the crisis, for having poorly trained volunteers, and for seeming to be disorganized. The ARC took in $1.8 billion in donations after Katrina. Four presidents resigned after 1991, citing conflicts with the perhaps overly large, 50-member board.

Hurricane Katrina: Ten Years Later

From 25–34 square miles of Louisiana land is swallowed each year by the Gulf of Mexico; this makes New Orleans closer to being a beach-front city, and therefore more and more susceptible to hurricanes. The hurricane season runs from summer through fall every year.

In tourist spots of New Orleans, like the French Quarter and the Garden District, one would never know there had been a Hurricane Katrina that had much of the city under water. The Ninth Ward, hardest hit by the ferocious storm, is not fully recovered, but there is progress.

Some residents of the Lower Ninth Ward, the hardest-hit and poorest neighborhood affected by Katrina flooding, have rebuilt their homes. Some had insurance; others were aided by families and friends, charities, churches, and some good Samaritans. The rebuilt homes are scattered over a huge expanse of land, larger than it seemed when it was densely populated. New Orleanians estimate that by 2015, it will look like a neighborhood again.

Actor Brad Pitt and his Make It Right Foundation built 150 homes for the Lower Ninth Ward. Pitt and producer Steve Big donated $5 million each; "Idol Gives Back" on TV's *American Idol* donated $10 million; more than $10 million more has been pledged by companies, organizations, and individuals. The homes are equipped with solar panels so residents can produce most electricity needed. Some are up and occupied. On narrow lots, they are long and narrow and stand 8 feet from the ground with rooftop escape hatches just in case there are future floods (Figure 4.12). Many in the Ward died because they could not get to their roofs in the 2005 flooding. Pitt's project calls for houses to cost no more than $150,000, and he hopes buyers will be able to put up 85 percent from insurance and government assistance. The Pitt houses, if placed in one corner of the vast wasteland left by the flood, would be the size of a postage stamp on a large envelope.

Because of the bargain real estate, new homeowners have purchased land and have built homes. But it's still not the same. The tall shade trees are gone. You don't see children on bicycles riding through the street to the candy store (Figure 4.13). A restaurant opened in 2012. However, residents complain that there are no grocery stores, no drug stores in the Ward, not even the little mom and pop stores that existed before 2005.

Reconcile New Orleans, an organization of concerned citizens in and near the Central City section, had already spent several years helping at-risk youth learn life skills when it opened Café Reconcile in 2000. The meals are prepared by youth trained for entry into the hospitality and restaurant business that makes New Orleans famous. Though it existed before Katrina, it grew appreciably afterwards, partly because the city needed trained employees to keep the restaurants and the tourist trade, and partly

HURRICANE KATRINA'S
13 CRISIS COMMUNICATIONS LESSONS

1. Heed prodromes.

2. Anticipate and plan for the worst-case scenario. You can always adjust down to a lesser crisis but not to a greater crisis.

3. Always have alternatives. If plan A cannot work, there must be plans B and C.

4. Align the crisis communications with crisis management. What you say should be what you do and vice versa.

5. Have several places preselected for a crisis center or work site. All sites should not be in the same neighborhood or even the same city.

6. Have an email address, phone number or voice-mail number (perhaps out of town), where employees may report their whereabouts.

7. If possible, monitor television, radio, Internet, and print news. The news media may know something you don't know.

8. Always, the most crucial action is protecting lives in jeopardy.

9. If the story is negative, it is best that the organizational spokesperson reveal it. Tell your own bad news.

10. Plan on not having electricity and other necessities like landline telephones and cell phones. Be prepared to utilize low-technology bullhorns, walkie-talkies, manual typewriters, etc. But have effective hi-tech equipment available. Have power packs.

11. Do not guess statistics. In a great tragedy, the news media will want to know how many people lost their lives. Any guess made is bad. A large estimate gets headlines, but you look uninformed when it's over. A low estimate also insults your knowledge of the situation.

12. If you will depend upon the resources of others (governmental and non-governmental agencies and organizations), know what you can expect from each and how to seek those resources.

13. Just because a crisis has never occurred does not mean it never will.

Figure 4.11 Communications professionals should learn these lessons from the miscommunications of the Hurricane Katrina aftermath in New Orleans.

Figure 4.12 One of the houses built by actor Brad Pitt's foundation in the Lower Ninth Ward of New Orleans. Notice the house is built high off the ground to offer protection against minimal flooding. Many residents have rebuilt but have been concerned about the height. Photo by Gerald Brown. Permission granted.

because the youth needed jobs. The eatery is a non-profit restaurant serving delicious and inexpensive midday meals including fried catfish, gumbo, bread pudding, peach cobbler, and other New Orleans cuisine. The youth, referred by school counselors and word of mouth, take turns serving as chefs, sous chefs, waiters, cashiers, dishwashers, and greeters. Some of the trainees plan to go to college and major in culinary arts; others want to get local jobs right away. They are required to take lessons in life skills for three weeks—being on time, appearances, and social graces. Then they do four weeks in the café and two weeks of internships. On graduation day, tips earned during the four weeks are divided among the trainees. Supervised closely at every step by Sister Mary Lou Specha, executive director Reconcile New Orleans and her staff, many students have graduated from the program and transitioned into employment in the local restaurant industry.

What Has Not Gone Well?

The *New Orleans Times-Picayune*, the 175-year-old daily newspaper that became famous for its prize-winning brave coverage of Hurricane Katrina and later the BP oil spill, announced that it would no longer be a daily, but would continue to publish on Wednesdays, Fridays, and Sundays.

Figure 4.13 Many houses in the Lower Ninth Ward sit just as they did after Katrina's waters damaged them. Local residents say some of the families never returned to see what happened to their houses . . . and, of course, some died in the flooding. Photo by Gerald Brown. Permission granted.

Additional coverage would be online. Newspapers have been battling for years over failing advertising revenues as businesses defected to the Internet. In addition, since the storm, circulation fell sharply from 260,000 in 2005 to 133,400 in 2012. Numerous jobs at the newspaper were lost. New Orleans became the largest city in the United States without a daily print newspaper.

Ray Nagin was mayor of New Orleans from 2002–2010. In 2013, he was charged with taking free travel perks, bribes, and gifts from contractors. The bribes were handed out to Nagin and others for city business contracts. Many of them pleaded guilty and testified against Nagin. Federal District Court Judge Ginger Berrigan said Nagin, who received $50,000 in the scheme, claimed a "much smaller share of the profits of the crime than any other member of the group," noting that he was neither the organizer nor leader of the crime (Johnson & Robinson, 2014). Still it was a crime and, in 2014, he was sentenced to ten years, years fewer than Judge Berrigan could have ordered. She instead praised his efforts to save the city. He began serving his sentence in a minimum-security lockup in Louisiana.

Meanwhile, a series of articles in the *Times-Picayune* in December, 2008, warned that Louisiana is the fastest sinking land in North America and that the Gulf of Mexico, to the south, is rising. And that does not take into account hurricanes.

Update/Case Study: Hurricane Katrina, New Orleans, and Brad Pitt

The Katrina flooding crisis spawned a sub-crisis. Houses built by actor Brad Pitt's charity "Make It Right" in the Lower Ninth Ward in 2006, a year after the flooding, were the center. A total of 109 homes, sold as floodproof, were architecturally interesting. To use a New Orleans word, they were "jazzy" and built on stilts higher than water would likely rise (Figure 4.12).

Residents purchased the homes below cost, starting at $150,000. They said that as soon as Pitt left the scene, others took over and the buildings began to deteriorate. The homes, they said, did not withstand torrential rains. Some had flat roofs. Some did not have rain gutters or overhangs. Most were not finished with waterproof paint. There was mold, leaks, rot, and electrical fires. They were trapped in houses they could not sell.

Owners of these post-Katrina homes filed lawsuits against Pitt and his now-defunct charity. In 2022, they succeeded in getting a $20.5 million settlement from the Brad Pitt Foundation to fund renovations and repair.

Ron Austin, lead attorney in the lawsuits, said owners did not blame Pitt but praise him for making the wrong right. "He's an icon kind of guy," Austin said. "They are still his fans." (Chan, 2022).

New Orleans is still lower than sea level and therefore stands a constant chance of severe flooding from hurricanes and storms. Scientists say, furthermore, that the city is gradually sinking and sea level is rising.

Bibliography

Case Study: Thinking Outside the Box

Anderson, N. (2021, May 12). COVID vaccine freebies: Companies offer rewards, incentives to those who got the shot. *Fox 8 Cleveland WJW*. Retrieved April 22, 2022, from https://fox8.com.

Cullen, D. (2009). *Columbine*, New York, Twelve Hachelle Book Group.

Dodd, S. & Henni, J. (2021, June 08). How to get promotions, prizes, and freebies with you COVID-19 vaccine. *People*. Retrieved April 22, 2022, from https://people.com.

Fox61 Staff. (2021, April 24). Cigna rolls out incentives to encourage vaccinations, expand access. *Fox 61*. Retrieved April 22, 2022, from www.Fox61.com.

Groppe, M. (2021, May 25). Federal government gives OK for states to offer lotteries, cash incentives for vaccinations. *USA Today*. Retrieved April 22, 2022, from www.usatoday.com.

Olson, J. (2021, May 27). Minnesota to announce vaccine incentives Thursday. *Minnesota Star Tribune*. Retrieved April 22, 2022, from www.startribune.com/jeremy-olson.

Parent, J. (2021, April 23). Legal questions arise on the role of workplace incentives. Retrieved April 22, 2022, from www.concordmonitor.com.

Powell, A. (2020, December 10). Fauci offers a timeline for ending COVID-19 pandemic. *Harvard Gazette.* Retrieved September 18, 2022, from https://news. harvard.edu.

Slavitt, A. (2021). *Preventable: The inside story of how leadership, failures, politics, and selfishness doomed the U.S. Corona Virus response.* New York: St. Martins Press.

Suddiqui, S. & Armour, S. (2021, May 11). Uber, Lyft to provide free rides to COVID-19 vaccine sites until July 4. *Wall Street Journal News.* Retrieved April 22, 2022, from www.wsj.com.

Tyko, K. (2021, May 11). McDonalds is bringing this COVID-19 vaccine awareness message to its coffee cups, times square billboard. *USA Today.* Retrieved April 22, 2022, from usatoday.com.

White House. (2021). *National strategy for the COVID-19 response and pandemic preparedness.* Retrieved April 22, 2022, from http://nhcnhc.org.

Will, M. (2021, May 13). Cash for shots? Districts take new tactics to boost teacher vaccinations. *EdWeek.* Retrieved April 22, 2022, from www.edweek.org.

Williams, R. (2021, March 22). Krispy Kreme serves sweet incentive for vaccinated customers. *Market Industry Dive.* Retrieved April 22, 2022, from www. marketingdive.com.

Zavert, M. (2021, May 26). New York's latest vaccination incentive: A full ride scholarship to a public state college. *The New York Times.* Retrieved April 22, 2022, from www.nytimes.com.

Case Study: Gander, Newfoundland and 911

Defede, J. (2002). *The day the world came to town.* New York: HarperCollins Publishers.

Moss, M. (2021). *Flown into the arms of angels.* St. Johns, NL: Flanker Press.

Update/Case Study: Columbine High School and the Shooting Tragedy: Preparing for the Worst

Brockell, G. (2019, April 19). Bullies, black trench coats: Columbine's most dangerous myths. *The Washington Post.* Retrieved March 24, 2023, from www.columbian.com/news/2019/apr/19/bullies-black-trench-coats-columbines-most-dangerous-myths/.

Depart, Z. (2023, March 20). "He has a battle rifle": Police feared Uvalde gunman's AR-15. *The Texas Tribune.* Retrieved March 23, 2023, from www. texastribune.org/2023/03/20/uvalde-shooting-police-ar-15/.

Education Week. (2022, January 27). *School shootings in 2022: How many and where?* Retrieved March 23, 2023, from www.edweek.org/leadership/school-shootings-this-year-how-many-and-where/2022/01.

Case Study: Hurricane Katrina and New Orleans

Bazar, E. (2005, September 1). Desperate message triggers calls from across USA. *USA Today,* p. 6A.

Blanco's state of emergency letter to president bush. (2005, August 27). *Archives of the Times-Picayune.* Retrieved from www.mondotimes.com.

Bourne, J. K., Jr. (2004, October). Gone with the water. *National Geographic Magazine* [online]. Retrieved November 13, 2006, from www3.nationalgeograpic. com/ngm/1410/feature5/.

Connelly, R., Hufner, R. & Spivak, T. (2005, September 8–14). Katrina and the waves. *Houston Press*, pp. 14–17.

Farhi, P. & Wiltz, T. (2005, September 1). Delivering news of the storm that stopped the presses. *Washington Post*, pp. C1, C7.

FEMA Emails. (2005, October 20). Retrieved October 27, 2005, from www. NYTimes.com.

Frey, J. (2005, September 1). TV networks navigate floodwaters to get on air. *Washington Post*, pp. C1, C7.

Hand, M., & Iacono, E. (2005, September 12). In hurricane's wake, New Orleans-based press relations still chaotic. *PR Week*, p. 1.

Johnson, A. & Robinson, C. (2014, July 9). 10-year term on graft charges for C. Ray Nagin, former mayor of New Orleans. *The New York Times* [online]. Retrieved January 26, 2015, from www.nytimes.com.

"Katrina kids sickest ever." (2008, December 1). *Newsweek*, p. 8.

"Katrina puts end to lull." (2005, August 27). *Times-Picayune*, pp. A1, A10.

"Katrina takes aim." (2006, August 28). *Times-Picayune*, pp. A21, A23.

Kimzler, S. (2005, September 3). AARP members putting party hats back on shelf. *Washington Post*, p. B1.

Mohammed, A. & Krim, J. (2005, September 1). Communications networks fail disaster area residents. *Washington Post*, pp. D1, D3.

Pierre, R. (2005, September 1). Helpless worry far from New Orleans. *Washington Post*, p. B1.

Rhoads, C. (2005, September 9). At center of crisis, city officials faced struggle to keep in touch. *Wall Street Journal*, p. A1.

Russell, G. (2005, September 11). Nagin: Mistakes were made at all levels. *Times-Picayune*, p. A1.

Scarritt, T. (2005, September 5). Paper sees future of reporting. *Birmingham News*, p. A1.

Sullivan, K. (2005, September 4). How could this be happening in the United States? *Washington Post*, p. A12.

Walker, D. (2005, September 24). The perfect storm coverage. *Times-Picayune*, p. C1. Retrieved from February 19, 2015.

Update/Case Study: Hurricane Katrina and New Orleans

Chan, W. (2022, August 15). Brad Pitt Foundation agrees on $20.5m settlement to owners of faulty post-Katrina houses. *The Guardian*. Retrieved May 10, 2023, from www.//theguardian.com.

Chapter 5

Communications to Prevent Crises

Warning signs, called *prodromes*, are crucial because prevention is the best cure for a crisis. Strong community relations programs that get positive coverage in the media and endear your company to its publics will help this effort. Actually, ongoing proactive public relations programs of any kind are insurance policies against crises.

A strong people-centered corporate culture, rather than a profit-centered one, is also an effective crisis prevention tool. Corporate culture is the way an organization does business—its unwritten but firmly established values. The corporate culture must be established in such a way that honest, open communication is a basic value. Problems such as the CEO not speaking to the head of public relations and ignoring complaints from consumers are signals of an impending crisis that can be devastating. Employees who are stressed from overburdened workloads can ignite a crisis, as well.

When on a fact-finding mission among internal publics to determine likely prodromes, listen attentively to others. You need to listen to what is said and to note how it is said, under what circumstances, and who said it. Watch facial expressions; they may be indicative of a story beyond the information you actually gather. Employees may fear reprisals from superiors or want to avoid "ratting" or whistle-blowing. There are numerous reasons for omissions, half-truths, and lies. A diligent researcher will see clues and hints of a need for further investigation.

An example of this was exhibited when a specific brand of automobile was found to be dangerously defective. It was discovered, after numerous cars had rolled off the assembly line and been sold, that the workers on the line knew about the defect. They were afraid to pull their supervisors' coattails, afraid of the workplace culture of "Kill the messenger of any news that causes a slowdown."

The News Media

Before a crisis, or at the onset of a crisis, you must anticipate what the news media need and want. Looking at the big picture, the media want to

DOI: 10.4324/9781003019282-5

sell newspapers and win ratings wars. Today's media give the public what it wants to know rather than what it needs to know. There is a fine line between news and entertainment, and crises make for entertaining news. The public is perceived to enjoy watching, reading about, uncovering, and lambasting organizations, companies, and individuals who might have done harm to people or, even worse, to animals.

Never say, "No comment!" to the news media; refusing to comment appears to be an admission of hiding information or even guilt. If you do not respond, the public does not hear your side of the story and will conclude, "Company X refused to comment and, therefore, it must have done something terrible." If there is some legal reason for not revealing certain information, explain this as much as possible and promise to reveal the information at a specific time. Do all you can to make that information available at the time you specified.

Do not assume that the crisis story will go away. The media can do their stories without you. They can build a case against your organization, portraying it as "the bad guy," by talking with disgruntled employees, volunteers, and customers, and, even more often, by seeking out disgruntled former employees, former volunteers, and former customers. The media can also use online databases and call up long-forgotten problems and mistakes and, in a few seconds, regurgitate them and place them before the eyes and ears of the public. The people thus hear the negative story.

In a TV interview, Carl Bernstein (1994), who with Bob Woodward investigated the Watergate crisis for the *Washington Post*, said, "There are always people, if you work hard enough, who will want to tell the truth." In other words, do not wage a war with an enemy who buys ink by the barrel and paper by the ton, and/or controls the airwaves.

Internal Publics

Companies and organizations are wise to develop programs designed to achieve the following objectives with internal publics, particularly with employees.

1. Employees must learn what positive performance is and how it will benefit the organization and the employee. Employees need job descriptions and perhaps instructions on how their jobs should be done. In some public relations departments, employees admit that they write news releases using a "monkey-see, monkey-do" system—they use previous news releases and make new ones fit the same format, a kind of formula writing. This may work occasionally, but each news release should have its own unique elements and style. If an employee needs a formula to write a news release, it may be time for writing classes. Demonstrations, practice, and special training or a reference manual may also be helpful.

2. Employees also need to know the consequences of a job well done and of a job poorly done, including consequences to the company and to the individual employee. It is important for all employees to feel as if they are part of the company. It's a feeling of "we" not "they."

3. Employees must learn what the job priorities are. Employees and management could have various opinions of which jobs or tasks are priorities. It is important for both employees and management to be on the same page. Either side may adjust to the other, but it is important that management and employees agree on priorities. This, again, requires effective communication.

4. Positive performance must be rewarded. Employees perform well when their work is recognized and rewarded. Conversely, they perform poorly when their work is not rewarded. Although managers say the paycheck is enough, they are the very managers likely to suffer crises arising from internal conflict. Research shows that positive reinforcement results in continued effective performance. Rewards may include money, trophies, certificates, an afternoon off, a free lunch, compliments, announcements on a bulletin board, a temporary parking place of honor, or other forms of employee recognition. Even a minor recognition in the form of a letter, memo, or email message can be effective and encouraging when it is provided on a regular, perhaps daily, basis. Such a message might say, for example, "You worked very hard to get that report completed on time, and I appreciate your hard work."

5. Conversely, poor employee performance should be punished. If an employee not doing his or her job well is never reprimanded, the good workers become discouraged. Proper communications with poor performers include formal or informal documents and face-to-face conversations, but they should never include public humiliation.

6. Punishment for good work must be avoided. Many times in companies, an employee who does work well is given more work to do. An employee who makes useful suggestions winds up having to carry out the suggestions. An employee who comes in early or stays late is despised by other workers. These are examples of punishing employees for exceptional work. First, communication is necessary to reward the good performance; second, an effort should be made to provide the training, mentoring, and advising necessary to bring the other employees up to the standard set by the exceptional worker.

7. Help employees cope with personal problems. Whether management likes it or not, employees will have personal problems that may interfere with their work. Management should learn to recognize the symptoms of a personal crisis. A personal crisis may exist when an employee does the following: spends an unusual amount of time on the telephone, makes an unusual number of errors, is unproductive, abuses equipment,

arrives late or leaves early, stares blankly into space, yells and is otherwise irritable, or spends excessive time in the restroom.

Because personal crises can turn into company crises, it is imperative to help employees cope with the issues affecting their performance. Allowing employees time off for personal business (with or without makeups) is one way to handle these situations; providing on-site psychologists and advisers is another. Some companies even have on-site physicians and dentists available to employees to save time away from the job.

Large companies have employee relations departments to cope with issues surrounding employee problems and employee benefits. Many companies provide outstanding benefits that are a real plus in earning employee loyalty. They may also provide stock options and extensive vacation time. J. P. Morgan grants a free lunch. Fel-Pro pays $3,000 a year to help send employees' children to college. Johnson & Johnson has a benefit whereby employees who have worked there for at least five years get an extra week's paid vacation when they get married. Johnson & Johnson also has a childcare center and on-site fitness center.

Customers/Consumers

Generally, a business has five primary objectives designed to build sales and gain loyal customers. These objectives are the following.

1. *Keep the old customers*: Longtime contented customers bring other customers. Programs such as frequent-flyer programs and exclusive discounts are examples of programs designed to reward consumers for loyalty to a company, brand, or product. Other communications, such as newsletters and individual letters, are also frequently used. Assuring loyal customers of the constant effort to have quality products and services as well as competitive prices is important.
2. *Attract new customers*: Good prices, excellent quality, and word-of-mouth referrals from loyal consumers help to attract new customers. Interpersonal contact with sales staff and other employees is also effective in this area. Open houses and other special events bring the company to the attention of potential customers. Publicity about the company's outreach programs also attracts new customers.
3. *Market new services and products*: Customers and consumers want to see that a company or organization is constantly making efforts to better itself in every area. They want to know what the new products and services are, why they are better than the older ones, and that prices are reasonable.

4. *Handle complaints swiftly*: A customer who complains and is subsequently satisfied will return and bring other customers. One who does not complain or is not satisfied after a complaint will switch loyalty to a competitor. If four people complain, one can usually assume that there are 24 others who were dissatisfied and did not speak out. Complaints in some organizations are handled by a middle person who mediates between the complainant and the company. He or she may simply say, "We're sorry and will make amends." Or a letter might be written explaining the company's actions. The overall message to the customer is: "We want you to be happy. We want your business."

5. *Educate customers*: Companies develop programs to educate customers about products and services. A store with a new line of cotton garments might inform customers—through ads, publicity, newsletters, and web pages—of the advantages of cotton, how to recognize well-made garments, and so on.

6. *Organize outreach programs.* In the area of community relations, companies and organizations adopt outreach programs in an effort to build loyalty among persons in the community surrounding its place of business. This may include making donations to non-profits, schools, and the like, or it may mean actually getting involved: A drug store may offer colon cancer screening. The police department might mentor fatherless teens. McDonald's runs the Ronald McDonald Houses providing temporary houses for families while their sick children are treated at nearby hospitals. The IRS includes photos of missing children on its income tax forms. In outreach programs, it is important to publicize your efforts—if your purpose is to build positive relationships with the community. Some organizations feel that publicizing their good deeds is bragging. If you do not publicize, only those people who have benefited will know about your actions.

The Nordstrom Consumer Policy

The Nordstrom chain is known for its "customer is first" policy, a prototype and model for other retail stores. A Nordstrom store manager said, "Employees are instructed to make a decision that favors the customer before the company. They are never criticized for doing too much for a customer, [but] they are criticized for doing too little" (Spector & McCarthy, 2000, p. 88).

The company works on the principle that if it takes care of customers' needs and concern first, the dollars will come. The corporate organizational chart shows customers at the top of an inverted pyramid and the co-chairs at the bottom. Perhaps the most well-known aspect of Nordstrom customer relations is its returns policy: If a customer is dissatisfied with a Nordstrom purchase for any reason, the store takes it back with no questions asked. Bruce Nordstrom advised his salespeople:

> If a customer were to come into the store with a pair of 5-year-old shoes and complain that the shoes were worn out and she wants her money back, you have the right to use your best judgment to give my money away. As a matter of fact, I order you to give my money away.
>
> (Spector & McCarthy, 2000, p. 98)

Although the returns policy invites consumer abuse, Nordstrom believes that 98 percent of its customers are honest and should not be punished for the dishonesty of a few. This policy has forced other retail stores to adopt a more liberal returns policy to compete with Nordstrom.

Employees, customers, and even other publics (boards of directors, advisory boards) may be included in regular communications through social media, such as Facebook groups.

Preventing Multicultural Crises

All crises have the potential to have a negative outcome, but few are as detrimental as those that involve race. Such crises have the potential to stir up a significant amount of unwanted attention from press, influencers and the community.

Kim L. Hunter, Founder, President, and CEO of
LAGRANT COMMUNICATIONS

Figure 5.1 Kim Hunter is CEO of LAGRANT COMMUNICATIONS, chairman and CEO of the LAGRANT Foundation, and managing partner of KLH & Associates—all in Los Angeles.

Source: Permission by Kim Hunter

Hunter's integrated marketing communications firm creates and executes comprehensive, culturally sensitive, and relevant advertising, marketing, and public relations campaigns targeting the African-American, Hispanic, and LGBTQ+ (lesbian, gay, bisexual, transgender, queer and other identities) markets. Following are his suggestions on how to prevent multicultural crises.

Crises that originate from racial discrimination have burned bridges among large companies like Sony Pictures Entertainment, CompUSA and Southern California Edison and the minority communities. Although, it is almost impossible to prevent crises, especially racial, from happening, there are proactive steps that can help prevent most.

Understand that there is no formula on how to handle a crisis successfully, but it's important to have policies and procedures set in place that are constantly being reviewed and tested. Working in a 24-hour news cycle, particularly with various social media platforms like Facebook, Twitter and Instagram, it's important your policies and procedures be a living and breathing document that is fully understood by the senior leadership and staff. Internally it's best to utilize a company's employee resource groups to test key messages and visuals before going public. Externally, it is expected that you have a spokesperson that represents each ethnic group and when necessary speaks the language of that group.

Hunter advises following the seven Page Principles, developed by the Arthur W. Page Society (AWPS), which capture key concepts that should be considered when determining how to develop a plan and respond to a crisis. They are as follows.

1. *Tell the truth*: Let the public know what's happening and provide an accurate picture of the company's character, ideals, and practices.
2. *Prove it with action*: Public perception of an organization is determined 90 percent by what it does and 10 percent by what it says.
3. *Listen to the customer*: To serve the company well, understand what the public wants and needs. Keep top decision-makers and other employees informed about public reaction to company products, policies, and practices.
4. *Manage for tomorrow*: Anticipate public reaction and eliminate practices that create difficulties. Generate goodwill.
5. *Conduct public relations as if the whole company depends on it*: Corporate relations is a management function. No corporate strategy should be implemented without considering its impact on the public.

The public relations professional is a policymaker capable of handling a wide range of corporate communications activities.

6. *Realize that a company's true character is expressed by its people*: The strongest opinions—good or bad—about a company are shaped by the words and deeds of its employees. As a result, every employee—active or retired—is involved with public relations. It is the responsibility of every corporate communications department to support each employee's capability and desire to be an honest, knowledgeable ambassador to customers, friends, shareowners and public officials.

7. *Remain calm, patient, and good-humored*: Lay the groundwork for public relations miracles with consistent and reasoned attention to information and contacts. This may be difficult with today's contentious 24-hour news cycles and endless number of watchdog organizations, but when a crisis arises, remember, cool heads communicate best.

Hunter continues:

These principles should always be incorporated when determining how to respond to potentially reputation damaging situations. Don't make the mistake of thinking that minorities are alike or that there is a "one size fits all" approach when dealing with a crisis. It's important for brands to have established relationships within the diverse communities to sustain a positive reputation.

This includes having regular visibility in the different communities and understanding who the key influencers, community-based organizations and major stakeholders are.

Hunter believes that the minority markets are keenly aware of brands that are not authentic. This is why brands should avoid only participating once throughout the year during national observances like Black History Month, Hispanic Heritage Month or LGBTQ+ and Pride Month, and should show commitment throughout the year. To be authentic and mitigate a crisis, it's important for a brand to learn as much as possible about the customer's traditions and beliefs. To build a better understanding of the African-American, Hispanic, and LGBTQ+ communities, Hunter notes some of the nuances in these communities (Figure 5.2).

African-American/Black Community

As their interests have historically been neglected, African-Americans have shown a high degree of loyalty to businesses that give back to their community. With a buying power of nearly $1 trillion in 2013, it's

Figure 5.2 Few crises are as detrimental as those that involve race.

important for businesses to understand that African-Americans are loyal to a company that invests in their community and supports it by educating, motivating, and empowering them. Having relationships with major civil rights organizations such as the National Association for the Advancement of Colored People (NAACP), National Urban League, National Action Network, and Rainbow PUSH Coalition is critical since they have historically been deeply rooted in the community. It's also important to note that the African-American/Black community is not a monolithic market and in addition to African-Americans, includes representation from West Africa and the Caribbean.

Hispanic/Latino Community

The Hispanic community is the largest and fastest growing minority segment in the United States and had a projected growth to 60 million by 2020. It is important to understand how culture defines the identity of the Hispanic person. If you do not understand what makes them unique, you will not understand why they remain loyal to certain brands and not to others.

Hispanics place a high significance on the family. The family is the most important social unit and is a close-knit group, which goes beyond the nuclear family. Spanish language also notes a strong connection to Hispanic heritage and is shared with the family and the community. When it comes to sources of information, Spanish-language media like Univision or Telemundo and Hispanic organizations like the National Association of Latino Elected and Appointed Officials (NALEO), Mexican American Legal Defense and Educational Fund (MALDEF), and Salvadoran-American Leadership and Educational Fund (SALEF) are seen as highly credible.

While there are similar traditions and values that are shared across the communities, there is also vast diversity within the Hispanic market. According to the Pew Research Center, the four major groups are Mexican, Cuban, Puerto Rican, and Salvadoran. There are tremendous differences between them all, and it is important to note that when determining how to respond to a crisis.

LGBTQ+ Community

The LGBTQ+ community supports brands that champion equality in the workplace, contribute to LGBTQ+ organizations like Gay and Lesbian Alliance Against Defamation (GLAAD) and the Human Rights Campaign, and supports political causes within the LGBTQ+ community. As the community continues to advocate for equal rights, they are cognizant of companies that are integrating LGBTQ+ imagery into their mainstream ads. They also have a special appreciation and loyalty to advertisers that support LGBTQ+ media with ads. They know that without advertising support, the publications on which they rely for LGBTQ+ news and perspectives would not survive.

As a final point, Hunter notes that developing a crisis communications plan that incorporates multicultural markets stands on the fact that you must understand their beliefs and values: "Understanding their values, gives brands the opportunity to empower diverse communities and sustain a positive relationship."

References

Bernstein, C. (1994, August 9). Interview. In *CBS This Morning*. New York: CBS.
Spector, R. & McCarthy, P. (2000). *The Nordstrom way*. New York: Wiley.

Chapter 6

Communications When the Crisis Strikes

When there is a crisis, there must be communication with the news media, social media publics, internal publics, external publics, and lawyers. All these communications should begin as soon as possible in the "golden hour," the first hour following notification that a crisis has occurred.

The International Telecommunications Union (ITU) estimates that 5.3 billion people, or 66 percent of the world's population, use the Internet, and the numbers continue to grow. There are still 2.7 billion people offline. According to ITU,

> In the countries of Europe, the Commonwealth of Independent States (CIS) and the Americas, between 60 and 90 per cent of the population uses the Internet, approaching universal use (defined for practical purposes as an Internet penetration rate of at least 95 percent). Approximately two-thirds of the population in the Arab States and Asia-Pacific countries (70 and 64 percent respectively) use the Internet, in line with the global average, while the average for Africa is just 40 percent of the population.
>
> (ITU, 2022)

Nevertheless, that does not mean social media and websites are more important tools of communication than the traditional news media. As much as Internet use has increased, we still cannot ignore that television is in 98 percent of homes in the United States. Some were lost when television went digital in 2009, but television is basically in all U.S. homes. The percentage is high in other countries, too (Media Trend Track, 2009). Another consideration is that television viewers get crisis information without seeking it. A family can be watching their favorite sitcom when breaking news interrupts (Figure 6.1). If people read newspapers—and there are still millions who do—they see news stories they were not necessarily seeking. Conversely, with online media, you don't get any information unless you actively seek it yourself.

DOI: 10.4324/9781003019282-6

Figure 6.1 Information about a crisis reaches publics through the media.

News can sometimes be circulated faster by social media than by traditional news media (see Chapter 7, "Social Media and Crisis Communications"). Reporters must spend time getting to a crisis site and then transmit a story while bloggers already at the site, with little or no expertise in reporting, can get information transmitted immediately. It may be accurate; it may be misinformation. The trained reporter, hopefully, will find more complete information than the blogger or the Facebook friend. He or she will know what questions to ask and what answers to seek.

Still, without doubt, both social media and traditional media must be targets of communications as swiftly as possible. Ideally, the two should be contacted simultaneously and immediately because if accurate data is not disseminated, inaccurate data is. If the crisis is online, then online communications is probably best (see "Mini-Case: Domino's Pizza" in Chapter 10). If your communications staff is too small to permit simultaneous communication, then a decision must be made as to which is more urgent for your business.

Communicating With the News Media

There are three possible results of a crisis: (a) The organization is put out of business, ruined, possibly sued, and key executives are possibly charged with crimes; (b) the organization continues to exist, but it has lost some image and respect in its publics' eyes, and perhaps a great deal of financial position; or (c) the organization, in a hard-fought battle, has won the war of public opinion and is seen as favorably as before, or perhaps more favorably.

Some types of organizations suffer crises, loss of reputation, and great financial loss but never seem to go out of business, no matter what they do.

Governments are usually in that category, and they often lose lead officials after a crisis—the captain must go down, but not the ship. Hospitals are also in this category—no matter what misdeeds they do, they usually stay in business.

Information about a crisis reaches publics through the media more than through any other means. An organization may have to work very hard to get the media's attention during normal times; its public relations personnel may struggle even to get a news release used. However, during times of crisis, it will be the media who will be seeking out PR personnel or other company representatives.

It is true, unfortunately, that bad news sells. This has always been true. Even Shakespeare wrote about it in *Julius Caesar:* "The evil men do lives after them. The good is oft interred with their bones." A negative story is deemed more newsworthy than a positive one; the media consider your positive news "puffery."

It is the PR practitioner's dream that every news publication and every electronic news outlet will run prominent stories saying, "Company A is the greatest. Its products and services are the greatest, and it has the best PR people imaginable."

Plan a system in advance whereby you are notified of erupting crises. You want to be among the first—if not the first—to know. This can be done by instructing company telephone operators (if they still exist) to reach you 24 hours a day, leaving a voice-mail greeting on your personal line during non-business hours, and cultivating friendly relations with key personnel in the media, the fire department, and the police department—people who can notify you in the event of a crisis affecting your organization.

Stages of a Crisis in the News Media

News media coverage of a crisis usually falls into four stages. The crisis communicators should realize these stages and be prepared to provide correct information and make explanations at each stage.

Stage 1 is breaking news. It is the immediately shocking or dramatic impact. Detailed information is usually not available; misinformation is often broadcast and printed. For example, in the Fort Hood shooting incident in November, 2009, the first news stories said the gunman had been killed; he had not. Reporters are covering the shock of it all.

Stage 1 ends when causes and explanation are presented. News stories then center on those explanations. This can mean one day on TV news and newspaper pages, not to mention social media conversations, or it can mean several days. The Exxon oil spill (see Chapter 3) stayed in Stage 1 for a long period of time because reporters were stuck in Alaska with nothing else to cover except the dead sea life.

Natural disasters also have prolonged Stage 1 news coverage. The January 2010 earthquake in Haiti suffered Stage 1 for a couple of weeks. As long as survivors were being pulled out of the rubble and as long as relief was delayed, the stories continued. Fortunately for Haitians, as people all over the world watched and read about the disasters, they felt inclined to make donations.

Stage 2 begins when concrete details are becoming available. In the Haitian tragedy, an accounting of the fatalities and the funds being raised was a sign of Stage 2. In the Columbine school shooting in Littleton, Colorado (see Chapter 4), Stage 2 began when descriptions of the personalities of the shooters and stories of survival became available.

Stage 3 often involves analysis of the crisis and its aftermath. How are victims coping? What is being done to remedy the situation? More is said about how and why. In the Columbine crisis, Stage 3 stories were about how the gunmen planned the attacks and about memorials for the victims.

Stage 4 is an evaluation and critique of the crisis. Were warning signs heeded? In most natural disasters and frequently in other crises, stories are done about how the company, city, or country was warned that the crisis would occur. Hurricane Katrina, the Asian tsunami, and the Haitian earthquake had warning signs. At Columbine, the youthful gunmen displayed signs of maladjustment. This stage also signals a return to normalcy and a consideration of what lessons have been learned.

Stage 4 usually includes anniversary stories—at first yearly, and then perhaps every 10 years, 20, 30, etc. The 9/11 tragedy is revisited every year in September. The 1941 attack on Pearl Harbor is still revisited each year but to a greater extent in 10-year increments. The 2000 Alaska Airlines crash over the Pacific Ocean was revisited in January, 2010 in Seattle newspapers, the headquarters of the airline. The news media keep "tickler files" to remind them to revisit crises.

Sometimes a crisis grows out of another crisis, and that also goes through stages. After the 9/11 tragedy, concern erupted about what was happening to the enormous donations made to survivors, and this became another crisis.

What the News Media Want to Know

- What happened?
- Were there any deaths or injuries?
- What is the extent of the damage?
- Is there a danger of future injuries or damage?
- Why did it happen?
- Who or what is responsible?
- What is being done about it?
- When will it be over?

- Has it happened before?
- Were there any warning signs of the problem?

If your organization has erred, it is usually best to reveal the mistake at once, apologize, and make amends. The story may end right away as long as the crisis itself is not continuing. Cover-ups make a crisis persist. Whether your company has erred or not, do all you can to get control of the situation as much as possible and as soon as possible. When you release your own bad news, you decrease the likelihood of rumor, supposition, half-truths, and misinformation.

If the disaster or crisis has already resulted in injury or death, or if it poses a threat to the safety or well-being of groups or individuals, contact the media immediately and indicate that you are looking into the situation, that you "just found out five minutes ago." This way, the media representative will realize both the crucial aspect of the problem and that your company cares about people and understands the media's needs. This action may buy you an ally as well.

If the situation is not urgent (be certain of this), it is advisable to look into the situation, make attempts to fully understand what took place, and have answers prepared for the media's questions.

If reporters contact you first and you are unaware of the crisis, do not rattle on without knowing details. Ask if you can call back in a few minutes, saying frankly, "I need to find out what's going on." Get the facts and then call the reporter back at the appointed time to communicate them.

Remember that the media and the public are entitled to have the facts about a crisis. The idea is to help the media cover the story accurately and with minimum criticism of the organization or company. The overall goal is to keep or get the public's trust through the media. The media need you for information for interesting stories. Your organization needs the media to communicate with the public en masse. By keeping this symbiotic relationship in mind, the public relations professional will be in a more proactive position during a crisis and feel more in control of the organization's bad news.

The spirit of cooperation must be established. In a crisis, there are the following three types of response to a media request.

1. We know, and here's all the information.
2. We don't know everything at this time. Here's what we know. We'll find out more and let you know.
3. We have no idea, but we'll find out and tell you.

Give the media access to the material they need: background information, statistics, photographs, and spokespersons.

Apology

Know the difference between an apology and an excuse. An excuse passes blame to others; an apology does not. Do not say, "We didn't realize . . ." when you should have realized. An apology is a sincere admission that you are sorry for whatever happened. When people, especially children, were sick and dying from the *E. coli* that had tainted Jack in the Box hamburgers (see "Containment" in Chapter 1), an excuse was not what the consumer public wanted to hear. Saying the meat packer was responsible for the *E. coli* infections was not an apology. If your company had sold such a product, you would owe the public an apology: "We are sorry. We will do everything we can to make amends. We take responsibility for medical treatments" (see "Apologia Theory" in Chapter 2, "Crisis Communications Theory").

Spokespersons

Identify one primary spokesperson for your company. Designating one primary spokesperson reduces the possibility of conflicting statements, organization values, or explanations being released to the media. Speaking with one voice is more crucial in a crisis than during normal operations.

The CEO is considered by most public relations professionals to be the spokesperson of choice during a crisis, especially if people have been injured, if there is danger of physical harm, or if there are millions of dollars in damages. The CEO usually has the most credibility with publics and the media. He or she is seen as a true representative of the company—as a person who can make decisions and speak for the company. If the company has a heart, it is the CEO's; at least, that is the public's perception.

Alternative spokespersons should be selected in the event the primary spokesperson is not available during a crisis. Supportive spokespersons— people who can speak authoritatively on technical subjects—are frequently of value, too. For example, if patrons of a restaurant get food poisoning, a physician might serve as a supportive spokesperson responsible for telling the public about symptoms and treatments.

External Experts as Spokespersons

When there is an opportunity to let impartial experts speak about your company's diligence, sense of responsibility, or innocence in a crisis, permit them to be spokespersons. In the Snapps restaurant case (see "Recovery" in Chapter 1), medical officials spoke at news conferences telling the public that AIDS could not be spread to food by an HIV-positive food handler after rumors spread that the fast-food restaurant's managers had spread the disease.

News Conferences

If a news conference is warranted and can be arranged swiftly, arrange one. Be certain to have a prepared statement read and distributed to the media. This assists you in setting the tone for the rest of the session.

Spokespersons—whether the CEO, other top executives, experts, or public relations professionals—should have major talking points. Also called *key messages* and *speaking points*, these talking points are one- or two-sentence summaries used to remind you of messages you want to be sure to get across to the public. They might provide details about the crisis or positive information about the company, such as the company's safety record, safety procedures, evacuation procedures, and other information that says, "We are very concerned; we care."

Be mindful during a crisis, however, that it is not the time to bring up unrelated community service projects, no matter how many you have. When lives are in jeopardy, no one wants to hear about how much money you give annually to scholarships.

Spokespersons should rehearse their statements and talking points enough to be comfortable with the information, to be comfortable in front of TV cameras, and so prepared that he or she need only glance occasionally at notes. Preferably, before a crisis, practice sessions should be held in which employees ask the most difficult, rude, pointed questions of the spokespersons to simulate an actual crisis news conference.

Do not prolong the crisis by calling an unnecessary news conference or by engaging in other activities that can keep the crisis in the news. During a crisis, you want to get off the news pages, broadcasts and social media.

Ten Dos for Media Interviews

When dealing with the media or when being interviewed by the media, whether in a one-on-one situation or at a news conference, note the following ten dos for media interviews.

1. Do listen to the whole question before answering.
2. Do use everyday language, not the jargon of your business or profession. Even if the reporters use the jargon, use the common vernacular unless the interview is with a professional publication.
3. Do maintain an attitude showing you are calm, courteous, responsive, direct, positive, truthful, concerned, and—if necessary—repentant and apologetic.
4. Do understand the reporter's job. Respect deadlines and return phone calls promptly.
5. Do be accessible and pleasant.

6. Do try to treat the reporter as a partner, an ally in maintaining or restoring the company's good image.
7. Do tell the truth, the whole truth. Misleading or omitted facts are also forms of lying. (Some seasoned public relations practitioners disagree with this position and even insist that no organization in a crisis is ever totally open and honest with the media or anyone else from the outside. This is an arguable point in a moot debate. Even these skeptics would agree that it is important to appear open and honest.)
8. Do look the reporter in the eye. In your response, address each reporter by name if possible.
9. Do use your crisis communications plan.
10. Do keep employees informed of the crisis. They may be volunteer spokespersons.

Ten Do Nots for Media Interviews

At the same time, there are "do nots" when dealing with the media, as follow.

1. Do not be a wimp! Being concerned and empathetic does not mean that you must shake in your boots.
2. Do not guess or speculate. Either you know, or you don't.
3. Do not get overly upset about being quoted out of context. Unless a complete transcript of your interview is printed, you are almost always quoted out of context to a degree. If the quote is completely wrong or libelous, that is another matter. Asking an editor for a retraction or correction is permissible if a reporter has been undoubtedly biased. A friendly letter delivered immediately and followed by a phone call is generally most effective. "Demanding" a retraction should usually be a lawyer's job, as is a charge of libel. Proving libel is difficult and costly.
4. Do not play favorites with the media. Always favoring one newspaper or one television station is bad business. It can haunt you later.
5. Do not pull advertising from a newspaper because reporters are not cooperative. The purpose of advertising is not to help the newspaper anyway.
6. Do not consider your news release "golden." It will be changed, except by small-staffed newspapers. If it is written well with real news, you have done the best you can do.
7. Do not stick to a story if it has changed just to be consistent. The media realize that things change. Johnson & Johnson experienced this during the Tylenol crisis (see Chapter 3). It had initially announced there was no cyanide in its plant but later discovered that there was.

Johnson & Johnson's public relations staff told the media the truth. No publication made a big deal about it.

8. Do not be trapped into predicting the future.
9. Do not wear sunglasses or chew gum.
10. Do not smoke—unless you are in a place such as Winston-Salem, North Carolina, where the economy is based on cigarette sales and smoking is a way of life.

Trick Questions (Rude Qs)

Although news reporters must make sure their information is accurate, communications professionals representing companies in crisis must be careful of their response to reporters. A media critic once said, "Being interviewed is like playing Russian roulette. You never know which question will kill you." Sometimes reporters stray from the typical "who, what, where, when, and why" questions. Metzler (1994) identified several types of questions that reporters have been known to ask. Metzler's questions as well as a few others follow.

Speculative questions begin with "if." These can be embarrassing and dangerous. For example, a reporter may ask, "If the earthquake had happened during business hours, how many people would have been killed or injured?"

Leading questions imply that the reporter already has the answer; you are merely to verify it. For example, "You do agree that the company could have avoided this tragedy, right?"

Loaded questions are designed to elicit an emotional response. Some television reporters thrive on these because responses to them make for more exciting videos. A sample might be, "Isn't it true that you knew there was asbestos in the ceiling and failed to do anything about it?" In the case of a loaded question, rephrase it and answer your own question. You could say, "Do you mean, 'Were we aware there was asbestos?' No, we were not."

Naïve questions indicate that the reporter has not done any homework and does not know what to ask. "Tell me, what does your company do?" is an example. Reporters who ask such questions are dangerous because they desperately need a story. Make sure they get the story you want them to have. Give them media materials such as press kits, "backgrounders," biographies, and news releases.

False questions intentionally contain inaccurate details. If the question is "You fired half of your over-50 staff, right?" the public relations professional, knowing the statistic is wrong, could counter with, "No, only 40 percent," not realizing the reporter was aiming for that information all along.

Know-it-all questions begin with "We have the story. I just need a few wrap-up facts." The reporter may want you merely to confirm an already formed viewpoint. He or she may not have a story at all but wants you to release only "the dirt."

Silence, or an absence of questioning, is used by reporters who want you to spill your guts, to talk on and on. Many people tend to babble because there is silence. Remember, silence is the reporter's problem, not yours. Use this opportunity to reinforce positive statements or continue to be silent.

Accusatory questions are designed to force you to blame others. Never fall for this. Maintain your innocence if that is true, but do not cast blame on others. The court of public opinion does not react kindly to this.

Multiple-part questions can be confusing to you, as well as to the public. Ask which part you should answer first. Then answer each part as a separate question. Also, you can say, "I'll take the first part first." Then restate it yourself the way you want to answer it. Do the same for each subsequent part.

Jargonistic questions are those in which technical words or professional jargon are used. In response, use everyday language. Jargon builds a barrier between you and your publics and erodes their trust.

Chummy questions are those in which the reporter, pretending to be your buddy, may ask, "Say, pal, off the record, what do you think . . . ?" The PR practitioner should remember that nothing is off the record and should be careful about supposed friendships.

Labeling questions aim to make issues negative or simplistic by seeming to ask for clarity, as in "Would you call the company's work schedule 'stressful'?" You should not accept the reporter's labels unless they are fair and accurate.

Goodbye questions are posed at the end of an interview and may even come after the camera or tape recorder is turned off. The reporter shakes hands and says, "By the way, . . ." Watch out for what follows. The interview is not necessarily over. Remember—in all media questioning—to be positive, concerned, empathetic, and apologetic, if necessary.

Reporters

The preceding discussion of trick questions may seem to be a warning that reporters are sinister creatures whose life goal is to harass public relations practitioners. This is usually not the case.

There are jerks in every profession, including the news media. If you stay in public relations long enough, you will come in contact with them. Know who the jerks and enemies are. Sometimes you can work around them by dealing with other reporters. Other times, you can follow the advice of former U.S. President John F. Kennedy: "Forgive your enemies, but never forget their names."

There are also those journalists who apparently make themselves feel better by labeling public relations people "flacks." There is no reason to take this to heart. Reporters do not hate you or your profession. In fact, many of them will seek public relations jobs.

Newspaper and broadcast journalists, in record numbers, are becoming public relations practitioners. Newspapers are failing. Most on-air personnel in television cannot expect to have jobs in their middle age. Everyone is downsizing. Public relations is the fastest growing communications profession, largely because of crises and the forecast of crises to come.

Reporters are frequently not knowledgeable about, or interested in, the issues they cover. A story may have been assigned to them. Their task is to bring back an interesting story, a story that will get them a promotion, a raise, an extended contract, an Emmy, or a Peabody. They want their stories prominently displayed in the newspaper or at the top of the broadcast. They want to get this award-winning story back before the deadline. All would rather that you assist them than be an obstacle to them. Obstacles make awards and raises difficult to obtain.

After reporters have filed stories, they are frequently finished with them. They do not write the newspaper headlines that you hate—that's the job of editors you rarely, if ever, see. Sometimes, if the story continues, other reporters will be assigned.

If you are breaking the news of a crisis or a development in a crisis and you know of reporters who are known to be fair and accurate, you can sometimes give them your story. This does not mean that if you dislike the reporter assigned, you can call another. This works only when no other reporters are involved and you thus cannot be charged with playing favorites.

Choosing the news outlet for bad news is not unheard of or a new tactic. When death was imminent, physicians attending to King George V injected lethal doses of drugs into his veins to hasten his death. They wanted him to die in time to make the deadlines of *The Times*, a morning newspaper in London, considered more responsible than what were, in 1936, considered the "inferior news organs of the afternoon."

In dealing with reporters, one must consider the pressures they are going through, especially when covering an emotional story.

Communicating With Lawyers

Lawyers frequently advise clients in crisis to: (a) be silent, say nothing, circle the wagons; (b) say as little as possible but reveal what information you have as quickly as possible; (c) deny blame and guilt; (d) shift blame to others or share it with others; and (e) remember that anything you say can be used against you in a court of law.

A public relations counsel suggests that a client be open and honest. "No comment" is perceived by the public as an admission of guilt. Anything you do not say can be used against you in the court of public opinion (Figure 6.2).

Both professions must be heard and considered. There are times when lawyers are right; spokespersons can speak too much. There are times when speaking up pays dividends in both courts of law and the court of public opinion.

Courts of law proclaim that a person is innocent until proven guilty, whereas the court of public opinion often declares a person guilty until proven innocent. When your company loses in the court of public opinion, it also loses its reputation, good name, and positive image—the very qualities that make for its success.

The public believes that an innocent person can answer a police officer's questions without having a lawyer present. After all, what does the person have to hide? The public also believes that this innocent person can go on the stand and plead his or her innocence, showing emotion in the process. However, lawyers frequently advise clients to refrain from all these actions and reactions. Some lawyers think public relations is publicity, getting somebody's name in the newspaper. Others know what public relations really is, but they choose to ignore it.

Sometimes lawyers may be cautious at a time when public relations professionals feel that open communication with publics is crucial to the positive conclusion of a crisis. The lawyer's job, after all, is to protect the company, organization, or individual. Sometimes public relations counsels may not anticipate threats to their own clients.

Figure 6.2 Courts of law are very different from the court of public opinion.

Lawyers know that any persons with knowledge of the organization in trouble can be called into court for depositions against the client. Sometimes communication with publics can put the organization in a perilous situation.

A case of law versus public relations occurred in 1985, when a Delta Airlines plane crashed. After the crash, high-ranking Delta employees showed great concern for survivors and families of victims. They sent flowers. They visited. They attended funerals. The company's public relations effort was so impressive that many lawsuits were avoided as a result. Nevertheless, some lawsuits were filed. In court, the lawyers for Delta were said to be vicious. They accused one plaintiff of being a cocaine addict and of having a child who was not her husband's. They implied that another victim, a homosexual, might have died soon of AIDS. Irate news stories resulted in the company being called a "monster." At least one newspaper wrote prominently of the airline's "Jekyll and Hyde" behavior.

Delta was upset about the negative publicity, but its lawyers insisted that they had to introduce relevant information, acquired legitimately, to fight money-hungry personal injury lawyers (Thompson & Hess, 1986). A solution to such a dilemma is a bond of mutual understanding, a marriage of the two fields, and a careful balance.

The legal profession is much older than the recognized field of public relations (although, in effect, public relations has been practiced for centuries). As a profession, public relations is moving toward a day when professionals will have to pass a kind of "bar exam." The APR credentialing offered by the Public Relations Society of America is a step toward this certification.

Lawyers are becoming more adept at public relations. The American Bar Association provides media training for its primary officers. It realizes that a defendant can win a battle in a court of law and lose it in the court of public opinion. In recent crises, lawyers have apparently learned the value of communicating. Rarely does a corporate spokesperson in a crisis refuse to address the news media. Usually, the company in crisis goes further and even puts information about the crisis on its website and in blogs and other social media.

In 1991, for instance, a crisis team consisting of public relations and legal representation for a Snapps restaurant in Florida made a decision not to prosecute or sue a teenager who had helped spread a rumor that caused a drastic loss of business. The members of the team decided that although they might win a victory in court, it would be a case of winning the battle and losing the war. The teenager had apologized publicly and admitted she was truly sorry that her actions had caused the crisis; she had simply been trying to warn her friends whom she believed might be in danger. The public might have boycotted the restaurant had further action been taken against her. It would have been a matter of the powerful restaurant ruining the life of a well-meaning child who made a mistake in judgment.

Conversely, a defendant can lose in court and win in the battle of public opinion. Sometimes the latter offers a brighter future. This was the case when Mayor Marion Barry of Washington, D.C., was convicted of a drug charge, served time in prison, and then returned to the nation's capital to resume his political career. Although few voters doubted that Barry was a drug user, there was resounding public resentment of the way he was supposedly "set up" for the arrest. Anger at those believed to be responsible for the "setup" translated into support in the court of public opinion for Barry, who was re-elected as mayor in 1994.

More and more, lawyers are influencing public opinion outside the courtroom. We have seen the results of this when a lawyer representing a prisoner convicted of a serious crime persuades *60 Minutes* or *20/20* to tell a story of the innocence of the client. The lawyer may have exhausted all legal channels or the client may have been unable to afford the legal battle. An effective letter to the television news magazine may change everything.

The public is often not aware of how the news magazine series got the story; true public relations professionals (or lawyers performing public relations acts) are more concerned with their client's needs than with promoting their own visibility. Thus, a televised account of a "poor, innocent" man imprisoned for years for a crime he did not commit is a public relations tool that appeals to the court of public opinion. In many cases, on the basis of the convincing television profile, viewers appeal to courts for new trials, or judges grant new trials in anticipation of public reaction. Sometimes the prisoner is subsequently freed.

The necessity of merging law and public relations leads to an even greater need for pre-crisis planning by representatives in both fields. Effective pre-crisis planning sets up scenarios for each type of crisis likely to affect the organization. Different strategies and tactics are outlined for each kind of crisis. Examples are reflected in such statements as these: "If there is a loss of life, we will . . ."; "If there is no loss of life, we will . . ."; "If the media are unaware of the story, we will . . ."; "If the media are pressing, we will . . ."

A balance between public relations and law should, as much as possible, be determined before the crisis. A balance often cannot be accomplished effectively after the manufacturing plant has exploded. The PR professional should communicate with the organization's lawyer before communicating with external publics, even if it is not a matter of getting permission.

Lawyers who have not adapted to public relations procedures should be advised that some key stakeholders can be dealt with personally, whereas some key stakeholders will get negative impressions from the news media and social media.

Refusing to talk to reporters will not make the story go away. Reporters will get a story—and it may not be the story the company wants told.

The board of directors of the United Way of America was not aware of this when, in 1991, its CEO, William Aramony, was accused of excessive spending. No one on the board would talk to the media. The story started as a brief section in a long, basically flattering article about Aramony in one newspaper. Editors of other newspapers read the article and focused only on the negative aspects, and soon public perceptions of misuse were nationwide.

The news media is a conduit to the public. The public rarely has any real evidence, or at least, not as much as juries in courtrooms do. Even though the public is well aware that reporters err, people still tend to believe what they see and read in the media. They make decisions based on sound bites and articles selected and written by reporters.

The court of law and the court of public opinion will remain crucial in deciding the fate of individuals, groups, organizations, and corporations. Both the public relations professional and the lawyer must learn to put clients in the best light in both courts to gain the best possible outcome to a crisis.

Communicating With Internal Publics

Internal publics include all classifications of employees—labor, management, hourly workers, interns—as well as retirees and stockholders. In a non-profit organization, volunteers are also an internal public. Internal publics are crucial in a crisis because they are the most believable spokespersons. Because internal publics may not be hired or paid to speak for the company, the news media seek them out for comment.

In many businesses, such as retail stores, employees are a link between the company and the consumer public. They are the principal representatives of the company and have the power to make a potential customer a loyal customer or to make a loyal customer a former customer.

Communication with internal publics before, during, and after a crisis is vital. For each internal public, you must choose the correct message and the correct medium.

Once a crisis has occurred, employees and other internal publics must be advised of what has happened early in the notification process. Whenever possible, internal publics should not learn of the crisis from the news media, and they should know about it before external publics do. If the crisis occurs after office hours, all managers notified are aware of others they should inform. Those notified by those managers have others to contact, and so on. The telephone tree must be in place before a crisis. As a crisis develops, the employee public, called a *functional public*, should be kept apprised of what is occurring at every step. Common methods for keeping employees informed include meetings, closed-circuit television programs, email, the public address system, and bulletin boards.

Many companies can utilize their intranet, which are internal networks designed to improve productivity and the circulation of proprietary information. The intranet is better than the Internet in the case of crises because it allows the company or organization to communicate only with its own people, whereas anyone can access the Internet.

Crisis communications researcher W. Timothy Coombs (1999, p. 85) advises that "the beauty of the intranet is the speed of accessing information." The crisis team can access information directly with keystrokes on a computer instead of going through telephone calls or through other means. Information may be stored on the intranet and updated regularly, and any employee can access it. Coombs also warns that all information cannot be collected by using the intranet. Some interpersonal communications may be necessary, but the relevant data can be stored there after it is gathered.

During a crisis, internal publics generally want to know what they can or should do. During the Snapps restaurant rumor crisis, managers volunteered to take AIDS tests to prove that no manager could have spread the AIDS virus through food products. If it is important for employees to make some effort to continue the business, convey that to employees and tell them why. If there are crisis tasks employees need to take on, they should be pre-advised and pre-trained. If the nature of the crisis eliminates jobs—either temporarily or permanently—employees need to be carefully told what options are available and what the future is likely to hold.

As in normal operating mode, it is crucial that employees feel a sense of "we-ness" during a crisis—that they are part of the battle. Many companies order employees to remain silent about company issues relating to the crisis; they are especially told not to talk to the news media. They are told to let the appointed spokesperson do all the speaking. Often, this is an advisable move; too many people can make for a confusing story. However, some companies and organizations do not fear the situation will get out of hand and encourage their employees to talk to the media, confident that employees like their jobs and their company.

Communicating With External Publics

External publics include consumers/customers, community members, government officials, labor unions, dealers, suppliers, trade associations, competitors, and other outside people related in some way to an organization. As in all types of communications, it is important to strategically plan the correct message and the appropriate medium for communicating with each external public, both before and during a crisis.

Organizations tend to form alliances with key external groups that will make members of these groups feel like they are part of the company.

The airlines have been very successful with the frequent-flyer programs, so much so that other businesses are trying "frequent" programs, too. Boards of directors and community advisory boards are also popular efforts at bridging the gaps between companies and organizations and between the business world and the community, respectively.

Organizations should communicate with loyal consumers more directly than through the news media to inform them of the crisis and progress toward normalcy. Various methods must be evaluated—social media networks are popular methods, also letters, newsletters, notices on websites, telephone calls, and so on. You want customers to remain loyal throughout the crisis and continue to patronize the organization. So tell them all the "Five Ws" of the crisis—who, what, when, where, and why.

Like consumers, community members will want to know what happened, what the cause was, what is being done, when the crisis will be over, and so forth. Community members can be reached through key community leaders on advisory boards. Flyers can be circulated in communities and posters can be put up in public places and on bulletin boards.

Labor representatives and government officials should be among the first notified. Key messages should be conveyed to them because these people, depending on the nature of the crisis, may be called on by the news media to comment.

Communicating With the Masses Directly

With new communications technology, it is possible to get information out to the masses. The Internet makes it possible to communicate with vast numbers of people through Twitter, Facebook, email, blogs, websites, and any new methods that have been developed since this edition was written. This is mind-boggling when people living today recall when the manual typewriter was the most modern writing tool. There was a job title called typist. Newspaper printing meant setting each letter in type on brass dies individually on a linotype machine. Newspaper boys delivered and persuaded people to buy the newspapers. Radio was the best broadcasting tool—not television, not satellites. When computers were born, they were giant machines that occupied a huge room. Now, in a flash, one person can send a message read by thousands—even millions—of people.

This is progress, but few people have considered how this swift dissemination of information should mean new policies of accuracy. Historically, research tells us that people believe the written word more than the spoken word. This is because the articles in newspapers go through layers of editors before they are published. Most books (except self-published books) go through fact checkers before they are published. People are therefore inclined to think of data on the Internet as factual when it's not necessarily so. Some information has gone through editors, but other information has come straight from the writer, who may be biased or wrong. Readers and researchers must discern what is true and credible.

Because information on the Internet remains primarily textual, some people may be inclined to think of it as factual. However, research findings from the Center for the Digital Future at the University of Southern California's Annenberg School suggest that experienced information-seekers rank media and government sites as more reliable than those published by individuals.

The growing demand for news has made the Internet a valuable source of supplemental information. The traditional news media are still the primary sources of news for the unwired American, but as many as two-thirds of Internet users have accessed some of their news online and about one-third do so three or more times a week. In addition, the tragedies of September 11, 2001 made it clear that news-seekers want more immediacy than newspapers, commercial television, cable television, and radio can offer.

On the morning of September 11, 2001, the 24-hour news services reported to more than 100 million people. According to Nielsen Media Research, nearly 50 percent of all television households watched CNN's coverage. The commercial stations also had high ratings that day. However, according to researchers Paul N. Rappoport and James Alleman (2003), the demand for more coverage and instantaneous updates led large numbers of people to the Internet. They say there is anecdotal evidence that the Internet, on that day, became overwhelmed and left users without access or reasonable connections, but when it did catch up, it was an effective means of supplementary news.

Between 9 a.m. and 10 a.m. Eastern time, MSNBC.com experienced a 50 percent increase in traffic, CNN.com, a 450 percent increase. The sites were ill prepared for such surges as more than 30 million people sought online news. Many sites urged people to go to television and some had a written statement saying, "Many online services are not available, because of high demand." Internet sources have and probably will become more capable of handling the task.

Nevertheless, researchers conclude that the public has accepted online news sites as sources of credible news, although most Americans obtain their news from television—local, network, and cable.

Among the values of Internet news sources, according to Rappoport and Alleman, are the following: (a) information sources may be tailored to meet the specific objectives of the user; (b) the user may get the news at any time—no more "News at 11"; (c) news may be linked to other sources; and (d) in-depth analyses may be available, even more in-depth than newspapers, because the medium is not restricted by column inches or minutes of airtime.

Organizational and corporate websites provide background information and, in a crisis, what the organization believes is the truth. This gives the information-seeker the organization's side of the story. A website is normally a one-way means of communications, but the Internet can easily link one to other points of view.

Blogs

Blogs, or weblogs, are a type of website that consists of commentary from an author (or authors) with comments from various readers. The writing style is usually more casual and often more personal than traditional organizational or corporate communication. Blogs are one form of personal publishing and have several distinctive characteristics, including the following.

* reverse chronological journaling (format);
* regular, date-stamped entries (timeliness);
* links to related news articles, documents, and blog entries with each entry (attribution);
* archived entries (old content remains accessible);
* links to related blogs (blogrolling);
* RSS (Really Simple Syndication) or XML (Extensible Markup Language) feeds (ease of syndication);
* passion (voice).

A website is rather standard as an organizational communications tool, and blogging is growing in usefulness and importance. Because blogs can easily facilitate dialogue between information-giver and information-seeker, they may be more believable than a traditional website. Blogs are good for public relations purposes to provide accurate information for persons seeking information about your organization.

Blogs are akin to buzz. Whatever subjects or issues are occupying the minds of the public can be brought to the attention of many on a blog. Political blogs are popular, but all kinds of blogs are developing—from commercial business to education to basic gossip. In addition, the person wishing to post his or her opinion about an issue will find the blog more accessible than other forms of electronic expression.

Companies and organizations are being urged to develop blogs to garner web-based commentary about their products or services from consumers. The number of blogs is growing constantly and they can be accessed by search engines such as Google, Yahoo!, Technorati.com, and GlobeofBlogs.com. Technorati is one of the oldest blog search engines, whereas Globe of Blogs classifies blogs by subject. Information published in blogspace is disseminated faster than more traditional forms of communications through a technology called RSS. Textual blogs have given birth to video blogs and audio blogs, often known as podcasts.

In some cases, companies may need to have a blog format to show their publics that they are savvy about current technology. Companies and organizations may also find a blog to be the preferred publishing medium when an issue is constantly changing and it is urgent to get the latest information out as soon as possible.

Blog expert Kathy Gill asked, "What does the audience expect when they visit the website?" If the public is technically savvy, it will expect information in a blog format. Gill also noted that the voice of a blog is "personal" and cautions that "personal" is difficult for some organizations that require various levels of approval and sign-off. They tend to distrust having an unmoderated voice speak for them. In blogspace and in a crisis, there is often no time for multilayered decisions.

Blogging software makes the process of creating and updating a professional-looking web page relatively easy and less expensive when compared to a webmaster setting up a site. Some companies offer free hosting for blogging services. These blogs can be linked to other data on the Internet, other blogs, a corporate website, news articles, photo images, and audio files. The blogosphere is the word for the blog network with blogs interconnected to other blogs on the Internet.

Following are five basic types of blogs.

1. *The corporate/organizational blog* provides commentary about a specific company or organization. Key executives usually are the bloggers, and their goal is to tell their own story and/or to correct misinformation of others. It is considered unethical for a corporate executive or employee to respond to a blog without revealing who he or she is and the connection to the organization. Will PR professionals ghost-write blogs? Probably. However, if the information seems like puffery, the readers will soon distrust it.

2. *Subject blogs* are comments relating to various subjects or issues written by experts on these subjects. Smudde (2005) writes that these blogs are like white papers or keynote addresses.

3. *Industry blogs* are centered on the status quo of a particular industry or field and otherwise are similar to subject blogs.

4. *Publication blogs* come from media sources such as newspapers, magazines, and other publications. Editors and reporters are the bloggers and sometimes readers. They are usually a way of keeping up to date on a continuing news story.

5. *Personal blogs* express opinions of individuals on any matter they choose to discuss, often politics, issues in the news, or products, especially high-technology ones. Smudde writes that personal blogs are the most potent type because subjects covered can be beneficial and helpful or hurtful to an organization's reputation.

The Harvard Business School's online tool "Working Knowledge" suggests the following reasons (in italics) for a company having its own blogs.

1. *You can influence the public conversation about your company*: Journalists can locate accurate information—the information you want them to have. You can correct misinformation and provide new information.
2. *You can enhance brand visibility and credibility*: This can give the company a human voice. Debbie Weil of BlogWrite for CEOs advises that companies not let their PR departments write blogs. This is true if the blogs are puffery, but not true if the PR writers can present the facts. Some PR firms are already offering expertise in "blog relations."
3. *You can achieve customer intimacy*: Customers can speak directly to you, whether positive or negative comments. This is a kind of electronic, immediate suggestion box.

Newspapers have begun to have blogs to supplement their publications. Different from an online edition of the paper, the blogs are updates on specific issues, continuing stories that may change several times before the next issue of the newspaper. Years ago, metropolitan daily newspapers used to print multiple editions throughout the day to always have the latest news; however, shrinking budgets and shrinking readership have ended that level of production.

Crisis communications researcher Amiso George (2005) at Texas Christian University writes of a newspaper's blog:

The *Nevada Appeal*, Carson City, Nevada, newspaper developed its first web log before breaking news on its website www.Nevada Appeal. com to keep the public updated on the Waterfall Fires of 2004. From the onset of the fires on July 14 until containment on July 20, the newspaper provided frequently updated information on the fires. The paper's editor, Barry Smith, said that the initial coverage of the story followed traditional news coverage format, until he realized quickly that merely updating the news was no longer enough . . . The paper updated the web log 50–60 times a day for the duration of the fire. Smith noted that the web log generated "terrific response" from people outside the Carson City and Reno, Nevada areas as people were interested in getting details of the fire and checking up on loved ones.

The *Times-Picayune* in New Orleans set up a blog for its readers. During the Hurricane Katrina disaster in September, 2005, the presses did not run for a few days. Instead, reporters and editors published only online and used blogging software to "report" the news. As in New York after September 11, 2001, local bloggers provided their own news of what was happening to New Orleans. Survivors told very poignant, graphic stories without having a reporter as an intermediary. It was a kind of participatory journalism; everyone can be a reporter in the blogosphere. (See also "Hurricane Katrina and New Orleans" in Chapter 4.)

Case Study: At Starbucks, Lawyers Can Prevent Crises

Crises caused by charges of racism are probably the most frequent in communities in the United States. Starbucks, the international coffee chain, made news in 2018 when it made an unprecedented decision and looked at itself in a mirror to determine what to do about an incident that management agreed was racist. In this era of cancel culture, one wrong move can be disastrous to a business.

Most people know the basic history. On April 12, two young Black men were handcuffed and arrested when the white female manager of a Philadelphia Starbucks (Figure 6.3) called police because they had not made a purchase and requested to use the restroom. White customers complained that the men had done nothing wrong. Some of them made videos of the arrest and confessed they don't always order, and that the two men who were waiting for an associate to have a meeting may have intended to order later. The video spread virally. Customers threatened boycotts and protests.

Starbucks would not press charges against the arrested men. So, they were released within a few hours. Then-CEO Kevin Johnson and his team not only had to satisfy the innocent men but a great number of segmented publics who were watching Starbucks' every move and needed to be satisfied. The wrong move could spark a disaster. Following is a partial list of the many publics who were concerned and were watching closely to see what Starbucks would do.

Customers who are patrons at Starbucks everywhere.
Customers at the site of the incident.
African-American customers globally.
The African-American community.
The Philadelphia City Council.
The mayor.
The people of Philadelphia.
Potential protestors.
Shareholders (who may or may not be actual consumers).
Police in the city and state.

Figure 6.3 This is the site of the Starbucks incident in a section of Philadelphia where earlier racial issues were reported.

Source: Photo by Jeremy Fearn

Starbucks employees, called "partners."

Neighbors and other businesses in Center City where the incident occurred.

Other coffee serving companies and competitors.

Individual protestors and civil rights organizations like the national and local NAACP, the Pennsylvania Legislative Black Caucus, the Congressional Black Caucus, Black Lives Matter protestors, and others.

Based on observations, one could describe the Starbucks culture, the prototype of the Starbucks consumer, and the average consumer in the United States and many cities abroad. In Honolulu, a group of writers gather weekly at a Starbucks to work on a project. In Washington, D.C., another group meets monthly at a Starbucks café to plan a college sorority reunion. In Seattle, a gathering of professional journalists has met at Starbucks Madison Park quarterly for years planning the annual scholarship competition. A man in Houston meets his financial planner regularly. A woman in Denver meets at Starbucks to have a friend read over her grad school application. Undergrad students work on term papers and group presentations. Starbucks customers are usually college graduates or headed in that direction. You must be somewhat bright to know how to order "a venti green tea Frappuccino with extra matcha, no added sweetener, and no whipped cream." A professor said he regularly ate breakfast and lunch in his local Starbucks café while working on his dissertation and sat in the same corner table, his "coffice" (coffee plus office).

There are rarely disturbances in Starbucks cafés where people are different human types than the folks drinking coffee outside a convenience store or inside a McDonalds. The Starbucks customer might buy a coffee in a pinch at McDonalds but he/she will buy it in a drive-thru line. Ask patrons in most Starbucks and they will agree that they should and do buy their favorite coffee drink when they go to Starbucks but they appreciate the fact that baristas do not demand it. Starbucks customers everywhere seem to know this, but the baristas and particularly the manager at the café did not on April 12, 2018.

Journalists for the *New York Times* reported after the story broke that Black Philadelphians told them that the arrest of Black men in Rittenhouse Square, the recently gentrified site of the Starbucks, was not an isolated incident.

> Statistics show that Rittenhouse Square, with its hotels, boutique museums and upscale shops, has the highest racial disparity in the city when it comes to police pedestrian stops. Although black people account for just 3 percent of the residents of that police subdistrict, they made up two-thirds of the people stopped by the police in the first half of 2017, according to figures collected by the American Civil Liberties Union.
>
> (Dias, Eligon & Oppel, 2018)

A Black woman said a security guard followed her as she shopped at Nordstrom Rack. A Black man said a security guard prevented him from leaving Barnes & Noble until it could be proven that the book in his bag was not stolen.

To stop the furor from growing, CEO Johnson and the leadership team knew they had to move fast. Zabrina Jenkins (Figure 6.4), a litigator who had been at Starbucks since 2005, said she was on vacation with relatives in Atlanta when she was called to get on a plane and fly to Philadelphia. She said she was planning to rest and relax so she had not packed business attire. She barely had time to go shopping. By Sunday night, all members of the Starbucks leadership team had arrived in Philadelphia and had begun a meeting at 1 a.m. Monday, a few hours before the scheduled 7 a.m. protest. Jenkins said, "We deployed everybody and everybody dropped everything. We didn't care about selling coffee at the time. We focused on preventing a crisis" (Interview with Jenkins).

Figure 6.4 Zabrina Jenkins began her career at Starbucks as a junior litigator in 2005. After the racial incident in Philadelphia, she was acting executive vice president and general counsel. As this volume went to press, she had been promoted to executive advisor to the office of the CEO. Her favorite Starbucks beverage is a tall Americano.

Jenkins, then head of the Starbucks litigation team, was interviewed by a crisis communications class at the University of Washington. Her memories follow.

Having this incident happen was hurtful to me as an African-American woman. I mention race because I think that it's being a minority that has allowed me to demonstrate empathy in many different situations. I talked to our CEO and I said, "We can easily just cut them a check but I think what's more meaningful, and what would be more helpful, is to help them advance their goals and their career." I asked him would he be willing to mentor them to try to provide them with more opportunities because they had an interest in real estate and they were trying to meet with a real estate developer at our café. I said, "Why not utilize our resources to help advance their goals?" Without reservation, he said, "Yes, let's build something. Let's talk about what that would look like." So that's how we were able to incorporate it into the resolution. We had to make a decision about the protests, "How do we face the fact that we've got protestors scheduled to arrive at our store at 7 a.m. Do we close the store at 7 a.m.?"

Our CEO, on Saturday night, started by filming a video apologizing to all employees via a memo. On Monday, he appeared on *Good Morning America*, again apologizing and accepting that change must come from within the company. He also met with local leaders, acknowledging fault and promising to do something. The customers' videos and the Starbucks security cameras allowed the leaders to see with their own

eyes what happened. We also had our government affairs team working to schedule meetings with the mayor's office and other politicians in
the city to get a better sense of how we can contain the issue and move
things forward. We needed to go out publicly and not place blame on
the police. [She said there are occasions when the police must arrest
customers who cause disturbances, so the police commissioner was loud
and clear that the police acted appropriately. Later, he recanted, saying
he would have used different words had he and his officers known that
Starbucks allows people to occupy cafés without making a purchase.]

We also did not want to place blame on Rashon Nelson and Donte
Robinson, the two Black men who had been falsely arrested. I was responsible for reaching out and trying to contact them. They had retained
lawyers and we kind of got a bit of a gift with that. The lawyers were
not interested actually in meeting with us. They were not appreciating
all that we were willing to do in terms of trying to help Donte and Rashon. I think it would have been easy for them to have said, "Let's stick
to whatever dollar amount you're going to pay." But Donte and Roshan
had the ability to see past what their lawyers were saying in terms of
how to resolve this. They were also pleased to see that I was Black. So
we met and talked for several days. We didn't want to close the store
that Monday morning because it might send a message that we were
running away from the issue but we couldn't risk having an incident
at the store. [The Starbucks leadership team arrived at the site before
the protestors. As the protestors held placards and chanted and posted
their ire on social media, CEO Johnson made a brief announcement that
basically said, "It was completely inappropriate to engage the police."]

We were there talking to people and honestly, listening. People have
a right to protest, so we were there to meet and listen. We were there to
show up and say "We're here. Talk to us. Help us move forward. Give
us your thoughts about what we should do differently." So that's what
we did. I would say it was a relatively peaceful protest to begin with
but momentum built, as more people showed up. The store is no bigger
than this classroom and we had to close but the demonstrators stayed
on until the afternoon. [A second protest took place a few days later
when about 100 members of Omega Psi Phi, an international primarily
Black fraternity to which Rashon has belonged since his college days,
demonstrated in support of him.]

After talking with Donte and Rashon, we circled up as a team and
we started to do some self-reflections like "How did this happen? How
did we get to the place where this would happen?" I know that it's just
one individual who placed the phone call, but what have we created in
our culture that allowed her to think that was OK? So, the decision was
made that evening that we would close all of our stores and have a day

Figure 6.5 This drawing depicts signs held by persons demonstrating outside the café. Most demonstrators were pleased with Starbucks' response to the racial charges.

Source: Drawing by Gina Arnold

of education where we could talk about these issues. On April 17, our CEO made the announcement of anti-bias training. The following day, Howard Schultz, our chairman and founder, went on *CBS This Morning* and again talked about how impactful this was to us as a company and to him personally as a person who has built the company.

Donte and Rashon agreed to a settlement with Starbucks for an undisclosed sum. In addition, they were offered the opportunity to complete their undergraduate degrees through the Starbucks College Achievement Plan, a then-four-year-old program that covers tuition for eligible U.S. employees for an online degree program offered by Arizona State University. In a separate arrangement, the men received a symbolic $1 each from the City of Philadelphia, as well as a promise from officials to establish a $200,000 public high school program for young entrepreneurs. This was a specific request from Donte and Rashon. Starbucks promised continued listening and dialogue with them.

The restroom issue was also explained by Schultz, as follows.

We don't want to become a public bathroom, but we're going to make the right decision a hundred percent of the time and give people the key, because we don't want anyone at Starbucks to feel as if we're not giving access because you are less than.

(CBS News, 2018)

Philadelphia Mayor Jim Kenney said in a statement, "This was an incident that evoked a lot of pain in our city, pain that would have resurfaced over and over again in protracted litigation" (Fortin, 2018).

As planned, Starbucks closed most of its 8,000 stores for an afternoon on May 29 to conduct racial bias training for 175,000 employees. Schultz said, "It will cost millions of dollars, but I've always viewed this and things like this as not an expense, but an investment in our people and our company. And we're better than this" (Hyken, 2018).

The training program for partners was prepared by various local and national experts on facing racial bias: Bryan Stevenson, founder and executive director of the Equal Justice Initiative; Sherrilyn Ifill, president and director-counsel of the NAACP Legal Defense Fund; former U.S. Attorney General Eric Holder Jr.; Heather McGhee, president of Policy Center Demos; and Jonathan Greenblatt, chief executive of the Anti-Defamation League.

Rapper/activist Common was scheduled to provide recorded remarks. The plan was for partners to explore bias in their daily work life.

Rodd Wagner, in Forbes.com, described the highlights of the training program (Wagner, 2018).

- The company called a full stop with a $4.4 million loss in sales.
- There was a team guidebook, a journal, and videos and all of them were well produced.
- The group workbook included real examples of real-life scenarios.
- Experts like Stanley Nelson, Jr., who produced an eight-minute video about the juxtaposition of "a black man concerned that people feel uncomfortable when I walk in" and "a white man saying I feel no such burden."
- The company aimed for a high level of empathy and understanding.
- It made clear where Starbucks leaders stand.
- The company did not feel the training was "mission accomplished," but agreed for additional training.
- Sentiments by most leaders on videos seemed heartfelt.

Partner response to the training was mixed. Some felt they did not need it, that they were already aware of most points. Others felt that it was effective because no one was exempt from the training. However, some of the employees felt as if nothing would change. They agreed that the Stanley Nelson video was the highlight.

Most publics were impressed by Starbucks' plan.

Shep Hyken, leading expert in customer service, Forbes.com, wrote:

There have been PR disasters as a result of poor judgement from employees, data breaches that impacted millions of customers, and more.

You'll find good examples to learn from. But, if you want the textbook perfect way to handle a crisis, look no further than the excellence demonstrated by Starbucks.

(Hyken, 2018)

Sarah Halzack, senior consumer editor, Bloomberg News, wrote:

Starbucks won't put out the fires overnight. But leadership is taking the right approach to make sure it isn't consumed by flames. That's a hopeful sign it can handle its more prosaic business challenges, too.

(Halzack, 2018)

Richard Quest, British editor, CNN Business, wrote:

You could say it was a textbook example of how to handle a PR disaster. But it's deeper than that for Starbucks . . . the CEO was simply practicing what Starbucks preaches. In trying to put things right, Johnson was making sure the company was living up to its principles. This is a lesson for every other CEO out there.

(Quest, 2018)

When asked about the Starbucks legal department's relationship with Starbucks communications, Jenkins replied,

As years have gone by, and we have more stores and more complexities in our stores, we started to elevate our presence in the press and social media. We have a global communications team and what we found is that the communications team would often receive media inquiries about legal cases or lawsuits we were managing and they would go to the press and make statements that often times were inconsistent with what we as lawyers wanted to communicate. Now, you have to keep in mind that when an incident happens, from a lawyer's perspective, we're always looking from the perspective of making sure that we are not saying something or doing something that may be against our interests in the future. So, we're trying to think sort of long-term strategy, what do we want to communicate. So, we started to develop a greater relationship with our communications team and in fact our relationship is such that when we received media inquiries about active litigation or potential litigation, we work hand-in-hand with them on what sort of messaging we want to put out.

Zabrina Jenkins became acting executive vice president and general counsel, Starbucks Corporation. Kevin Johnson resigned from Starbucks in 2022. Founder Howard Schultz preceded and succeeded him as CEO. Laxman Narasimhan took the position in 2023.

Bibliography

CBS News. (2018, May 11). Starbucks overhauls bathroom policy after racial firestorm. Retrieved March 7, 2022, from www.CBSnews:com/news/starbucks-overhauls-bathroompolicy-after-racial firestorm.

Coombs, W. T. (1999). *Ongoing crisis communication*. Thousand Oaks, CA: Sage.

George, A. (2005, October 20). Blogs as transformational corporate communication tool: Implications for crisis communication. Paper presented at the annual meeting of the Association for Business Communication, Irvine, CA.

International Telecommunications Union. (2022). Two-thirds of the world's population uses the Internet, but 2.7 billion people remain offline. *Fact and figures 2022*. Retrieved from www.itu.int/itu-d/reports/statistics/2022/11/24/ff22-internet-use/.

Media Trend Track. (2009, September 30). *TV basics television households*. Retrieved November 23, 2009, from www.tvb.org.

Metzler, K. (1994, March). Shooting it out with the media. *Hemispheres*, pp. 51–53.

North America Internet Usage Statistics. (2009, September 30). *Internet usage and population in North America*. Retrieved November 23, 2009, from www.internetworldstats.com.

Rappoport, P. N. & Alleman, J. (2003). The internet and the demand for news: Macro and microevidence. In A. M. Noll (Ed.), *Crisis communications: Lessons from September 11* (pp. 149–166). Lanham, MD: Rowman & Littlefield.

Smudde, P. M. (2005). Blogging, ethics, and public relations: A proactive and dialogic approach. *Public Relations Quarterly*, 50(3) 34–38.

Thompson, T. & Hess, J. (1986, November 15). Delta accused of Jekyll—Hyde behavior in wake of crash. *Atlanta Constitution*, pp. 1–10.

Wagner, Road. (2018, June 1). "The Philadelphia incident was terrible: Starbucks' response was admirable." *Forbes.com.*, 2018, June 1. Retrieved March 7, 2022 from www.forbes.com/sites/roddwagner.

World Internet Usage Statistics. (n.d.). Retrieved May 11, 2010, from www.internetworldstats.com.

Case Study: At Starbucks, Lawyers Can Prevent Crises

Barnes, T. (2018, May 29). Starbucks closes 8,000 stores to give staff diversity training amid race storm. *The Independent*. Retrieved March 5, 2022, from www.independent.co.uk>world>americas.

Calfas, J. (2018, May 30). Was Starbucks bias training effective? Here's what these employees thought. *Time Magazine*. Retrieved March 7, 2022, from https://time.com.

Creary, S., Boyd, H. & Gilly, M. (2018, April 20). What brands can learn from Starbucks' crisis response. *Knowledge at Wharton (podcast)*. Retrieved March 7, 2022, from http://knowledge.wharton.upenn.edu.

Dias, E., Eligon, J. & Oppel, R. (2018, April 17). Philadelphia Starbucks arrests, outrageous to some, are everyday life for others. *New York Times*. Retrieved March 7, 2022, from www.nytimes.com/2018.

Fortin, J. (2018, May 2). 2 black men settle with Starbucks and Philadelphia over arrest. *New York Times*. Retrieved March 7, 2022, from www.nytimes.com/.

Halzack, S. (2018, April 18). The CEO of Starbucks just passed his biggest leadership test. *Bloomberg News*. Retrieved March 7, 2022, from www.bloomberg.com/gadfly.

Hauser, C. (2018, April 16). Starbucks employee who called police on black men no longer works there, company says. *New York Times*. Retrieved March 7, 2022, from www.nytimes.com.

Hyken, S. (2018, May 10). Starbucks gets an A in crisis management. *Forbes*. Retrieved March 6, 2022, from www.forbes.com./sites.

Neuman, S. (2018, May 3). Men arrested in Philadelphia Starbucks reach settlements. *NPR*. Retrieved March 7, 2022, from www.npr.com/sections.

Quest, R. (2018, April 20). Starbucks: Crisis response done right. CNN Business. Retrieved March 6, 2022, from www.money.cnn.com.

Chapter 7

Social Media and Crisis Communications

As this book went to press, Twitter and Facebook were the most popular of the social media used in crisis communications. (Owner Elon Musk recently renamed Twitter to "X," but we felt that the Twitter name might return or perhaps some other name might be applied. The communications world is using Twitter still as this book goes to press). Professionals say Instagram, YouTube, Snapchat, Pinterest, WordPress, and LinkedIn are also vitally important (Figure 7.1). Aaron Blank, president of the Fearey Group, said "The tools will change. MySpace was hot and it died. Foursquare was in and it's now out. Facebook will be around if it continues to innovate. When it stops innovating, it will disappear" (Interview with Aaron Blank). Pam Miller, principal of numoon communications says "an omni-channel presence is critical these days, and it is important to understand the various channels, and their advantages and disadvantages" (Interview with Pam Miller). Marilyn Hawkins of Hawkins and Company, agrees with both Blank and Miller on the hot social media, but she warns, "They don't replace traditional media. Students must remember that" (Interview with Marilyn Hawkins).

Writing Social Media Messages

Social media is not only an effective method for monitoring and participating in proactive public discourse but also a tool for participatory crisis or emergency communications. The basic difference between crafting messages for more traditional methods of communicating and crafting messages for social media is the speed with which one can communicate information and misinformation.

Blogs, Twitter, Facebook, and podcasts are used to convey messages. They can build trust or they can destroy trust, depending upon how they are used. More than ever, rules of writing are important and they will remain important no matter what social media are created.

DOI: 10.4324/9781003019282-7

Figure 7.1 The Big Four social media logos are displayed here—TikTok, Instagram, Twitter (or X), and Facebook.

Source: Hideki Yoshihara/AFLO/Shutterstock.com

The following are guidelines for social media writing. Most—marked by *—are also guidelines for traditional media.

- *Know your subject well. If you don't, research it well. Talk to experts.
- *Know your public(s). What knowledge do they have about the subject? You don't want to talk down to them, but you want to use all information needed to get them on your side.
- *What is the best method of communication? What is the best way to reach your targeted publics? Which social media network(s) should be used? Or is your public reached best by other methods? Believe it or not, there are still people who do not live by social media. One agency learned that baby boomers, its primary public, do not spend much time on the Internet even though they have computers and Internet service.
- *Don't forget ancient tools such as telephones and direct mail. If your public is not large, a personal phone call could make a consumer feel important to the company; long-distance calling is relatively inexpensive or free these days. The same might be true of a real letter delivered by the U.S. Postal Service or other couriers. Letters can have more permanence than any computer-generated product.
- Monitor social media to see what is being said about your subjects and who is communicating. Participate in the discussion. In Twitter, you may have only a few followers, but all your followers may have dozens or hundreds. By communicating, you are building relationships, building a community. Some PR agencies make lists of tweets and blogs about their clients and give the list to the clients weekly so that they will know what the issues are.

- *When you begin to write, have the reader in mind. If you have monitored and participated in discussion, you have a good idea of who the reader is.
- *Think before you write. You need to think of your objective. What do you want to happen as a result of this effort?
- *Adopt a style. The most frequently used style book is the *Associated Press Stylebook*. Make sure you have the most recent edition. There are differences and changes in accepted style.
- *Make sure everything is accurate. Good writing is moot if the facts are wrong. If you make a mistake in social media, it is possible that thousands of readers are misinformed forever. There are no editors as in traditional media.
- *Make sure everything is clearly understood. A reader should not have to read something more than once to understand it. Social media are rapid methods of communication—rapid writing, rapid reading. People comprehend immediately or they don't read.
- *Be brief. Brevity is important in all social media. Each word should be essential.
- *Watch noun/pronoun agreement. This is the mistake made most by novice writers. A singular noun takes a singular pronoun; a plural noun takes a plural pronoun. For example, the following sentences are wrong. "The company tries to satisfy their consumers. They send them coupons every month." The word "company" is singular. It takes a singular verb "tries" and can be substituted by the pronoun "its" and in the subsequent sentence another "It." So the sentences should be, "The company tries to satisfy its consumers. It sends them . . ."
- *Do not use redundancies. "The company hired a new technology manager." The word "new" is not needed; the company did not hire an old one. It could be "hired a second technology manager" or "hired its first technology manager" or simply "hired a technology manager."
- *Don't use emoticons—such as smiley faces—and abbreviations (such as "icur" for "I see you are") in business communications.
- *Do use legitimate abbreviations (such as "PR" in place of public relations).
- *Don't rely on your spell-checker. It doesn't find all typos. When "public relations" becomes "pubic relations," you're in trouble.
- *Edit and proofread. It is often effective to have a second party proofread. The writer has been looking at the document too long (even if the writing is swift) to notice errors. Be careful of multiple editors and writing by committee. Remember, a camel is a horse designed by a committee.

Social Media in Strategic Organizational Communication

Ever since social media such as Facebook, Twitter, YouTube, Flickr, Instagram, blogs, and other communication technologies have emerged, organizations and educational institutions have incorporated social media into their organizational communication activities. As popular peer networking tools, many large and small businesses—as well as non-profit celebrities and other public figures—have also harnessed the social networking power of these technologies, in many cases using them to bypass the traditional mass media and communicate directly with fans, customers, and constituents.

Multiple sources identify a mix of entertainers, politicians, and athletes as having close to—or more than—100 million Twitter followers each. At the top of the list are people like former U.S. President Barack Obama, who political newshounds may recall was the first presidential candidate in history to announce his vice-presidential running mate via text message and email when he first ran for the presidency in 2008 (Nagourney & Zeleny, 2008), as well as Justin Bieber, Katy Perry, Rihanna, Cristiano Ronaldo, Taylor Swift, and Lady Gaga. Keep in mind that popular social media stars may change with the times as new names rise to the top and familiar ones fade.

Kevin Kawamoto, Ph.D., has been studying the social impact of information and communication technologies since the early 1990s; more recently, he has been looking at the uses of social media by businesses, organizations, and celebrities—for better and for worse. In the following subsection, he offers ten thoughts, tips, and tactics for those who are currently using or plan to use social media as a strategic communication tool.

Thoughts, Tips, and Tactics

Question 1: Are social media here to stay?

Answer: By now, it is clear that social media technologies are no passing fad and have an important role to play in organizations for both external and internal communication, but as mentioned earlier, the specific social media platforms will evolve. Like the social media celebrities themselves, over time, some platforms will rise to dominate the industry and others will fade away. Having said this, I think they will continue to be viable tools for relationship building and for increasing brand loyalty among people who are more "connected"—or at least believe they are—to a person, group, or institution via online social networks, especially as the assortment of consumer-oriented information and communication devices provide more ways to make that connection. Even journalists are using social media to develop relationships with their audiences, as well as to use as source material for news and feature articles.

If you look around you in the United States and many other nations, it is rare to find a person in the teens to young adult age group without a smart phone or laptop computer. Go to any public setting and the chances are that a significant number of people are using some kind of Internet-based hand-held device (which is why they so often need to be reminded to turn it off or put it on silent mode when such devices could become a distraction to others).

Among social media options, Facebook and YouTube are among the most popular with Internet-using adults. In 2021, a Pew Research Center survey of American adults, 81 percent reported using YouTube and 69 percent Facebook (Auxier & Anderson, 2021).

Today, the traditional or legacy media can operate in sync with social media, as fans of the Super Bowl commercials know and have demonstrated. While more than 113 million viewers watched the Super Bowl LVII football game on television in 2023 (Nielsen.com, 2023), many thousands of them were also on their favorite social media platforms commenting on the game and often legendary ads that are eagerly anticipated each year. The social media platforms are referred to as "second screens," the additional layer of media that serves as an adjunct to the primary focus of attention: the television screen.

In 2022, many of the commercials were criticized by social media commentators as failing to take risks and be edgy at a time when there was much social upheaval occurring in society, including in regard to race relations. There were some exceptions, such as the ad for Google's Real Tone software, which claims to capture Black skin tones better on the Google Pixel 6 phones. Lizzo's powerful voice and lyrics provided an appropriate musical context for the technology. "And if you love me," she belted out, "you'll love all of me," as the text "Everyone deserves to be seen as they really are" was superimposed on her photo in the center of the ad, gradually revealing a montage of diverse faces with dark complexions. The Super Bowl 2022 halftime show was considered to be the most Black-centric in history, featuring Dr. Dre, Snoop Dogg, Eminem, Mary J. Blige, Kendrick Lamar and surprise guest 50 Cent (Deggans, 2022).

Super Bowl ads have long generated buzz before, during, and after their air date during the game. After the 2015 Super Bowl XLIX between the Seattle Seahawks and the New England Patriots, for example, a game that had viewers on the edge of their seats right up to the end, social media users posted messages about the game and the commercials in record numbers. Various web analysis sources provided a picture of what people were talking about the most online in regard to the Super

Bowl and what commercials were getting the most attention. The "Like a Girl" ad by feminine-product brand Always, McDonald's, Budweiser, Nationwide, and others were heavy hitters on social media.

Facebook reported that 65 million people posted 265 million posts, comments, and likes related to the game, and YouTube reported that its users spent 4 million hours looking at Super Bowl-related ads and teasers. These were significantly higher than the previous year (Shields & Marshall, 2015). There were reportedly 28.4 million Super Bowl-related tweets (Oreskovic & Saba, 2015). The concept of multiple screens is at play here. It's not just watching the game on television, but at the same time engaging in related media activities using web-based media.

So yes, social media are here to stay and can be used by organizations in a variety of innovative and complementary ways to traditional media, but whether the current crop of the most popular social media tools remain dominant or are replaced by something else—which is what happened when Facebook supplanted MySpace as the dominant social media tool—remains to be seen. Today, Facebook is the household name and MySpace has become the tool many people "used to use a long time ago." More recently, in 2019, Google decided to shut down its once-heralded consumer (or personal) version of Google+, a social network, due to an assortment of challenges meeting customer expectations, but there were alternative social networks for consumers to transition to in its absence (Google, n.d.). In short, the concept of social media will endure and remain an important part of our evolving communication infrastructure, but as with all information and communication technologies (hereafter referred to as ICTs), the specific features and industry or platform leaders may change—and perhaps dramatically so—in the future.

Question 2: So businesses and other organizations should use social media as part of their external and internal communication strategies?

Answer: If it makes sense to do so, yes. But what has happened in many cases is that businesses and organizations incorporate social media without much thought to strategy, and—perhaps more importantly—to "quality control," if I might use an overused term. A not-too-uncommon scenario is for an organization to hire what it perceives to be a social media geek-type person who is not necessarily well-rounded as far as public relations knowledge and skills are concerned, and then give that employee free rein—with some loose parameters—over the social media activities of the organization. That's a recipe for disaster, in my opinion.

That's a potential crisis waiting to happen because the person fronting the social media operations should also be a knowledgeable, ethical, and conscientious public relations professional. They should be able to discern what kind of social media content is beneficial to the organization and what might be controversial and even self-destructive to the organization, and then know when to consult with peers and senior management before posting such content. These well-rounded potential employees are not going to be difficult to find as more public relations and communication programs at colleges and universities across the country integrate social media type courses into their overall curriculum. Social media skills are not just technical, but also involve intellectual, ethical, legal, strategic, and other types of components.

Students who want to become serious social media professionals should consider taking classes in public relations, journalism, media or communication ethics, and media or communication law, if they can get into them, or at least self-study these subjects to enhance their knowledge and skills as professional communicators—as well as decrease the chances of getting themselves or the organizations that they represent into trouble.

Government agencies and offices at all levels should be using social media when it makes sense to do so. Government produces collateral material such as brochures, posters, websites, and so forth to strategically communicate with various publics. Social media tools can also be used for public communication. Some government programs have sponsored contests whereby young people produce public service videos on topics related to public health and safety. During the COVID-19 pandemic, public health agencies in the United States and throughout the world had to engage in an all-hands-on-deck approach to public awareness and education campaigns to help deter the spread of this contagious virus and its variants. Social media and social media influencers played an important role in this effort.

Question 3: So what should organizations look for in a social media professional?

Answer: First, it's important to develop an organizational mindset that recognizes the power of social media, and that you don't want to simply invest that power in just anybody off the street who happens to use social media a lot. That shouldn't be the criterion used for hiring. The use of social media for strategic organizational communication in a professional setting should not be a casual undertaking, even though the technologies involved may have gained a reputation for accommodating a breezy and informal—if not spontaneous—style of communication. In a professional setting, the content of social media may be presented differently from traditional business communication, which might get vetted multiple times up a chain of command before that content is released to the public, but social media content (which tends to get posted much more quickly and frequently) still needs to adhere to standards of ethical communication, such as honesty, accuracy, and fairness.

As mentioned earlier, social media professionals, if they call themselves professionals, need to know the relevant laws regarding invasion of privacy, libel, slander, obscenity, copyright, and fair use, as well as freedom of speech protections, and so forth. Journalists and public relations professionals have their professional codes of ethics, as all public communicators should have.

A person who works in public communications needs to be on top of current events. There are certain subjects that should not be treated in a humorous or playful way if they connect audiences to tragic real-life incidents. For example, in September 2014 a marketing campaign for a DVD release of the television show *Sleepy Hollow* encouraged fans to send ecards in observance of National Beheading Day, which was meant to evoke images of the Headless Horseman in the fictionalized story. However, the campaign was launched around the same time a terrorist group was in the news for real-life beheadings of hostages, making the campaign seem insensitive and macabre, although that was not its intent. To its credit, the publicity firm quickly stopped the campaign and apologized for its unfortunate timing, but by then the promotion was already being widely discussed on social media (Stedman, 2014).

Sometimes things that happen on social media leave you scratching your head. In April 2014, a US Airways tweet contained a link to a pornographic image. It was up long enough for people to take a screenshot and circulate it. US Airways apologized for the incident and provided an explanation of how it happened, ending the statement with, "We deeply regret the mistake and we are currently reviewing our processes to prevent such errors in the future." It appears the post was accidental but highlights the need to be particularly careful when sending messages out from an organizational account (Cutway, 2014). There are so many examples of when unintended content was mistakenly tweeted by organizations, with the worst offenses remaining forever retrievable from digital archives.

The actual technical qualifications of a social media professional are, in my opinion, almost secondary. Whether someone is a prolific user of Facebook, Twitter, Instagram, TikTok, and other social media tools says nothing about their understanding of strategic organizational communication and public relations. It certainly tells you nothing about their critical thinking skills, discernment process, social skills *offline*, character, personality, or ability to act sensibly in a crisis situation, or their competence as a communication strategist and tactician. These are all key qualifications for an effective social media professional.

Question 4: What are some of the dangers to an organization's or a public figure's reputation as a result of social media use?

Answer: Social media are a strange breed of animal, so to speak. Social media technologies often reflect a hybrid or agglomeration of different communication approaches, with elements of mass communication, interpersonal communication, and small group communication integrated into a dynamic system whereby the boundaries among these different approaches sometimes get blurred. There have been a number of high-profile cases in which public figures and private citizens alike have gotten into trouble after indiscreet posts on social media.

The case of former New York congressman and mayoral candidate Anthony Weiner, for example, comes to mind. Although this incident happened years ago, its lessons are timeless.

The Anthony Weiner case brought the phenomenon of "sexting," or the act of sharing sexually explicit content of oneself with one or more people online or via a cell phone, into the living rooms of America's news consumers and onto the pages of some of the nation's most respected news publications. The once up-and-coming politician was a seven-term congressman who resigned from office due to a sexting scandal that derailed his political ambitions at the time, which many people agree were promising.

According to media reports, Weiner—who was married—used Twitter to send a racy photo of himself to a college student in the state of Washington. He initially denied he did it, but later publicly admitted to the deed, and eventually resigned from office. A future bid for mayor failed amid a series of additional sexting allegations.

The details of Weiner's sexting scandal can be found in many articles online, but the takeaway message for organizations and individuals alike is that social media should be regarded, in all instances, as public communication, despite the fact that there are elements of private communication built into the social media environment.

Even when inappropriate content is quickly removed from a site within minutes of being posted, someone somewhere may have taken a screenshot of that content with the intention of sharing it with others. The combination of a well-known politician (from any political party), sexual indiscretion, and scandal almost ensures that the content will go viral.

The ease and rapidity with which social media content is shared with hundreds, thousands, and even millions of social media users are unprecedented in the history of communications technology. This can be a good thing, as the social media-driven "Ice Bucket Challenge" demonstrated when it raised more than $100 million in the span of a couple of months for the ALS Foundation during the summer of 2014, a phenomenon that one Forbes.com contributor described as a "philanthropic blockbuster" (Diamond, 2014). The money the foundation raised in 2014 was reportedly a 3,500 percent increase from its previous fundraiser a year earlier.

As with most technologies throughout history, social media tools have their upside and downside. The downside is that damaging content can travel just as easily and rapidly as empowering content, as many organizations and individuals have learned the hard way. There has been a handful of cases in which rogue employees have recorded themselves or been recorded doing unsanitary things in their places of employment. The sensational nature of these activities—even though they may be isolated and not sanctioned by company policy—can be harmful to a company's reputation and brand if the videos go viral. And of course like real viruses, the kind that make a person sick, once a video goes viral, it is difficult to rein it back in. The horse has left the gate, as they say. These are the times when an organization has to practice diligent crisis communications and respond appropriately to public consternation.

In some cases, people have lost their jobs as a result of the public shame they cast upon their organization, as happened when surveillance video surfaced showing a company CEO kicking a dog in an elevator, as well as when a U.S. congressman's communication director insulted former President Barack Obama's daughters Sasha and Malia Obama in a Facebook post (Figure 7.2).

In 2020, social media users turned their ire on a white woman in Central Park, New York City, who called 911 on a bird-watching Black man and said that he was threatening her. The man, who had asked the woman to leash her dog, recorded the incident on his phone and posted it on social media, where it was viewed millions of times and attracted the attention of mainstream news media, as well as the white woman's employer. She lost her job as a result of the incident. As part of a restorative justice program, misdemeanor charges against her were dropped, but the incident serves as a reminder of how even seemingly private conflicts between individuals can have much broader exposure—and implications—when social and traditional media are involved (Booker, 2021).

There are also numerous websites where people complain about bad customer service or about a bad experience they had with a company—maybe a cruise ship, an airline, or a phone company. People find out about it and pretty soon the site is overflowing with complaints, with the site serving as a kind of online, asynchronous gripe session. From the consumer's point of view, this site could be very useful in learning what other people's experiences have been with a company, product, or service. From a company's perspective, however, the site may be harmful to the company's

Figure 7.2 A Republican congressman's communications director, in 2014, apologized and resigned after she posted on Facebook an attack of then-U.S. President Barack Obama's daughters, Sasha, 13, and Malia, 16, who did not seem excited about participating in their father's traditional Thanksgiving pardoning of the White House turkey The post said "Try showing a little class. At least respect the part you play. Then, again, your mother and father don't respect their positions very much . . . ." On social media, many complained that the children of the president should be off-limits to critics.

Source: NICHOLAS KAMM / AFP via Getty Images

reputation—and by extension, its sales potential. If the company's service or product is genuinely poor, it deserves that outcome, but if the comments are unfounded or the problems have been corrected, that message may not be getting across and needs to be communicated.

Question 5: What should an organization do if it is maligned in some way by social media?

Answer: It really depends on the actual situation because there is no cookie-cutter response plan that will be appropriate in every case. In general, an organization has to quickly and as thoroughly as possible research the situation and what damage might be caused by the social media content. If there is intense media interest in the case, the organization or—in the case of a restaurant chain, for example—the parent company should address the situation in a way that reassures the public that it takes the matter seriously and is either cooperating in an investigation or conducting an investigation of its own, especially when the public's health is concerned. If it's found that false or misleading information is at the heart of the controversy, take immediate measures to clear the air with the facts. If there is truth to the damaging social media content, address the problems forthrightly and explain the company's resolution to correct misconduct and impropriety.

When a security video surfaced showing a Pizza Hut district manager in West Virginia urinating in one restaurant's kitchen sinks, the story (and the video) not only circulated on social media but was also picked up by national news media and aired nationwide. Although this was one incident in one restaurant, it reflected poorly on the Pizza Hut brand in general, and the company responded quickly. A spokeswoman was quoted as saying that the company was "embarrassed by the actions of this individual."

The company also released a statement saying:

> Pizza Hut has zero tolerance for violations of our operating standards, and the local owner of the restaurant took immediate action and terminated the employee involved. While the isolated incident occurred during non-business hours and did not involve any food tampering, we follow strict safety and handling procedures and the restaurant has since been closed permanently. We apologize to our customers of Kermit, West Virginia and those in our system who have been let down by this situation.
>
> (Kim, 2013)

Note the key terms in the statement: "zero tolerance," "operating standards," "took immediate action," "isolated incident," "did not involve any food tampering," "strict safety and handling procedures," and so forth. Pizza Hut's response can be fashioned into a more general template that other organizations could use if faced with a similar situation.

Pizza Hut is not the only restaurant whose reputation was stung by rogue employees committing unsanitary acts in food preparation areas. Burger King, Domino's, McDonald's, Taco Bell, KFC, Chili's, and Wendy's have also garnered unwanted public attention because of employees caught on camera behaving badly (Kim, 2013). Social media can keep the story "alive" for a long time as video footage is stored on YouTube indefinitely and people (including journalists) share links to that footage over and over again because of the sensational nature of the offensive behavior.

Organizations need to prepare a timely and effective response to these kinds of situations *before* they occur, carefully studying other cases and learning from other organizations' best practices. As part of their scenario planning in a comprehensive crisis communications plan, organizations should assume that a well-publicized breach of company policy by an employee is probable, and then plan what the organization's response should be, given a series of different circumstances.

The current media environment can be much more harmful to an organization's reputation due to the rapid-fire nature of social media communication and the fact that social media—such as Facebook, Twitter, YouTube, and others—essentially serve as a digital archive these days. Unlike a television news story which may disappear and be difficult to trace once it airs, social media stories and images remain easily accessible through simple web searches. An organization's strategic response to a crisis is likewise archived and may remain a part of the public record in social media for perpetuity.

Of course, there are times when online comments about a company, product, service, or person are so egregiously inaccurate and harmful to reputation that they may be defamatory. Organizations may need to resort to legal action to cease further injury to a brand. Lawsuits are showing up when social media are involved, usually involving libel, but online libel on social media is still an evolving area of law and not one that is always clearly understood. Someone even coined the word "twibel," which refers to libel on Twitter.

It should be pointed out that lawsuits are not the only way to resolve this kind of problem. Harmful content is sometimes voluntarily removed from the web by persuasive communication with a system administrator or other party authorized to make those changes.

Organizations need to be extremely careful and strategic about how they respond to a controversy that concerns them, however. An over-reaction can increase the attention that is focused on the controversy and even be fodder for ridicule.

Question 6: A number of celebrities have been caught up in a maelstrom of bad publicity over the years. Is social media a useful tool for celebrities?

Answer: Social media tools can be both a gift and a curse for public figures, including celebrities. As mentioned earlier, many celebrities have legions of followers on Twitter. It's a great way for celebrities to connect directly with fans, bypassing the traditional news and entertainment media. I'm sure there are celebrities who have a public relations professional or maybe a close associate handling their social media activities under the guise that it is the celebrity herself or himself doing the posting, but there are other celebrities who appear to do the postings themselves. Posting to Twitter and Facebook is not a complex task and does not require a high degree of technical skill.

But a freewheeling, indiscriminate approach to public communication can have its consequences. A celebrity may make a thoughtless, offhand comment via social media that offends a certain class of people. This kind of comment might not get a lot of attention if posted by someone who is not in the public eye, but the news media and others tend to scrutinize every word that emanates from a public figure. Twitter, Facebook, and other social media tools are not the same as a private conversation in a private space, but sometimes it might feel that way because comments are usually posted in private and can be done without much forethought or filtering, and it is especially risky if the person posting the comment is not in a normal state of mind.

Examples of tweets that have triggered a public backlash include teenage celebrity Kylie Jenner's offhand remark that used the word "bipolar" in relation to her indecisiveness about her hair color. Some people criticized her cavalier use of this word that actually describes a serious mental health disorder, although others came to her defense to say that it is a word commonly used in other contexts. But she is only one of a growing number of celebrities who have been criticized for their posts—words and photos—because some have found the posts to be offensive, insulting, crude, ignorant, or offering too much information (TMI) about private matters.

Many of these are easy to find by using a search engine on the web and searching for terms like "worst celebrity tweets." *The Huffington Post* produced a slideshow on this topic with specific examples. The slideshow was called, "Think Before You Tweet" and included eyebrow-raising posts from celebrities including Ashton Kutcher, Alicia Silverstone, Jenny McCarthy, Jessica Simpson, the Kardashians, and others (Huffington Post, 2014).

Whether these kinds of social media posts actually hurt a celebrity's brand, so to speak, is questionable. In some cases, such controversy can generate media attention and online chatter that is helpful in maintaining a celebrity's public persona. But when the line is crossed, and it's difficult to generalize where that line is drawn, the backlash can be severe, and then the celebrity often offers a mea culpa of some sort to try to smooth things over. This might include an apology, a correction, a retraction, an explanation that provides context, maybe something sincere, or maybe something forced and half-hearted to avoid financial repercussions. Sometimes it is too little too late.

The late comedian Gilbert Gottfried posted a series of offensive tweets making light of the devastating and deadly tsunami that hit Japan in 2011. Although he deleted the "jokes," he was fired as the spokesman for Aflac insurance, which does robust business in Japan. Both Aflac and Gottfried apologized for the offensive posts. It is difficult to comprehend how Gottfried could have imagined those posts would have resulted in anything other than what actually transpired. Yes, "think before you tweet" is good advice, but the ability to comment and post on just about any topic, anytime, anywhere, to hordes of followers is a little too intoxicating for some people who make their living seeking the public's attention.

It should also be noted that social media companies are under increasing pressure by the public and government regulators to monitor the content on their platforms to identify illegal content and disinformation. Consequences for egregious and repeated violations can result in warnings, fines, a suspension of one's social media account, or even a permanent expulsion from the social media platform.

Question 7: How has social media affected public relations?

Answer: By this point in time, social media tools should be part of a public relations professional's toolkit. As mentioned earlier, however, social media need to be used strategically, not haphazardly, as a professional PR tool. Back in the old days preceding the rise of interactive digital media, before the mid-1990s, a lot of public figures relied on public relations professionals to deal with their publics. The PR professional, or publicist, would be a sort of filter between an organization or public figure and the public. If an organization or a celebrity wanted to communicate something important to the public, the PR professional could provide wise counsel or at least begin a thoughtful conversation that studied the potential effects of specific public communication messages.

These days that vetting process, so to speak, may be dispensed with and the organization or celebrity can simply "unload" on social media directly without careful consideration of strategy and consequences. This may be good for spontaneous communication—over-management of communication messages can come across as contrived and insincere—but it can also lead to disastrous public image problems.

Organizations need to carefully think through social media campaigns, because a campaign can have unintended consequences, which is what happened when the New York Police Department invited the public to post photos of themselves with police officers. Photos of unflattering encounters with police officers began to appear, including some that appear to depict police brutality. A spokesman for the department addressed the outcome with finesse, saying, "The NYPD is creating new ways to communicate effectively with the community. Twitter provides an open forum for an uncensored exchange and this is an open dialogue good for our city" (Ford, 2014).

Question 8: Are there interesting examples of celebrities or organizations using social media in a constructive way?

Answer: There are lots of examples, many more so than the negative examples mentioned previously. Celebrities can use social media to call attention to important causes they care about, using their celebrity status and massive following to raise both money and awareness. Lady Gaga, Queen Latifah, Angelina Jolie, Bono, Brad Pitt, Ellen DeGeneres, George Clooney, Leonardo DiCaprio, Michael J. Fox, Oprah Winfrey, Susan Sarandon, the late Betty White, and many others have contributed much in the way of helping improve the lives of people, animals, and the environment. While they may not all be avid social media users, the attention they generate by associating themselves with causes and charities has been carried by social media hosted by others.

We already talked about ALS and the "Ice Bucket Challenge" fundraising tactic. Most social media fundraising campaigns will not reach that level of success, which is noteworthy because it was an anomaly, but organizations do raise substantial amounts of money from web- and social media–based campaigns. Crowdsource fundraising is an innovative and often effective way of raising money for good social causes. There are nonprofit organizations that use social media to promote socially constructive causes, activities, and public awareness efforts.

For years now, corporations have participated in cause-related marketing activities and tactics. Social media can definitely be used to harness a lot of the good that exists out there in society. Some social critics have observed that civic engagement has been on the decline since the late 1970s in the United States. That may be true, but I also think that in more recent times, civic engagement has found its way back into contemporary society through social media.

Question 9: What is the future of social media?

Answer: We can expect social media to be further integrated into our contemporary communication and media environment but not necessarily in the same ways that they exist now. Information and communication technologies are constantly evolving. I think social media will be even more mobile, wearable, multifaceted, and internetworked than they are today. They can be used for crisis communications in an assortment of ways. Imagine a natural or human-caused disaster that has disabled traditional lines of communication such as telephones, television, radio, and so forth. Social media can exist on more robust communication networks and allow people not only to get information but also how to find or receive help. But they can also co-exist with traditional media and complement so-called "low-tech" communication such as amateur radio or ham radio in a disaster. Governments are already integrating social media into their crisis communications plans. But citizens can help each other, with or without the government's participation.

In the near future, we will wear our social media, if we want to, when we leave the house, which many people already do to a certain extent as they travel with their smart phones. The concept of social media may include not only communicating with other people but also with intelligent machines. You are already seeing commercials where this is happening. Our definition of "social" will expand.

Question 10: How do we keep on learning about the role that social media will play in our lives?

Answer: The information sources are numerous and include government, businesses, academic institutions, civil society, and the bright thinkers and innovators that exist in all of these sectors and elsewhere. Social media started as a way of keeping track of friends' comings and goings, not necessarily trivial matters but not necessarily seen as groundbreaking and revolutionary, either. It will evolve into much more. I think it will play an important role in healthcare and social welfare, as well as in education and civic engagement. So we have to look at developments in all of these areas. YouTube has become an important tool in my and many other people's lifelong learning. When I have a question about how to do something— everything from using a software application to re-threading my grass trimmer—I turn to YouTube. Inevitably, I will find the answer there. This simple reality should make organizations take note about how to identify and reach new target audiences. Millions of people are out there at any given moment in search of something they need or want. The COVID-19 pandemic also seems to have bolstered the use of social media among people who were unable to physically gather with their peers but still sought out social interaction online.

Crisis communications professionals should regard social media as representing an opportunity to reach and engage with target audiences in the pre-crisis, crisis, and post-crisis stages, all done with an eye to increase preparedness and effectiveness in managing a crisis and reducing risk of harm to public safety and the organization's reputation.

Mini-Case Studies in Social Media Crises

Critics of social media claim that the relatively new method of communications causes too many problems. The media don't cause the problems; the users do. Polly Keary, a former doctoral student at the University of Washington, gathered here the following stories of crises started in social media.

Applebee's Controversy Over Fired Waitress

Social media administrators of Applebee's, an international restaurant chain, made a bad situation worse in February, 2013, by taking a defensive stance against online criticism following the firing of a waitress who had publicly shamed a poor tipper. Applebee's has a policy of adding an automatic 18 percent gratuity to checks on tables of more than six people, but one diner who took exception left an injudicious note. "I give God 10 percent, why do you get 18?" the note read, and the gratuity sum was scribbled out.

Waitress Chelsea Welch posted a photo of the receipt, including the diner's signature, on Reddit.com. The post went viral, prompting the diner, Pastor Alois Bell, to call the restaurant and complain; Welch was fired, generating considerable media coverage. Applebee's posted a status update on the company Facebook page announcing that the company had fired Welch for violating company policy and expressing regret for the violation of the customer's privacy.

Within hours, the status update drew more than 17,000 comments, and indignant supporters of the waitress launched Facebook pages and Twitter campaigns to have her reinstated. At about 3 a.m., an administrator of the Applebee's Facebook page posted an explanation of Applebee's decision in the comments under the status update; this was a poor strategy, as comments left on such a busy status update are soon buried under new comments.

As people continued to post critical comments, Applebee's administrators responded by cut-and-pasting the defensively worded explanation into the comment thread over and over, tagging people who had left critical comments. The administrators also began arguing with individuals who had commented, which provoked additional hostility.

Between the first status update and two subsequent updates that unsuccessfully attempted to defuse the controversy, Applebee's social media sites got 1,400,000 views and more than 41,000 comments, mostly negative, as well as international media coverage of its social media faux pas.

KitchenAid Tweet on Obama's Grandmother

KitchenAid curtailed a potential public relations crisis by quickly apologizing and taking responsibility for a staff member's use of the company Twitter account to post a tasteless quip during a 2012 presidential debate.

The employee, who apparently forgot to log out of the company account before sending the tweet, made light of the death of Obama's grandmother, who had died four years earlier, just days before Obama won the office. "Obamas gma even know it was going 2 b bad! She died 3 days b4 he became president," read the tweet, posted from @KitchenaidUSA, which had about 25,000 followers. By the time the company deleted the tweet eight minutes later, it had already been retweeted hundreds of times and was generating considerable negative commentary

Cynthia Soledad, the company's senior director, introduced herself on Twitter and posted, "Deepest apologies for an irresponsible tweet that is in no way a representation of the brand's opinion." About an hour later, Twitter mentions of the gaffe peaked at about 1,800 mentions per 10 minutes, then sharply declined.

Soledad continued to address the incident late into the evening, explaining that the employee responsible would be held accountable, but also taking responsibility for her team, and tweeting an apology to the president and his family. Soledad's quick response was well received, and the company ended up with about 1,000 new followers by the end of the night.

The Burger King Twitter Hack

Burger King got a relatively gentle lesson in the importance of having strong social media security measures when someone hacked the company's Twitter account and began posting bizarre tweets. Twitter users began to notice something amiss when the company's profile picture was changed to the McDonald's logo and it was "announced" that McDonald's had purchased Burger King.

Twitter users flocked to the feed to witness the debacle unfold, as for the next hour the hackers tweeted tasteless humor and attempts to promote their friends' music and Twitter accounts. The tweets were so obviously the work of a hacker that Burger King ultimately gained sympathetic goodwill from many, including rival McDonald's, who tweeted support.

When Burger King finally got Twitter to temporarily freeze its account, Burger King issued a statement apologizing for the inappropriate tweets followers had been getting. Administrators also tweeted that it had been an "interesting day" and expressed the hope that Burger King's many new followers would stick around.

American Apparel's Tumblr Use of Challenger Disaster Image

Just before the Fourth of July, 2014, a social media administrator for American Apparel posted to the corporate Tumblr page an image of a thick, twisting column of smoke spiraling across a digitally altered red sky, along with the hashtags #clouds and #smoke. Outraged social media users swiftly protested the use of the image, a photograph of the 1986 explosion of the space shuttle Challenger in which seven astronauts were killed.

American Apparel removed the image and posted the following apology:

> We deeply apologize for today's Tumblr post of the Space Shuttle Challenger. The image was re-blogged in error by one of our international social media employees who was born after the tragedy and was unaware of the event. We sincerely regret the insensitivity of that selection and the post has been deleted.

DiGiorno Pizza Misappropriation of #WhyIStayed

Frozen pizza maker DiGiorno has built a brand around snarky public comments on social media, many under the hashtag #DiGiorNOYOUDIDNT. The branding strategy, largely hailed as creative and edgy, backfired when an administrator failed to check why a certain hashtag was trending before appropriating it to sell frozen pizzas.

After TMZ found and posted video of football player Ray Rice knocking his wife Janay Rice unconscious at a casino, a national discussion of domestic violence followed. Many questioned Janay Rice's decision to stay with her husband. In response, abuse survivors took to Twitter to tell their stories under the hashtag #WhyIStayed.

DiGiorno's drew social media fire by carelessly tweeting "#WhyIStayed You had pizza." The administrator spent the next several hours responding to people, apologizing for not clicking on #WhyIStayed to see what it was about before posting.

NYPD's and the Redskins' Miscalculations of Twitter Responses

Two large organizations gaffed when, badly misreading their audiences, their solicitations for supportive Twitter posts yielded the opposite. The Washington Redskins NFL football franchise, long embattled over the pejorative racial implications of the team's name, erred when trying to turn their supporters on Nevada Sen. Harry Reid, a vocal critic of the team name.

They asked fans to tweet messages with the hashtag #RedSkinsPride to @SenatorReid, explaining what the team meant to them. The vast majority of the several hundred opinions subsequently tweeted called for the team name to be changed.

An attempt at social media outreach on the part of the New York City Police Department similarly backfired when the department, through its official Twitter account @NYPDNews, asked New Yorkers, "Do you have a photo with a member of the NYPD? Tweet us & tag it #myNYPD."

City residents did so, but the images were not all what the department had in mind; many posted images of police arresting demonstrators and using violence and weapons on suspects. The #myNYPD hashtag trended worldwide, and similar threads were started under hashtags such as #MyNOPD, #MiPolicia, and #MyLAPD. New York Police Commissioner Bill Bratton defended the campaign, saying that he welcomed the attention and that the images depicted the difficulty of the job of police officer.

Pinterest's Humorous Apology Over Engagement Congratulations Gaffe

Pinterest is a popular venue for wedding planning, with thousands of users collecting images of wedding catering, fashion, venues and more. In a bid at creative self-promotion, Pinterest sent an email blast to some of those users, congratulating them on their engagements and suggesting they look at images posted by top designers, photographers, and other brides-to-be.

Unfortunately, many of the people who got the emails were not engaged or even in relationships. Most of the ensuing social media commentary was wryly amused, and Pinterest followed up with a humorous email apology, concluding, "We're sorry we came off like an overbearing mother who is always asking when you'll find a nice boy or girl."

Not Every Occasion Is Appropriate for Brand Use

A common error that companies make on social media is using holidays, news events, or sensitive issues to promote their brands. Nyquil apologized after drawing ire for posting a tweet on Martin Luther King Day, 2014, that said, "Today is the day for dreaming. Happy MLK Day."

The British Embassy in Washington, DC issued an embarrassed apology after tweeting a photograph of a cake decorated with a figurine of the White House flanked by British and America flags and the message "Commemorating the 200th anniversary of burning the White House. Only sparklers this time!" In spite of some effort on the part of U.S. diplomatic staff to see the humor in the post, offended retweets and comments prompted a chastened apology from the British Embassy staff.

Epicurious made a serious mistake by attempting to capitalize on the Boston Marathon bombing, tweeting "Boston, our hearts are with you. Here's a bowl of breakfast energy we could all use to start today," along with a link to an image of a company product. A second tweet suggested that buying the company's cranberry scones would be a good way to honor New England and Boston. The company withdrew the tweets and apologized, but ill will lingered.

IAC Exec Twitter Rant

Career-destroying controversy can unfold in a matter of a few hours, as Justine Sacco, director of corporate communications with Internet media company IAC, learned in December, 2013, upon making a Twitter comment many found offensive. As she prepared to board a plane for South Africa, she tweeted that she hoped she didn't get AIDS, then joked that she wouldn't because she was "white."

Figure 7.3 Elodie Fichet is head of Brand Accessibility at Amazon where she also raises the bar on disability representation. Fichet earned a Ph.D. in communications from the University of Washington. Her dissertation focused on how crisis communicators balance crisis planning with the necessity of being flexible. She has worked for the Americans with Disabilities Act (ADA) National Network as a communications director.

Source: Permission by Elodie Fichet

IAC, owner of the video platform Vimeo and the news and entertainment website *Daily Beast*, among other properties, immediately issued a statement condemning the tweet, but saying that until Sacco's plane landed and they were able to communicate with her, they would not take further action, which led to the hashtag #HasJustineLandedYet trending while she was on the 11-hour flight. Upon arriving and learning of the demise of her career, Sacco deleted all of her social media accounts and made a lengthy apology to a South African newspaper, claiming she had only meant to mock what a racist would say.

Unfortunately, there are still no hard and fast rules governing producing and distributing social media. There are, however efforts that should be made and acts that should not. Elodie Fichet (Figure 7.3) makes the following suggestions.

Social Media Etiquette for Organizations and Individuals to Prevent Social Media Crises

Social media have been proven to be excellent multidimensional communications tools, and although they are free, they do come with a cost: the potential ruin of an organization or a person's reputation. As Schadenfreude would say, Internet justice is swift and ruthless; therefore, organizations need to make diligent efforts to put the odds in their favor. To do just that, there are several things to consider and accomplish, as well as many others to avoid, no matter what.

The following suggestions are things you must "do" and are followed by suggestions of what you should "not do."

Do

Know Your Audience

Contrary to what may have been popular belief in the early days of social media, an impactful (think return on investment [ROI]) social media presence is labor intensive. Do your research and identify who your core audience is. Note, "gen pop" is not enough. This will help cater your messages to who you are trying to reach and anticipate what can be perceived as a faux pas.

Be Thoughtful

Probably the most important aspect of social media channels management is the idea of being thoughtful. The adage "Turn your tongue seven times before speaking" very much applies to posting on social media. Because social media know no geographical boundaries, their reach can be worldwide; thus, using the right tone, in the right voice at the right time, is essential. As we have often seen, perception prevails over intent, so ask yourself, "How will this be perceived?"

Be Authentic

Social media trends have stepped away from content that is contrived or overly polished messaging. While your communication on other channels (e.g., your website) may be more professional or dry, it's OK for your social media channels to have a more conservational and casual tone. Companies that are more personable, even fun (e.g., Wendy's, Spark Notes, Netflix, among others) get more attention and foster a greater number of friendlies.

Be Inclusive at All Costs

BE MINDFUL OF DIFFERENT BACKGROUNDS AND CREEDS, INCLUDING RACIAL, CULTURAL, RELIGIOUS, AND ETHNIC

This goes back to being thoughtful. Whatever the message, communicators should make a conscious effort to avoid offending at all costs—and not solely their known publics but whoever has an Internet access. For example, do not focus solely on Christian-centric holidays, and avoid things like "digital blackface" defined as when non-Black people use the images and voices of Black individuals to express emotions or situations.

BE ACCESSIBLE

According to the WHO, about 15–20 percent of the world has a disability, whether visible (e.g., paraplegia) or non-apparent (e.g., autism). In the United States alone, 25 percent of the adult population has some type of disability (Elodie Fichet). Certain types of disability affect how a person consume content. For example, someone who is blind or has low vision might use an assistive technology called a screen reader. A screen reader is a software that reads what is on the screen of a device (e.g., JAWS, NVDA, VoiceOver on Mac, and TalkBack on Android). It is an essential tool for blind people to be able to consume content. Another example is the use of captioning for people who are deaf or hard of hearing—but not just. Studies have shown videos with captioning tend to get more views and be watched for longer.

While social media platforms have made progress on the accessibility of their platform, end users (you) need to make a concerted effort to ensure their content is accessible. While each platform provides basic tutorials on how to implement accessible practices (e.g., how to input alternative text for images), all social media managers and content creators need to familiarize themselves with accessibility best practices. To get started, see the Bureau of Internet Accessibility (www.boia.org).

Social media accounts that nurture inclusion and foster a sense of belonging *for all* through thoughtfulness, diversity, and accessibility do better in general. Put crudely, diversity and inclusion are good for business, and great for preventing crises.

Have Clear and Thorough Social Media Policies and Approval Processes

Using social media professionally without official, written (and understood!) policies is a disaster waiting to happen. Put the rules in the book and make sure that everyone involved in social media knows what these rules are. Policies should include all social media platforms and their handling, troubleshooting and processes to follow in case of problematic situations, as well as the extent to which employees might be allowed to use social media to discuss work-related matters (blog, Twitter, etc.).

Laurel Papworth, named one of the "Top Social Media Influencers" by Forbes in 2012, compiled a list of different companies' social media policies, from IBM to the U.S. Air Force, which details how these organizations use and plan social media strategies but also how they would handle non-routine situations (on LaurelPapworth.com: "Behavioral and etiquettes guidelines for organizations").

When it comes to governments, social media policies take a different shape. One of the most crucial aspects is the capturing and archiving of social media content to permit retrieval in the case of public record requests. The type of capture needed for the different social media channels and the capital invested determine what tools can be selected.

When it comes to official posts, define a process for vetting posts (a few pairs of eyes are always better than just one). Also, make sure that each post complies with copyright laws on social media, and be clear on what company/product information can and cannot be shared on social media.

Secure Your Accounts Externally and Internally

Strong passwords stored in secure locations (if truly needed) is just one aspect of account security. Keep an up-to-date list of employees who have access and ensure that their access is revoked promptly if they switch teams, leave, or are terminated: cybersecurity crisis is much more likely to be caused by a disgruntled employee than a hacker.

Be Part of the Conversation and Respond Quickly

Social media, on any platform, are a fast-paced environment in which something seemingly small can become big quite quickly. Don't linger when addressing issues and making announcements about your organizations. In February 2022, the online messaging app Slack experienced a major outage which prevented users from accessing the platform. The moment Slack identified the issue, it started providing updates to users every half hour.

On the flip side, in October 2022, Adidas took two weeks to react and announce the ending of their partnership with Kanye West after his numerous anti-semitic rants and generally hateful language. While an incident may not have started on social media, it will likely make its way there quickly.

Have a Sound and Tested Social Media Crisis Plan

It goes without saying that whichever their nature, organizations should include social media in their crisis plan—whether to help manage and resolve the crisis, or on the other hand, in case social media instigate or aggravate a crisis. Because sometimes it is social media themselves that generate the crisis, all possibilities need to be considered, planned for, and regularly updated. One of the first steps to designing a social media crisis plan is asking "what is a crisis for my organization?"; plans must be tailored to your needs—crisis plans are never one size fits all. Remember, do not ever capitalize on another crisis.

Create a Social Listening Program and Monitor What Is
Being Said About You

To be kept in the loop, and hopefully never be the last one to know, set up recurring ways of monitoring what is being said, both about your organization and about its employees. There are several ways to do that. Once again, it is the size of the organization and its budget that will determine which monitoring methods can be used; nevertheless, there are several excellent free tools available.

One of the first steps is to decide what should be tracked (company name, website uniform resource locator [URL], products, specific events or campaigns, higher management names, and such).

GOOGLE ALERTS

Setting up one or several Google Alerts are the most basic ways to be kept aware of what might be said about your organization. By simply doing a Google search that includes your company's name, you will be prompted to *create an alert* (at the bottom of the page) to receive an email each time something new gets referenced in Google. It is recommended to create several separate Google Alerts combining the company's name with common negative words (or other relevant terms pre-determined), "{Company X} awful; wrongdoings; scandal."

Again, depending on the size of the company, it might be judicious to set up alerts for employees as well; using search words such as: "John Doe {Company X}" and remembering to keep these alerts active even if the employees get laid off. Other tools, such as Brandseye.com or Naymz.com, also allow to calculate influence and compare reputations against peers across LinkedIn, Facebook and Twitter, and to manage personal branding.

SOCIAL MEDIA MONITORING TOOLS

Depending on the company's budget, there is an array of social media management tools available that not only allow for content posting and scheduling but also for hashtags tracking. HootSuite and TweetDeck, both offering unpaid versions, let users set up hashtags or keywords tracking. Other social media tracking tools include SocialMention.com, Trackur.com, HyperAlerts.com for Facebook, PinAlerts.com for Pinterest, ImageRaider.com for images, and BackType.com for blogs.

WIKIPEDIA

Because it is a free-access encyclopedia, if an organization or person is the subject of a Wikipedia article, it should imperatively be checked regularly for accuracy. Having an editor account already created and ready to update content is crucial to expedite the process in case modifications are promptly needed.

ALWAYS HAVE SOMEONE "ON CALL" TO MONITOR SOCIAL MEDIA CHANNELS

Working with social media is not a 9-to-5 job. Because people are free to leave comments at any time and from any time zone, be sure to have access either directly to social media channels or to alerts (from Google or any other monitoring tool) at all times—including weekends and national holidays. Don't do the following:

Delete Unfavorable Comments

Bad comments and criticism are never pleasant and can sometimes have a snowballing effect, which might turn out to be difficult to handle. However, negative comments should not be deleted, unless they contain certain parameters, such as racial slurs. In any case, be sure to document the instance by taking a screenshot of the comment. Respond quickly and keep your cool: don't pour oil on the fire. An organization's social media policies should clearly state the specific process to be followed to handle such occurrences systematically and efficiently.

Have Professional and Personal Social Media Accounts on the Same Social Media Management Platform

For instance, do not let employees mix professional and personal social media accounts on Instagram or on HootSuite. This is just begging for a mistake to happen. An oldie but a goodie is from ARC Senior Officer of Humanitarian Engagement Gloria Huang and her tweet intended for her private account was sent from the official ARC Twitter handle. It read, @RedCross: "Ryan found two more 4 bottle packs of Dogfish Head's Midas Touch beer . . . when we drink we do it right #gettngslizzerd." The Red Cross quickly removed the tweet, and tweeted out "We've deleted the rogue tweet but rest assured that the Red Cross is sober and we've confiscated the keys." Huang then personally apologized for the confusion. Although called "an honest mistake" by the Red Cross, this could have been easily avoided by not mixing professional and personal accounts.

Manage a Government Facebook Page From a Personal Account

For two main reasons, government employees should never associate their personal Facebook accounts with a governmental Facebook page. First, access to a government Facebook page should not be protected by an individual's password that may be a simple "password123" used across all personal accounts. Second, as aforementioned, because of the eventuality of public record requests. Who wants their personal Facebook content scrutinized and possibly publicized simply because it is linked to a governmental page?

Let Your Accounts Become Zombies

Unmonitored, never-updated, half-dead accounts are highly detrimental for an organization's reputation. This is not only because queries, questions, and critiques remain unanswered for all to see, but also because it shows an inherent lack of commitment from the business or individual—which is never a good thing to show.

Be Cautious

Watch Out When Scheduling Content

Scheduling non-neutral content in advance comes with great risks. A few years back, the TV show *Sleepy Hollow* made a ghastly bang. To announce the release of the new season, the marketers had planned a promotion to encourage people on social media to celebrate "National Beheading Day" using the hashtag #HeadlessDay or through commemorative eCards in reference to the show's Headless Horseman character.

However, the campaign content was released on the same day ISIS claimed to have decapitated American journalist Steven Sotloff. Although it was never intended to make reference to the awful event, the harm was done. As soon as the juxtaposition of events became apparent, Think Jam, the publicity firm hired for the campaign, quickly retracted and apologized—but #HeadlessDay was already trending on social media.

Joining and Capitalizing on Trends

Unless clever and thought through, forcing your organization's content by appropriating a fun popular hashtag may not be a good idea. Furthermore, it is immoral to use sensitive hashtags to push content and gain viewership.

Using Humor

What you find funny or what seems an innocuous humorous comment may not be to everyone. Gilbert Gottfried's tweets following the Japanese earthquake and tsunami in 2011 are extreme but relevant examples:

@RealGilbert: "I was talking to my Japanese real estate agent. I said 'is there a school in this area?' She said 'not now, but just wait.'"

What Is Posted Cannot Be Taken Back

Although most social media platforms allow you to delete your post or at least edit it (Twitter, Facebook, etc.), what is put out there cannot be taken back. It only takes a second for someone to take a screen shot. Before posting, therefore, check for relevance (in terms of content and audience), importance, and potential varied interpretations and consequences.

Despite All This, a Crisis Occurs—What Do I Do?

- Acknowledge the issue, follow your crisis plan, and use your best judgment. If you can, don't go at it alone. If you have to be creative and address an unanticipated issue, run your post by someone else before publishing.
- Stop all scheduled content. You don't want a planned promotion or a #WednesdayWisdom to pop up amid official statements or resolution status updates.
- Keep the broader team and leadership in the loop.
- Once resolved, learn, learn, learn: what was the exact situation, what did we do well, what did we not do so well, what will we do differently in the future? Also, *update your crisis plan.*

The numbers of communities continue to increase and people see and find communities in which they are comfortable. They share views, problems, interests with other people in their communities. Social media expert Susan West (Figure 7.4) explains with the following.

Turning Online Communities Into Crisis Communications Vehicles

It's common to visit social media channels, but have you joined an online community? What is an online community? People feel a connection with others on specific social networking sites. They check the site often for new posts and updates on previous ones, and post their own thoughts, photos, or videos. They read, share, and participate in conversations and the exchange of ideas and opinions. They also sell things, give things away, and ask for donations or help. They learn about each other and form friendships, loyalty, or even rivalry that leads to online debates. They keep coming back or say they won't, but do. The online community becomes a way of life, part of people's daily routine. They depend on it as a tool to gain information, awareness, education,

Figure 7.4 Susan J. West is an executive communications professional who has provided expertise to Amazon in King County, Washington. She was mayor of the city of Normandy Park, Washington. She earned a B.A. from the University of Washington and an M.A. from George Washington University. As an anchor, reporter, and producer, West worked in TV news for nearly 20 years and was Emmy nominated.

Source: Permission by Susan West

entertainment, and to network. It replaces a phone call or an in-person visit. It becomes a virtual home where people feel comfortable and eager to return.

In the small city where I live, 3,574 neighbors joined an online community called Nextdoor.com which notifies members when others have posted. Some call it a blog, a listserv, a social media channel, or a social networking service. Either way, this site has become a powerful and influential online community. People talk about the site and other's posts at city meetings, in the grocery store, in emails, over coffee, and at home. It has become a modern version of a water cooler or café where people gather each morning to chat and catch up on each other's lives.

I roam the site every day, as if it has replaced the Sunday newspaper. I find urgent posts about lost or found pets, power outages, downed trees, and election results. I come across people who give away furniture, books, and even a frog. People debate local political issues about the city, school bonds, and council members. They offer solutions to problems, provide support when someone is down, and congratulate others on a job well done. They disagree, argue, and become emotional about issues near and dear to their heart. It becomes more than a community and more like a family.

Why do I scour this site? For one, I'm curious. I'm a longtime resident, and know many of the people who regularly post. Others I do not know, but I want to know what they have to say about local issues.

Second, I am a community reviewer which means I review posts that others report as alleged violations of Nextdoor's policies. I then vote with other community reviewers on whether the post should be removed or not. Third, if an emergency occurs, people on this site will immediately discuss the situation and share thoughts, opinions and information. The site becomes an instant crisis communications vehicle for me as a resident and as a volunteer for my city. I was mayor of my city and chaired the communications committee which focused on crisis communications. My background is in media relations, crisis communications, messaging, social media, strategy building, and TV news. Online communities can be potential communication gold mines for the city if a significant issue or emergency occurs. Important information could be instantly conveyed to the hundreds of people who use the site. That could mean fewer phone trees, postal mail, or knocking on the house next door to tell neighbors about the latest news in the neighborhood. The information is instant and before our eyes.

Should companies, agencies and organizations participate in online communities like Nextdoor.com? Yes, if this is where their targeted audience resides. Online communities offer them an opportunity to participate in conversations and become part of the virtual community. As their online relationship builds, people will begin to turn to them for information. The spokesperson becomes a trusted source and that is important when they need to convey urgent information. Should the spokesperson ever say "No comment" to the online community or ignore posts? They should never say no or ignore posts. If the spokesperson is still seeking information about an emergency or issue, then they should let the online community know. Give a timeline of when information will be updated online. Keep the conversation going. If the spokesperson does not provide the information, then people will ask someone else. In other words, someone else will take over and own the messaging. The spokesperson has lost control of the information and the audience. To avoid this situation, prepare a crisis communications plan prior any issue or emergency, and before the spokesperson joins the online community. The plan's template should include the following sections.

1. Identify the issue.
2. Conduct a SWOT analysis—strength, weakness, opportunity, threat.
3. Identify those affected, and who will receive messaging. Who is your audience and the stakeholders?
4. How will information be conveyed in addition to the online community (i.e. news media, press release, door-to-door with flyers,

all-staff email, text alerts through community or employee sign-up, virtual or in-person all-team or community meetings, phone hotline messages, etc.)?

5. Identify DEI (diversity, equity, inclusion)/ESJ (equity, social justice) accommodations needed, including translation.
6. Identify the chain of command (i.e. leadership, communications team, etc.) for determining, writing, approving, and posting the information about the crisis and responses to audience comments and questions.
7. Create a tracking chart that shows who will and has posted updates and responses to audience, and when (this could be 24/7, depending on the emergency).
8. Anticipate frequently asked questions (FAQs) by the media, public, and targeted audience.

A well–thought-out crisis communications plan provides a path for efficiency, effectiveness, and consistency in providing information to the online community and audiences through the other communication tools mentioned in bullet point 4 of the preceding list. Most of all, it builds trust with the recipients of your information.

What is my final reason for following my city's online community? I am truly fascinated with the power of online communities. I have watched Nextdoor.com and other sites grow over the years. I have seen the influence that posts have on people's decisions and the power posts have to open other's eyes to new perspectives. Many have stayed with the site in my city while some have opted out due to the frustration and emotions that online communities can spark, primarily due to political debates. Online communities are not for everyone. You have to find the online community that fits you or your company, agency or organization best—and when you find it, you will know because it will be difficult to step away for too long.

Bibliography

Social Media Etiquette

6 Painful Social Media Screwups. (2011, April 7). Retrieved March 14, 2015, from http://money.cnn.com/galleries/2011/technology/1104/gallery.social_media_controversies/3.html.

American Red Cross. (2011, February 15). *We've deleted the rogue tweet but rest assured that the Red Cross is sober and we've confiscated the keys:* [*Twitter post*]. Retrieved from https://twitter.com/RedCross/status/37748007671832576.

Applebee's. (2013, January 31). *We wish this situation hadn't happened.* Retrieved March 9, 2015, from www.facebook.com/applebees/posts/10151383621179334.

Auxier, B. & Anderson, M. *Social media use in 2021*. Retrieved October 18, 2022, from www.pewresearch.org/internet/2021/04/07/social-media-use-in-2021/.

Booker, B. (2021, February 16). Amy Cooper, white woman who called police on Black bird-watcher, has charge dismissed. *NPR.com*. Retrieved October 18, 2022, from www.npr.org/2021/02/16/968372253/white-woman-who-called-police-on-black-man-bird-watching-has-charges-dismissed.

Borreson, K. (2014, September 5). That time Pinterest congratulated women on their non-existent weddings. *The Huffington Post*. Retrieved March 8, 2015, from www.huffingtonpost.com.

Bratton on Twitter fail: I welcome the attention. (2013, April 24). *NBC New York*. Retrieved March 8, 2015, from www.nbcnewyork.com.

Chasmar, J. (2014, May 29). #RedskinsPride Twitter campaign targets Harry Reid, draws derision. *Washington Times*. Retrieved March 8, 2015, from www.washingtontimes.com.

Cutway, A. (2014, April 15). US Airways' pornographic tweet and other social media fails. Retrieved February 7, 2015, from www.orlandosentinel.com/features/the-list/os-social-media-fails-20140415-post.html.

Deggans, E. (2022). The best (and worst) Super Bowl commercials: Lizzo, cranky Zeus and more. *NPR.com*. Retrieved October 18, 2022, from www.npr.org/2022/02/14/1080516128/super-bowl-commercials.

Diamond, D. (2014, August 29). *The ALS ice bucket challenge has raised $100 million—and counting*. Retrieved January 29, 2015, from www.forbes.com/sites/dandiamond/2014/08/29/the-als-ice-bucket-challenge-has-raised-100m-but-its-finally-cooling-off/.

Duggan, M., Ellison, N., Lampe, C., Lenhart, A. & Madden, M. (2015, January 9). *Social media update 2014*. Retrieved January 29, 2015, from www.pewinternet.org/2015/01/09/social-media-update-2014/.

Ford, D. (2014, April 24). *#D'oh! NYPD Twitter campaign backfires*. Retrieved February 7, 2015, from www.cnn.com/2014/04/22/tech/nypd-twitter-fail/index.html.

Google. (n.d.). *Frequently asked questions about the Google+ shutdown*. Retrieved October 18, 2022, from https://support.google.com/googlecurrents/answer/9217723#whatshappening&zippy=%2Cwhy-shut-down-google-for-consumers%2Chow-can-i-stay-in-touch-with-my-google-followers.

Griner, D. (2012, October 3). KitchenAid mistakenly tweets joke about Obama's dead grandmother. *Adweek*. Retrieved March 9, 2015, from www.adweek.com.

Hsu, T. (2012, October 4). KitchenAid apologizes over tweet about Obama's grandmother. *LA Times*. Retrieved March 11, 2015, from www.latimes.com.

Huffington Post. (2014, November 14). *These celebrities really need to think before they tweet*. Retrieved January 30, 2015, from www.huffingtonpost.com/2013/11/14/celebrity-twitter-tmi-think-before-tweet_n_4275390.html.

Kim, S. (2013, February 20). *Pizza Hut manager pees in sink leads top 10 grossest fast-food moments*. Retrieved January 29, 2015, from http://abcnews.go.com/Business/pizza-hut-manager-pees-kitchen-sink-latest-grossest/story?id=22600828.

KitchenAid Twitter crisis. (2012, October 4). Retrieved March 9, 2015, from www.oursocialtimes.com.

Mayhew, C. (2013, February 19). Burger King hack shows not all social media "disasters" are bad. *Social Media Today*. Retrieved March 8, 2015, from www.socialmediatoday.com.

McDermott, J. (2013, January 30). It's not delivery: It's DiGiorno trolling delivery. *Digiday*. Retrieved March 8, 2015, from www.digiday.com.

Memmott, M. (2012, October 4). KitchenAid apologizes for "offensive tweet" about Obama's grandmother. *NPR.org*. Retrieved March 8, 2015, from www.npr.org.

Nagourney, A. & Zeleny, J. (2008, August 24). *Obama chooses Biden as running mate*. Retrieved January 28, 2015, from www.nytimes.com/2008/08/24/us/politics/24biden.html?_r=0.

Nielsen.com. (2023, February 14). Super Bowl LVII totals more than 113 million viewers, ranks second most-watched game ever. *Nielsen.com*. Retrieved February 25, 2023, from www.nielsen.com/news-center/2023/super-bowl-lvii-totals-more-than-113-million-viewers-ranks-second-most-watched-game-ever/.

Olenski, S. (2013, April 19). Epicurious tweets inappropriately after Boston Marathon tragedy. *Social Media Today*. Retrieved March 9, 2015, from www.socialmediatoday.com.

Oreskovic, A. & Saba, J. (2015, February 2). *Facebook, Twitter lock horns in post-Super Bowl battle of the statistics*. Retrieved February 6, 2015, from www.reuters.com/article/2015/02/03/us-nfl-super-socialmedia-idUSKBN0L703B20150203.

Papworth, L. (2009, April 24). *Enterprise: List of 40 social media staff guidelines*. Retrieved March 14, 2015, from http://laurelpapworth.com.

Pilkington, E. (2014, August 25). British embassy sparks anger for tweet celebrating 1814 White House burning. *The Guardian*. Retrieved March 9, 2015, from www.theguardian.com.

Porter, C. (2013, February 5). US restaurant Applebee's commits "social media suicide." *The Australian*. Retrieved March 8, 2015, from www.theaustralian.com.au.

Rawden, J. (2014, September 2). *So, Sleepy Hollow's headless campaign didn't go over so well, obviously*. Retrieved March 14, 2015, from www.cinemablend.com/television/Sleepy-Hollow-Headless-eCards-Don-t-Go-Over-67078.html.

Schroeder, A. (2014, January 20). Joe Mande is once again retweeting MLK Day brand fails. *The Daily Dot*. Retrieved March 9, 2015, from www.dailydot.com.

Shields, M. & Marshall, J. (2015, February 2). *How the Super Bowl resonated across digital and social media*. Retrieved February 6, 2015, from http://blogs.wsj.com/cmo/2015/02/02/how-the-super-bowl-resonated-across-digital-and-social-media/.

Stampler, L. (2014, September 9). DiGiorno used a hashtag about domestic violence to sell pizza. *Time*. Retrieved March 8, 2015, from www.time.com.

Stedman, A. (2014, September 2). *"Sleepy Hollow" marketers sorry for "National Beheading Day" stunt*. Retrieved February 6, 2015, from http://variety.com/2014/tv/n.

Stollar, R. L. (2013, February 2). Applebee's overnight social media meltdown: A photo essay. *R.L. stollar////Overturning tables*. [Web log post]. Retrieved March 8, 2015, from www.rlstollar.wordpress.com/2013/02/02.

Stopera, M. (2011, March 14). *The 10 worst Gilbert Gottfried tsunami jokes*. Retrieved March 14, 2015, from www.buzzfeed.com/mjs538/the-10-worst-gilbert-gottfried-tsunami-jokes#.xbg8340wg.

Strange, A. (2013, December 21). IAC confirms firing of PR exec Justine Sacco. *Mashable*. Retrieved March 9, 2015, from www.mashable.com/2013/12/21.

Taylor, C. (2013, December 21). Twitter turns ugly over PR person's idiotic tweet. *Mashable*. Retrieved March 9, 2015, from www.mashable.com/2013/12/20.

Washington Redskins. (2014, May 29). Tweet @SenatorReid to show your #RedskinsPride and tell him what the team means to you. *Twitter post*. Retrieved March 8, 2015, from https://twitter.com/Redskins/status/472088588251721729.

Wasserman, T. (2013, December 21). Wi-Fi provider Gogo apologizes after commenting on Justine Sacco saga. *Mashable.* Retrieved March 9, 2015, from www.mashable.com/2013/12/21.

We've deleted the rogue tweet but rest assured that the Red Cross is sober and we've confiscated the keys. (2011, February 15). *American Red Cross.* Retrieved from https://twitter.com/RedCross.

White House. (2013, June 19). CB...Oh, baby! at.wh.gov/mbyRI #Immigration Reform. *Twitter post.* Retrieved from https://twitter.com/search?q=from%3Awhitehouse%20since%3A2013-06-18%20until%3A2013-06-20&src=typd.

Withnall, A. (2013, December 22). PR executive Justine Sacco apologises after losing job over racist AIDS "joke" provoked #HasJustineLandedYet Twitter storm. *The Independent.* Retrieved March 9, 2015, from www.independent.co.uk.

Wood, S. P. (2014, July 7). American apparel mistakes Challenger explosion for fireworks. *Adweek.* Retrieved March 9, 2015, from www.adweek.com.

World Health Organization. (2022, December 2). Disability. Retrieved from www.who.int/news-room/fact-sheets/detail/disability-and-health.

Chapter 8

Culture Crises
Foreign and Domestic

The cases studied in this chapter center on crises within the United States and those in other countries. All cope with communications either with publics in that country or with publics in other countries. First, the HIV/AIDS crisis continues to cause deaths in many African countries, and tactics for battling the disease and convincing public to utilize prevention protocols are necessarily challenging to develop and put in place. We take a look at how communications helped African countries when they first suffered from COVID-19 on top of the dominance of HIV/AIDS. In the case study "Nut Rage," there's a lesson in culture and employee relations in South Korea. The case study "Yuhan-Kimberly and Baby Wet Wipes" tells the story of one company's determination to satisfy culture above finances. The case study "Saginaw Valley State University and the Theater Controversy" relates a story of how one university handled a situation honoring the LBGTQ+ community.

Case Study: AIDS in Africa

The conversation at the World AIDS Day in 2014 was the possibility of ending AIDS worldwide by the year 2030. Those gathered urged every country and every person to do their part to make the goal a reality. Efforts to stop the spread of HIV/AIDS globally have been slowly successful, but about 40 million people had died as of 2023. The numbers of newly infected people declines each year and is down about 38 percent since 2001. In sub-Saharan Africa, hardest hit by the disease and the site of the origins of the disease, the reduction was significant—35 percent (UNAIDS, 2014). But the crisis remains.

The 2014 GAP Report (UNAIDS, 2014) revealed that one public has been largely ignored: persons over 50. Evidence shows that older people have lower levels of HIV-related knowledge than younger groups and are less likely to have tested for HIV. So the second goal was that by 2020, 90 percent of all people living with HIV will know their status and 90 percent

DOI: 10.4324/9781003019282-8

of all people with diagnosed HIV infections will receive antiretroviral therapy (ART).

This case study looks at crisis communications aimed broadly at Africans in various countries, people who have HIV and need to accept treatment, and those who are not yet infected and need to accept prevention techniques.

Considering that abstinence and safe sex are determined to be the methods of preventing AIDS and that medical treatments can help infected persons to live with HIV, communications to persuade people to take these actions is necessary. As in all crises, to be effective, the communicators—whether organizational leaders or communications experts—must choose the best message targeting the precisely segmented publics by the best possible method of communications.

Compounding this is the urgency of considering the culture of the publics to be reached and served. Cultural backgrounds and traditions, including sexual practices, have remained constant for generations. Even educated Africans say, "We cannot ignore our elders." So, although medical science searches for cures and treatments for HIV and AIDS, social scientists must research this previously seldom studied subject of African cultures. Sexual myths, taboos, and traditions cannot be easily combated.

A *disconnect* is sure to occur if well-meaning persons from other countries are sent to African countries to basically change a way of life. This communications process is called *parachuting*. To avoid parachuting, it is necessary for foreign professionals to partner with local organizations, agencies, or officials who understand the culture and the people and are trusted by the people. Too often, "do-gooders" sympathize with the African plight when they should empathize. Sympathy is feeling compassion and concern for others, whereas empathy is more intellectual; it involves the understanding of thoughts and feelings and sensitivity. Even in one's own country, it is important to empathize when communicating with people of other races, religions, social status, and walks of life. Often people say to others suffering some loss, "I know how you feel." Actually, they don't know; they can't know. They can imagine how one feels. They can have concern, compassion, or sympathy. But empathy is not that easily achieved. It requires carefully studying a culture, a plight. It's more than a simple feeling.

Some of the practices and taboos of African countries will seem strange to outsiders. Some practices in your culture are strange to people in other countries. A person who feels superior with an attitude of "I shall help these unfortunate souls because I am so above this problem" is likely to fail in the communicating process.

One must accept the fact that for generations—more generations than there has been a United States of America—people have followed tribal traditions that are precious to them because of their longevity. Their lives are built on love for ancestors, elders, traditions, and history. True, some practices must change for them to survive, but getting them to make these changes requires a careful plan sensitively executed.

Cultural Practices, Beliefs, and Challenges

Some of the taboos, cultural practices, and traditions follow. They are not specific to one country and are not manifested exactly the same way in each country. These practices, identified by various organizations and individuals researching the HIV/AIDS crisis, are not characteristic of all persons in any country or region, but have been determined to be problematic in the fight against HIV/AIDS when they do occur. The challenge of the communicator is to help eliminate a specific practice or belief while respecting and sustaining the culture.

1. A man who is HIV positive can be cured if he has sex with a virgin; most virgins are, obviously, little girls.
2. There is great sexual inequality. Women feel powerless to reject or disagree with their husbands about sexual acts. "Women's lib" is a concept they do not know.
3. A person known to have AIDS is often stigmatized or physically abused by others. Wives are often terrified to tell their husbands they are HIV positive even when their husbands infected them. A woman in South Africa admitted on television that she had AIDS. When she returned home, she was beaten to death by people in her village.
4. Men say, "Having sex with a condom is like eating a banana with the peel."
5. A man buys a bride from her family, making her his property. If a wife dies, the man can demand to marry (and sleep with) her sister because he has paid to have a wife.
6. In some countries, when a man dies, his wife is automatically the property of his brothers, just like his house, land, and cattle. Many wives are infected in these inherited marriages when their brothers-in-law are HIV-positive.
7. "Sugar daddies" are appealing to young girls who want material possessions; the girls who are very poor often see no possibility of ever having a simple change of clothing unless they perform sexual favors. These sugar daddies often carry HIV.
8. If a person is well dressed and clean looking, he or she could not possibly have HIV.
9. If someone dies of AIDS, relatives blame the death on witchcraft from an enemy.

10. Nursing mothers who are HIV positive continue to breastfeed their babies, exposing them to the virus, because the stigma of being known to have the virus is unbearable.
11. In six countries, approximately 15 million people are at risk of starvation (Maskalyk, 2002). These countries are Zimbabwe, Zambia, Swaziland, Lesotho, Malawi, and Mozambique. The convergence of hunger and HIV increases vulnerability to infection and disease. Malnutrition and HIV weaken the immune system. Also, hunger is immediately felt and women will do anything—including prostitution—to feed themselves and their families.

The rest of the chapter addresses these countries: Uganda, Botswana, Zambia, South Africa, Zimbabwe, and Swaziland. The culture, including facts about geography, government, and languages, is mentioned, as well as the tactics used to fight HIV/AIDS. Crisis communicators supposedly considered these facts before planning the tactics. For example, if 75 percent of HIV-infected people have no access to television, it would be senseless to make television the primary method of communications. If people do not trust outsiders, it would be senseless for strangers to try to change their practices.

Uganda

AIDS, commonly called "slim disease," emerged in Uganda in 1982. Great human suffering resulted, as elsewhere in sub-Saharan Africa. Approximately 2 million people died; the government estimated that 1.5 million children were orphaned. Uganda became a leader in working to reduce the AIDS rate. However, more recently, the country has seen about 140,000 new HIV infections per year, pushing the infection rate to about 7.2 percent. It is estimated that 80 percent of those living with HIV in Uganda are not aware of their status and more than 100,000 are newly infected each year.

Yoweri Museveni seized power from dictator Milton Obote in 1986 and became president of Uganda. He learned of the dreadful HIV/AIDS statistics and was appalled. He established the country's first AIDS Control Program. He also asked for help from researchers and public health organizations worldwide, announcing that Uganda would participate in African vaccine trials. He involved religious and traditional leaders, community groups, and non-governmental agencies in a unified effort to slow the spread of the disease and provide care and support for the victims (Figure 8.1).

The program had some success. In 1994, the president's efforts resulted in survey results showing that there were fewer cases of casual sex, more frequent condom use, and youth who waited until an older age to become sexually active. More importantly, the HIV infection rate dropped.

Figure 8.1 In Uganda, billboards exhibit encouragement to take HIV tests and treatments. The country's HIV epidemic one of the highest in sub-Saharan Africa. More than 1.4 million Ugandans live with HIV.

Source: AFP / Stringer via Getty Images

Since 1993, HIV infection rates have been halved for pregnant women, a prime indicator of the spread of the disease, and decreased by a third among men seeking treatment for sexually transmitted infections (STIs). In Kampala, the capital, the HIV rate of pregnant women seeking prenatal treatment declined from 31 percent in 1993 to 14 percent by 1998. The rate for men studied went from 46 percent in 1992 to 30 percent in 1998.

Cultural Practices, Beliefs, and Challenges

Nevertheless, there is and has been a high risk of infection due to cultural practices and factors. Consider the following cultural practices and challenges.

1. It is acceptable that the groom's father has sex with the bride. Sometimes other members of the groom's clan may also have sex with the bride and nothing is said. It is possible that these men may have HIV.
2. A widow can be inherited by any of a man's surviving brothers. However, wife inheritance, along with polygamy, has begun to fade owing to HIV/AIDS and exposure to Western culture.
3. A 16-year-old girl said she was "heir" to her aunt. This meant that when her aunt died, she had to marry her uncle (her aunt's husband) and care for his children. Both the aunt and the uncle were HIV positive, and the girl also became infected by her husband-uncle (who also

died) and subsequently infected one of the two sons she bore. She was not promiscuous; it was her duty; it was tradition.

4. Truck drivers stop regularly for sex from women who need the money to feed their families. This, too, is tradition. The women infect their husbands and boyfriends who then infect other women.

5. In rural areas (88 percent of the population), people value appearing wealthy. This includes owning livestock, bicycles, and—still to a degree—multiple wives.

Additional cultural practices may affect communications—particularly religion and sports. Most Ugandans are Christian—Catholics and Protestants primarily, but some are Pentecostals. Sudanic people in the West Nile region (one of four main linguistic lines) are primarily Muslim.

Strategies and tactics have had to be developed to change traditions and alter tribal culture.

Strategy

Some say Uganda used the "ABC" strategy to prevent the sexual transmission of HIV. "A" stands for abstain, "B" stands for be faithful, and "C" stands for condomize. The use of ABC as a slogan seems to have originated in Botswana, but Uganda did use the elements of the ABC approach in its successful program.

There are various definitions of the ABC approach. UNAIDS, the United Nations AIDS agency, defines "A" as abstinence or delaying first sex, "B" as being safer by being faithful to one partner or by reducing the number of partners, and "C" as correct and consistent use of condoms for sexually active young people, couples in which one partner is HIV positive, prostitutes and their clients, and anyone engaged in sexual activity with partners who may have been exposed to HIV. The President's Emergency Plan for AIDS Relief (PEPFAR) defines "A" as abstinence for youth until marriage, "B" as being tested and being faithful in marriage and monogamous relationships, and "C" as correct and consistent use of condoms for those with high-risk behaviors. The latter includes prostitutes, substance abusers, and couples in which one partner has HIV, but does not include youth in general.

The government of Uganda launched a media campaign aimed primarily, but not exclusively, at youth. They were encouraged to abstain from sex if they were virgins and to return to abstinence if they were sexually active. Persons who were sexually active, whether married or not, were encouraged to adopt a policy of "zero grazing," which means staying with one partner and not having casual sex. Those who would not or felt they could not abstain were encouraged to use condoms. All the population—not just youth—were encouraged to use condoms.

Tactics

An aggressive media campaign was launched. Radio broadcast the message and the urgency. Rallies were held; posters were put up in key spots. Teachers were trained to educate students on HIV and AIDS. Community leaders and faith-based organizations, especially churches, were encouraged to work with the government in getting citizens to reduce the increase of HIV cases and eliminate the tradition of death.

Messages were drafted differently to impress different groups, depending on their cultures and needs and their ability to comply. Discussion groups were organized to answer questions and to hear challenges. Questions regarding fear and stigma of having the disease were anticipated and addressed so that people would not hesitate to be checked and treated.

A television medical drama, *Centre 4*, was produced and aired in 13 episodes. Aimed at men and women aged 18–36, the production aired in 2002. An audience of 110 million in Uganda and 20 other African countries could see the drama. HIV/AIDS and other crucial health issues such as malaria immunization and safe childbirth were explored in the storylines. The initial design began with a workshop for representatives of the Uganda Ministry of Health (MOH) and other health organizations. Mediae (a television production company) and Johns Hopkins University Center for Communications Programs collaborated on the production.

In 2001, flyers publicizing the TV drama were distributed in Uganda seeking persons to apply for training positions as scriptwriters, directors, sound technicians, camera operators, editors, and other production staff members. Also in the same year, profiles of the main characters and storylines were developed for each of the episodes. Three Ugandan scriptwriters participated, as well as health specialists from MOH.

Communication through personal and social networks of friends and family was dominant as far back as 1989. Aunts and other relatives were instrumental in talking to young girls and in creating a dialogue about sexual behaviors and HIV.

Religious leaders and faith-based organizations served as educators and developed prevention activities early in the fight.

Population Services International (PSI), based in Washington, DC, launched clubs for Uganda university women called Go Getters, in 2004. The clubs worked with 669 women in their first year at three universities and used 60 peers to encourage the women to gain confidence in themselves and to set long-term goals. There were presentations by women who were role models. Employment opportunities were revealed, as well as information on how to get the skills for those jobs. Internships were offered. More than 40 girls found employment as a result of the Go Getters clubs.

Numerous workshops and websites were organized for key publics. One was an AIDS website competition involving 60 Ugandan schools. Teachers participated in workshops in Cape Town, South Africa, and Washington, DC. AIDS orphans were offered a workshop to help them learn to generate income and entrepreneurship skills. There were many other workshops.

Uganda used between 80 million and 100 million condoms annually. Safe sex and the use of free condoms was widely considered the reason for the success of the prevention program that helped reduce rates from as high as 30 percent of the population in the early 1990s to about 6 percent in 2005. However, a 1995 study showed that 48 percent of men and women in Uganda reported that they stuck to one partner; 11 percent of women and 14 percent of men said they stopped all sex; and 2.9 percent of men and 12.5 percent of women said they had started using condoms. If this study is accurate and if it is representative of the entire country, it means that the success of the campaign was not based on condoms but on abstinence or being faithful.

Under U.S. President George W. Bush's Presidential Emergency Plan for AIDS Relief, Uganda was funded by about $31.8 million. The cornerstone of the Bush prevention strategy was the promotion of sexual abstinence, not safe sex. The Ugandan First Lady, Janet Museveni—said to be an extremely conservative evangelical Christian—attacked the use of condoms and those who distribute them. After years of success, there was a fear that condom use would become restigmatized, according to the Center for Health and Gender Equity.

In October 2005, a condom shortage in Uganda was reported. Apparently both the U.S. government and the Uganda government had allowed the condom supplies to decrease. A reported 32 million quality-approved condoms remained impounded in government warehouses. AIDS activists in Uganda wrote a letter to the MOH claiming that for more than a year, access to condoms had decreased dramatically and that programs should embrace a full range of HIV prevention (condoms) instead of focusing only on abstinence.

Virgin Scholarships

In 2005, a Ugandan lawmaker, Sulaiman Madada, proposed a plan to promote a new morality among young girls in the Kayunga district of Uganda. This district has one of the highest HIV/AIDS infection rates in the country. Girls who could prove they were virgins would have their university fees paid by him.

Madada said his purpose was to counteract the attraction of young girls who see sex as a way out of poverty. One 13-year-old girl said that an older man had offered to take care of her in return for sex. Because she owned only "one dress and one knickers," she said she was "thinking about it. I want to take a sugar daddy and just go. I need someone to take care of me." Her mother, who had been forced into marriage at 15, wanted her daughter to stay in school and said, "Don't go to the old men."

Said Madada, "Our area has high incidences of early marriage and defilement and sugar daddies." He said he hoped the program would grow and help steer young women away from sexual arrangements that could ruin their lives and often cause their deaths.

Government billboards went up reading, "Saving yourself for marriage is the right thing to do." Posters in schools read, "Beware of sugar daddies." The United States gave Uganda grants to promote abstinence.

The scholarships were offered to teenaged girls who could prove their virginity through gynecological exams. This stipulation caused some concern among Ugandans who say the virginity tests are not always accurate and that if girls fail them, they may be ostracized. Other critics say the testing is traumatizing and could stigmatize girls who have been raped.

Billboards, television and radio spots, wristbands, and viral text messages encourage people to be "Reliable, Exceptional and Dependable." The campaign pushes for what they call "passionate fidelity ambassadors." Supporters wear something red to signal their backing of the program, titled "Go Red."

Another program encourages those infected to secure the future of their children by teaching them to write wills and record information, advice, and other messages for their children. Older children are trained to care for younger siblings and to manage households. This program is challenging because in many places, it is taboo to discuss death.

The Stay Negative Campaign is aimed at encouraging people to protect themselves and their partners. It advocates conversation and being tested, and it distributes free condoms. All of this is communicated through popular music and through leaders' speeches with the theme "Get Tested. Stay Healthy. Stay Negative."

Strategy and Tactics Since 2010

Uganda's president, Yoweri Museveni, in 2014, signed into law the HIV and AIDS Prevention and Control Act which criminalizes the transmission of HIV and enforces mandatory testing. Museveni and his wife were tested for HIV in public to encourage all Ugandans to do the same.

Botswana

Botswana is one of the countries hardest hit by the AIDS pandemic, largely because the disease was ignored for so many years. As of 2011, there were an estimated 300,000 living with HIV/AIDS, or one-quarter of the population aged 15 and over. There have been positive changes in that the life expectancy rose to 53 years from 49 in 2002. New infections declined by 71 percent between 2002 and 2011.

Cultural Practices, Beliefs, and Challenges

1. Women feel that they do not have the power over their husbands to control decisions about sexuality. They also feel pressured to conform to tradition by their parents, their in-laws, and the elders in their tribes.
2. Traditional healers use herbal medicines and charms and provide widely respected alternatives to modern medicine.
3. Many skilled health professionals in Botswana have taken jobs elsewhere—many in the United States, where there was a shortage of nurses and considerably higher salaries and benefits. Consequently, 90 percent of the physicians are from other countries and do not speak Setswana, the primary local language. English is the official language of government and education, but more people speak Setswana. The foreign physicians also do not understand the culture of the country.

Positive Conditions

1. Independent newspapers have freedom of the press and wide circulation, an opportunity for communications. Also, schools receive copies of the *Daily News* from the government.
2. In 1987, school fees were eliminated for primary and secondary schools, so education is offered to most children, making the schools a good source of AIDS education.

AIDS Strikes Silently

The first case in Botswana was reported in 1985, and at that time AIDS was considered essentially a male homosexual disease affecting people elsewhere. In the late 1980s, screening of blood through blood transfusion was instituted. From 1989–1997, information about how the disease is spread was circulated, but the target public was still not focused. President Festus Mogae and his government developed the Botswana National Policy on AIDS.

The government adopted the ABC approach (see "Uganda" in this chapter) and had billboards reading "Avoiding AIDS disease is as easy as Abstain, Be Faithful, Condomize." Posters and billboards were plentiful all over Botswana. One health official said, "The country has been bombarded with HIV messages, but there hasn't been a change in behavior." The problem was the publics who needed to be targeted by the slogan did not understand what it meant and it was not clear what publics were targeted. The disease became known as the "radio disease" because people heard about it on the radio but paid no attention. HIV and AIDS were spreading while Botswana was not looking.

Between 1997 and 2002, there was an effort to identify key publics after realizing the disease affected all levels of society. Botswana was the first African country to provide ARV to its citizens. The government of Botswana is credited with lessening the stigma because it supports free ARV therapy and the Prevention of Mother to Child Transmission (PMTCT) program. In the latter, mothers go into ARV therapy, and their infants are provided with formula so that the women will not breastfeed and thereby pass the virus to the babies.

By the end of 2004, more than 35,000 Botswanans were receiving ARV drugs thanks to organizations such as the Bill and Melinda Gates Foundation and the Merck Company; each committed to $50 million through the African Comprehensive HIV/AIDS Partnership (ACHAP). ACHAP is a collaboration between the Gates Foundation, Merck, and the government of Botswana.

Tactics

Botswana has had at least two television shows with AIDS prevention themes. One is the show *Talk Back*, a product of the Botswana Ministry of Education and its Teacher Capacity Building (TCB). It is a one-hour weekly program broadcast live that features interactivity between teachers and viewers through phone-ins, email, and letters. The show includes a documentary or video clip on HIV/AIDS shot in different areas of Botswana in Setswana and in English. This makes the show a countrywide participation show. Then, there is further interaction and feedback through workshops and seminars at various education sites around the country.

Another weekly television show is *Re Mmogo* (meaning "We are together in this"), which is an educational HIV/AIDS awareness program. It reveals and examines new approaches to win the war against the disease and tackles issues that might contribute toward positive behavior change. The show hopes to further destigmatize the disease.

There is also a radio drama, *Makgabaneng*. It is similar to a soap opera in the United States, and the characters were developed to draw the listener into wanting to know what happened to them next. The characters lived in a small town where one-third of the inhabitants are HIV positive. The HIV storyline was introduced gradually, so listeners would be so engaged in the dramatic entanglements of the characters that they would not realize there was a hidden lesson. It was a sneaky but effective method of getting listeners to pay attention, and the 100 episodes of the drama were therefore a combination of entertainment and education.

Stellar among the programs in Botswana is a beauty pageant called "Miss HIV Stigma Free." All the contestants are women who are HIV positive and of a variety of sizes, shapes, and ages. The winners are seen as spokespersons and a symbol of the fact that a full life is possible even with AIDS. The pageant is featured on CNN and the BBC each year, and is a model for other African countries.

The Youth Health Organisation (YOHO) is a non-governmental organization (NGO) that provides sex education through school plays and other Botswana-specific AIDS-related materials. Discussions about prevention, living with AIDS, and caring for AIDS patients were encouraged by improving the knowledge of teachers, who could thereby help to take the mystery and stigma out of the fight against AIDS. This meant challenging cultural beliefs and traditions.

Peer education was a strategy in getting males and females to buy condoms. These sessions were set up at shopping malls, night spots, fairs, and festivals, as well as schools.

"Know Your Status" was a campaign to get Botswanans aged between 18 and 49 to be counseled and/or tested voluntarily. Many centers in convenient places were provided for this service; results were immediate and confidential. The target public learned about the centers from bus stop signs, print ads, billboards, banners, and radio programs. Between 2000 and 2003, 65,000 citizens used the centers. Botswana was therefore the first country in Africa to have national voluntary routine HIV tests.

Educational videos were released to educate citizens about the impact of ARV drug therapy. They were shown to patients in waiting rooms and in presentations at hospitals and clinics, thereby reaching HIV-positive patients and families of HIV patients. Approximately 90 percent of patients in the drug regimen adhered to it, so the videos did their job.

The "Get-Involved" campaign used mass media to facilitate behavior change. It called for ads at bus shelters; the ads showed photographs of persons engaged in high-risk behavior, with Botswanan proverbs and a hotline number giving the target audience an opportunity to call and get help or to volunteer to help. Volunteers received training in how to be grassroots counselors. They distributed condoms and informational materials.

The Botswana government developed a campaign to circumcise 500,000 men by 2012 and an additional 460,000 by 2014, which, according to the *Journal of the International AIDS Society*, will prevent nearly 70,000 new HIV cases by 2025. The campaign is publicized through television and radio advertisements to encourage circumcision at local clinics.

The National MCP (Multiple and Concurrent Partnership) Campaign was proposed in 2009 with the goal of an AIDS-free generation with zero infections (new) in 2016. The campaign targets young women, ages 18–24, who are engaged in MCP for personal or material gain; men, 25–35, engaged in MCP for sexual variety; and cross-generational sexual partnerships between older men and young vulnerable women.

After gathering data from numerous qualitative studies, it was determined that both deep-seated cultural traditions and modern phenomena are drivers of MCP.

The following are some of the messages designed for the target groups.

- overlapping sexual relationships are risky;
- masculinity is not defined by the numbers of sexual partners one has;
- men must learn to communicate about sex and relationships with their sexual partners rather than seek additional partners;
- young girls must be empowered to refuse sexual advances from older men offering gifts and money;
- girls should be encouraged to seek social support from authorities.

Methods of communicating were to be:

- churches and faith-based organizations;
- community theater and debates;
- mass media spots and jingles;
- peer education;
- small group discussion;
- one-on-one discussion;
- sports, music, and other leisure activities.

New Tactics

UNICEF, the United Nations Children's Fund, granted Botswana TeachAIDS funding to support the development of culturally appropriate and medically accurate HIV/AIDS prevention materials. The goal of the project is to reach persons not aware of their status. The people seem to have HIV fatigue, so there is an effort to make more interesting and engaging teaching materials. The project targets learners from 6–24 years of age in schools, churches, after-school programs, village outreach programs, and boys' and girls' clubs.

Zambia

Zambia, in the heart of subequatorial Africa, has some of the world's most devastating statistics about HIV/AIDS. Out of its population of 11 million, 1 in every 6 adults is infected. More than 14.3 percent of the population was HIV positive in 2009, or 1,100,000 Zambians. More than 600,000 children are orphans.

Unlike other countries with high incidence of the disease, HIV does not merely affect the underprivileged; there is a high rate among the wealthy.

The country's first reported AIDS case was in 1984. By the end of 2003, 89,000 had died and 820,000 were living with the disease or the infection. Most of the victims were female. Life expectancy at birth is less than 40 years. The deceased left 630,000 orphaned children. Half the population is under 15, and 85,000 children are infected.

Unlike many countries in Africa, Europe, and the West, most Zambians with the disease are not the underprivileged and uneducated. Numerous teachers and other educated professionals have the virus. Nevertheless, there are great numbers of poor, uneducated Zambians who are in need of information and training on how to manage their lives with HIV.

Cultural Practices, Beliefs, and Challenges

As in other African countries, most HIV infections in Zambia result from unprotected sex. There are numerous cultural practices that compound the prevention problem; following are some of them.

1. Gender inequity prevails. Women and girls are expected to be submissive. Older women teach young girls, sometimes through song and dance, how to please their husbands. The bride learns to obey and cannot refuse her husband sex, even if she knows he is HIV positive. If women are infected, they can and do infect their unborn children and are stigmatized by the community for promiscuity even if their husbands had the disease first.
2. Extended families exist in which a father's brothers are also considered fathers and a mother's sisters are also considered mothers. All of the children of these extended fathers and mothers are considered as sisters and brothers, not cousins as U.S. culture dictates. The father is the traditional head of the family, but if the father must work out of town, it is not unusual for women to head the household. Often while striving to survive under dire circumstances, guidance in how to prevent disease is lacking. Sometimes, if AIDS has taken adults in the family, the older children head the household.
3. Many Zambians mix indigenous beliefs with the practice of Christianity or Islam. Approximately 80 percent of Zambians are Christians and about 10 percent are Muslim. A smaller number practice only indigenous beliefs; among them witchcraft remains strong, especially in villages.
4. Sex for sale is prominent in Zambia. Nearly one-third of the male population has had sex with prostitutes. Nearly one-fifth of the female population has sold sexual favors as a regular way of living or for occasional needs of money. Truck driving, a popular occupation in Zambia, causes drivers to be away from home for long periods. Some are HIV positive and engage in temporary relationships and spread the disease.
5. Soccer is the most important sport. Zambians play mankala, a strategy game with marbles and stones. Church activities are important in rural areas (60 percent of the population).

6. Zambians value education, but often cannot afford to send children to school. The government pays teachers' salaries, but parents must buy uniforms and books.
7. Television is available in cities and large towns. Rural areas get radio, and much news is passed by word of mouth. Newspapers are not distributed in rural areas, but if someone gets one, it is passed around.

In the late 1980s, Zambia began an aggressive educational campaign (Figure 8.2). The slogan, "Sex thrills, but AIDS kills," was circulated on posters and pamphlets. The warnings were out there, but many misconceptions remained, including the following.

1. HIV/AIDS cannot be avoided;
2. mosquitoes carry the virus;
3. the virus and disease come from witchcraft or sorcery, and it is imperative to find out who is responsible;
4. sharing a meal with an HIV-positive person will put one at risk;
5. people who get HIV have "weak blood."

The challenge is to change attitudes and behaviors to curtail the spread of the infection and to teach Zambians how to have responsible sexual

Figure 8.2 In Zambia, signs remind people that children become victims when their parents die of AIDS even if the children have not been infected. Millions of orphaned children in southern Africa have been left parentless after both parents die of the disease.

Source: Louise Gubb / Corbis Historical via Getty Images

relationships. Because much of the population is under 15, children are a primary public. The Ministry of Education was slow to get started with the campaign, but in recent years, there has been an effort for more support. There are problems involved. One is that 72 languages are spoken in Zambia and AIDS-related materials must be translated into these languages and into Braille. Another problem is that if parents cannot afford school uniforms and books, only the oldest boy goes to school, so often girls, the main victims of HIV/AIDS, are not in school to see and hear the warnings and advice.

The third problem is that many teachers and school officials have the virus or the disease. Teachers once threatened a strike because they did not get their paychecks. Of the two government officials responsible for payroll, one was ill from an AIDS-related illness and the other was attending the funeral of a colleague who had died from the disease. These problems create a crisis within the crisis because schools are often the best way to reach uninfected youth and to persuade them to reject old ways of life and accept new attitudes.

Tactics

A study of how Zambians acquired information about sexual warnings, HIV, and AIDS reveals that most found out from friends, family, overheard conversations, gossip, and word of mouth—not from schools. So AIDS activists in Zambia determined that they must reach the youth through means beyond the school chalkboard.

There was a stigma attached to those who are known to have the virus, so many people were afraid to take the tests. Some had the virus and were unknowingly exposing others to it. Then, two well-known politicians—former President Kenneth Kaunda and Vice President Nevers Mumba—consented to take the HIV tests publicly. Both tested negative. This inspired others to take the test, learn their status, and, if necessary, seek confidential counseling and treatment.

Television, radio, and the press were used for people in cities and large towns, but only radio is available in rural areas. In those areas, interactive sessions using music and drama or role-playing or group discussions were organized.

Anti-AIDS clubs organized by both schools and outside organizations were used with 25,000 students. In these clubs, games, dramas, and role-playing were used to get the points across. Organizations also used trained peer educators to work with street children, commercial sex workers, and the military.

The Washington, DC-based organization PSI implemented a prevention program called Corridors of Hope in 35 African nations, including Zambia. The intention was AIDS prevention by the social marketing of condoms. Activities centered on prostitutes, truckers, informal traders, uniformed officials, and adolescent girls. Zambia's Society for Family Health promoted the program and made efforts to remove the stigma attached to the use of condoms. The condoms were promoted as part of a very successful safe sex awareness campaign through radio, television, print, and outdoor advertising. Large musical events such as "Chirundu Live" delivered the message about prevention and the use of condoms. The show was so successful that it expanded to other cities in Zambia.

At the end of 2007, 46 percent of the 330,000 people who needed antiretroviral drugs were receiving them. But nearly two-thirds of youth, ages 15–24, could not identify ways of preventing HIV, nor could they reject misconceptions about HIV transmission. Only 28 percent of Zambians aged 15–49 knew their status. Education of youth is considered the "window of hope" for Zambia.

There are conflicts over whether young people should be told about condoms at all. Many say abstinence should be the goal until they marry. Consequently, there are many campaigns to persuade youth that condoms do not work.

In 2005, the Zambian government admitted it does not encourage mandatory testing as suggested by Zambia's National AIDS Council (NAC), but it did agree to encourage voluntary testing and routine testing for at-risk patients.

In April, 2009, the NAC launched an organizational website aimed at disseminating information on HIV/AIDS to stakeholders. Health Deputy Minister Mwendoi Akakandelwa hopes to better address concurrent sexual partners, discordant couples, male circumcision, and men having sex with men. It is believed that Zambians will feel this site is more credible to their culture than external sites.

In 2007, evidence was revealed that condom ads and radio and television programs on family planning and HIV were successful in reaching large numbers of Zambians. The results also show that condom campaigns were more effective for males than females.

Also in 2007, a radio serial drama *Gama Cuulu* was launched in the Southern Province. The drama is managed by the U.S. Centers for Disease Control and Prevention (CDC) and is funded by the U.S. President's Emergency Plan for AIDS Relief (PEPFAR). The show encourages listeners to adopt safer behaviors and to encourage and to talk more openly about HIV/AIDS issues. With a script in the chiTonga language, it has six main characters who face hurdles as they strive to practice healthy behavior.

New Strategies and Tactics

The country waged one of the more aggressive and innovative educational campaigns. In 2012, a program was instituted called the U-Report which permits the Zambian people to sign up to get information about their HIV status via a mobile phone. A video first explains how the program works and thereby gives people privacy. At the end of 2011, 82 percent of 510 persons needing ARV treatment were receiving it. The goal was to make that number 100 percent.

South Africa

The first two official deaths from AIDS in South Africa were recorded in 1982. In 2009, 5–7 million were living with HIV and AIDS, more than in any other country. In 2012, an estimated 6.1 million people were living with HIV, with 240,000 South Africans dying from AIDS-related illnesses. One-fifth of South African women of reproductive age are living with HIV.

The country is the worst affected because of several factors. Among them are the following: poverty and unemployment, low status of women; high mobility (mostly migrant labor), what persons in the West would call sexual promiscuity, the legacy of apartheid, stigma and discrimination, misconceptions about HIV/AIDS, cultural beliefs and practices, and lack of leadership. Educational organizations say there are difficulties delivering prevention services to sex workers due to police harassment.

There is a high prevalence among men who have sex with men, which makes up an estimated 9.9 percent of new infections. There is also a high rate among sex workers which accounts for 19.8 percent of new infections.

Ex-President Thabo Mbeki, unlike presidents of most countries in sub-Saharan Africa, did not lead the fight against the disease. He is reported to have said that widely used anti-AIDS drugs are "poison," that prevention and treatment programs are plots by the West to eliminate Black Africans, and that AIDS might not be caused by HIV.

Making the fight against HIV more difficult to understand, Roman Catholic bishops from South Africa, Botswana, and Swaziland—all hit hard by AIDS—held a semi-annual meeting in South Africa in 2001. Realizing that the Pope disapproved of condoms, the bishops' purpose for meeting was to determine whether they would approve the use of condoms for AIDS prevention. After five days of closed-door meetings, they emerged and announced that promotion of condoms was immoral, that condoms undermined abstinence and marital fidelity and that condoms might even spread the disease. Most South Africans are Christians, so this was shattering. This was doubly shattering and shocking to AIDS prevention activists, because the Catholic Church provides more direct care for AIDS patients and their loved ones than any other institution. Churches were urged by proponents of condoms to not speak of condoms in a negative manner.

In 2002, former U.S. president Jimmy Carter and Bill Gates, Sr. (the father of Microsoft's Gates) went to South Africa and offered Mbeki what Carter called "a chance to be a hero instead of a villain" through introducing antiretrovirals for treatment and adopting a prevention plan. Carter and Gates expressed disappointment with their meeting. Mbeki said the ARV drugs were too expensive, difficult to take, and dangerous, and that South Africa was and should be more concerned about poverty that still remained after white rule ended.

In August 2003, activists at the opening of a national AIDS conference in Durban, South Africa, jeered the country's health minister, Tshabalala-Msimang, yelling, "Shame on you!" They displayed signs and placards reading "Save Our Youth, Save Our Future, Treat AIDS Now." Tshabalala-Msimang said that she advocated a diet of beetroot, olive oil, African potato, and garlic for HIV victims. She became known as Dr. Beetroot. Mbeki told the *Washington Post* that he didn't know anybody who had died of AIDS. In late 2003, the Mbeki government made a decision to initiate a HIV/AIDS program that included the distribution of free ARV drugs, yet critics say it was late—too late.

Cultural Practices, Beliefs, and Challenges

Even with the plan to use the antiretroviral drug, the challenges—mostly cultural—remained. Among them were the following.

1. Men are socialized to believe that women are inferior, and women are socialized to be submissive, meaning they have no power to insist on condoms or to refuse sex at all.
2. Abstinence and monogamy are often considered unmanly. Violence against women is manly.
3. A South African woman has a 1 in 3 chance of being raped, so the country has the highest sexual violence statistics in the world. Genital injuries resulting from forced sex increase the likelihood of HIV infection.
4. Women who have no male partners are the lowest in the class system. This encourages women with abusive husbands to keep them at any cost. Also, women who have "too much knowledge" about sex are considered immoral. So, if a woman insists on the use of condom, she is either considered too informed or suspected of having an extramarital affair.
5. The early fight against HIV/AIDS was lost while South Africans fought against apartheid, which was a longtime issue and a passion for most Black South Africans. Blacks comprise 77 percent of the population. When Nelson Mandela was freed and the country erupted in celebration as he became president, HIV infections were growing rapidly.

6. Millions of men work as miners in a migrant workers program left over from apartheid, during which the government relied on cheap Black labor. Away from home for long periods of time, the men live in hostels and are given easy access to commercial sex workers and little access to condoms. They are infected by the virus and then go home and pass it to their wives.

7. Homosexuals are subject to violent attacks, so few admit their sexual preference or identity and are fearful of seeking protection or treatment.

8. About 80 percent of South Africans consult traditional healers and use traditional health remedies. These healers treat symptoms successfully—though temporarily—and claim to have cured their patient.

Tactics

Various organizations, both external and internal, are engaged in crisis communications tactics. Some of the communications are through the mass media, but in many cases the publics targeted do not have access to the broadcast media or newspapers, especially in countries with high rates of poverty, so organizations must strive to find the best method to deliver their messages to the segments of the broad public that will benefit.

The following are some of the tactics used.

1. The government made efforts to integrate traditional healers into the national healthcare system. This was necessarily one-on-one communication, as well as getting community organizations to work with the healers in counseling, testing, and promoting good nutrition. Later, some of the healers even recommended patients to clinic workers and vice versa. This effort shows signs of sustained success, although the battle is not won.

2. The Medical Research Council set up free HIV testing and free condoms for miners. Couples counseling was offered, as well as education awareness and ARV treatment. Mining companies are being urged to make family-friendly housing so that families may remain close.

3. Former South African President Nelson Mandela went public in 2005 and announced that his 54-year-old son had died of AIDS. This was considered a brave move because use of the term AIDS was taboo. Associates of Mandela, 86 at the time, said he knew of his estranged son's illness but refrained from discussing it openly, though he visited his son in hospital. He said, "We must not hide." Later in 2005, Mandela began a "46664" (his number during his 27 years in prison) anti-AIDS campaign. He was MC of a pop concert in Norway attended by more than 15,000 people and held to benefit the AIDS fight. Musical celebrities from around the world entertained.

4. To reach persons worried about stigma, the International Cricket Council and its players in South Africa embarked in 2004 on a series of activities designed to help reduce the stigma attached to the epidemic. They wore red ribbons as a sign of solidarity and were joined by cricket players from Australia, West Indies, England, Sri Lanka, India, and Pakistan. On their HIV/AIDS Awareness Day, the players visited an AIDS center and garnered attention from the news media.

5. Another program utilized the mass media. An estimated 99 percent of South Africans have access to radio, 75 percent have access to television, and 7 percent read newspapers. As many as 69 percent of young people (40 percent of the population is under 20) watch television five or more days per week. Consequently, a national campaign using television, billboards, newspapers, and magazines was launched. Knowing South African youth are attracted to American culture, sexy ads and branding techniques were used to advocate LoveLife, a lifestyle that is cool and hip and safe. The images were like those on a rap album and were designed to compete for attention with products such as Coca-Cola or Levi's. Slogans that encouraged teens to discuss sex with their families were also included. Nelson Mandela endorsed the campaign; critics said the ads were too sophisticated or too subtle. Research determined that young South Africans recognized the effort, and of those, two-thirds said they have delayed or abstained from sex as a result.

In 2009, there were more than 5.7 million HIV/AIDS cases in South Africa, with as many as 1,800 reported daily, and 900 deaths daily. New infections among mature age groups in South Africa are still high, but infections among teenagers seemed on the decline in 2009.

A study by the Harvard School of Public Health in 2008 revealed that the South African government could have prevented 365,000 AIDS deaths in the early years of this century if it had provided antiretroviral drugs. This failure resulted from President Thabo Mbeki's and Minister of Health Tshabalala-Msimang's denials that HIV causes AIDS.

In 2008, President Mbeki resigned and was replaced by Kgalema Motlanthe, who was to complete Mbeki's term, due to end in May, 2009. He hired Tshabalala-Msimang ("Dr. Beetroot") as Minister in the Presidency. Jacob Zuma was elected president in May, 2009. He promised a new era in the fight against the disease and to expand testing and treatment for HIV/AIDS.

In 2008, at least 90 percent of people carried a mobile phone—and that number was increasing, so Project Masiluleke was set up to send text messages by the millions and in all 13 of the country's languages to increase HIV/AIDS awareness, testing, and treatment. Pilot projects saw immediate results with a decided increase in the numbers of calls to the National AIDS Helpline.

Local celebrities Sipho "Hotstix" Mabuse, Seiphemo Rapulana, soccer star Shoes Moshoeu, and comedian Kenneth Nkosi participated in a roundtable discussion at the fourth Southern African AIDS conference in 2009, and agreed to urge their peers to help spread the messages of HIV prevention and safe sex.

In 2009, the Khuza Award, determined by a vote of 3,000 youth aged 8–22, went to the animated campaign "Scrutinize" and HIV prevention programs. The Khuza is South Africa's biggest research-based youth marketing and communications award. Young people indicated they love the humorous ads, and the campaign also had a high "talkability" factor.

A survey asking men to tap answers into a PalmPilot device revealed that 1 in 4 men in South Africa admitted to rape and confessed to attacking more than one victim. The Medical Research Council of South Africa says the responses were very frank and provide hope that this may be a first step in changing the culture where sexual entitlement of men is rooted in the ideal of manhood.

Strategies and Tactics Since 2010

Voluntary male circumcision became a drive because research showed that this can reduce the risk of HIV transmission up to 60 percent. A report showed a 76 percent reduction in the risk of HIV infection for circumcised men compared to uncircumcised men. The goal was to offer the procedure to all HIV-negative men aged 15–49. By 2011, more than 150,000 operations had been conducted.

"Soul City" and "Soul Buddyz"—two government multimedia campaigns targeting adults and children, respectively—continued to broadcast TV and radio drama in prime time. "Soul City" is widely regarded as the leading course of information on HIV and AIDS in South Africa, reaching 72 percent of the viewing public. "Soul Buddyz" reached 67 percent of 6–12-year-olds (about four million children) and was judged to be the most successful TV show produced in South Africa.

Khomamanih, an AIDS program launched by the Department of Health, used situational sketches on TV and announcements on radio to reduce the rate of new infections by 50 percent.

Zimbabwe

About 15 percent of the population in Zimbabwe lives with HIV/AIDS, but incidence seems to be on the decline—in fact, by 50 percent between 2001 and 2011. Still, in 2011, there were one million children orphaned by parents dying who had the disease. Average life expectancy is 53.

Zimbabwe also suffered other crises—a severe cholera epidemic, a stressful political and social climate, a severe rise in inflation, and high rates of unemployment.

Children orphaned by AIDS number more than 980,000, and 120,000 children are living with HIV infection. Of the total of all hospital admissions, 70 percent are HIV related. Infection rates are highest for people aged 25 or under, especially teenagers and women who are most vulnerable.

HIV/AIDS activists, attempting to be as optimistic as possible, say that although 25 percent of the population is infected, 75 percent of the population is HIV negative, and it is these people they need to reach with safe sex and abstinence programs.

Cultural Practices, Beliefs, and Challenges

There are sociological findings that contribute to the challenges. Among them are the following:

1. The population is largely Christian and more Roman Catholic than any other denomination. The Vatican is opposed to condoms, and many of the people are therefore confused as to whom to believe.
2. English is the official language of the educated population, but people in rural areas speak in their native languages—usually Shona and Ndebele. Many healthcare workers cannot speak those languages.
3. The country is crippled by drought, a shortage of food, unemployment, and poverty. Concern about a confusing and mysterious disease is not as urgent as having food to eat.
4. The meaning of the term "be faithful" is difficult to comprehend. Being faithful to one person is only effective if one's partner is also faithful and uninfected. The culture in Zimbabwe has long permitted men—but not women—to have multiple sexual partners. Also, young people consider faithfulness to mean dating one person at a time—no matter how frequently one relationship may follow another. Actually, this is also a source of confusion in the United States. When the advice is that people with multiple sex partners are more likely to be infected, many do not realize that if the one partner they have sex with in their entire lives is HIV positive, they might be infected, too.
5. The school system is a major center of fighting the virus in Zimbabwe and a major center of the crisis. Teachers are the career group with the highest infection rate, so they are not effective role models. They have not been adequately trained in coping with HIV/AIDS themselves. Also, sick teachers lose their jobs after excessive absences. Some, therefore, force themselves to meet their classes even when they are chronically ill, so the quality of education also suffers.

6. Long distances between home and school result in some students—especially girls—seeking temporary housing closer to schools. This is called "bush boarding," and it often results in prostitution, which increases the risk of HIV infection. When girls have sex with older men in return for shelter or money, it is called "food for work" or "survival sex."

7. School enrollment levels are also affected because girls—who are more susceptible to the disease—often drop out to care for the sick in their families or they are often unable to pay school fees because of sicknesses in their family, or unemployment or abject poverty.

8. Research shows that persons not in school are five times more likely to have sex than those in school, so children are urged to stay in school not only to get an education that will make them more upwardly mobile but also to learn the lessons of HIV/AIDS.

9. The schools in 80 percent of Zimbabwe, in rural areas, do not have televisions or access to any electricity, so training programs that require electronic equipment are not useful. Urban schools and homes may have television. Most people even in rural areas have radio at home and can comprehend if programs are broadcast in their native languages.

Tactics

The Zimbabwe National Family Planning Council (ZNFPC), with technical assistance from Johns Hopkins University's Population Communication Services, launched a program aimed at getting young people to adopt new behaviors: abstinence or the use of condoms. The campaign was based on the Steps to Behavior Change framework that has five stages: knowledge, approval, intention, practice, and advocacy. Effective communications campaigns determined at which stage the segmented publics would become targets of "approval" campaigns. Once publics approved, they would be targeted by "intention," and so on. Each step led to the next. For example, the youth campaign (for those aged 10–24) was at the knowledge stage and the slogans mentioned in all its activities and printed matter were "Have self-control," "Value your body," and "Respect yourself."

More than 10,000 posters were distributed with slogans such as "You may think you are ready for sex, but are you ready for the consequences?" Leaflets were produced on abstinence, saying "no" to sex, and postponing sex; 19,000 were distributed. Most youth in Zimbabwe had access to radio, so a one-hour radio variety series, *Youth for Real*, was produced and broadcast nationwide weekly. The episodes mixed entertainment such as music and drama with advice. There was also a segment in which listeners could call in and ask questions of counselors or physicians. Two community theater troupes performed interactive dramas daily at schools, churches, and shopping centers. Peer educators were trained to advise people in their own age group, mostly in schools.

Other organizations also joined in with the knowledge and approval stages. The Grassroot Soccer Foundation (GRSF) trained 14 well-known soccer players to educate at-risk youth about HIV/AIDS in nine schools in Bulawayo, Zimbabwe. GRSF targeted seventh-graders to improve their knowledge, attitudes, and perceptions of HIV/AIDS. Students reported that they intended to use their knowledge. The program was completed by 3,000 children.

In an exchange program funded by the American Federation of Teachers, "Teachers Helping Teachers, Combat HIV/AIDS in Africa," teachers from Zimbabwe and Kenya came to the United States for intensive two-week sessions of learning about HIV/AIDS and how it spreads. The teachers from Zimbabwe and Kenya also shared their various experiences with the disease, though Kenya's statistics (a 13.5 percent prevalence rate) were less troubling. They were all encouraged to return home and teach other teachers and students. The same program produced a Zimbabwe publication, *Teacher's Voice*, which also aims to educate teachers about the disease. Each edition explores a basic fact.

To reach the HIV positive in Zimbabwe, PSI received funding from US-AID to do an anti-stigma media program titled, "Don't Be Negative about Being Positive." It was featured on television, radio, newspapers, and posters, beginning in 2005. Persons who are HIV positive are provided with a platform to frankly discuss their situation and to challenge discrimination.

In 2007, Zimbabwe, though still in crisis, had a drop in HIV rates, one of the most significant declines. Despite a high level of awareness, HIV/AIDS remains highly stigmatized in Zimbabwe, but people feel that the stigma is diminishing. The "Don't Be Negative about Being Positive" campaign won the 2005 Global Media Award for its organizers.

The statistics are worse for women than men because of social inequality. According to UNAIDS, in 2006, 60 percent of adults in Zimbabwe with HIV were women. Women are poorer, less educated, and more dependent. Programs that ignore these facts are doomed to fail.

Women's football (soccer) teams made up of openly HIV-positive players are increasing in number. Two top teams are the ARV Swallows and the Sporting ART (ART stands for antiretroviral treatment). They are positive role models because they are open about being infected, and their success in the sport shows how healthy one can be while taking HIV drugs. They distribute literature and male and female condoms at the games; the supply is depleted after every game.

A public health television commercial featuring Davies Mazodze, a college lecturer speaking openly about his HIV status, is a popular mass media campaign and has generated dialogue and discussion about everyone's vulnerability to HIV.

More than 70 barbers and 2,000 hairdressers in Zimbabwe have been trained to provide information about male and female condoms and to sell them. They earn a small commission on all they sell.

In 2009, the Children's Performing Arts workshop in Harare presented a participatory theater production to address issues related to HIV/AIDS and young women. "Act Out: Tackling HIV and AIDS through Theatre Communications" fused theater with discussion to engage the audience. At a high school in St. Augustine, students participated in a workshop run by a Zimbabwe theater group.

One hope for beating the disease is that more and more information may be disseminated online. Internet penetration in Zimbabwe increased from 6.7 percent to 10.9 percent between 2005 and 2008. Most people access the Internet through colleges, schools, cybercafés, workplaces, and some access it at home.

New Strategies and Tactics

Research shows that about half of the people living with HIV were infected during adolescence or young adulthood, so currently, children are taught about the disease in schools. Tests show that half of young people ages 15–24 have knowledge of the disease but that knowledge does not translate into action. Most of them fear learning their result. Others fear depression and suicide, stigma, dying faster, or feeling that they are not at risk.

Young people complained that the testing centers are not youth-friendly, that they are crowded with adults. Consequently, mobile testing facilities visit schools and clinics.

After a clinical trial determined that male circumcision reduced female-to-male transmission of HIV by 50 percent, Zimbabwe's most famous poet, Albert Nyathi, and his son volunteered to be circumcised to encourage others; many men did agree, but the numbers are still not enough to make a difference.

Swaziland

In 2012, the Kingdom of Swaziland still had the highest rate of HIV infection in the world. The first case of AIDS there was reported in 1987. Since then, the disease has spread rapidly.

About one-fourth of the 480,000 adult Swazis are HIV positive out of a total population of 1 million. The age group from 20–30 is the most affected. Out of young people aged 15–19, 29 percent are HIV positive. Of adults aged between 30 and 39, 40 percent tested positive. As many as 42.6 percent of pregnant women tested were HIV positive.

Cultural Practices, Beliefs, and Challenges

1. Unlike some other African countries (such as Uganda), it is still taboo to admit HIV-positive status in Swaziland. Polygamy is still practiced and supported by the royal family, and people still think they can avoid the infection and practice polygamy. In the old tradition, boys are expected to seek sex and girls are expected to comply, but the new environment is beginning to shun that tradition.

2. Research reveals that poverty and culture are the biggest issues in the fight against HIV/AIDS. Swazis are warm people, but they have some lack of trust in foreigners and persons in the political arena.

3. Extended families, headed by the eldest male (usually a grandfather if there is one), make decisions involving the entire family. Adult unmarried children and some married sons remain in the extended family. Women have little voice, but they are beginning to take jobs out of necessity. HIV/AIDS has affected the family structure.

4. Churches and other faith-based organizations are coming forward to help the fight against HIV. Swazis are primarily Christians who mix religious principles and indigenous practices. The goal was to convince churches that AIDS is not about sin.

5. ARV drugs have been introduced, but many health workers fear that HIV prevention is being ignored while treatment is emphasized.

6. Swaziland's National Emergency Response Council on HIV/AIDS (NERCHA) determined through research that when targeting people between the ages of 20 and 30 who had already had sexual experiences, the anti-AIDS effort should concentrate on encouraging self-protection and not on abstinence.

7. The epidemic affects Swazi children in two ways. First, they are orphaned, and then they often contract the disease through child abuse. There was a 50 percent rise in reported cases of incest between 2003 and 2005. This does not mean a drastic increase in cases, but rather that reporting became more acceptable.

8. Protectors were put in place in some urban areas. These were people whom children could trust and could tell them about abusive incidents. The protectors would tell them how to recognize dangers and what to do, and that they did not have to accept abuse—but in villages in rural areas, it was not possible for outsiders to be accepted.

9. The people of this country are very mobile traveling across the country and outside for work. This would include migrant miners who may be away from home as long as a year. Many travel to South Africa to work in mines. Most of these men encounter commercial sex workers.

10. In 2005, Swazi King Mswati III abandoned a campaign to urge girls to remain virgins. The campaign began in 2001 and urged young girls to avoid marriage and remain virginal for five years. It was a modern version of the tradition of "uMcwasho, the badge of the virgin." No reason was given for the king's action, but it is believed that the program was not popular among youth. In a jubilant ceremony, thousands of young girls removed the "virgin tassels" they wore to signify chastity.

Tactics

Billboards and posters were installed by NERCHA in schools, clinics, and libraries, at bus stops, and as full-page ads in newspapers. They showed a confident, smartly dressed professional woman. The message was, "I am not going to share my partner with anybody." The organization's communications director explained, "The woman cannot control what her partner does, but she is warning him that if he does take another girlfriend, he will lose her." It's a message of independence—that a girl can stand up to cultural pressures and say "no" to men despite the cultural pressures.

NERCHA's program is built on the hope that many women will respond as Gcebile did.

A UNICEF representative, Alan Brody, used folklore traditions to communicate with Swazi children aged 12 and older. A story titled, "How the Children of Chakijane Put an End to Brother Snake's Abuse" was first performed by professional actors in churches. Later, children played the roles themselves. The characters in the play are animals; a deceitful snake convinces a rabbit that bedding his 12-year-old daughter is acceptable. There is humor in the play, but the overall effect is devastation. The daughter rabbit dies, the father is banished, and the villagers behead the snake. However, it leads to much more open discussion than real-life abuse can bring about. When done in a village, the discussion often leads to the audience electing a village protector who tells the story to other children from a book published by UNICEF. This way, bonds of trust and resulting communication develop.

The play has been done for various adult groups also—the unemployed, community elders, Christians, male groups, female groups. Each time, the audience can translate the allegory to their own lives.

Posters read, "Be faithful to your polygamous family." If all the partners are faithful to each other, then HIV is not a threat. However, if one partner strays and is infected, all the partners are at risk.

On a visit to Matsapha, Swaziland, in July, 2005, U.S. Global AIDS coordinator Randall Tobias and principal secretary of Swaziland's Ministry of Health and Social Welfare Dr. John Kunene underwent public AIDS testing from a PSI center to show the Swazis how easy the test is.

There was a slight decline when the prevalence rate dropped from 42.6 percent in 2004 to 39.2 percent in 2006. There seems to be conflict among Swazis over whether prevention is possible. Some say condoms are advised; men have them, but they do not use them. The government pushes condoms; community leaders push abstinence. They call condoms "unSwazi."

In 2009, the AIDS Healthcare Foundation (AHF) launched a free "Love Condom" campaign utilizing television and newspapers. There was early indication that those who saw the coverage requested condoms.

In June, 2009, the Partnership Framework on HIV and AIDS was formed. The purpose of this five-year (2009–2013) collaborative effort of the government of the Kingdom of Swaziland and the government of the United States was to provide a strategic agenda to contribute to the PEPFAR goals for prevention, care, and treatment. A key intervention area in the plan called for focusing on better linking mass media approaches with sustained community-based prevention activities.

PEPFAR also launched a "love test" to encourage couples to be tested for HIV as a way of showing love for each other.

New Tactics and Strategies

Polygamy is rampant in Swaziland, as is child marriage. This contributes highly to early sexual experiences and early infections. Though the president has spoken out in favor of taking precautions and getting tested, he has 14 wives and therefore sets a poor example. A spokesman from a civic organization in Swaziland said when Western NGOs put out a message about using condoms, someone will speak on the radio and say, "Don't be silly. Our job is to produce children" (Smith, 2012).

Programs to get newborn boys circumcised have been successful. As many as 78 percent of HIV-infected people can get antiretroviral treatments, so the death rate is decreasing but more people are becoming infected. Campaigns targeting young people through billboards, radio, and print media with slogans like "Because tomorrow is mine" continue.

Conclusion

Worldwide, the HIV/AIDS crisis has not ended; it just happens to be worse in African countries. The essential evaluation of the fight is a measurement of whether there are fewer cases of infections and fewer deaths. This will require years to determine. Earlier positive indications will be celebrated—an increase in the use of condoms and a decrease in the pregnancy rate of young girls, which is a signal of abstinence—and people verbalizing their concern about the crisis and their determination to do something about it.

What Could Have Been Done If Social Media Had Existed

Actually, there is a social media boom in Africa. Many who study Internet usage say there is major shift to mobile Internet use, with social media driving the shift. Facebook, the most popular, was used by 15 percent of the continent's population in 2010. Twitter and YouTube uses also are increasing in number. There were 100 million social media users at the end of 2010, meaning that 1 of every 10 is an Internet user. Prohibitive costs are the primary reasons that the numbers are not greater. Facebook has versions in the major African languages—Swahili, Hausa and Zulu.

African programmers are designing, testing, and launching their own platforms to continue the online conversation. However, even though technology increased methods of communications, this has not affected the battle against the HIV/AIDS epidemic because the challenge is not that people don't know about the disease. They do. It's because they believe they cannot live the lives they think they should and want to live. Warnings of HIV workers conflict with years of traditions and ancient beliefs. How can a 280-character tweet compete with that? Other methods of persuasion and enlightenment must be applied.

Update/Case Study: HIV/AIDS Plus COVID-19, a Syndemic

When COVID-19 spread quickly all over the world early in 2020, people faced with saving their own lives and the lives of their families and friends did not notice how countries far away might be affected. Students who read previous editions of this book followed the HIV/AIDS crisis in Africa but when COVID-19 began to cover the world, people naturally turned their attention to their own survival. The situation is dire.

The continent of Africa, already battling HIV/AIDS, consisted of many communities where people had poor access to treatment which they also could not afford. Misconceptions were abundant; communications to dispel misconceptions were often not available and difficult to understand or not heeded because they were new concepts.

Nevertheless, there was a plan to fight the crisis—but that plan did not include having to fight another pandemic.

UNAIDS, in 2014, set a goal called "90–90–90" which meant that 90 percent of the population of Africa, those living with HIV (PLHIV) would know their status by the year 2020; at the same time, 90 percent of people with knowledge of their infected status would be enrolled in an antiret-roviral therapy (ART), and 90 percent of patients on ART would have a declining viral load. The overall goal was to eliminate new infections and thereby stop the spread.

At the beginning of 2020, it was obvious that the goal would not be reached by all 54 countries. There was progress in getting people to learn their status. In sub-Saharan countries, great strides had been made, but this was not the case in Western and Central Africa.

At this point, testing and treatment had been improved, and follow-up of patients was better organized, but goals had not been reached in most of the countries followed in this text. Only Botswana and Rwanda (not stud-ied in this text) achieved the 90 percent goal. Uganda, Zimbabwe, South Africa, Mozambique, Zambia, and Eswatini (often seen as eSwatini, for-merly Swaziland and renamed in 2018) had not. There were issues in most countries where people continued to fear the stigma of being labeled with the disease. They were afraid of sexual rejection and verbal abuse. they also feared discrimination if their status was revealed. In some countries, there was still sexual violence. Women, following cultural norms, felt duty bound to submit to sexual violence of men, even relatives.

In Zimbabwe, as many as 23 percent of women still believe they do not have the right to ask their sex partner to use a condom. Botswana, an upper middle-class country compared to other countries, lost valuable funding from donors because decisions were made falsely that the country did not need help.

On the positive side, in Eswatini, a free condom distribution titled "Got it. Get it" was somewhat successful. Radio turned out to be a more effec-tive method of persuasion and communication for young people because 95 percent of people have access to radio, while only 21 percent have access to television. Botswana, one of the most affected countries, gained access to free ART. Also a long-running radio drama in Botswana titled "Mak-gabaneng," mentioned earlier in the chapter, continued with themes on faithfulness, treatment, and HIV services. The drama also now outreaches to health fairs and roadshows. Zambia has developed a door-to-door test-ing and mobile outreach program to reduce stigma.

Despite improvement and a decrease in new cases in many African countries, a difficulty to depart from longstanding cultural norms is hard to fight—so UNAIDS, in 2020, reset the goals for "95–95–95" in the same categories: recognizing one's status, enrolling in ART, and getting virally suppressed. These goals must be reached by 2025 to end the spread of AIDS by 2030.

Then COVID-19 hit the continent in March, 2020, in the midst of all the efforts to reach the UNAIDS goals. Then there were two epidemics. Two or more epidemics equal one syndemic, making a greater burden of disease—a syndemic made up of two devastating diseases linked by cultural crises. Adding COVID-19 was a great setback. The new disease demanded social distancing and that did not coordinate with the practice of peer support groups meeting to solve HIV/AIDS infection issues.

When the COVID-19 virus struck the continent of Africa, two-thirds of the total number of persons in the world infected by the HIV/AIDS virus were in Africa.

Cameroon-born Dr. John Nkengasong, director of the African Centers for Disease Control and Prevention (Figure 8.3) noting that the continent had fought HIV-AIDS for more than 40 years and lost more than 37 million people, said "The potential social, health, economic, and security devastation that COVID could cause in Africa should be enough of an incentive for African governments to invest immediately in preparedness for the worst case scenario" (Looming threat of COVID-19 infection in Africa: Act collectively and fast, February 27, 2020). He was able to get 400 million doses of COVID-19 vaccine at a time when the vaccine was hard to get.

Compounding the culture crises, sexual violence—a long-accepted condition that reformers were trying to eradicate—increased because of the stay-at-home mandate of COVID-19. Men were at home for longer periods, so women and girls had to be taught to say "No" to sexual aggression at home.

Some countries, including South Africa and Uganda, had a triple epidemic. Both had to cope with tuberculosis (TB). People living with HIV are 20 percent more likely to develop TB than people without HIV because both are fueled by weakened immune systems. Added to the three-fold

Figure 8.3 Cameroon-American Dr. John Nkengasong, once the chief virologist of the World Health Organization (WHO), headed the battle against COVID-19 in Africa by coordinating with heads of states, including U.S. President Joe Biden.

Source: MICHAEL TEWELDE / AFP via Getty Images

disease is malaria. Thirty-one of the 54 countries have seen increases in malaria cases due to a lack of prescription drugs. Fifteen have an increase of 40 percent: Mozambique, Zimbabwe, and Zambia are among those suffering malaria.

Misinformation also created a greater crisis as people said they "heard" or "saw" that COVID-19 was not able to survive in a tropical climate. Also, some believed certain races would not be affected by the virus. This misinformation was passed around in the United States, but Dr. Anthony Fauci and the CDC quickly disputed this claim—and the death toll backed them up.

It was determined that a healthy attitude toward COVID-19 prevention resulted in fewer cases of HIV, as well.

Following is the HIV status (as of 2021) of the counties studied in this text (AVERT, 2018) and also the constantly changing COVID-19 statistics as reported by the WHO. Many experts feel that the COVID-19 statistics are underestimated because reporting of cases and causes of death were limited due to a lack of resources.

Botswana (with a population of 2,351,627) had 4,100 deaths and 380,000 living with HIV. It has the highest rates of HIV of all African countries but it reached and exceeded the UNAIDS 90–90–90 targets. The country had 329,000 cases of COVID-19, with 2,795 deaths.

Eswatini (with a population of 1,160,164) had 2,600 AIDS-related deaths, and 210,000 known living with HIV/AIDS. More women than men have the disease, and 91 percent of those infected are on ART. This newly named country had 1,422 deaths from COVID-19 and 74,000 additional cases.

South Africa (with a population of 59,308,690) has had 51,000 AIDS-related deaths, 7.5 million infected with HIV, and 1.2 million on ART. South Africa reached the 90–90–90 targets for 2020. This country lost 102,371 and had 257,000 cases of infection of COVID-19.

Uganda (with a population of 45,741,007) had 17,000 AIDS-related deaths, 1.4 million living with HIV, and 1.2 million on ART. The country had 3,630 deaths from COVID-19, and 170,000 cases.

Zambia (with a population of 18,383,955) lost 19,000 to AIDS-related deaths, has 1.3 million living with HIV/AIDS, and 1.2 million on ART. The country lost 4,057 citizens from COVID-19 and had 338,000 cases.

Zimbabwe (with a population of 2,351,627) lost 20,000 to AIDS-related deaths, has 1.3 million with HIV/AIDS, and 1.2 million on antiretroviral treatments. This country lost 5,637 to COVID-19, with 260,000 cases.

The continent of Africa lost more than four million souls to COVID-19 by January 19, 2023.

Case Study: Nut Rage and Korean Airlines

A Korean Air jet bound for Seoul from Kennedy Airport in New York, was moving toward the runway when a junior flight attendant served Cho Hyun-ah macadamia nuts in a plastic bag. This simple incident on December 5, 2014, started the crisis that came to be called "nut rage" all over the world. Three things need to be understood to see this nutty case clearly:

1. Cho Hyun-ah (aka Heather Cho), then 40, was an executive with Korean Airlines. She had earned a bachelor's degree from Cornell University and an MBA from the University of Southern California. She was also key in the family-run conglomerate business that owns and operates Korean Air.
2. The nuts, according to the airline service manual, should not be served unless a customer indicates he/she wants them. Cho didn't ask.
3. Also, according to the manual, the nuts should be served on a plate, not in a bag.

Cho was so alarmed at the poor service that passengers said she erupted loudly, asking, "What kind of service is this? Are you following proper procedure?" When the flight attendant said she was, Cho summoned the purser (who supervises flight attendants) and asked him to check the service manual. When he couldn't find that regulation readily, witnesses said, Cho shouted insults at him and hit him with a binder. A Korean Airlines spokesperson said Cho raised her voice but did not insult. Cho later admitted she shoved the flight attendant. The purser said he and his colleague even kneeled before Cho and that she yelled at the crew to "Stop the plane! I will stop the plane from leaving!"

Cho was determined to return to the airport to oust the purser. The pilot did not disagree with her. And why would he, since Heather Cho was the eldest daughter of the Chairman of Korean Airlines, Cho Yang-ho? Chairman Cho subsequently died, but that's another story in the update to this chapter (See pp. 263–264).

The flight was delayed by 11 minutes. Airline industry experts said the "ramp return" maneuver is only executed when there is an emergency or when the wrong cargo has been loaded. Cho's ranting spread quickly on social media, causing embarrassment for her father and family. The whole world was talking, but no one was as angry as Koreans who were concerned that this was another example of spoiled brats from large conglomerate families.

Apologies Abound

As the furor grew all over the world, Cho stepped down from her corporate post and said she would apologize to the purser and cabin crew involved in the incident. She eventually said, "I beg forgiveness of those who may have been hurt by the actions, and offer my apologies to our customers" (Lee, 2015).

Chairman Cho Yang-ho made a deep bow to the journalists in the crowded lobby of the airline's headquarters. He said he regretted he didn't raise her better. He also said, "I apologize to the people of the country as Chairman of Korean Airlines and as a father for the trouble caused by my daughter's foolish conduct" (Park, 2014, December 12). As for the purser, "I feel greatly sorry for what he underwent and apologize as Korean Air chairman." He further vowed that no disadvantage would befall him (*Korea Times*, 2015, January 30).

Korean Air Public Relations

Korean Air responded to the initial incident by telling the news media that Cho did not insult the purser, but she did raise her voice. Obviously, the announcement followed what Cho told the communicators. It was also announced that Cho had the support of the pilot.

On December 8, a statement "We are sorry about the inconvenience to passengers," was disseminated. It noted that the plane was less than 10 meters from the gate when the decision to return was made.

Bloomberg indicated that two calls to Korean Air headquarters in Seoul seeking comment went to an automated answering service (Park, 2014, December 9). After the incident went viral and the apologies admitting guilt had been made, there wasn't much public relations could say. It couldn't agree or disagree with the widespread public opinion. There was a negative mark on the company name, but it was clearly one person at fault, not the whole company.

Court Hearing and Decision

Heather Cho was taken into custody on December 30, and tried in court for forcing a flight to change its route, obstructing the flight's captain in the performance of his duties, and forcing a crew member off a plane. She was found guilty and ordered to serve a year in prison.

Her lawyer said she deposited considerable sums of Korean currency for the purser and flight attendant "as a sign of her sincerity as she was unable to apologize in person due to her arrest." The purser and flight attendant reportedly refused the money (*The Chosun Ilbo*, 2015).

The cabin crewmembers testified in court that Ms. Cho (Figure 8.4) was "like a beast" who treated them like "feudal slaves" (Nam, 2015). To Koreans in the uproar, family conglomerates, known as *chaebol*, often act above the law. Chaebol leaders convicted of white-collar crimes usually receive suspended sentences and are even often pardoned. The reasoning

Figure 8.4 Cho Hyun-ah, also known as Heather Cho, once a vice-president of Korean Airlines, makes a deep bow of apology, a tradition in Korea. She was also sentenced to a year in prison for having ordered a plane turned back to the gate because flight attendants did not serve macadamia nuts properly. Her father was head of Korean Air.

Source: Chung Sung-Jun via Getty Images

seems to be that these people have made such strides on behalf of the country in making it a recognized economy.

Whang Sang-mi, a psychology professor at Yonsei University, said "Most second or third generations of chaebol in South Korea think of themselves as members of royal families or in a special aristocratic class." The judge said, "If she were considerate to people, if she didn't treat employees like slaves, if she could have controlled her emotion, this case would not have happened" (Picchi, 2014). And she also said, "This is a case where human dignity was trampled upon" (Nam, 2015).

The South Korean news media called Cho a princess and some Koreans said she was an international embarrassment to her country.

Outside of South Korea, this story might have evoked amusement. Passengers in first class on U.S. domestic flights are served warm mixed nuts in a bowl, but the culture of the United States and South Korea are so different that if the nuts showed up in a plastic bag, most passengers might say to the flight attendant, "Oh, you're out of bowls today?" and go right on munching. Actually, passengers on the Korean Air flight might have had the same reaction; it was just Heather Cho who couldn't cope. Passengers in coach on U.S. airlines would be so pleased to be served nuts at all that the situation seems ridiculous.

What this case demonstrates is the importance of professional conduct in dealing with one's associates, subordinates, and customers. In this case, it was even more important because of cultural considerations, such that citizens of Cho's home country were apt to be less forgiving of this outlandish display of social power. Cho's executive position with the airlines, prior to her resignation, involved the oversight of inflight service. Nevertheless, she should not have created a public spectacle that demeaned employees of her organization, even if she did feel superior to them, and violated safety laws. She had other options for correcting what she considering to be inadequate inflight service. Instead, she lost her cool and misused her authority, which ultimately came back to haunt her in the days, weeks, and months following this notoriously heavy-handed "nut rage" incident.

The job of flight attendant, once one of the most popular among job-seekers, has lost its popularity in South Korea. Students at training schools say passengers treat flight attendants like servants and that the Korean Air incident exemplifies that the flight attendant is basically a waitress in the sky. Korean Air was, at one time, the most popular carrier in Asia.

There was a great increase in South Korea in the sales of macadamia nuts after the "nut rage case." It would be difficult to say that the incident made people buy macadamia nuts. Perhaps those who didn't know about them wanted to see what the big deal was. Maybe people who know and like them were reminded about how good they are. At any rate, macadamia nut producers in Australia and Hawaii were presumably pleased.

Update: More Family Rage

Heather Cho was sentenced to two years in prison; she served five months. Her younger sister Cho Hyun-min, or Emily Cho, Korean Air senior vice president, later berated a business associate during a corporate meeting. Some said she threw water on the man's face. She apologized on social media and in email to company employees. The company's unions were not satisfied with the apology.

The father of the sisters, Company CEO Cho Yang-ho (Figure 8.5) announced that the daughters were removed from their executive positions. He said, "I feel miserable by the immature behavior of my daughters" (Puckett, 2018). Koreans say the daughters were merely moved from one executive position to another. Lee Myung-hu, the mother of the Cho daughters, was accused of being verbally and physically abusive to employees. She was also believed to have smuggled luxury items into the country.

Cho Yang-ho was ousted from the board of Korean Air after the series of scandals. He was indicted on a number of charges ranging from embezzlement to tax evasion. The company's reputation was at an all-time low, according to shareholder/activist-turned-lawmaker Chae Yi-bai, who criticized the Cho family for its "czar-like management style" (Yang & Jin, 2019). The elder Cho died in 2019 in a Los Angeles hospital. The cause of

Figure 8.5 Korean Airlines Chairman Cho Yang-ho answered questions from the news media after being charged with tax evasion and other crimes connected to the troubled family business. He died later in a U.S. hospital of natural causes.

Source: JUNG YEON-JE / AFP via Getty Images

death was not revealed in the Twitter announcement, but he was known to have been treated for a lung ailment.

On the positive side for his people, Cho was instrumental in the movement to bring the 2018 Winter Olympics to South Korea. He led the organizing committee and secured the bid in 2011.

The Cho family sparked a social movement "gapjil," an abusive relationship that happens in unequal power relations. South Koreans are calling for an end to it—but the third generation of the Cho family is still a chaebol, as the son Cho Won-tae became president of Korean Air.

Case Study: Yuhan-Kimberly and Baby Wet Wipes

Yuhan-Kimberly is a leading health and hygiene company that manufactures and sells diapers, tissues, sanitary napkins, and wet wipes. The company was established in Seoul, Korea in 1970 as a joint venture of Kimberly-Clark and Korea's Yuhan Corporation. Its major products make up more than 50 percent of the market share in Korea.

SeungWoo Son is public relations manager for Yuhan-Kimberly, and EunWook Lee is vice president.

The 2005 crisis centered on the Yuhan-Kimberly product, Huggies baby wet wipes. Wet wipes were originally classified as a cosmetic product in the United States, Europe, and several Asian countries. Because Yuhan-Kimberly also sells diapers, the wet wipes were marketed in Korea for baby care.

The crisis began March, 2005, when a consumer activist organization discovered through its research that there was formaldehyde in Yuhan-Kimberly wet wipes. It announced its findings through the mass media—newspapers, TV cable channels, and radio—all over Korea.

Son said there was a standard of formaldehyde used in cosmetics, but there were no regulations in place for wet wipes for babies. Yuhan-Kimberly took the position that the wet wipes had only one-tenth of the formaldehyde permitted in cosmetics, and that there was therefore no danger.

Cultural Concern

In order to comprehend Yuhan-Kimberly's position, Son said one must first understand aspects of the Korean culture. The Ministry for Health, Welfare and Family Affairs reveals that the Korean people consider the ideal birth rate to be 2.54 children per family. However, the actual birth rate is lower than what people consider ideal; it is 1.19 children per family. The reasons, according to Son, are financial burdens, including the value and importance of private education and insufficient infrastructure for childcare. In addition, public opinion can quickly spread through Internet networks due to Korea's 80 percent use rate and top-class IT infrastructure.

Consequently, Son said, parents are extremely sensitive about the safety of babies and want to take all precautions and no risks to protect babies from illnesses and infections.

This does not suggest that parents in other countries do not care as much for their children, but the formaldehyde scare did not arise in other countries where wet wipes were sold, probably because they were marketed as a cosmetic product.

The level of formaldehyde in Yuhan-Kimberly's wet wipes did not please parents, even though it was one-tenth of the permitted level. Nearly 50,000 consumers filed complaints via telephone, email, and a website bulletin board. In addition, comments were posted on portals and community sites; a protest website was launched. This put Yuhan-Kimberly in a challenging situation. Not only was there concern for the sales of wet wipes, but also fear that sales of other products would drop. Yuhan-Kimberly is also the leading diaper manufacturer. In fact, it began manufacturing wet wipes for hygiene purposes as an extension of its Huggies diaper business, which accounted for 60 percent of the market share of all diapers sold in Korea. As consumers complained about the wet wipes, there was concern that the diaper business would begin to fail because they were connected. The market share of the wet wipes went from 50 percent to 26 percent and 21 percent in April and May, respectively. The possibility of widespread criticism of the company was a dire situation.

유한킴벌리 물티슈는 안전합니다.

물티슈 제품은 미국, EU 등 선진국에서는 화장품류로 분류되어 일반공산품보다 더욱 엄격한 품질과 안전성 관리를 받고 있습니다. 이때 허용되는 포름알데히드의 기준은 2000ppm입니다.

국내 화장품의 허용 기준 역시 미국, EU, 캐나다, 호주 등과 같이 2,000ppm이며, 유한킴벌리의 아기용 엠보싱 물티슈는 이러한 기준보다 훨씬 강화된 품질관리와 안전성관리를 통해 생산되어 지난 5년 이상 최고의 소비자 만족도를 지켜왔습니다.

한편, 소비자시민모임의 최근 조사결과에 따르면 유한킴벌리의 엠보싱 물티슈에서 210ppm 정도의 포름알데히드가 검출되었다고 합니다. 이는 앞서 언급한 주요 선진국 및 우리나라의 화장품류 허용 기준 2,000ppm의 약 10분의 1 수준으로, 안전성을 재 확인 받았습니다. 다만, 소비자시민모임에서 물티슈의 자율적 검사제도인 항균(S)마크를 위해 정한 가이드라인 30ppm을 국내 제품에서 맞추기를 바라는 요구가 제기 된 바 있습니다.

이에, 유한킴벌리는 주요 선진국 물티슈 및 국내 화장품 허용기준에 따라 생산 판매된 회사의 엠보싱 물티슈 제품의 안전성을 거듭 확신하고 있지만, 국내 항균(S)마크의 자율적 사용을 위한 가이드라인을 존중하는 입장에서 원하는 거래선과 고객들께 반품, 교환을 해 드리기로 결정하였습니다. 고객들께서는 사용하시던 제품은 그대로 사용해도 무방하며, 원하실 경우 교환해 드릴 것입니다.

별도로, 주요 선진국의 공통적인 허용기준이자 국내 화장품의 허용 기준인 2000ppm과 상기 국내 자율 안전마크 사용을 위한 30ppm의 가이드라인 간에 있는 현격한 차이에 대해서는 향후 관련 기관 및 단체와 긴밀히 협의해 나갈 것입니다.

Figure 8.6 This is the message, in Korean, used on the news release to explain the wet wipes situation. There was never a danger, but consumers did not understand this. Courtesy of Yuhan-Kimberly.

Son said, "Yuhan-Kimberly is one of the most respected companies in Korea and has earned high consumer confidence as a company that is strongly dedicated to fulfilling its corporate social responsibility." CSR is very important to Koreans, who have high expectations of ethical

YUHAN-KIMBERLY WET WIPES ARE SAFE!

In the developed countries such as United States, EU, and etc, wet wipes is classified as cosmetics and its quality and safety are rigorously controlled by administration than any other industrial products. Here, the maximum permissible level of formaldehyde in cosmetics is 2,000 ppm.

Use of formaldehyde in the local cosmetics is also allowed by 2,000 ppm just like United States, EU, Canada and Australia. With much reinforced quality and safety control than regulation, Yuhan-Kimberly's baby wet wipes has become the most loved one over the past 5 years.

According to the recent examination of one consumer organization, 210 ppm of formaldehyde as detected in the Yuhan-Kimberly's baby wet wipes. As noted before, this amount is only 1/10 of both local and other developed countries' regulation, and it had been reconfirmed as being safe. However, the consumer organization asked the local companies to adjust the amount not exceeding 30 ppm once in the past, which falls into the guideline for the 'voluntary safety mark' of the wet wipes.

Though Yuhan-Kimberly is convinced of the safety of baby wet wipes, we decided to accept return or exchange products, with respecting the 'voluntary safety mark' guideline. The consumer who is currently using the product can either keep it or replace.

Separately, we will closely work with the related organizations to close the gap between 2000 ppm, which is the common regulation in both of the developed countries' and the local cosmetics, and 30 ppm, which is the 'voluntary safety mark' guideline.

Figure 8.7 This is the news release in Figure 8.6 translated into English by Yuhan-Kimberly executives. Courtesy of Yuhan-Kimberly.

behavior in large companies. CSR asks for a high standard of social contribution in addition to fulfilling ethical and environmental requirements. Just before the crisis in 2005, the company ranked sixth on the list of "Most Respected Companies in Korea" by the Korea Management Association. "We did not want to lose this position in the eyes of consumers," said Son.

Customers had begun asking for refunds on wet wipes and then also began asking for refunds on diapers. There were signs that consumers were planning to launch a boycott campaign of all products. "Whereas companies with a good image can achieve high marks from consumers, when consumers are disappointed, the effect can be much more negative in relative terms," said Son.

Crisis Management and Communications Plan

Yuhan-Kimberly had a crisis management policy that included crisis communications. It included crisis prevention and crisis response if a crisis developed.

When the formaldehyde issue became problematic, the company set out to follow its plan.

Step 1: The company created the crisis management team, which included the CEO, a spokesperson, and the business leader.

Step 2: The spokesperson (EunWook Lee) was responsible for communication with all publics, external and internal, to be certain to have what Yuhan-Kimberly calls "one voice, one channel."

Step 3: The crisis management team oversaw the monitoring of all reports in newspapers, television, radio and Internet sources, particularly websites. Persons directly monitoring media made reports back to the crisis management team. Internal publics were informed of outlooks and outcomes. A product safety survey was conducted by authorized research facilities.

Step 4: A standby statement was carefully written as swiftly as was possible. Q&As were prepared for each stakeholder: employees, news media, customers, vendors, government, and consumer protection organizations. There was great concern to protect Yuhan-Kimberly's reputation and the confidence publics have in the company. There was determination to avoid any public misunderstanding and thereby minimize the impact of the crisis.

Step 5: In an effort to convince the publics that the product was safe, data was collected to prove the points and avoid further widening of the crisis. This data was written in a news release to the media. Questions were anticipated and interviews with staff members, shareholders, and partner companies were conducted to add to the persuasion. One interview with experts was posted on the website for consumers who sought details online. In addition to the standby statement, medical and chemical professionals gave objective evidence of product safety on a video interview. They had studied safety regulations of Korean and international agencies.

Step 6: The company refrained from making individual responses to prevent friction and the dissemination of ungrounded data. The team did, however, make efforts to control information on anti-company websites by politely providing the site webmaster with the company's position and objective data to resolve misunderstandings. In response to the third-party complaints on the web, the team used the standby statement, as well as convincing information from the medical professionals.

Step 7: If consumers made requests for exchanges or refunds after learning of the explanations, the company complied with their requests to prevent the spread of complaints. The company handled its own exchange and refund process rather than turning it over to external agencies, so that the crisis would be contained and the "one voice" could be maintained. Also, the company delivered its statement and Q&A to wholesalers and direct accounts including discount stores, and asked for their cooperation in dealing swiftly with exchanges without inconveniencing consumers.

Step 8: The business leader prepared his department for development of wet wipes without formaldehyde, even though legal regulations did not make this requirement.

Step 9: A rebuilding program was executed to recover corporate and brand reputation. There were five steps, all designed for a return to normalcy.

1. Maintain consistency in communications until the close of the crisis.
2. Develop and launch a new product that not only meets legal standards but also consumers' expectations.
3. Re-examine social commitments such as ethical management, environmental management, and CSR.
4. Expand social contributions activities and reinforce public relations activities. Reinforce corporate public campaign "Keep Korea Green," which existed before onset of the crisis.
5. Make an announcement on the increased investment and enhance reporting on the company and products.

Observations

1. The crisis was kept at a minimum by speedy communications and effective crisis management. The market share recovered in a short period of time. The wet wipes market share recorded 50 percent in February, 2005, and dropped to 21 percent two months later; however, it recovered after that and recorded 30 percent in June and 40 percent in October. The 2008 market annual share recorded was greater than 46 percent. The general evaluation is that the company's communications program received high trust due to the company's reputation of being concerned with the consumer.

2. Although the reputation of the company was partly damaged, consumer confidence was recovered in a short period of time thanks to prompt and consistent response, a reputation rebuilding program, and the longstanding high reputation of the company.

3. In the list of Korea Management Association's "Most Respected Companies in Korea," Yuhan-Kimberly slipped from No. 4 in 2004 to No. 6 in 2005. It recovered the No. 4 position in 2006 and advanced to No. 3 in 2008 and 2009.

4. Research in 2009 conducted by crisis management experts headed by Professor Hyun Ou Lee of Hanyang University revealed that Yuhan-Kimberly's longstanding good corporate image had helped it withstand the crisis, with less damage to its corporate reputation than a company with a not-so-stellar image.

Conclusions

Yuhan-Kimberly's reputation based on social contributions and responsibilities is the best asset and value in the face of a crisis (Figure 8.6, Figure 8.7).

Approach With a Human Face Is the Basic Message of Crisis Communications

Setting crisis management techniques and appointing a spokesperson swiftly minimizes confusion. Even prior to the crisis in 2005, Yuhan-Kimberly had a well-managed crisis management system, including a crisis management team. However, the company took the opportunity to be stronger when facing a crisis. The company reinforced crisis prevention activities and an early warning system with issue monitoring and tracking.

Prompt Responses Minimize Negative Opinion

Yuhan-Kimberly's crisis management was successful in that it minimized negative public opinion and sentiment efficiently with clear and honest communication, and it also prevented problems, all according to its prepared crisis manual.

In 2014, the company, in order to build trust with consumers in foreign markets, as well as in Korea, adopted a safety policy of disclosing ingredients used for baby products. In partnership with U.S.-based Kimberly-Clark, the company has been focusing on overseas baby care markets. It exports baby wipes, wet tissues, and other products to Australia, New Zealand, China, and Singapore, countries with strict safety standards.

Case Study: Saginaw Valley State University and the Theater Controversy

Saginaw Valley State University (SVSU) is located in the heart of the Tri-Cities of Saginaw, Midland, and Bay City in mid-Michigan, about 90 miles north of Detroit.

Not as famous as the Big Ten football powerhouse University of Michigan, 90 miles to the east, SVSU is proud of its football team, a member of NCAA Division II which made six playoff appearances in a ten-year period and had five players go to the NFL in 2008.

SVSU, the youngest of the state's 15 public universities, is also proud of its phenomenal growth since its birth in 1963. It is proud to be the most affordable public university in Michigan, with annual tuition and fees at $6,900 in 2009–2010. It prides itself on personal attention to students, with an average class size of 25 students, and it is proud of its numerous programs—among them its Theater Department.

In January, 2010, the Theater Department, for the second straight year, hosted the regional Kennedy Center American College Theater Festival. More than 1,500 participants from colleges and universities in five states (Illinois, Indiana, Michigan, Ohio, and Wisconsin) attended the competition.

Each year, the Theater Department—faculty and students—plans a schedule of plays to be presented. The goal is to present a wide variety to showcase the talents of theater majors and also to attract an admiring audience.

In the 2006–2007 school year, the plays selected were the following: *Fat Pig*, *A Christmas Carol*, *The Princess and the Pea*, and *Angels in America, Part One: Millennium Approaches*. The selection was intended to have some fare for everybody. Some patrons would choose one or more of the plays; serious theatergoers would see them all. *Angels in America* won a Pulitzer for playwright Tony Kushner. Its themes are homosexuality and the early days of the HIV/AIDS crisis.

The crisis for SVSU began after the play's director, Professor Richard B. Roberts, enthusiastically spoke with *Saginaw News* reporter Janet I. Martineau about the upcoming play. He told Martineau and she wrote, in the April 14, 2007 edition of the newspaper, that the play was one "clearly no community theater north of Detroit would touch. And not only is it untouchable but it's also X-rated and suitable only for ages 16 and up." Roberts was referring to conservative individuals and groups in small towns and rural areas outside of Detroit, the state's only large and clearly diverse city.

The play features full-frontal male nudity and the actors frequently use the "F" word—"without either being gratuitous," Roberts told the reporter. "And we are doing it all. It is our responsibility to provide our students with cutting-edge material to perform, with shows that stretch them."

Numerous colleges and universities across the United States have produced *Angels in America*, and some have had problems resulting from conservative publics. Kushner recalls problems at the Catholic University in Washington, DC, Wabash College in Indiana, and Kilgore College in Texas, among others. Professor Anthony Hill, of the Department of Theater at The Ohio State University, said both *Part One* and *Part Two* of the larger work have been produced successfully and without furor on the stage of the Thurber Theater. He said, "Students and faculty are usually accepting of cutting-edge drama and the city of Columbus is known to be 'gay-friendly.'"

Of the two lead actors in the SVSU production (Figure 8.8), one is gay and the other straight. Caleb M. Knutson, then 19, is straight, but said, "I figured if I can play a role I don't 100 percent believe in, then I will stretch 100 percent as an actor." The other actor, Chad W. Baker, then 21 and publicly gay, said:

> When I was cast, . . . I was afraid the actor cast opposite me, if he were straight, would be uncomfortable with me being gay. And we, as actors, need to look comfortable because, in the play, we've been lovers for four years.

In addition to playing homosexuals, a female was cast as a rabbi and a white person as Black.

The play was scheduled to run two consecutive weekends, April 20–22 and April 27–29. Roberts also mentioned in the article that ran in the April 14 edition that "we are the only theater in mid-Michigan that can get away with it because while we want people to come see the show, we're not tied to ticket sales to survive."

This was true because the production was part of the university's academic program. However, there was also no intention to alienate local patrons. Still, he did not want to hide the controversy from the public. He knew the value of producing plays that cause people to think, to discuss, to grow and perhaps change attitudes that help develop harmonious relationships within the community. Controversy was the reason for the play.

Nevertheless, the reference to not being tied to ticket revenue was what Eugene Hamilton, special assistant to the university president and head of government relations, calls "the spark that lit the firestorm that would follow."

Phone calls and emails began to come in to the president's office. On April 19, a letter signed by several Michigan state legislators, spurred

Figure 8.8 Chad W. Baker (left in T-shirt) and Caleb Knutson played the leads in the gay-themed play *Angels in America, Part One: Millennium Approaches* at the Saginaw Valley State University Theater for Performing Arts in 2007. They both faced challenges as actors in that Baker is gay and Knutson is not, but were determined to do it. *The Saginaw News*, 2007. All rights reserved. Reprinted with permission. Credit: Eric Gilbertson

by their constituents, arrived expressing "disappointment that the university would sponsor a play with this content [full-frontal nudity and vulgar language]." It further said they were "appalled that our tax dollars would have any part in funding such a display." One lawmaker sought to withhold all of the university's state funding ($28 million) if the play opened.

Realizing his response to the emails, phone calls, and letters would be identical, President Eric Gilbertson and J. J. Boehm, Director of Media Relations, crafted an open letter responding to the issue on the SVSU website.

Basically, the open letter spoke about the wide variety of plays done by the Theater Department. The key point was the following:

All in all, our students have had a wonderful range of opportunities to experience the varieties of theater. But part of any comprehensive range of performance art must also include pieces that may be more controversial, unnerving, occasionally even raw. Their experiences would be sheltered and incomplete without exposure to contemporary plays that raise troublesome questions—even in controversial ways.

Hamilton said, "Whenever an individual or a media outlet asked questions about the play, they were referred to the website. There were no press conferences and the president did no interviews."

Boehm, on the other hand, said he did dozens of interviews, including one on WJR Radio in Detroit. "I simply answered the phone in my office and I was immediately on the air live in a conversation with the state representative seeking to withhold our funding." Boehm said the news coverage of the play before and after it opened was as far away as New York and San Francisco, a wider circle of coverage than SVSU normally receives: "My comments quickly spread across the Internet, showing how rapidly word can travel in today's information age, especially the following remark, 'This is a Pulitzer Prize-winning play, not some piece of second-rate sleaze we picked up somewhere.'"

The play went on as scheduled to capacity audiences, great applause, and several curtain calls. Martineau of the *Saginaw News* wrote in her review, "There is nothing more fun or pleasurable, after 40 years in this reviewing business than discovering a great play for the first time and getting lost in its magic." She went further to tell her readers, "There is nothing to fear about this work other than dealing with your own fears." She also pointed to the "sarcastic witty dialogue" and praised the actors saying, "There are no misses in the cast of 14."

Playwright Kushner wrote two emails. The first, just before the second weekend, was to the cast, urging the actors to stay focused despite the "mean-spirited attacks that can be upsetting, infuriating, even frightening, and which can make it difficult to stay focused on the reasons you decided to do the play in the first place."

The second email was to President Gilbertson on the final day of the production saying he admired his integrity, his decision to "accept as part of his job description protecting the atmosphere of open discussion, free

AN OPEN LETTER

I appreciate your thoughtful expression of concern. It is a freedom of expression issue, but some additional context may also be helpful in your assessment of our theater program at SVSU.

Our Theater Department has attempted to give our students a balanced and varied array of performance opportunities. In the past few years, they have performed children's productions ("Princess and the Pea," "Young Black Beauty"), musicals ("Oliver," "Man of La Mancha," "Fiddler on the Roof"), comedies ("I Ought to be in Pictures," "I Love You, You're Perfect, Now Change"), seasonal works ("A Christmas Carol"), and even informal performances for kids at the Saginaw Children's Zoo.

All in all, our students have had a wonderful range of opportunities to experience the varieties of theater. But part of any comprehensive range of performance art must also include pieces that may be more controversial, unnerving, occasionally even raw. Their experiences would be sheltered and incomplete without exposure to contemporary plays that raise troublesome questions—even in controversial ways.

"Angels in America," is such a play, but it was carefully chosen.

It also won a Pulitzer Prize and several other awards, and has served as the basis for a television mini-series.

In the local news report about this production, the Director tried to give the readers fair warning as to what was in the play so that all of us could make an informed judgment about whether we wanted to attend. I appreciate his doing that. Certainly no one should be lured into a performance only to be offended.

And so, I suspect we may simply have to remain in disagreement about this matter. But even as I am not willing to censor this kind of artistic expression, you too are free to express your disapproval. And I do respect your point of view in this regard.

Again, thank you for your message and your thoughtfulness in expressing it.

Sincerely,
Eric Gilbertson

President
Saginaw Valley State University

Figure 8.9 When some members of the community questioned whether a controversial play should be produced at Saginaw Valley State University in Michigan, the university president posted this open letter on the campus website and all doubters were referred to it. Saginaw News. Reprinted with permission.

Source: The Saginaw News. Reprinted with permission. Credit: Eric Gilbertson

What Could Have Been Done If Social Media Had Existed

While Saginaw Valley State University (SVSU) effectively messaged its support of the play *Angels In America, Part One* through statements from the university president and an open letter on its website, it could have leveraged Facebook and Twitter to share this message with a broader audience.

SVSU could have posted the letter in its entirety on Facebook, and allowed the community to share its feelings through the commenting feature, with the caveat that threatening or offensive language would not be tolerated. SVSU's media relations director could have reviewed comments to note themes or common questions that he could use to proactively craft additional media and social media messaging—messaging that could not only answer community questions but could provide additional, easy-to-use material (such as an FAQ) for local media covering the theater controversy.

Additionally, SVSU could have used Twitter to share snippets of the president's message, and to link users to the full message on the university website and/or Facebook page.

Facebook and Twitter could also have been used to post statements of support for the play from members of the cast, from university faculty members or elected officials who supported SVSU's decision to produce the play, or even from theater directors nationwide wishing to voice support for SVSU.

To track and monitor rumors, misinformation, or community comments about the play, SVSU could have proactively created a hashtag (such as #SVSUAngels or #SVSUTheatre) to track these comments across social media platforms. This would allow SVSU to gauge not only how well their statements were received by social media users, but keep tabs on how the discussion changed over time as the university released additional information. This would have allowed SVSU to not only monitor the conversation in real time, but would have provided proof-of-performance data afterward so the university could understand its successes in messaging and areas for improvement.

Bronlea Mishler, Community and Media Relations Officer, City of Marysville, WA from intimidation, essential to the life of the mind." He criticized state representatives for having "nothing better to do with their time than trying to censor a college theater production."

On May 8, after the play had closed, the *Bay City Times* said, in a short editorial titled "Freedom of Expression at SVSU Stands Against Gusts of Intolerance":

> One man's filth is another's fertilizer. Most Americans can appreciate that; well, anyway, those not handicapped by whatever blinders they choose to wear. The play's opponents were free, of course, to vent their raging intolerance. Pres. Gilbertson and the university didn't bend an inch. The show went on as scheduled. Bravo!

President Gilbertson received additional emails, mostly positive, thanking him for supporting the production despite opposition, applauding his leadership and support of the arts and freedom of speech. Standing on principle is admirable, but it is also important to know one's publics. Who are the patrons? How do taxpayers and community leaders feel? What will be the reaction of the news media? There are places, colleges included, where such a play would not be as successful. Gilbertson knew the people SVSU serves. That is the best advice: to be well acquainted with the people you serve.

Boehm received the Ruby Award from the First State Bank—awarded to "the brightest professionals under the age of 40 who have made their mark in their professions and are having an impact throughout the Tri-Cities"—for his public relations work, including crisis communications for this theater project. He said, "While $28 million is no insignificant sum, to SVSU its reputation and image are infinitely more valuable and these emerged from the ordeal intact." On top of that, the university did not lose the funding.

Playwright Kushner said in 2014:

> The amount of progress in the last decade is absolutely breathtaking. I thought gay marriage would someday be legal, but didn't realize once there was a big Supreme Court decision (U.S. v. Windsor) in its favor that barriers would topple so fast. But behind that breathtaking speed was decades of incredibly dedicated work by many, many people who helped prepare the way . . . . When we did (the play) in New York in 2010, with actors who weren't even born when the epidemic appeared, it was very moving to see them discover how terrible the time was.
>
> (Berson, 2014, pp. H1–2)

Bibliography

Case Study: AIDS in Africa

African Comprehensive HIV/AIDS Partnerships. (n.d.). Retrieved August 30, 2006, from www.achap.org.

Ahaibwe, G. (2013, November 15). Halting and reversing the spread of HIV/AIDS in Uganda. *Africa in focus.* Retrieved February 12, 2015, from www.brookings.edu.

AIDS Healthcare Foundation/Uganda Care's Stay/Love Condoms Campaign Kicks Off in Uganda. (2009, August 6). *Medical news today.* Retrieved December 8, 2009, from www.medicalnewstoday.com.

Albone, R. (2014, November 28). World AIDS Day 2014: Ensuring older people don't fall through the gaps. *Help page.* Retrieved February 14, 2015, from www. helppage.org.

Bell, G. (2005, June 12). Mandela, stars rock out against AIDS. *Seattle Times,* p. A18.

Bobb, S. (2009, December 1). South African President announces expansion of HIV/AIDS testing, treatment. *VOA News.com.* Retrieved December 25, 2009, from www1.voanews.com/English/news/South-African.

Bollinger, L.A., Stover, J., Musuka, G., Fidzani, B, Moeti, T., and Busang, L. (2009). The cost and impact of male circumcision on HIV/AIDS in Botswana. *Journal of the International AIDS Society,* 12, 7. https://doi.org/10.1186/1758-2652-12-7

Christiansen, J. (2000). AIDS in Africa: Dying by the numbers. *CNN in-depth specials.* Retrieved August 30, 2006, from www.cnn.com/specials/2000/aids/stones/overview.

Corridors of Hope. (2005, April 28). *PSI health areas.* Retrieved August 30, 2006, from www.psi.org/our-programs/coh.html.

Coulson, N. (2004, October 6). Developments in the use of the mass media at the national level for HIV/AIDS prevention in South Africa. *SoulBeat Africa.* Retrieved August 31, 2006, from www.comminit.com.

Cramer, R. (2003, September). *Misconceptions, folk beliefs, denial hinder risk perception among young Zambian men.* Washington, DC: PSI Research Brief.

Cullen, D. (2009). *Columbine.* New York: Hachette Book Group.

Danielson, C. (2005, October 17). PSI wins population institutes Global Media awards. *PSI online.* Retrieved August 31, 2006, from www.globalhealth.org/news/article/6747.

DeYoung, K. (2002, March 15). Mbeki pressured to lead South African fight against AIDS. *Washington Post Online.* Retrieved August 31, 2006, from www. washingtonpost.com/wp-dyn/world/issues/aidsinafrica.

Ebikeme, C. (2014, May 7). Selling circumcision for HIV prevention at the epicenter of the global epidemic. *Huffington Post.* Retrieved February 12, 2015, from www.huffingtonpost.com.

First Lady of Uganda rolls out next phase of campaign to stop HIV infections among children. (2013, September 17). *UNAIDS.* Retrieved February 14, 2015, from www.unaids.org.

Global Challenges/Report estimates significant impact of widespread circumcision effort in Botswana. (2009, May 29). *Henry J. Kaiser family foundation.* Retrieved November 11, 2009, from http://kaisernetwork.org.

Goosby, E. (2009, November 27). No hold on PEPFAR funds for Uganda. *Newsweek online; The human condition blog.* Retrieved December 8, 2009, from http://blog.newsweek.com/thehumancondition/archive/20009/11/27.

HIV and AIDS in South Africa. (n.d.). *AVERTing HIV and AIDS.* Retrieved May 18, 2010, from www.avert.org/aidssouthafrica.htm.

HIV and AIDS in Swaziland. (n.d.). *AVERTing HIV and AIDS*. Retrieved December 2, 2009, from www.avert.org/aids-swaziland.htm.

HIV and AIDS in Swaziland. (2012). *AVERTing HIV and AIDS*. Retrieved February 12, 2015, from www.avert.org.

HIV and AIDS in Uganda. (n.d.). *AVERTing HIV and AIDS*. Retrieved December 7, 2009, from www.avert.org/aids-uganda.htm.

HIV and AIDS in Zambia. (n.d.). *AVERTing HIV and AIDS*. Retrieved December 2, 2009, from www.avert.org/aids-zambia.htm.

HIV and AIDS in Zimbabwe. (2012). *AVERTing HIV and AIDS*. Retrieved February 12, 2015, from www.avert.org.

HIV and AIDS in Zimbabwe. (n.d.). *AVERTing HIV and AIDS*. Retrieved May 18, 2010, from www.avert.org/aids-zimbabwe.htm.

Irin Plus News. (2009, December 8). *Uganda: Campaigns tackle "the complexity of sexuality"*. Retrieved December 8, 2009, from www.plusnews.org/report.aspx?Reportld=84944.

Kanabus, A. & Noble, R. (2005, August 17). *The ABC of HIV prevention*. Retrieved from www.avert.org/hivprevention.htm.

Keller, B. (2005, March 16). AIDS infects education systems in Africa. *Education Week*, pp. 22–23.

Kim, Y., Kols, A., Nyakauru, R., Marangwanda, C. & Chinatamoto, P. (2001, March). Promoting sexual responsibility among young people in Zimbabwe. *International Family Planning Perspectives*, 27, 1.

King abandons campaign for virgin girls to remain abstinent, avoid marriage. (2005, August 23). Retrieved August 30, 2006, from www.kaisernetwork.org.

Koehler, J. (2004, June 9). *Soulbeat Africa*. Retrieved August 31, 2006, from www.comminit.com/Africa/experiences.

Long, J. (2004, September 18). *Top players help raise awareness of HIV/AIDS*. Retrieved August 31, 2006, from www.icc-cricket.com.

Louw, M. (2005, September). *HIV danger to migrant workers*. Retrieved August 31, 2006, from www.health24.com.

Machinchick, K. (2003, February 21). *Zimbabwean teachers travel to U.S. for HIV/AIDS awareness programs*. Retrieved August 31, 2006, from www.usembassy.it.

Mandela's grief. (2005, January 24). *People*, p. 88.

Maskalyk, J. (2002). Southern Africa's famine far worse than anticipated. *Canadian Medical Association Journal*, 167(11). Retrieved February 4, 2024, from https://www.ncbi.nlm.nih.gov/pmc/articles/PMC134147/.

Molomo, B. (2009, May 29). *National campaign plan: Multiple concurrent partnerships*. Retrieved November 2, 2009, from http://comminit.com/en/node/304747/36.

Moyo, J. (2013, November). Fear of HIV testing among Zimbabwe's teens. *IPS News*. Retrieved February 15, from www.ipsnews.net.

National Center for Biotechnology Information, National Library of Medicine, National Institutes of Health. (2020, February 27). Looming threat of COVID-19 infection in Africa: Act collectively and fast. https://Ncbi.nlm.nih.gov.

Paulet, L. (2014, August 27). HIV prevention act angers Ugandan AIDS activists. *VOANews*. Retrieved February 14, 2015, from www.voanews.com.

President's Emergency Plan for AIDS Relief. (2009, October 29). *AVERTing HIV and AIDS*. Retrieved November 22, 2009, from www.avert.org/pepfar.htm.

Qayyum, A. (2015, January 12). HIV/AIDS: What's behind the decline in new infections. *CS monitor*. Retrieved February 14, 2015, from www.csmonitor.com.

Ramey, C. (2008, July 31). Cell life update: Using mobiles to fight HIV/AIDS. *Mobile active*. Retrieved November 2, 2009, from http://mobileactive.org/.

Reducing the HIV stigma by speaking up. (2009, August 24). *USAID for the American people*. Retrieved December 2, 2009, from http://Kenya.usaid.gov/stories/zimbabwe.

Reuters. (2005, August 4). AIDS summit opens with accusations. *Washington Post Online*. Retrieved August 31, 2006, from www.washingtonpost.com/wp-dyn/world/issues/aidsinafrica.

SAPA (2014, November 20). AIDS: Uganda's success prompts worry. *IOL scitech*. Retrieved February 14, 2015, from www.iol.co.za.

Singizi, T. (2007, November 6). Multiple community programmes simultaneously fight HIV/AIDS in Zimbabwe. *UNICEF online*. Retrieved December 2, 2009, from www.unicef.org/infobycountry/zimbabwe.

Smith, D. (2012, April 11). HIV/AIDS and ignorance thrive as Swaziland struggles for funds to fight disease. *The Guardian*. Retrieved February 14, 2015, from www.theguardian.com.

Socio-cultural aspects of HIV/AIDS in South Africa. (2005, April 8). Retrieved August 30, 2006, from www.Health24.com.

South Africa has the biggest and most high profile HIV epidemic in the world. (n.d.). *South Africa info*. Retrieved February 14, 2015, from www.Southafrica.info.

South Africa's HIV/AIDS battle plan. (n.d.). *AVERTing HIV/AIDS*. Retrieved February 14, 2015, from www.avert.org.

Sternberg, S. (2001). Uganda: Deadly traditions persist. *USA Today Online*. Retrieved September 28, 2001, from www.usatoday.com.

Swaziland: Folktales to address modern problems. (2005). Retrieved August 30, 2006, from www.irinnews.org.

Swaziland: New anti-AIDS campaign targets young people. (2005). Retrieved August 30, 2006, from www.irinnews.org.

Swaziland: Tobias undergoes HIV testing. (2005, August 23). Retrieved August 30, 2006, from www.psi.org/news/0805d.html.

Text messages are new tool for AIDS education in South Africa. (2009, March 9). *PBS online newshour*. Retrieved November 2, 2009, from www.pbs.org.

Ugandan condom crisis: Basic facts. (2005, August). Retrieved August 30, 2006, from www.genderhealth.org/uganda.pho.

Ugandan lawmaker to reward virgins with scholarships. (2005, October 16). *Mail & Guardian Online*. Retrieved October 16, 2005, from www.mg.co.za.

Uganda: Protect, don't punish, people with HIV. (2010, May 19). *Human rights watch*. Retrieved February 14, 2015, from www.hrw.org.

UNAIDS. (2014, July 16). *GAP report*. Retrieved February 4, 2024, from https://www.unaids.org/en/resources/documents/2014/20140716_UNAIDS_gap_report.

UNAIDS (n.d.). *Zambia*. Retrieved from www.unaids.org.

UNAIDS: Sub-Saharan Africa. (n.d.). Retrieved May 14, 2010, from www.unaids.org.

Van Rossem, R. & Meekers, D. (2007, December 18). The reach and impact of social marketing and reproductive health communication campaigns in Zambia. *BMC Public Health*, 7, 352.

Vickers, S. (2009, October 13). Zimbabwe women combat HIV stigma. *BBC online*. Retrieved December 2, 2009, from http://news.bbc.uk/sport2/hit/football/africa/8304292.

Wax, E. (2005, October 10). Virginity is commodity in AIDS fight. *Concord monitor online*. Retrieved August 31, 2006, from www.concordmonitor.com.

World Health Organization. (2023, July 13). *HIV and AIDS: Key facts*. Retrieved February 4, 2024, from https://www.who.int/news-room/fact-sheets/detail/hiv-aids.

York, G. (2009, November 16). South Africa radically shifts thinking in HIV/AIDS. *The Globe and Mail*. Toronto, Canada, p. A16.

Youth Love to Scrutinize. (2009, July 6). *All Africa global media*. Retrieved November 2, 2009, from http://allafrica.com.

Zavis, A. (2005, September 29). U.S., South Africa fight AIDS in military. *Los Angeles Sentinel*, p. A–13.

Zimbabwe: Chipawo to present new HIV production (2009, June 15). *All Africa global media*. Retrieved December 2, 2009, from http://allafrica.com.

Zimbabwe Country Report of the United Nations. (n.d.). *Secretary-general's task force on women, girls, and HIV/AIDS in Southern Africa*. Retrieved August 31, 2006, from www.rockofafrica.org/news.htm.

Update/Case Study: HIV/AIDS Plus COVID-19, a Syndemic

AVERT. (2018). HIV and AIDS in east and southern Africa regional overview. *AVERT*. Retrieved January 12, 2023, from https:www.avert.org.

Case Study: Nut Rage and Korean Airlines

Airline exec resigns over nut dispute. (2014, December 9). *CBS News*. Retrieved February 4, 2015, from http://cnsnews.com.

Airline heiress resigns vice-presidency over "nut rage". (2014, December 11). *The Chosun Ilbo*. Retrieved January 9, 2015, from http://english.chosun.com.

Chappell, B. (2014, December 9). Nut rumpus prompts Korean Airline exec to apologize and resign. *NPR*. Retrieved March 3, 2015, from www.npr.org.

Crew in Korean Air nut rage says he was insulted. (2015, January 9). *Yahoo News*. Retrieved February 13, 2015, from http://news.yahoo.com.

Gale, A. (2015, January 7). "Nut rage" reignites backlash against South Korea's family-run conglomerates. *Wall Street Journal*. Retrieved February 4, 2015, from www.wsj.com.

Jung, Y. (2014, December 15). Korean air scandal causing huge social repercussions. *Business Korea*. Retrieved February 4, 2015, from www.businesskorea.co.kr.

Korean Air chief apologizes to steward allegedly assaulted by his daughter. (2015, January 30). *Korea Times*. Retrieved February 17, 2015, from www.koreatimes.com.

Korean Air executive resigns over "nut rage". (December 9, 2014). Korean Air executive resigns over "nut rage". *The Korea Herald*. Retrieved February 4, 2015, from www.koreaherald.com.

Lee, J. (2015, January 9). Former Korean air VP asks for forgiveness over "nut rage". *Youhap New Agency*. Retrieved February 4, 2015, from http://english.youhapnews.co.kr.

Nam, I. (2015, February 12). Former Korean Air executive found guilty over "nut rage" incident. *Wall Street Journal*. Retrieved March 2, 2015, from www.wsj.com.

Park, J. (2014, February 15). "Nut rage" prompts South Korea to consider law against highhanded conduct. *Reuters.com*. Retrieved March 3, 2015, from www.reuters.com.

Park, J. (2014, December 12). Korean air executive apologizes after nuts incident sparks national outrage. *Reuters.com*. Retrieved March 3, 2015, from www.reuters.com.

Park, K. (2014, December 9). Korean Air vice president forces plane back to gate over nuts. *Bloomberg*. Retrieved February 4, 2015, from www.bloomberg.com.

Park, M. & P. Hancocks. (2015, February 12). Korean Air executive jailed over "nut rage" incident. *CNN*. Retrieved March 2, from www.cnn.com.

Picchi, A. (2014, December 12). Korean air chairman apologizes for "nut rage" daughter. *CBS News*. Retrieved February 4, 2015, from www.cbsnews.com.

Taylor, A. (2015, December 9). CEO's daughter loses job after "nut rage" incident on Korean Air flight. *Washington Post Online*. Retrieved February 4, 2015, from www.washingtonpost.com.

Yang, H. & Jin, H. (2019, March 26). 'Nut rage' fallout: Korean Air chief ousted from board in landmark vote. *Reuters*. Retrieved February 4, 2024, from https://www.reuters.com/article/us-korean-air-shareholders-idUSKCN1R803E/.

Update: More Family Rage

Puckett, J. (2018, April 23). *Korean Air CEO fires his daughters after a pair of scandals*. Retrieved April 5, 2022, from https://thepoints guy.com/news/Korean Air.

Yang, H. & Jin, H. (2019, March 26). "Nut rage" fallout: Korean Air Chief ousted from board in landmark vote. *Reuters*. Retrieved March 9, 2022, from https://reuters.com.

Case Study: Saginaw Valley State University and the Theater Controversy

Berson, M. (2014, August 10). A Q&A with Tony Kushner on his 'Angels in America', revisiting the Intiman Theatre. *Seattle Times*, pp. H1–2.

Chapter 9

Transportation Crises

This chapter involves crises and near-crises relating to transportation. They show that crisis communicators must cope with near-crises and preventing crises, and that job is nearly as demanding as coping with actual tragedies.

Case Study: Holland America Line and Cruise Crises

This crisis features the multitude of crises one corporation can face. It advises and warns all organizations to be aware and prepared for all possibilities.

When cruise lines do crisis communications and crisis management plans, the worst-case scenario is the sinking of a ship and lives lost. The last luxury liner to sink was the *Andrea Doria* in 1956. It collided with another ship (the *Stockholm*) en route from Italy to New York. Unlike the *Titanic*, there were enough lifeboats for all passengers—though 46 fatalities (out of 1,706 persons aboard) resulted from the collision.

Like the *Titanic*, the *Andrea Doria* was considered "unsinkable." Because of these two sea tragedies, cruise lines don't use the word "unsinkable" in their marketing. Advances in shipbuilding and strict safety precautions have made the loss of lives due to sinking very unlikely.

However, cruise lines (as well as many other companies and organizations) must expect the possibility of numerous crises, and publics expect a response from their crisis communicators. Crises or negative news stories about any one cruise line can affect future bookings. Any crisis at sea deters potential passengers from taking cruises on any cruise line. Unlike flying, cruising is an elective form of travel; no one has to cruise. Therefore, cruise lines such as Holland America Line must do their best to persuade past, current, and future customers that cruising is safe, luxurious, relaxing, exciting, and enjoyable—all the positive adjectives that add up to making cruising popular.

Some call cruise ships floating hotels, but others go so far as to describe them as contained floating cities. As a form of transportation, almost

DOI: 10.4324/9781003019282-9

anything can happen. Storms, hurricanes, collisions, hijackings, drunkenness, missing persons, person overboard, fire onboard, sickness of many kinds, food poisoning, natural deaths, spousal abuse, airport shutdowns, power outages, oil spills, kidnapping, theft, and violence are just some of them.

Holland America Line is owned by Carnival Cruise Lines and is registered in the Netherlands. In 2010 there were 15 ships offering nearly 500 cruises to 320 ports in more than 100 countries in all seven continents. Passengers come from all over the world. The ships must follow law in the Netherlands and typically the United States as well as in the countries of port cities.

Under the leadership of Sally Andrews, Holland America Line manages its crises and issues through the Public Relations Department. Sally and director Erik Elvejord (Figure 9.1) act as its primary crisis communicators and spokespeople. The department includes the following areas: media relations, social media, crisis communications, internal communications, corporate giving, event planning, inaugural events, and writing.

Each area serves the company proactively in building good relationships with publics—customers, travel agents, port officials and employees, news media, and others. Each area also serves to prevent crises. If all the areas run smoothly, crises are less likely to occur. However, when a crisis does occur, the PR team is usually front and center as the primary spokespersons and communicators. The Public Relations Department reports to the Executive Vice President, Marketing, Sales and Guest Programs, and to the CEO of Holland America Line, who reports to the CEO of Carnival.

Figure 9.1 Erik Elvejord is Director, Public Relations, Holland America Line. He works with staff members like Mary Schimmelman who was Project Manager, Marketing and Creative Services.

Mini-Case 1: Passengers as Non-Expert Experts

The *Titanic*'s officers had to use Morse code to notify other ships that it was in trouble, and the world did not know the full story until the surviving passengers reached New York, days after the ship sank. Just a few years ago, the company and the Public Relations Department would be notified by ship personnel when a crisis occurred. Today, with cell phones and computers, news media and people worldwide often know of an incident at sea before the cruise line company does. This compounds the crisis, because people frequently do not get the facts correct, and undoing false information is extremely difficult. Non-expert experts are people who speak as if they are knowledgeable and have authority when actually their appeal is based on emotions and excitement (see the Chapter 4 subsection "Update: Subsequent Commentary" in the case study of the Columbine High School shootings). These passenger non-expert experts are the spokespersons who often use exaggeration when describing situations to the news media.

Also, the news media, especially television news reporters, seek stories from "real people" because they are perceived to be more interesting than a boring spokesperson with facts.

Onboard illnesses such as the Norwalk-like virus (NLV) are probably the most expected crisis when hundreds of people are gathered in one place for a long period of time. The ships take precautions by washing down the ship after each cruise; they even wash the poker chips in the casino and throw away the playing cards. Viruses are spread when individuals, even though they are warned, do not take precautions to avoid communicable diseases. So the diseases spread despite the fact that the cruise ship staff do all they can to prevent them.

Elvejord was in San Diego in spring, 2009, to meet the news media at the port where a Holland America Line ship had Norwalk virus victims. A passenger had sent emails to the news media that two people had died, 200 were sick, and the ship was in quarantine. The "facts" were erroneous. No one had died, there were 106 who were affected during the entire length of the cruise. The ship was not quarantined. The passenger spokesperson also falsely claimed to be sick and quarantined. When Elvejord arrived, he found reporters who wanted to believe the passenger—the non-expert expert—and not the cruise line as it was a much more interesting news story, so he had to battle cameras and a barrage of questions.

Elvejord checked the websites of three of the news organizations and found the incorrect facts and also a quote attributed to him that he knew nothing about. He was quoted as saying, "They were puking, having diarrhea and in quarantine." Holland America Line received many calls from other news organizations and individuals who had seen this misinformation.

Knowing that the reporting was misinformation, he contacted the news organizations and corrected the information. He said that after that incident, he always checked the websites first and made sure the online information was correct sooner.

Mini-Case 2: The Bungee Jumper

A 36-year-old would-be stuntman/daredevil sought to get attention to his bravery and skills by jumping from the middle span of the Lions Gate Bridge in Vancouver, British Columbia, Canada, to Holland America Line's MS *Veendam* as it passed under the bridge.

There was a stuntmen's convention nearby, and the man, Dean Sullivan, thought if he succeeded at the stunt, he would get the attention of people at the convention.

Sullivan said, "This was no way some whimsical thing." He said he had planned it for more than two years. He checked traffic flow charts figuring out how to get to the bridge on time, reviewed tide times and boat layouts including the location of boat mainstays. He said, "The planning also included security protocols for the port of Vancouver and research on where people stood on cruise ships leaving the port of Vancouver." He found out that people gather at the bow or the stern, so he prepared to reach the ship in a less populated spot so no one would get hurt. He said, "I would rather hurt myself than someone else." He studied weather and itineraries for the ship, had custom anchors for the bridge built, two-way radios secured, and he said he practiced.

On the chosen day, the weather was overcast, which was perfect for Sullivan because few people would be on the deck. He had a driver get him to the bridge on time, secured himself to the span with 227 feet of rope in a custom-made bag. He knew the *Veendam* would pass under the bridge 270 feet above the water. He had a knife attached to himself so he could cut the rope once onboard. So he jumped.

The bag holding the rope did not deploy on time, putting the jump off by mere seconds. By the time he jumped, the ship had traveled about 12 knots. He said, "Holy s***! I was flying toward the deck of the ship at an incredible speed." He bounced off the netting covering the ship's tennis court, struck his head on a railing, and the ship sailed off, leaving him dangling in mid-air. He was not seriously injured; a witness said he saw him light a cigarette after being picked up by a water taxi. He said his face was "cut pretty good." He was arrested and charged with criminal mischief. Evaluating his feat, he said he was on the ship's netting for about two seconds, so technically he made it. If he had not lost those few seconds and landed successfully, he had planned to stay onboard until he was forced to leave.

Passengers on the back deck of the ship saw the incident and told the crew. The Coast Guard, advised by passersby, told the captain. It could have been so much more unfortunate. A man hitting the side of a cruise ship is similar to a mosquito hitting the windshield of a moving car. Sullivan was very lucky. This could have been a tragic story with the Holland America Line name in it, something the cruise line would never welcome though it was totally innocent.

Elvejord was contacted by a Vancouver television station. He answered questions about the ship's route, what was happening onboard, that no one on the ship was injured, etc. He told the news media that the ship followed standard procedure, that the incident slowed the ship down—inconveniencing passengers—because the Coast Guard asked the ship to dock.

Mini-Case 3: Immigrant Rescue

Holland America Line experienced a crisis of sorts after a ship's crew members thought they spied a man overboard and soon found themselves involved in rescuing refugees immigrating to seek a better life.

The MS *Noordam* was approaching Kusadasi, Turkey, in the Aegean Sea early one morning when crew members cleaning the deck heard a shout in the distance and saw a person in the water. Notifications were made and personnel began its man overboard (MOB) procedure, returning to the site of the sighting. The captain sent a fast rescue boat to search for the person in the water. Then, suddenly, they saw three persons wearing life jackets yelling for help on the port side of the ship, then there were more on the starboard side and others in front of the ship.

One officer said he thought they were survivors of a sunken pleasure boat. The rescue boat holds only six passengers and there were many more people needing to be rescued. The MS *Noordam* sent a Mayday signal asking for assistance, but no other vessels would stop. The ship's hotel manager explained, "The other vessels are so used to people in the water that if they have brown skin, they just call the Coast Guard." So the MS *Noordam* sent out additional rescue boats and plucked 22 persons out of the sea. One infant had drowned.

The survivors were taken to non-public areas of the ship, fed, clothed, and seen by a medical team. They were from Somalia, Iran, Iraq, and Palestine and had been in a refugee house in Turkey. They wanted to go to a Greek island where they hoped to get jobs and live under human rights laws, but the motorboat they hired had capsized in rough seas.

Over the last decade, thousands of people have died attempting to get to better lands of opportunity in unseaworthy boats. The ship morally was obligated to save the refugees from what would have been certain death, but it was obligated by international law to disembark rescued persons at the next port of call, which was in Turkey, from where the people had fled.

Holland America Line held the ship in Kusadasi an extra day while diplomats from the Netherlands, the United States, and the United Kingdom took up the issue of repatriating the refugees with the Turkish government. This delayed the ship's schedule and meant that the cruise would have to skip one of its ports of call, angering passengers who were looking forward to going to Malta. Some of them may have considered Malta to be the highlight of the trip, and now they would not get there. It also meant that Holland America Line would lose revenue on shore excursions and vendors in Malta would suffer economically.

Andrews said:

> Holland America Line has a very deep sense of its humanitarian role as well as a commitment to service and our guests. As this situation played out, we kept our guests informed so they understood the situation. Even though we missed a port, they did understand the reasons behind it and nearly everyone supported this.

The ship's hotel manager said they sent out to guests several statements from the captain, both written and verbal, to apologize and give partial refunds. At the end of the cruise, the ship's officers and staff made a presentation to the passengers relating details of the incident, and they received a standing ovation.

The Public Relations Department issued a news release to travel media and those who were following the story.

Nature's Crisis

Cruises are often affected by severe storms and hurricanes. Executive management and crisis teams make decisions about alternate routes and changes of itineraries to ensure the safety of passengers while providing them with a pleasurable experience. Crisis communicators regularly disseminate messages to several stakeholders.

Key among them are: persons aboard ships directly affected by an impending storm, employees who live in the path of a storm, families of employees who live in the path of a storm, travel agents with clients currently aboard affected ships, travel agents whose clients' future travel plans may be affected, and the travel industry news media.

Elvejord and Andrews say they use virtually all news media, travel desks, and news desks:

> We use PR Newswire and post on our website if the event is large enough, then we keep a log of those working the story to always send updates. We now use social media—Twitter and Facebook—though we did not at that time. Other publics we have to reach are port officials, airlines, travel agents, vendors, visitors, and shore excursion operators.
> (Erik Elvejord, personal communication with author)

Mini-Case 4: Hurricane Changes Ship's Itinerary

September 2

When Hurricane Frances threatened the coast of Florida in September, 2004, the staff on the MS *Zuiderdam* delivered a letter to passengers on September 2, reading that the Coast Guard had closed Port Everglades (at Fort Lauderdale) to incoming vessels. The ship would be unable to dock there as the scheduled point of disembarkation two days later.

The letter indicated that Holland America Line would re-book passengers on later airlines if flights were missed. Also, Holland America Line would provide motor coaches to other airports when it could dock in Fort Lauderdale. Further, it gave passengers a website and a toll-free phone number they could pass on to family and friends to keep them updated on the changing situation.

On the same day, letters were sent to travel agents with clients booked on the September 4 sailing, informing them that the cruise would be shortened from seven to six days and there would be one less port stop. It gave each passenger a choice of a total refund or a discount and onboard credit for a future cruise. Whenever passengers are inconvenienced, benefits are offered.

A news release to consumers, the travel trade, local reporters, and the website was sent announcing the itinerary change due to the hurricane and why. It stressed that safety was paramount and that the passengers were enjoying an extra day of cruising in calm seas away from the storm.

September 3

By the next day, Hurricane Frances had weakened, and the plan was that the ship would dock in Fort Lauderdale on the morning of September 5—a Sunday—a day later than scheduled. The letter that day also offered passengers an opportunity to stay onboard for the next sailing at a reduced rate. Several took advantage of the opportunity.

A letter went to travel agents with clients aboard the then current cruise advising them of the situation and the air travel issue. A letter went to

Holland America Line employees and their families living in the path of the hurricane; the letter informed them that if they were thinking of evacuation, they might think of evacuating to the safety of the *Zuiderdam* at a greatly reduced rate ($149 per person for a one-week cruise) since several passengers would likely cancel. Employees enjoy those special benefits regularly.

September 4

An early letter on September 4 indicated that the plan was still to dock in Fort Lauderdale the following morning, and that, until then, the ship would be navigated far from the storm and would cruise the beautiful calm seas and sunny skies of the Gulf of Mexico until it could safely approach Fort Lauderdale. However, it was later announced that nature had made its own plans and that the ship could not dock until Monday, September 6 and that the scheduled Saturday departure would depart on September 6, two days later than scheduled and with a change of ports of call.

Again, passengers were offered an opportunity to stay onboard for the next cruise if staterooms were available, anticipating that some of the booked passengers would cancel because they were unable or unwilling to take the delayed shortened cruise and/or unable to get to Fort Lauderdale.

Another announcement news release went out explaining the extended delay and the change of ports.

September 5

The *Zuiderdam* actually reached port on Sunday, September 5, a day earlier than predicted, and delivered letters to thank guests for their patience and give them instructions to make disembarkation and rebooking of flights easier.

Some stayed onboard for the Monday embarkation and a five-day cruise. Some Holland America employees made quick decisions to take a few days off and join the cruise at a discounted rate (a perk of the job). The company communicated with cruise customers through sales representatives so that they received the communications in their own languages.

(Eric Elvejord, personal communication with author)

Crisis Management Also Includes Communications

Holland America Line's 13,500 seagoing employees on all 15 ships must participate in fire and "abandon ship" drills monthly. Upon boarding a vessel, crew members receive crisis management and human behavior training in accordance with the Standards of Training, Certification and

Watchkeeping (STCW) convention mandated by the International Maritime Organization (IMO). Key issues taught are for crew members to be firm in their actions and self-assured.

An example of problems faced in the training is that 60 percent of guests in an emergency situation do nothing at first. They find the situation unbelievable and continue to gamble, drink, sleep, eat, do whatever they were doing or maybe just stare into space, so the crew must be able to persuade them to take action swiftly.

For those employees who are shore-based, Michiel Versteeg, Director, Compliance Programs, manages the Incident Command Center and organizes periodic drills and exercises so that, in the unlikely event of a shipboard emergency, adequate assistance can be provided.

There are various contingency plans for different types of crises. There may be incidents on board ships or ashore, or there may be natural disasters such as earthquakes, tsunamis, and mudslides that affect company employees. International maritime law requires a ship to render assistance whenever another ship is in distress. Rescue Coordination Centers all over the world have the authority to do so. In particular, cruise ships with large numbers of supplies, medical assistance, and other facilities onboard are likely to be assigned to take charge of on-scene rescue until the Coast Guard arrives. As an example, one of Holland America Line's cruise ships was called to the site of a cargo ship taking on water off the coast of Cuba. The crew members rendered assistance by providing dewatering equipment, which kept the cargo ship afloat.

Rescuing persons at sea is an expected but not common event, but it is a part of maritime law. Elvejord said, "You help your brothers, like using your cell phone when you see an accident on the freeway."

So assimilated drills and exercises are critical for emergency preparedness and Holland America Line's business operation. Some are as long as two days; others take two or three hours. Participants in shore-based exercises not only include land-based employees but may also include external partners such as the U.S. Coast Guard (USCG), U.S. Customs and Border Protection (CBP), FBI, FEMA, state (Department of Public Health, state troopers, Department of Environmental Conservation), and local agencies (firefighters, police, etc.).

To facilitate any interaction with these agencies, the cruise line adopted the Incident Command System in accordance with the National Incident Management System. This provides a systematic, proactive approach to guide departments and agencies of all levels of government, non-governmental organizations and the private sector to work seamlessly to prevent, protect against, respond to, recover from, and mitigate the effects of incidents regardless of cause, location, or complexity in order to reduce the loss of life and property and harm to the environment.

In August, 2009, a simulated exercise was held in Juneau, Alaska, aboard Holland America Line's MS *Veendam*, together with the local authorities. The created scenario was that there was a fire aboard the cruise ship, and the local fire department as well as the Coast Guard participated. For 3½ hours, the participants tested communications, equipment, and response skills and simulated getting passengers away from the fire and the ship, and safely evacuating them to a nearby school.

A larger multiagency two-day exercise was conducted in April, 2009, and organized by the USCG, Holland America Line, C BP, and local authorities in Ketchikan, Alaska. The exercise consisted of a tabletop exercise and an actual simulated exercise involving about 100 volunteers who acted as guests and responded to a simulated incident with a large passenger vessel.

Each organization in the drill had its own set of objectives in the drill, plus objectives shared by all participants. The shared objectives included but were not limited to the following:

- Coordinating rescue and assistance action plans for the evacuation and transportation of evacuees from the incident site to designated landing/ recovery sites.
- Accounting for passengers and crew with 100 percent accuracy by the end of the exercise.
- Implementing a shore-side support plan for evacuees that included triage and medical services, local transportation, sheltering, and personal care.
- Establishing and operating a joint "media plan" for response to an elevated public affairs demand to the given scenario.
- Establishing timely communications and information exchange between the ship, industry Emergency Operations Center, response agencies, and impacted port community.
- Establishing an Emergency Call Center and an industry website to serve as a point of information for family and friends and crew members sheltered at the location.

Holland America Line's objectives included the following:

- Improving overall Incident Command Center readiness and effectiveness.
- Activate an Emergency Call Center and a Holland America Line website to serve as a point of information for family and friends of guest and crew members.
- Coordinating a public affairs plan for the planning and execution phases of the event.

- Establishing video conferencing with the Coast Guard command. Exercise and evaluate the system if the technology is available.
- Providing all Holland America Line Crisis Action and Emergency Response Team members with incident response training.

Incident Command Center

The company also maintains a fully equipped, ready to use Incident Command Center in case of major news-making crises or disasters. The center has established stations for various department representatives (media relations, guest programs, risk management, etc.) who will need to be present during a crisis. The stations have computers and telephones, supplies, liquid crystal display (LCD) television screens that can be tuned to different networks and cable stations, video conferencing equipment, surround systems, organizational charts, and clocks set for various time zones, including the site of the crisis—everything needed. Employees from Public Relations such as Andrews and Elvejord need only come into the office and they can immediately begin the media relations aspect of the crisis communications. Every four weeks, the equipment is tested for readiness.

The center is located in Holland America Line's headquarters in Seattle; Versteeg said the company is looking toward establishing a similar setup offsite in case of the unlikely event that the headquarters office is not usable. This is an advisable preparation, as businesses in New York's WTC realized after the 9/11 tragedy. When there is no office, no command center, no phones or computers, what happens? Management needs to communicate not only with the news media but also with employees, and perhaps their families as well as other publics.

Holland America Line has consistently been rated among the top cruise lines by *Condé Nast Traveler* Readers' Choice Awards and *Travel & Leisure* World's Best Awards. It earned the High Deluxe Five-Star Rating by the World Ocean & Cruise Liner Society, and for 17 consecutive years it was the Best Overall Cruise Value by the World Ocean & Cruise Liner Society and *Ocean & Cruise News*.

Update/Case Study: Cruise Ships and COVID-19

An iceberg caused a famous ship to sink in 1912, but a disease threatened to sink entire cruise companies a little more than a century later. During the first months of the COVID-19 outbreak in 2020, there was concern that cruising might be a pleasure of the past. First, the British ship *Diamond Princess* with 3,711 souls aboard had 700 stricken with the disease and nine died. Soon after, 40 ships had reported cases. By summer, 50 cruise lines and 270 ships stopped operating.

Some ports did not permit ships to dock. Some ships were idle at sea. Would-be cruisers were advised to avoid cruising to save their lives. The news media termed cruise ships "floating petri dishes." Thousands of people on board ships were stranded and far away from home. More than 200,000 jobs depending upon cruise ships, including tourists at ports, were lost. Cruise workers—often from countries like India, Bangladesh, and the Philippines—were not entitled to U.S. government stimulus checks and could not provide for their families.

Thousands of people were infected; more than 100 died. In the second quarter of 2020, Carnival, the largest cruise company, reported a net loss of $4 billion; as much as $650 million was lost each month. Carnival sold six ships as scrap to cut costs.

Could the industry survive bankruptcy? How can thousands of people practice the mandated social distancing on ships with confined indoor areas and minimum medical facilities? Well, today, the cruise industry is fully functioning. What happened?

The cruise industry knows its primary publics, passengers, very well (Figure 9.2). It knew the passengers love cruising and most definitely wanted to return. Where else can you find leading chefs, great bars, gambling, entertainment—all within a few yards of your bed? So, the

Figure 9.2 Holland America and other cruise lines studied their primary publics, those who love cruising, and worked out marketing deals to keep them making travel plans after the pandemic protocols were lifted. Many people thought the cruise industry might have gone out of business.

Source: SOPA Images / LightRocket via Getty Images

passengers who were on ships at the time of the shutdown were offered the choice of a refund or credit toward future trips. A huge percentage opted for the credit. In addition, the Cruise Lines International Association found that 82 percent of previous customers were eager to return. (Anderson, 2022).

After a 15-month shutdown, cruising was on its way back. At first the CDC established a strict safety protocol program and worked closely with the industry. There was more distance between tables in dining areas. There were fewer people on elevators. The ships added more sinks for handwashing and more hand sanitizing stations. Some ships offered—for additional costs—premium accommodations with fewer people, like private dining and smaller bars with limited capacity. Then later, around July, 2022, each ship set its own protocols.

The marketing and public relations programs targeted groups other than the usual senior citizen passengers—first-time cruisers, singles, adults only, young couples, and people who seek all-inclusive fare. Cruise shoppers went for the deals.

Beth Bodensteiner, senior vice president and chief commercial officer for Holland America, a division of Carnival, said considering challenges in air travel, they developed shorter cruises that do not require long flights for passengers to connect to ships. She also said:

> During the pause, we worked to carry out protocols that helped make cruising among the safest forms of travel, and we offered guests a "worry-free promise" so they could feel confident booking a cruise, knowing they would be covered if their plans changed. . . . Our team members and guests are thrilled to be on board again.
>
> (Pratesi, 2023)

Disney Cruise Lines added its largest ship, the *Disney Wish*, in 2022, the same year that Royal Caribbean, the second-largest cruise company, added the largest ship in the world, the *Wonder of the Seas*.

Case Study: US Airways and "The Miracle on the Hudson"

James Olson joined US Airways as Vice President, Corporate Communications, in April, 2008, from Waggener Edstrom Worldwide, a technology-focused PR agency based in Seattle.[1] One of his first tasks was to consider the company's crisis communications plan. The plan had been developed years before and basically suffered from additions deemed important by later teams. It was 125 pages and Olson said, "Every name was out of date."

So, in October, 2008, he and his department organized to make the plan more user-friendly. It was cut to fewer than 15 pages and included only elements needed if there was a crisis "now."

In mid-December, 2008, the company had a "tabletop drill." The drill was a simulated catastrophic accident. The corporate communications team also had a half-day summit that involved first-responder teams from other areas of the company, including marketing, emergency planning, information technology (IT), and the external crisis response agency, Weber Shandwick.

The drill was just in time. Each executive and each member of the communications team recalls where they were and what they were doing on January 15 when they learned that US Airways Flight 1549 leaving New York's LaGuardia Airport for Charlotte, North Carolina, was down.

Elise Eberwein (Executive Vice President, People and Communications) was on a flight from Phoenix to Charlotte heading for a vacation. As soon as she landed, she abandoned thoughts of vacation and took the next flight to LaGuardia.

Michelle Mohr (Senior Manager, Corporate Communications) was in her office at the Charlotte hub. The troubled plane was heading to Charlotte, so Mohr began to prepare for the local news media that would descend on the airport.

Morgan Durrant (Senior Manager, Corporate Communications) was based in Philadelphia and was in his office. On hearing the first report, he caught the next flight to LaGuardia to provide on-site support.

CEO Doug Parker was in the Tempe, Arizona, headquarters company boardroom meeting with bankers. Senior Vice President of Public Affairs C. A. Howlett entered the room and told Parker there was a report that a plane was down. Parker dashed back to his office and saw the Airbus 320 floating in the Hudson River on television. He told the bankers the problem and dismissed them immediately; the boardroom was the designated corporate command center.

Olson was meeting in his Phoenix office with the IT director to discuss the technology and phone demands and needs of the war room should there be a crisis. The IT director had just said that it would take about three months to install the needed equipment.

Suddenly, a colleague burst into the office and said, "Jim . . . sorry to interrupt but I think you'll want to take this call. It's Reuters [wire service] wanting a comment about one of our planes floating down the Hudson River." Olson turned on the television, which is generally always on CNN. Without a word, the team went about setting up the crisis war room. The phones were installed within minutes (rather than months).

Participants in the December drill were warned that despite the company's sophisticated notification system, if there were an actual crisis, they would probably be notified by the news media. Reuters called and they tuned in to CNN and received confirmation when they saw the plane afloat.

Olson and the communications team activated the emergency response plan immediately. He said his BlackBerry was "burning in my hand with people seeking information."

He rushed back to the office where the rest of the Phoenix-based Corporate Communications staff of six were already writing the first news release. Olson said:

> It is our goal that the initial news release should go out within 15 minutes of a crisis. There are templates for press releases that were available, but this was a "moving accident site." All the templates did not fit the situation.

The site and the information were changing rapidly, so updates were made as information was confirmed. Information had to be substantiated by the airline before it could be distributed. News media often go with one source in the interest of immediacy and beating the competition, but the Corporate Communications team at US Airways was determined to be more accurate than fast.

Even though numerous media outlets were reporting that all passengers were safe within 90 minutes of the emergency landing, US Airways could not make that announcement on its website or on social media networks until it had confirmed personally with each passenger or a family member. This could not be done immediately because the ferries that rescued passengers took them to various places. As the ferries took them to both sides of the Hudson River, the passengers dispersed to hotels or the homes of friends and family, and some even headed back to the airport to catch the next flight to Charlotte.

The news media, especially television and online media, often get facts wrong in their quest to be first rather than factual. An organization in crisis cannot afford to take this chance. It serves its customers and employees first or it will lose customers and the respect of employees—reactions organizations cannot or should not risk. It cannot guess or estimate when lives are in question.

When News Is Wrong—When Experts Are Not Experts

An illustration of this dilemma took place on November 5, 2009, when 12 people were killed and 31 wounded at Fort Hood, the military base in Killeen, Texas. CNN—on the air with continuous coverage—and networks reported that Maj. Nidal Hassan, the gunman, was himself killed by civilian police.

For more than four hours, this "fact" was reported over and over. Also, the anchors advised viewers repeatedly that there would be a news conference "at any minute." At about 9:15 p.m. EST, Fort Hood finally held the news conference, led by spokesperson Lt. Gen. Robert Cone. Cone and the public affairs staff had without doubt monitored television news, saw the errors, and felt the pressure to make announcements. Nevertheless, they did not come forward until they had facts. The first fact was a correction of the error made all evening. Hassan was not killed, but was injured and in custody. Cone said, "I would say his death is not imminent."

A few minutes later, the *Larry King Show* was broadcast, and King mentioned again that the gunman was not deceased and said something about how it is expected that errors will be made in breaking news. That seems to be the nature of today's news media, in the post-Cronkite era.

King's show that night had as guests Dr. Phil McGraw, former POW Shoshana Johnson, and Tom Kenniff of the U.S. Army. The conversation was why Hassan had shot so many people, or shot anybody. Certainly none of them knew why, but it was exciting conversation about a timely issue. Kenniff said Hassan was an Islamist committing a terrorist act. The others were incensed at Kenniff and said Hassan had a mental health problem. None of them actually knew. All of them were *non-expert experts* in this arena.

The non-expert expert, seen on television and frequently online, appeals to viewers on emotion not fact, a threat to any organization or individual in crisis. The term "non-expert expert" was coined for the first three editions of this textbook in a case titled "Cellular Phones and the Cancer Scare." Ken Woo, then a media relations manager for Cellular One, used the term to describe David Reynard, a recent widower and a father whose wife had died of brain cancer. On the *Larry King Show*, he blamed the cancer on her usage of a cellular phone, which, he said, she held near the tumor. Also on the show was a scientist who had studied cellular technology for years and said the power output from cellular phones was too low to damage human tissue. However, viewers chose not to believe any of her scientific data because, after all, Reynard's wife had died. He was sad. He had a motherless child. The show even showed video of the wife before she died saying she used the phone "a lot." As the phone calls poured in, the cellular phone crisis was born for cellular carriers. They all developed crisis communications campaigns, but basically the crisis ended because people did not really want to give up the convenience of cell phones.

Getting It Right Takes Time

So US Airways wanted to get the facts right. An emergency response "bridge line" was established, through which key company personnel—Operations,

Customer Relations, Corporate Communications, Legal and Regulatory teams—were either participants in the phone calls between key first responders who were communicating with the crew and the Federal Aviation Administration (FAA) or listening to the conversations.

It was during this call that Olson learned that all 150 passengers and the five members of the crew had been safely evacuated. Olson said,

> One of our guys at the OCC [Operations Control Center] came on the line and said, "This is preliminary, but I just spoke to the captain [Sullenberger] and he tells me he walked up and down the aisle and he thinks everyone is off the plane safely."

People watching television news and computer reports also heard about Capt. "Sully" Sullenberger going back through the plane to make sure all were off. Fear at US Airways turned to relief shared by people everywhere as they watched the passengers standing along the slightly submerged wings seemingly standing on water.

Corporate Communications put up its customer and media website dedicated to Flight 1549 within 30 minutes of notification of the accident (Figure 9.3, Figure 9.4). This was the initial primary source for customers and the news media. The first news release was issued in 45 minutes. The CEO conducted a press briefing covered by nearly every network and news outlet within about 90 minutes. As more information was learned, additional news releases and internal messages followed in the hours and days that followed.

Olson recalled,

> The Corporate Communications team also worked with our marketing team to leverage search engines like Yahoo and Google by purchasing key word terms related to the Flight 1549 emergency landing and directing them to the dedicated Flight 1549 micro site.

Several crisis management/communications actions emanating from the company took place immediately. The Care Team of employees trained from various work groups was dispatched to New York, where they provided cell phones and clothing for passengers, and to Charlotte, to provide on-site support to family members. The Family Support Hotline was a special toll-free phone number set up for family members to call to get information on the status of their loved ones. The Passenger and Crew Manifest Reconciliation is a crucial process of confirming the whereabouts and safety of all passengers and crew. The confirmation from Capt. Sullenberger was assumed to be correct, but each and every person had to be accounted for and confirmed to have survived. Someone had to determine

---

US AIRWAYS PRESS RELEASE

US Airways Flight 1549 Initial Report

Tempe, Ariz.—(Business Wire)—Jan. 15, 2009—US Airways (NYSE: LCC) flight 1549, an Airbus A320 en route to Charlotte from LaGuardia, has been involved in an accident in New York approximately 3:03 p.m. Eastern Time.

Airline officials are in direct contact with local, state and national authorities and are cooperating fully with emergency response efforts. US Airways' primary concern at this time is for those on board the airplane and their families.

US Airways is confirming passenger and crew on board the aircraft and will issue additional information as soon as possible. At this point, no additional details can be confirmed.

Individuals who believe they may have family members on board flight 1549 may call US Airways at 1–800–679–8215 within the United States. This number can be reached toll-free from international locations though AT&T's USADirect®. Then contact an AT&T operator—please visit www.usa.com/traveler for USADirect® access codes.

US Airways will provide additional information as it becomes available. Please monitor usairways.com for the latest information. (LCCG).

—LCC
CONTACT:
US Airways
Media Relations
Source: US Airways

Figure 9.3 This news release was the first one that US Airways disseminated after Flight 1549 made an emergency landing in the Hudson River. Courtesy of US Airways.

where they all were and make contact with them. Olson (Figure 9.5) said this process took 24 hours.

Later, in an article in *BusinessWeek*, writer Dean Foust praised the airline's care of passengers, calling the process "a model of crisis management" (Foust, 2009). In the article, James J. Hanks, Jr., a Baltimore attorney, was quoted as praising not only the pilot and crew but also the

CONTINUING PRESS RELEASES

Our goal is to issue the first press release (which acknowledges the accident and provides initial details) within 15 minutes of notification.

Press Release #1: Initial report. Flight number, aircraft type, O&D, location of accident, time, time zone

Press Release #2: Includes initial report information, adds number of passengers and crew

Press Release #3: Follow-up release containing remarks from initial press conference

Press Release #4: Information on aircraft (age, hours, last checks)

Press Release #5: Details on crew

Figure 9.4 As new information was available, that information was added to subsequent news releases.

US Airways Care Team for providing free hotel rooms, warm meals, and dry clothing.

The Go-Team consisting of CEO Parker, a managing director of the Finance Team, members of the Care Team—about 50 employees altogether—carried special emergency credit cards and cash to first responders to be used to book hotel rooms and to buy clothing and other essentials for passengers whose personal belongings, including wallets, were left on the plane. Passengers were ordered to leave everything not attached to them on the plane.

Before the day of the emergency landing was over, New York Mayor Bloomberg informed officials that there would be a news conference the following morning, and he wanted CEO Parker to be present to honor the crew as well as the first responders.

The January 26 news conference was announced in a news release along with the CEO's remarks applauding the crew, police, ferry boat operators, water taxis, EMTs (emergency medical technicians), the Office of Emergency Management, the ARC, the Salvation Army, and others.

On January 17, a letter from the CEO was sent to Flight 1549's passengers informing them how they might get their personal belongings from the plane and what the process would entail. A check for $5,000 was enclosed to cover immediate expenses and a separate check to reimburse the costs

FLIGHT 1549 LESSONS LEARNED

Be Prepared.
* Have an integrated plan.
* Test it!
* Use It!

Be Fast.
* First press release issued 40 minutes after accident.
* First CEO press briefing within first two hours of accident.

Be Accessible.
* 100+ calls an hour answered.
* Established media war room within ten minutes of accident.
* Established PR presence at origin, destination and crash site (in part through PR agency support and local team members).

Be Engaged.
* Share information with employees early and often.
* Partner with NTSB, FAA and manufacturer PR teams.

Be Compassionate.
* Balance facts with emotion.

Figure 9.5 James Olson, US Airways Vice President, Corporate Communications, developed this list of lessons learned based on challenges he faced in handling crisis communications after the emergency landing. Courtesy of James Olson.

of the original airfare. The services of the airline's Family Support Center were offered.

Another letter went to passengers on January 21, again offering the services of the Customer Care Team and promising to make efforts to recover personal items from the submerged plane. All passengers were informed that they would be extended Chairman's Preferred status, the airline's most prestigious frequent flyer level, through March, 2010.

There was some success recovering passengers' belongings. YouTube showed a dramatic video of the plane being raised.

The Corporate Communications team's work was not done even after passengers and crew were safely at home. The entire Flight 1549 crew appeared on CBS's *60 Minutes* about a month after the incident. They were interviewed by Katie Couric in one of the airline's maintenance hangars in Charlotte. In the 12 months after the emergency water landing, the crew conducted dozens of interviews and were reunited in New York City with many of the passengers and first responders on the one-year anniversary (Figure 9.6). Captain Sully again made news when he returned to the cockpit on October 1, 2009. The one-year anniversary activities included a trip back out on the Hudson River at the precise time of day and the precise location where the plane landed a year earlier.

FLIGHT 1549

Returning [to Charlotte] from the New York-based investment company that she is president of, [Maryann] Bruce had schlepped through LaGuardia Airport with a . . . laptop, briefcase, purse, a mink coat and a carry-on suitcase.

The diamond ring she . . . received on her 25th wedding anniversary ". . . must've smashed my finger," says Bruce. "By the time I got to the plane my finger was black and blue."

So she stashed the ring in a jewelry pouch in her carry-on in the overhead compartment. When the plane landed and the flight attendant ordered everyone off, "I knew I had to get off the plane even though the ring was up there."

"After being rescued, I thought I might get my suitcase back," she says "but I thought someone might steal the jewelry . . ."

. . . US Airways' [Deborah] Thompson flew to Charlotte to personally deliver Bruce's . . . ring . . . and [it] looked like new. "Oh my God, I got it back," Bruce says she thought.

. . . Another item that came back, a little worse for wear but still legible: Bruce's boarding pass for seat 5D, Flight 1549.

"I plan on framing that," she says.

Excerpt from "Belongings Once Lost are Found Again" by Marilyn Adams, *USA Today*, Wednesday, May 20, 2009

Figure 9.6 This excerpted story in *USA Today* tells a positive story of the efforts US Airways made to satisfy customers on flight 1549 (Adams, 2009).

The incident soon became known as "The Miracle on the Hudson," a term that Parker does not like. "I believe that 'Pride' is a better characterization," he said. There was nothing miraculous about the flawless efforts of the crew. He preferred to think that all US Airways pilots and crews would perform in the same excellent manner. As Capt. Sullenberger (Figure 9.7) said, "I know I can speak for the entire crew when I tell you we were simply doing the jobs we were trained to do."

The company hosted an employee ceremony praising the many employees who were directly involved in the response. A special video of the event and media coverage was distributed.

US Airways merged with American Airlines in 2015 and discontinued the US Airways brand name. The final flight from San Francisco to Philadelphia on October 17, 2015 made news and aviation history. Jim Olson had already left the airlines to lead global corporate communications and public affairs at Starbucks in Seattle. In early 2016, he departed Starbucks to be senior vice president of corporate communications at United Airlines.

Update/Case Study: Airplanes and Bird Strikes

After Captain Sullenberger maneuvered his US Airways jet to a safe landing on water, air safety officials have studied the phenomenon of bird strikes

Figure 9.7 Captain Chesley "Sully" Sullenberger became a celebrity after he skillfully landed the US Airways commercial jet to land on the Hudson River after a bird strike. He was in demand for news interviews and public appearances after the accomplishment. He retired and US Airways merged with American Airlines.

Source: Henry Lamb/BEI/Shutterstock.com

and other wildlife strikes. (Small airports have had reports of collisions between taxiing planes and deer.)

The first bird strike was reported by aviation pioneer Orville Wright in his diaries. Birds approached as he flew over a neighbor's cornfield and one bird fell on top of his plane and fell off. In 2003, 4,300 bird strikes were reported by U.S. Air Force pilots and 5,900 by U.S. civil aircraft.

There were more reports of bird strikes after the 2009 incident, mostly because pilots report them more often than they did in the past. Most bird strikes occur during takeoffs and landings or during low-altitude flight. Denver International Airport withstood more strikes than any other major city, followed by Dallas/Fort Worth, Chicago O'Hare, JFK, and Memphis. Denver suffered 9,000 strikes through the end of 2022; 42 caused damage to the planes, but no aircraft were destroyed. There were no injuries to passengers. The birds were not so fortunate.

Large birds like turkey vultures and white pelicans cause the most damage, and birds like Canada geese, doves, larks, and gulls are the most frequently involved in strikes.

In 2021 at Atlantic City International Airport in New Jersey, a bald eagle (an endangered species) collided with a plane engine. A fire resulted and there was damage. The plane with 102 persons aboard aborted the flight. However, eagle strikes are rare.

Since 2009, the FAA has invested $30 million into research to find ways of detecting birds in the path of aircraft. There also has been an effort to modify lights on planes that would help the birds detect planes and avoid them.

Note

1. Interview with James Olson by email and phone.

Bibliography

Holland America and Cruise Crises

Anderson, C. (2022, November 28). Has the cruise industry been hit by the perfect storm? *Company Debt*. Retrieved May 15, 2023, from www.companydept.com.

CBS Miami Team. (2022, September 6). With new ships in 2022, cruise industry shows recovery after pandemic. Retrieved May 15, 2023, from www.CBSMiami.com.

Pratesi, G. (2023, March 10). Have cruises recovered from the pandemic? *Reader's Digest*. Retrieved May 15, 2023, from www.RD.com/article/cruise-chip-covid.

Shah, S. (2023, March 16). The cruise industry is back—and breaking pre-pandemic travel records. *Time*. Retrieved May 23, 2023, from www.time.com/6263225/cruise.

Yeginsu, C. & Chokshi, N. (2021, July 28). The cruise industry stages a comeback. *New York Times*. Retrieved May 15, p. 202.

Update/Case Study: Airplanes and Bird Strikes

Adams, M. (2009, May 20). Belongings once lost are found again. *USA Today*, pp. IB, 4B.
Caruso, D. (2023, March 1). Reports of bird strikes on planes are increasing: Here's why you're actually safer since the Miracle on the Hudson. *USATODAY.com*. Retrieved May 15, 2023, from usatoday.com/story/news.
Foust, D. (2009, February 19). US airways: After the "Miracle on the Hudson". *Business Week*. Retrieved June 20, 2009, from www.businessweek.com/magazine/content.
McCartney, S. (2009, February 18). The middle seat terminal. *WSJ Blogs*. Retrieved June 23, 2009, from http://blogs.wsj.com/middleeast/2009.

Chapter 10

Truth and Privacy

The case study immediately following centers on the difficulties a crisis communicator had to endure to fight for the truth he knew existed, even though the public he served was not so sure. The second case is a re-write of a case study in the first edition of this book. It was brought back by popular demand because privacy laws have changed.

Case Study: Wendy's and the Finger-in-the-Chili Hoax

Denny Lynch, as senior vice president of communications for Wendy's International, faced a crisis that innocent food-based companies fear—a consumer commits a vicious act that causes other patrons to turn away from the restaurant or product.[1]

In March 2005, Anna Ayala, then 39, a Las Vegas resident visiting San Jose, California, went to a Wendy's with relatives. She ordered a bowl of beef chili. She said she bit into a spoon of chili and "suddenly I chew something that's kind of hard, crunchy. I spit it out." She said that's when she realized the crunchy item was a 1½-inch human finger with a well-manicured nail. She hired a lawyer and sued.

Lynch received a phone call that night from Bob Bertini, Wendy's director of communications, explaining what happened. Lynch said he had no time to make a plan of action; he had to act immediately—the news media were calling. For the next 60 days, Lynch and Bertini spent many hours talking to the news media. Lynch said, "The pace was nonstop. Even when Pope John Paul II died, the incident still got coverage."

At first, sympathy was with Ms. Ayala. The Santa Clara County Health Department said she was ill and distraught. The spokesperson said, "She was so emotionally upset once she found out what it was. She was vomiting." It also hurt Wendy's efforts when the health department immediately released photos of the finger to the news media. This made the picture people imagined very real, and national news coverage intensified. The

DOI: 10.4324/9781003019282-10

health department did announce that there was no public health risk, but that was never the issue anyway.

Lynch was not new to crisis communications. In his 25 years at Wendy's, he was on the job when five workers were shot and killed in a Wendy's in Queens, New York.

So a Wendy's regional management team set up a makeshift crisis command center in a franchise office in San Jose. The local police were involved, as was the coroner. Wendy's cooperated fully with the police and health officials, and did everything possible to assist them with their investigation from the earliest stages of the crisis.

As the news spread, patrons fled. A human finger found in food was not life-threatening—as in the Tylenol case when capsules had been laced with poison (see Chapter 3)—nor was it as frightening as a fear of AIDS—as in the Snapps case when restaurant patrons heard a rumor that a manager with AIDS had bled into a hamburger. However, it was still a picture that people could not get past. "It was the gross-out factor," Lynch said. People could not eat chili without imagining there was a finger in it. Even people who knew it was extremely likely that it was a scam were still affected by the gross-out factor.

Wendy's (Figure 10.1) is based in Dublin, Ohio, with 6,600 locations in North America. All its restaurants were affected, but particularly those in the San Francisco Bay area. The company lost 20–50 percent of its business in the Bay area in the first month after the incident.

The *New York Times* called the crisis campaign "CSI: Wendy's." Wendy's checked its own employees and the employees of all its suppliers and

Figure 10.1 Wendy's restaurants all over the country lost sales when a woman charged that she found a human finger in their popular chili. The news media loved it. People all over imagined seeing fingers in chili. It was the "gross-out" factor.

Source: Wiwit Ahmad/Shutterstock.com

quickly determined that no one in Wendy's supply plants or the restaurants had a missing finger. Lynch announced to the press, "All of our employees have ten digits." In addition there had been no reports made to the Occupational Safety and Health Administration of injuries at any supplier of the ingredients of Wendy's chili. (Wendy's chili is made from scratch in each restaurant.) The employee who prepared the chili had been with the same restaurant for ten years and was respected for his dutiful work.

Wendy's crisis management strategy centered on the following four areas.

1. Conducting due diligence to establish that the brand was not at fault.
2. Ensuring that Wendy's key company values drove all decisions and activities.
3. Briefing and mobilizing team members for quick action and response as events unfolded.
4. Building a post-incident campaign that enhanced Wendy's brand.

"Our position was that based on all the information we had, we strongly believed Wendy's was not responsible," Bertini said. "We cautioned the news media not to jump to conclusions, while deliberately avoiding fraud accusations against Ms. Ayala. We did not want to do anything that could jeopardize the police investigation."

So, feeling confident about Wendy's position, it became necessary to find out to whom the finger had belonged and vindicate the company publicly. In the spirit of a true TV mystery, talk went to "Where is the rest of the body?" Wendy's offered a $50,000 and later a $100,000 reward for information leading to positive identification of the finger, and announced that to the news media. Wendy's also contracted with an outside source to man a "tip line" operating ten hours each day for reports.

Copycat cases sprang up with people claiming to have found other items in food at Wendy's—bones and fingernails were mentioned. The finger was fuel for jokes on late night TV talk shows and conversation for daytime call-in radio shows. Jay Leno, on NBC's *The Tonight Show with Jay Leno*, said "I didn't know Wendy's sold finger food."

Immediately following the alleged incident, Ms. Ayala scheduled an appearance on ABC's *Good Morning America* to tell her story. This was the only such national program to have booked an interview with her. Wendy's tried to dissuade ABC from airing the interview because the story, at that point, would make Ayala look credible and would give her a national forum. However, the show refused to curtail its plans, and Wendy's representatives opted not to appear on camera with Ayala.

Nothing good could come from a conversation about the incident, especially as the police investigation was ongoing and the origin of the finger was still a mystery. Nevertheless, Lynch spent three hours on Easter Sunday night preparing a written statement that was read in its entirety on the show. The company's basic position was that the finger did not enter the food chain in its ingredients.

The employees at the San Jose restaurant had all their fingers, and no suppliers of Wendy's ingredients had any hand or finger injuries. If a Wendy's spokesperson had appeared, it could have left the viewing public with the attitude "Big company attacks poor innocent woman and won't admit it is wrong." Still, Ms. Ayala and her lawyer appeared, and anyone who had never heard the story before now heard it, and she was still considered the victim in the case.

People began to claim the finger and the reward. In one of the many bizarre twists in the case, a woman claimed she lost a finger in a leopard attack at an animal compound near Las Vegas. The woman said she last saw her middle finger when it was packed with ice in a plastic bag in hopes of reattaching it. When doctors told her it could not be reattached, she said she had "no idea what happened to the finger." The hospital confirmed that she was there for a leopard attack and that it could not account for where the finger was. Her lawyer came forward saying, "She wants to participate in DNA testing and any final resolution of that matter." He stressed that his client had no connection with Ayala. This was investigated, but the woman's finger was longer than the one supposedly found in the chili, and the fingerprints did not match.

Then the story began to turn. The police continued to investigate, and the coroner began an investigation. In considering the preparation of the chili, first, the raw meat is turned into ground beef at the meatpacking plant. Nothing as long as one inch survives the process. The ground beef used in the chili is chopped into small chunks with a spatula, not even a sharp knife. The beans, from cans, are added along with seasonings and tomatoes. Then, the chili is made in a 22-quart pot and cooked for 4–6 hours; it is stirred every 15 minutes. The coroner said (and the health department concurred) that the finger "was not consistent with an object that had been cooked in chili at 170 degrees for hours."

The police discovered that Ms. Ayala was experienced at filing lawsuits against companies. She had been involved in at least six such cases, some in the San Francisco Bay area. One involved a sexual harassment suit against an auto dealership. That case ended when she had a dispute with her lawyer.

In another suit, she won a settlement against an El Pollo Loco restaurant in Las Vegas. She charged that her daughter became ill after eating in the restaurant, and she was paid for medical expenses. Police investigators said they found 13 civil actions involving Ayala and her children. She was involved in a criminal complaint charging that she sold a trailer she did not own to a woman in San Jose.

In early April, police went to Ayala's home to question her and, according to Ayala, she asserted that they were out to get her and were unnecessarily rough as they executed a search warrant at her home. The Associated Press reported that she said, "Lies, lies, lies—that's all I am hearing. They should look at Wendy's. What are they hiding? Why are we being victimized again?" A few days later, her lawyer said she had decided not to sue.

In mid-April, there was a press conference with Wendy's officials and the police. The police told the news media that they considered the claim a hoax. Ayala was arrested and held without bail at Clark County jail in Las Vegas. She was charged with attempted grand theft stemming from the fact that Wendy's had lost millions of dollars in sales because of a hoax devised by her.

Police said they found in their investigations that two people who knew Ayala (Figure 10.2) said she described putting the finger in the chili. The descriptions were similar and the two people did not know each other. Also, Ayala's family members who were with her at Wendy's said they did not see the finger in her mouth and noticed it only after she pointed to it in the cup. Two family members said they saw her spit it out and she vomited, but there was no evidence of that at the scene.

Figure 10.2 Wendy's and police knew that Anna Ayala had planted a finger in her cup of chili. No employees had lost fingers, and the cooking process would have destroyed a finger. However, it was necessary to prove it before they could announce that she was fraudulent.

Source: John G Mabanglo/EPA/Shutterstock.com

Full Vindication at Last

In May 2005, Wendy's was fully vindicated when police discovered the owner of the finger. A phone call to the hotline tipped police to speak to a male friend and coworker of Ayala's husband, Jaime Plascencia. The friend—Brian Rossiter—had lost a finger in an industrial accident the previous December. The finger was positively identified as belonging to Brian Rossiter, who had sold it to Plascencia for $100. Rossiter cooperated with police and told them the couple had offered him $250,000 to keep silent. The husband was arrested on identity theft charges unrelated to the Wendy's case, but was later also charged with conspiracy to file a false insurance claim and attempted grand theft with damages exceeding $2.5 million.

San Jose Police Chief Rob Davis declared, "The jig is up! The puzzle pieces are beginning to fall into place, and the truth is being exposed."

Soon afterwards Wendy's, made a customer relations move, reaching out to customers in 50 Bay Area restaurants and offering each one a free Frosty and coupons. The approach was later expanded nationally, with Wendy's giving away more than $15–18 million during a weekend to thank customers for their loyalty. A column by Wendy's Chairman Jack Schuessler appeared that same week in the *Wall Street Journal* explaining how Wendy's defended its brand, at great cost, and would emerge stronger and better.

Both Ayala and Plascencia entered guilty pleas in September. At their sentencing hearing in January 2006, the Wendy's cashier, Jose Pacheco, said Ayala had asked whom he killed to get the finger and made him bear the brunt of her complaints. Hector Pineda, who made the chili, said "I felt so bad for the fear of what people would think of me. We are the ones who suffered."

Ayala was sentenced to nine years in prison, while her husband received a 12-year sentence. However, a court glitch reduced the prison sentence. They also were required to pay $170,000 in restitution for the San Jose Wendy's workers' lost wages and $21.8 million to Wendy's International and JEM Management, which owns the restaurant. Both corporations agreed not to collect from the couple if they never benefited from the scam, including books and movies.

Lynch asked the judge to send a message that "consumer fraud is a serious crime that demands a severe penalty."

Ayala didn't get the lesson because in 2012 when her son accidentally shot himself in the foot, she filed a false claim that he had been shot by two men. During police questioning, she admitted the false claim. She and her son were again arrested and sentenced to prison terms.

Looking back at the crisis, Lynch said

> We (Wendy's) moved from a place where many people thought we were guilty to a point where they realized our employees and our brand had

been victimized. Because of our actions, we hope people also now see us as a company that stood by its principles and endeavored to do the right thing when faced with enormous challenges.

In talking to *USA Today* about the crisis, Schuessler said, "We believe our reputation is the most important thing we have." He also said that during a crisis situation, companies have to have a set of core values because "there's no playbook that's been written."

Wendy's was widely praised for its crisis communications, including the following experts who made additional comments:

Jeremy Pepper, who blogs for many PR matters, thinks that if Wendy's had blogged before the finger had been identified, it would have opened itself up to unwanted jokes and comments since the late night talk shows were already making jokes about the finger in the chili.

Jonathan Bernstein, a crisis communications expert, advises that Wendy's should have offered the free Frosties as soon as the finger story hit the news—that this might have embraced customers sooner.

What Could Have Been Done If Social Media Had Existed

Given the modern Internet's seemingly unlimited capacity to excite itself, it's easy to imagine that the PR nightmare endured by Wendy's in 2005 would have only been worse if it had happened today. Social media gives everybody a voice and escalation is often the default course. Twitter is pretty lax on fact-checking. Can you imagine the memes? Luckily, brands have the same powerful tools of communication as everyone else, and Wendy's would have been engaged in the conversation right from the start. By actively monitoring the channels, crisis response can happen in real time, with dynamic strategies ready and in place. Instead of a "tip line," they might have set up a dedicated website, perhaps with a dose of humor to offset the implications of the crisis and play off the ridiculousness of the claim.

And since the online conversation includes everyone, the same voices that can work against a brand can also work for it. It's as much fun to dogpile on a fraud as it is a brand. It is entirely possible that Ms. Ayala's credibility would have been independently challenged, investigated, and ultimately discredited. Her litigious propensity was a matter of public record. There are entire online communities dedicated to such treasure hunts. An online conversation can include many different perspectives, and it is important to consider them all.

Effective crisis communication, like any conversation, starts with good listening. Modern channels allow brands to keep an ear to the ground like never before, allowing them to be among the first voices heard. But the core strategies are essentially the same as they've always been: listen, engage, repeat.

In the age of social media when conversations can change in an instant, it's more important than ever for brands to keep a finger firmly on the pulse (and out of the chili).

Aaron Blank, Principal, The Fearey Group

Mini-Case: Domino's Pizza

Wendy's gross-out crisis was trumped in 2009 by a Domino's Pizza chain crisis that played out and was appropriately battled on social media networks.

Two Domino's employees (a man and a woman) in a Conover, North Carolina, restaurant filmed a tasteless, extremely graphic prank and posted the video on YouTube. As the man defiled the delivery foods, the woman provided voiceover while operating the camera saying:

> In about five minutes, it'll be sent out on delivery where somebody will be eating these, yes, eating them, and little will they know that the cheese was in his nose and that there was some lethal gas that ended up on their salami. Now, that's how we roll at Domino's.

The video soon became the hit of YouTube and was seen by millions of viewers and, no doubt, described to numerous others. Though disgusted, people would still look and still talk, even though reviled. At the time, a search of Google for "Domino" turned up stories of the incident on five of the 12 results on Page 1. There were many discussions about it on Twitter.

A blogger alerted Domino's, and the two employees were immediately fired and arrested on felony charges. The woman issued an apology, which, naturally, was not accepted by Domino's or its consumers. The two said the tainted food products had not been delivered, yet that disclaimer was not enough to prevent serious damage to Domino's reputation or its financial stability.

Domino's spokesperson Tim McIntyre said, "We got blind-sided by two idiots with a video camera and an awful idea. Even people who've been with us as loyal customers for 10, 15, 20 years are second-guessing their relationship with Domino's, and that's not fair."

At first, Domino's chose to lay low and let the controversy die, but that didn't work—even though YouTube removed the video. "What we missed was the perceptual mushroom effect of viral sensations," said McIntyre.

Scott Hoffman, chief marketing officer, Lotame, a social media marketing firm, said, "In social media, if you think it's not going to spread, that's when it gets bigger." In that respect, social media can be a modern form of spreading rumor.

Questions on Twitter were basically, "What did Domino's do about it?" So Domino's created a Twitter account to address comments. It also posted its own YouTube response featuring President Patrick Doyle who said:

We thank members of the online community who quickly alerted us so we could take immediate action. The independent owner of that store is reeling from the damage that this has caused and it's not a surprise that this has caused a lot of damage to our brand. It sickens me that the actions of two individuals could impact our great system where 125,000 men and woman work for local business owners around the U.S. and more than 60 countries around the world.

The store has been sanitized from top to bottom. Nothing is more sacred and important than our customers' trust, and we're examining our hiring practices to make sure that people like this don't make it into our stores. We have auditors in our store every day of the week making sure our stores are as clean as they can possibly be and that we're delivering high quality food to our customers, day in and day out.

Case Study: Mr. Famous Dead Person and Privacy

Estelle Taylor is a fake name for a real person, a former communications director for a major medical center in the State of Washington. Taylor shares the following experience not very many years ago:

It was midnight and a nurse on duty at the medical center telephoned Taylor saying, "Someone was brought in to ER and everybody says he's famous, but he just died."[2]

"What is his name?"

The nurse responded and Taylor said, "Yes, he is famous but obviously not to your age group. Thanks for calling."

Taylor knew him immediately but we shall call him Mr. Famous Dead Person (FDP). This is a story about privacy. Soon after, someone from Mr. FDP's family called Taylor and she was able to confirm with him what she could say in a news release and that a news conference was acceptable the next afternoon. Taylor contacted the hospital CEO and he also approved of the news release (standard procedure) and the planned news conference.

Having taken care of crucial tasks, she went back to bed. "But that was a mistake," she said, "I should have taken a shower and gone to the office because at around 1 a.m. West Coast time, the East Coast morning network news and interview shows were gathering information. It was a bigger story than I estimated and apparently had been rushed from the police wire when the patient was picked up."

"I had never dealt with the national media in a situation like this. I could not tell them much, but I should have been prepared to explain what I could and that was that he died in our medical center last night."

The simple news release Taylor prepared included name, age, and apparent cause of death and was distributed by PR Newswire, Facebook, and Twitter. This was the pertinent information the family wanted released— nothing more. When a person dies, the personal representative who is executor or administrator of the estate or the person who is legally authorized by state law or a court to act on behalf of the deceased individual may also receive protected health information (PHI). In this case, the family and agent acted together and made decisions about information released. They also prepared an obit about Mr. FDP's life and career.

Just before the news conference, Taylor briefed the gathered family members and the agent explaining what questions the news media would likely ask. She advised them they were not required to divulge personal information and suggested that they should confer with each other on possible answers and who would be spokesperson, etc.

The news media gathered in the appointed place while the family viewed the body. When the family entered, Taylor introduced them one by one and also the hospital CEO and the physician who declared Mr. FDP dead. There were reporters from all news media—local, national, international. There were questions answered and politely refused, and the reporters respected the family privacy.

They were not as kind to Taylor afterwards. "Where was he when he had the heart attack?" That was the question she knew was coming and she knew the answer. Mr. FDP's heart attack took place in a bed that was not his wife's. She said she didn't know, even though she did. She felt no regrets because the hospital was only concerned with treating him medically. She said it would have been a great feeling if he had survived, a plus for the hospital. But it was clearly not her place to answer that question. It is considered tasteless to mention to reporters gathered at such a somber occasion to mention medical advances the hospital may have recently achieved.

However, the crisis communicator can use the occasion to show the news media how organized she/he may be. Tomorrow, reporters may be looking for your proactive news. The communicator is always strengthening relationships with the news media before that relationship is urgent.

Taylor said she followed this procedure.

Make sure information is correct and complete as possible, words and names are spelled correctly. Be a resource person if you can. Make it clear they can contact you even if they are not certain you are the right source. Establish that you are a person in the know. If a living patient gives permission for the news media to get information, find out what questions they would like answered and what their deadline is. If there are national and local media present, remember to treat local reporters as fairly as visiting reporters who may consider themselves more prestigious.

Reporters called for days asking questions, one even a year later. They seemed to be determined there was a story untold but she could not help them. Hospitals, cities, and states have various rules about privacy of patients (Figure 10.3). They differ, but there is one set of practices that is national. These are regulations set forth by the Office of Civil Rights of the U.S. Department of Health and Human Services pursuant to the Health Insurance Portability and Accountability Act of 1996, popularly known by the initials HIPAA. The HIPAA regulations are minimum standards for the release of PHI. Hospital policy and/or state and/or federal law may establish stricter standards, but not less strict standards.

According to federal law, all patients admitted to a hospital have an option regarding inclusion in the patient directory. If a patient chooses to opt out of the directory, his/her condition cannot be provided to others. Celebrities often opt out, but that privilege is available to all regardless of fame or status in life. If a patient chooses not to opt out of the directory, only a one-word condition can be provided to the news media and that is only if the media agency asks for a patient by first and last name. Also, patients

Figure 10.3 When a celebrity or anyone dies in a hospital, the communications department is limited to revealing a minimum of information to the news media. This is part of the national HIPAA privacy rule. Additional informational limitations may be local.

Source: JUSTIN LANE/EPA-EFE/Shutterstock.com

must give written permission to be interviewed and/or photographed for statements about his/her conditions.

If the news media or any other person asks about a patient's condition, the hospital communications department can only reply with one-word descriptions suggested by the American Hospital Association. They are as follows.

Undetermined, meaning a physician has not evaluated the patient.

Good, meaning the patient's vital signs are within normal limits. The patient is conscious and comfortable.

Fair, meaning vital signs are not within normal limits. The patient is conscious but may be uncomfortable. Indicators are favorable.

Serious, meaning vital signs are not within normal limits. Patient is acutely ill. Indicators are questionable.

Critical, meaning vital signs are not within normal limits. Patient may be unconscious. Indicators are unfavorable.

Treated/released, meaning patient was treated but was not admitted.

Deceased.

The term "stable" is not suggested to describe a condition.

The death of a patient is considered PHI under HIPAA. Thus, the condition of death may be released for deceased patients who have not opted out of the directory. Even under these circumstances, hospital communicators are urged to notify the next of kin before releasing information about the cause of death. That information must come from the patient's physician and must be approved by a legal representative of the deceased. When a death is investigated by the county coroner, questions about the cause of death should be addressed to the coroner's office.

There are very few exceptions to the HIPAA regulations. However, there is a case in which a "covered entity" (like a hospital, a clinic, a physician, or a PR spokesperson) may seek help from the news media in which case information must be shared. The news media may be instrumental in assisting the hospital or physician in locating the next of kin when the patient is incapacitated and not identified. This may be crucial in treating the patient.

The regulations are not simply guidelines. Covered entities found in violation of HIPAA standards may be at risk of civil monetary penalties. The U.S. Secretary of Health and Human Services may impose fines through the Office of Civil Rights (OCR). Research reveals that violations have resulted in millions of dollars in fines. A hospital in New York allowed news media to film its facilities, revealing the identity of a patient. It agreed to pay a fine of $2.2 million. A Texas hospital revealed a patient's name in a news release and faced a HIPAA settlement of $2.4 million (Stanger, 2017).

If the OCR believes that the exchange of individual health information has risen to the level of criminal activity, the matter may be submitted to the Department of Justice. The penalties may be fines, as well as prison sentences.

The key personnel in the hospital including the communications director and the news media answer to the codes of ethics in their fields. Communications professionals follow the Code of the Public Relations Society of America (PRSA) which in this case vow "to protect the privacy rights of clients, organizations and individuals by safeguarding confidential information." Also they "protect privileged, confidential or insider information gained from a client or organization" (www.prsa.org).

Professional journalists look to the Code of Ethics of the Society of Professional Journalists, Sigma Delta Chi which reads: "Conscientious Journalists from all media and specialties strive to serve the public with thoroughness and honesty. Professional integrity is the cornerstone of a journalist's credibility" (www.spj.org/ethics_code.asp).

Physicians advocate the American Medical Association Principal of Medical Ethics, which reads, in part: "Whatever I see or hear in the lives of my patients, whether in connection with my professional practice or not, which ought not to be spoken of outside, I will keep secret considering all such things to be private." The nursing profession instructs members to honor The American Nurses Association Code of Ethics, which reads that "information pertinent to a patient's treatment and welfare is disclosed . . . only to those directly concerned with the patient's care (Burkle and Cascino, 2011). As old as the Hippocratic Oath is, most medical students still look forward to graduation when for the first time, they can swear to it. One part of it reads, "I will respect the privacy of my patients, for their problems are not disclosed to me that the world may know."

Notes

1. All facts came from Denny Lynch.
2. Interview with communications director in 1995.

Bibliography

Case Study: Wendy's and the Finger-in-the-Chili Hoax.

Curtis, K. (2006, January 19). California couple get prison for finger-in-the-chili scam. *Seattle Times*, p. A4.

Goldman, A. (2005, April 14). *Wendy's finger finder won't sue*. Retrieved from http://signonsandiego.printthis.clickability.com.

Kaplan, T. (2013, June 5). San Jose finger lady to get ten years for new hoax. *San Jose Mercury News*. Retrieved from April 3, 2015.

LaGanga, M. L. & Simmons, A. M. (2005, April 23). Fast-food, finger-finder arrested; hoax alleged. *Seattle Times*, pp. A1, A12.

Police call Wendy's chili finger case a hoax. (2005, April 24). Retrieved August 31, 2006, from www.KTVU.com.

Richtel, M. & Barrionuevo, A. (2005, April 22). CSI: Wendy's restaurants. *The New York Times Online*. Retrieved August 31, 2006, from www.nytimes.com.

Ritter, K. (2005, April 9). Woman in Wendy's finger case has litigious past. *Pittsburgh Post Gazette*, p. A8.

Sandoval, G. (2005, May 14). Finger in Wendy's case traced to man's hand. *Seattle Times*, pp. A1, A2.

Search continues for owner of missing digit. (2005, March 24). *MSNBC Online*. Retrieved from www.MSNBC.com.

Wendy's off hook in finger case. (2005, April 22). *CBS News Online*. Retrieved from www.cbsnews.com.

Mini-Case: Domino's Pizza

Clifford, S. (2009, April 16). Video prank at Domino's taints brands. *The New York Times Online*. Retrieved April 16, 2009, from www.nytimes.com/2009/04/16/business/.

O'Hern, M. (2009, April 17). Domino's defends online reputation via Twitter and YouTube response. *Marketing Shift*. Retrieved April 17, 2009, from www.marketingshift.com/2009/4/dominos-defends-reputation-online-via.cfm.

Case Study: Mr. Famous Dead Person and Privacy

Burkle, C. & Cascino, G. (2011, December). Medicine and the media: Balancing the public's right to know with the privacy of the Patient. *Mayo Clinic Proceedings*. Retrieved March 3, 2023, from www.NCBI.nlm.nib.gov/pmc/articles/pmc3228620.

Stanger, K. (2017, May 24). HIPAA and disclosure to media. *Insight*. Retrieved March 3, 2023, from www.hollandhart.com/hipaa-disclosure-tomedia.

Sullivan, J. (2004). *HIPAA a practical guide to the privacy and security of health data*. Chicago: American Bar Association.

Chapter 11

The Basic Crisis Communications Plan

Crisis Inventory

Before an organization can develop a crisis management plan or a crisis communications plan, it must determine which crisis or crises the organization is most likely to face. A crisis communications plan's usefulness is directly associated with how specific it is to a particular type of crisis.

The workbook for this text takes the user through a step-by-step process of developing a crisis communications plan. Although there are several items in the plan that are mutual to all types of crises, varying information is needed for each type of crisis for maximum effectiveness. For example, a restaurant chain may decide that food poisoning and fire are its most probable crises. If a food poisoning crisis occurs, the media will want—and the public relations department should have—the following items readily available and in its crisis communications plan: recipes, a list of ingredients stocked, a list of vendors used, kitchen precautions and procedures, names and contact numbers of chefs and all other personnel handling food, and a list of medical experts for consultation and as spokespersons.

If a fire occurs, the public relations department should have—in a specific crisis communications plan—information about its evacuation procedures, its policy on using nonflammable decor items (such as window coverings and tablecloths), the floor plan of the structure, and fire experts for spokespersons.

The following list (Table 11.1) enumerates common types of crises. There are, of course, numerous others. Companies and organizations are advised to consider the list carefully and add other types of crises specific to their operations. Some crises will involve more than one of the types listed, such as workplace violence and fatality, or boycott and sexual discrimination.

Perhaps the involvement of the entire company or of representatives from each department can help determine the crises the company is likely to face. Then each unit's selections could be compared and compiled into

DOI: 10.4324/9781003019282-11

Table 11.1 Common Types of Crises

acquisition	kidnapping
age discrimination	lawsuit
alcohol abuse	layoffs
bankruptcy	merger
boycott	murder
bribery	negative legislation
chemical spill or leak	plant closing
computer failure	product failure
computer hacking	protest demonstrations
contamination	racial issues
cyber attacks	robbery
data loss/theft	sexual discrimination
drug abuse	sexual harassment
drug trafficking	strikes
earthquake	suicide
embezzlement	takeover
explosion	tax problems
fatality	terrorism
fire	tornado
flood	toxic waste
hacking	transportation accident
hurricanes	transportation failure
kickbacks	workplace violence

a company-wide list. When done properly, this can be an effective proactive employee relations program, a way of creating "we-ness," a way of including all of the employees in the company's decision-making. Janitors, executive assistants, blue-collar and white-collar workers, mid-level executives, and top executives can have a say. After all, each employee stands to suffer if the company should go under after the most serious of crises. Furthermore, employees in each position classification have unique perspectives on things that can go wrong. Janitors are more aware of heating and cooling equipment, possible gas leaks, and so on. Workers on an automobile assembly line know more about the quality of cars than managers in carpeted offices.

However, if a company-wide crisis identification program is not feasible, a meeting of key employees familiar with all facets of the operation can determine the crises the company is likely to face. Such a meeting should certainly include more than public relations staff members. You do not want the company blaming the public relations staff for the failure to recognize a possible crisis.

Frequently, ascertaining probable crises can point out problems that prevent crises from occurring. This is the primary reason for company-wide involvement. The second best reason is being able to manage a crisis once it occurs.

Every company and organization can experience many types of crises. Two questions must be answered: (a) how likely is this crisis?; and (b) how devastating can the crisis be? Crisis communications plans should be developed for all crises believed to be both most probable and most devastating. To do this, the public relations department, with its key executives, must take an inventory. Each possible crisis must be ranked as follows.

0—impossible; that is, the crisis has basically no chance of occurring;
1—nearly impossible;
2—remotely possible;
3—possible;
4—somewhat probable (has happened to similar companies);
5—highly probable (may or may not have previously occurred in the company, but warning signs are evident).

Each crisis also should be ranked according to its potential damage to the company. The rankings in this category are as follows:

0—no damage (not a serious consequence);
1—little damage (can be handled without much difficulty, not serious enough for the media's concern);
2—some damage (a slight chance that the media will be involved);
3—considerable damage (but still will not be a major media issue);
4—considerable damage (would definitely be a major media issue);
5—devastating (front-page news, could put company out of business).

For added security, when in doubt, rank a crisis in the next highest category. For instance, Company Z determines that there are five crises it could face: workplace violence, fire, protest demonstrations, negative legislation, and tax problems. Each of these crises might be ranked, as shown in Figure 11.1.

Keep in mind that a crisis you determine to be unlikely simply because it has never happened before can happen tomorrow. Both human nature and Mother Nature are very unpredictable, so natural disasters (e.g., earthquakes, floods, and hurricanes) and human failures should be expected to some degree.

After rankings for probability and damage are made, bar graphs should be made to clearly see and consider each crisis and compare it to others. (Bar graphing can be done on various computer programs or by hand.) At the base of each graph, write the name of each type of crisis. Plot the height of each bar according to numbers attributed to each crisis in the probability and damage rankings. Choose different colors or shadings for probability bars and damage bars.

When Company Z plots its data on a bar graph, it resembles Figure 11.1. Considering Company Z's graph, we see that the probability and

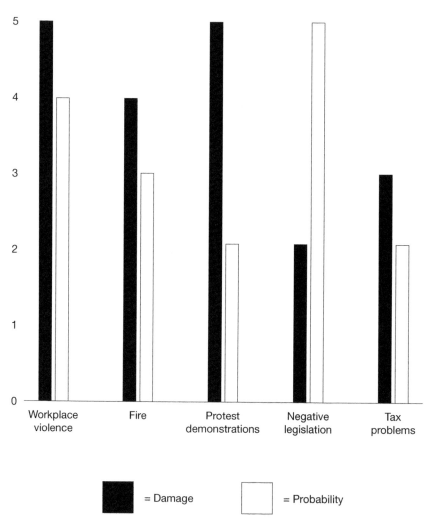

Company Z's Crisis Inventory

= Damage   = Probability

Figure 11.1 A sample bar graph showing how an organization might assess the probability of, and degrees of damage resulting from, various types of crises.

seriousness of a crisis relating to tax problems is not as crucial as in the other crises. This does not mean that a crisis plan is not important for tax problems; it's just not as important as for other issues, and not a priority.

According to the graph, the possibility of Company Z suffering a crisis resulting from negative legislation is likely, though not particularly critical. On the other hand, protest demonstrations are critical, although not very likely. Workplace violence and fire seem both likely and critical.

Most organizations plan for crises ranked high in both probability and damage. In this case, Company Z would probably develop crisis management and communications plans for workplace violence first, then for the other crises in descending order of importance: fire, protest demonstrations, negative legislation, and tax problems.

Sometimes, organizations make crisis plans for the most devastating crises—no matter how probable or improbable they may be. In this case, Company Z would develop plans for workplace violence first, followed by protest demonstrations, then fire. Naturally, a version of Murphy's Law can be expected: That crisis for which you have no plan will likely happen. However, you will find that any plan, and the process of developing that plan, will make you more prepared for crises generally.

Some organizations, having several crises classified with similar rankings in all categories, make general crisis communications plans with detailed information for all types of crises, although sometimes the detailed information is omitted.

Many companies, fearing all possibilities of crises equally, merely adopt a policy of "open and honest response" with the media and all publics, and plan to be in a total reactive mode during a crisis.

The importance of the crisis inventory is to force organizations to think about the possibilities. Sometimes the most ridiculous crisis occurs, something no one in the company could predict. Pepsi probably never dreamed that it would have a crisis about hypodermic syringes in its cans. On the other hand, Foodmaker, Inc. and Jack in the Box could certainly have anticipated children dying from eating hamburgers, and Exxon could have anticipated a devastating oil spill.

The ranking procedure may introduce ideas for prevention programs. You also may realize that your organization is more vulnerable than you anticipated.

Considering that the toll of stress and emotion during a crisis necessarily affects one's thought processes, a carefully developed crisis communications plan is the best substitute for a fully functioning brain. Even if you remain cool and calm under pressure, others in the company may not. The crisis communications plan alleviates this problem, too.

Developing the Crisis Communications Plan

Once likely crises have been identified, the crisis communications plan can be written. A crisis communications plan can be part of a larger crisis management plan (CMP) or it may be a stand-alone document to help public relations practitioners handle crises more effectively.

The CMP includes information such as evacuation procedures, emergency staffing of various departments of a company, and places to purchase or rent emergency equipment, tools, or vehicles—all the things a company may need in a crisis.

Public relations during a crisis focuses on communications with the company's publics during the crisis—for the most part, the same publics to which normal PR activities are directed.

The CMP is sometimes a large volume of instructions, whereas a crisis communications plan should be a more manageable, easier-to-read document. After a crisis has erupted, employees are likely to look at a large volume and say, "We don't have time to read this now" and then proceed to handle the crisis by "winging it." The crisis communications plan should be organized in such a way that the practitioners can quickly turn to each section. Some professionals use tabs in a notebook; others use a table of contents. Keeping the crisis communications plan only on a computer can be dangerous because many crises prevent access to offices (fire, earthquakes, explosives, etc.).

Many companies (such as Johnson & Johnson after the Tylenol crisis) urge employees to keep copies of the plan in various key spots—the office, at home, near the nightstand, or in the car. That way, the odds are good that at least one copy will be readily available should a crisis or disaster occur.

If a crisis inventory determines, for example, that there are three likely crises, the organization should draft a crisis communications plan for each type. A plan for an earthquake must be different from a plan for a product failure. The publics may be different; the media may be different; the message must be different.

The crisis communications plan states purposes, policies, and goals, then assigns employees to various duties. It generally makes communication with publics faster and more effective and should help end the crisis more swiftly than would happen without a plan.

When a crisis communications plan is ineffective, it is usually because the type of crisis was not anticipated or because variables arose that were not anticipated. For example, spokespersons or supplies may not be available. The crisis communications plan sometimes fails because it is outdated. Such plans should be updated regularly.

Even if unanticipated variables do arise, the crisis communications plan should be more effective than having no plan at all. Still, it must be remembered that a crisis communications plan is not a manual guaranteeing success, with everything done "by the book"—but rather a guide that must be flexible.

An effective crisis communications plan should have the following components, arranged in an order that best suits the organization and the particular crisis or disaster:

- cover page;
- introduction;
- acknowledgments;
- rehearsal dates;
- purpose and objectives;
- list of key publics;
- notifying publics;
- identifying the crisis communications team;
- crisis directory;
- identifying the media spokesperson;
- list of emergency personnel and local officials;
- list of key media—print, broadcast, and social;
- spokespersons for related organizations;
- crisis communications control center;
- equipment and supplies;
- pre-gathered information;
- key messages;
- website;
- blogs and social media;
- trick questions;
- list of prodromes;
- list of related Internet URLs;
- evaluation form.

Cover Page

The cover page of a crisis communications plan is similar to the cover page of a term paper. There are as many ways of doing one as there are ways of doing crisis communications plans. It should include at least the date when the plan was written, as well as revision dates.

Introduction

The head of the company or organization usually writes the introduction (or the PR practitioner ghostwrites it for the CEO with his or her approval). The purpose of this component is to persuade employees to take the crisis communications plan seriously. It stresses the necessity and importance of the plan, and it emphasizes the dire results possible when a plan is not followed.

Acknowledgments

This crisis communications plan component takes the form of an affidavit signed by all crisis personnel as well as by key executives, indicating that they have read the plan and are prepared to put it into effect. The signatures assure management that its personnel have read the plan.

Rehearsal Dates

Dates of rehearsals for all crises are recorded here. The most damaging and most likely crises should be practiced at least annually if not every six months. Rehearsal for any type of crisis is helpful, even if an eventual crisis turns out to be somewhat different.

Purpose and Objectives

The purpose statement details the organization's policies toward its publics. It might say, for example, "In a crisis, an open and honest disclosure with the media shall be stressed." The purpose is an expressed hope for a recovery and return to normalcy, to get out of the media. The objectives are responses to the question, "What do you hope to achieve with this plan?" Objectives should not be overly ambitious in difficulty or number. For example, a company may adopt the following goals.

1. To be seen in the media as a company that cares about its customers and employees.
2. To make certain that all communications are accurate.

List of Key Publics

The key publics list should include all publics, both external and internal, with which the organization must communicate during the crisis. The list varies with organizations, but may include the following, as well as others.

- board members;
- shareholders;
- financial partners;
- investors;
- community leaders;

- customers;
- clients;
- suppliers;
- vendors;
- neighbors of physical plant(s);
- competitors;
- key management;
- employees;
- legal representation;
- media;
- union officials;
- retirees;
- government officials (city, state, county, federal).

Although all publics need not be notified in every crisis, the list of key publics should be comprehensive. It is easier to eliminate unneeded publics at the time of crisis than it is to think of all the crucial publics during the stress of a crisis.

Publics fall into the following categories:

- *Enabling publics*—those people with the power and authority to make decisions: the board of directors, shareholders, investors, and key executives. Notifying enabling publics is a priority.
- *Functional publics*—the people who actually make the organization work: employees, unions, suppliers, vendors, consumers, and volunteers in the case of non-profit organizations.
- *Normative publics*—those people who share values with the organization in crises: trade associations, professional organizations, and competitors.
- *Diffused publics*—those people linked indirectly to the organization in crisis: the media, community groups, and neighbors of the physical plant.

Notifying Publics

To notify publics, a system must be devised for contacting each public (Figure 11.2), and that system should be described in the crisis communications plan. Social media networks such as Facebook groups can be used if people use computers constantly. For internal publics, many companies use a chain procedure, such as a telephone tree, in which each person is specifically designated to call others. The person who learns about the crisis first notifies the CEO, the head of public relations, and the head of the department that may be involved. The chain should be clear and error-free, even in the event that certain individuals are not reached.

An appropriate means of notification must be decided on for each public. A news release, for example, is appropriate primarily for the news media, not for other publics.

Board members are often reached by telephone or fax. Email or other computerized communications are also used. The media can be notified by way of telephone, wire service, fax, press conference, email, or news release. Other methods used for notifying publics include telegrams, personal visits, letters, advertisements, bulletin boards, and meetings.

Identifying the Crisis Communications Team

The crisis communications team members, along with backups, should be pre-selected. The team manager is usually—but not always—the head of public relations. He or she has specific responsibilities: communicating with top management, making decisions, drafting or approving major statements, and notifying the rest of the crisis communications team.

YOUR COMPANY

MESSAGE: There has been an explosion in the plant. There are injured employees. We do not know, at this time, the cause of the explosion or the extent of the injuries of the employees. An investigation is underway.

Methods of Communication

PUBLICS	TELEPHONE	EMAIL	FAX	LETTER BY MESSENGER	LETTER BY MAIL	NEWSLETTER	BULLETIN BOARD	PERSONAL VISIT	NEWS RELEASE	MEETINGS
EMPLOYEES		*J. Naas				*J. Naas	*J. Naas			
EXECUTIVES	*Nelson J.	*Nelson J.						*Nelson J. M. Yerima		*Nelson J.
CUSTOMERS						*Damien L.				
BOARD OF DIRECTORS	*Nelson J.			*Damien L.					*Gina A.	
ELECTRONIC MEDIA	*K. Stone		*K. Sone						*Gina A.	
DAILY NEWSPAPERS	*Gina A.								*Gina A.	
WEEKLY NEWSPAPERS			*Gina A.		*Damien L.					
SHARE HOLDERS		*Ann C.				*Ann C.				
COMMUNITY LEADERS			*Karen N.			*Karen N.				

*Staff member responsible for communications and followup

Figure 11.2 A sample chart showing how an organization might plan to communicate with key publics during a crisis. It includes key talking points and ways of communicating. The lists of publics and types of communication can be longer, shorter, or otherwise different depending on the organization's needs.

The assistant crisis manager assumes responsibility when the manager is unavailable (a second backup may be beneficial, if possible). The control room coordinator sets up the room with necessary furniture, equipment, supplies, and tools. An efficient executive assistant can be appointed for this position.

Other PR personnel have the responsibilities of preparing news releases and statements, contacting the media, and reporting all actions to the crisis communications manager. These people may notify employees or volunteers through letters or by writing telegrams to the mayor and governor, by telephoning union officials and others, and so forth.

Crisis Directory

The company should prepare a crisis directory, listing all members of the crisis team, key managers in the company, and key publics or organizations, along with titles, business and home telephone numbers, cellular phone numbers, and fax and email addresses, as well as business, home, and vacation addresses. It is also helpful to list the phone numbers of friends, neighbors, and relatives who are frequently in contact with persons crucial to the crisis recovery.

The crisis team should be large enough to get the job done, but no larger. Having too many people involved makes it difficult to get tasks completed and decisions made. There is no time for egos in a crisis; each person must be a team player. It is also preferable that crisis team members be generally healthy and capable of working under stress. They should be reliable professionals, whether gofers, interns, or assistants.

Identifying the Media Spokesperson

The media spokesperson must be selected carefully. To the public, this person *is* the company or organization.

Actually, sometimes several persons are spokespersons. This is an arguable point in the public relations profession. Some argue for one spokesperson per crisis, usually the CEO. Others argue for several spokespersons, depending on area of expertise. Clearly, the decision is a matter of what suits the company and type of crisis best.

Even if the CEO is an effective spokesperson, he or she may not be particularly knowledgeable about a technical aspect of the crisis. For example, during an oil spill, the company CEO is not the only important spokesperson; also needed is a person qualified to talk about what will be necessary for the cleanup. Frequently, university professors are called on for their specific knowledge about technical aspects of a crisis and for their credibility.

Another school of thought is that CEOs have no credibility because they have too much to lose. However, if lives are lost or in danger—including the lives of animals—most professionals agree that the company head must be the chief spokesperson.

In all cases, at least one—and preferably two or three—backup spokespersons should be preselected in case the preferred person is unavailable at the time of the crisis. Crises can occur when people are on vacation, on business trips, or sick with the flu. When the 1989 San Francisco earthquake struck, for example, the first two designated spokespersons for the Pacific Gas and Electric Company were at the World Series baseball game at Candlestick Park. The third spokesperson on the list was called and pressed into service.

An effective crisis spokesperson must have some position in the company. It is usually not the PR head, even if the PR person is normally the company's spokesperson. The spokesperson must also be articulate, powerful enough to make decisions, accessible throughout the crisis, able to talk clearly in concise sound bites, and pleasant to the eye of a camera. Moreover, the spokesperson in a crisis must appear rational, concerned, and empathetic. He or she should be pre-trained, rehearsed well in advance of the crisis, and briefed prior to the crisis response. The organization's legal adviser should be consulted before statements are made.

If the public relations department is a small or one-person operation, it may be beneficial to have capable, trustworthy volunteers to perform some tasks. Outside public relations firms that specialize in crisis planning and handling might be used. A non-profit organization can often get PR firms to help pro bono (the work performed or donated without charge). Many non-profit organizations have PR practitioners on their boards of directors, anticipating the need for their assistance during a crisis.

At times, one person may be required to perform all communications roles. On the other hand, in large companies, several people may perform each role.

List of Emergency Personnel and Local Officials

If the crisis is a disaster or emergency, various emergency personnel need to be contacted. A list should be made of contact numbers for police, fire officials, hospitals, the health department, utilities, and paramedics.

If the crisis affects large numbers of people or is a threat to the safety of people, government officials must be contacted. This list should include contact information for the mayor, governor, city council members, county officials, state legislators, and U.S. senators and representatives.

Sometimes union officials must be notified, and they should therefore be listed, as well as key citizens groups and community organizations.

List of Key Media—Print, Broadcast, and Social

After key executives are called, the media are the next most important public to notify about the crisis. A list of media contacts—newspapers, television, radio, wire services—should be completed and listed in order of importance. If particular editors or reporters are important to telling the story to the organization's benefit, a list of their home numbers and emergency numbers will be advantageous.

The media list should contain contact information for metropolitan dailies, certain weeklies, all TV news stations, the Associated Press, news networks, Reuters, all radio news stations, trade publications, and other relevant outlets. It also should include all social media on which your company has a presence. These change, so it is imperative to tailor this task to your own needs.

Spokespersons for Related Organizations

If an organization suffers a severe crisis, there may be spokespersons outside the organization who may be questioned. It may be effective to make a list of who these people might be and how to contact them at any time of day. It also might be effective to meet with them so that they are familiar with your company; with how you will handle a crisis, if it occurs; and with how to reach you.

Sometimes, other spokespersons have information you don't have. This information may help you communicate more effectively, so you need to be able to reach them. Because most people have cell phones, this could be a simple task.

Crisis Communications Control Center

The location of the crisis communications control center must be determined in case regular office space is unavailable. After disasters and emergencies, offices are often damaged, without power, or inaccessible.

Several possible sites should be listed in the crisis communications plan, as well as the persons instrumental in gaining access to these locations. Suppose, for example, a local church has offered its conference room. Who gave permission to use the room? Who can unlock the doors of the church and conference room? Does the permission include use of electrical outlets and furniture? Does the site have adequate space for the media to work?

Equipment and Supplies

Determine and list all of the equipment and supplies needed by the crisis team, media, and visiting publics. The list could include, but is not limited to, the following:

- chairs and desks;
- bulletin boards;

- flip charts and chalkboards;
- computers or typewriters (perhaps manual typewriters in case power is a problem);
- computer printers and paper;
- landline telephones and cellular phones with chargers;
- battery-powered televisions and radios;
- maps of the plant or crisis area;
- battery-powered flashlights and lamps;
- police radios;
- walkie-talkies;
- company letterhead, pens, and pencils;
- telephone directories;
- contact lists and media directories;
- press kits;
- CMPs and crisis communications plans;
- street and highway maps;
- food and beverages;
- copying machine(s) and paper;
- first-aid kits;
- cameras and film and/or memory cards;
- extension cords and generator power packs.

Pre-Gathered Information

Prepare and gather various documents that may possibly be needed during a crisis. Keep identical sets of documents in various locales to ensure availability. The types of documents that can be gathered in advance include safety records and procedures, annual reports, photos, company backgrounders, executive biographies, company maps, branch office locations, quality control procedures, product manufacturing procedures, and company fact sheets (including such data as numbers of employees, products manufactured, and markets served).

Skeletal news releases can be prepared as long as the PR practitioner anticipates the type of crisis and can make a statement on behalf of the company. As shown in Figure 11.4, a news release can be written in advance with blank spaces left for data to be filled in (such as the magnitude of the crisis and relevant dates and names).

Key Messages

Under the stress of a crisis, it is easy to forget—or at least fail to state properly—the main points you want to convey to publics or to a specific public. Even when there is no crisis, experienced spokespersons prepare in

---

NEWS RELEASE

For Immediate Release

Date _____

Contact: _____

(name/phone number)

_____   (name of celebrity) DIES

(SEATTLE) _____ (full name and title) _____ died today of _____ (cause of death) at _____ (time of death) _____ at Swedish Hospital Medical Center in Seattle. He/She was _____ (age).

Further details will be released by _____ (name of person to make announcement—family member or professional contact) at a news conference scheduled for _____ (time of news conference), at Swedish Hospital, Glaser Auditorium, 747 Summit Ave.

# # #

Figure 11.3 A sample fill-in-the-blanks news release.

advance the primary information they want emphasized in what are called key messages or speaking points.

The act of preparing key messages will help you organize your thoughts and will provide consistent information to publics. Each message must be accurate, brief, easy to use in a quote, and memorable. The spokesperson must be easily able to work the key message into responses to questions. Such messages also help reporters—who are looking for great quotes—to do their jobs.

Effective key messages help avoid misquoting, enable the spokesperson to tell his or her side of the story, and give the spokesperson a way to answer trick questions comfortably. Most of all, they establish credibility for the organization in crisis.

Website

Placing news on the organization's website and pre-appointing webmasters to keep updated information on the site will reduce both the number of phone calls from publics and the amount of time put into crisis recovery. The news put on the site should be brief or detailed, depending on the nature of the crisis. In the event of an airplane crash, for example, the airline's website would, at first, merely acknowledge the crash. After families of victims are notified, the names of victims would be listed. Regular notices of progress in the investigation would also be posted.

The concern of the company should be expressed and prominently displayed. A statement from the highest executive in the company is expected by the public. The website is an ideal venue for keeping safety rules, security precautions, and health policies posted. Restaurants might keep information posted on training new employees about cooking burgers at the proper temperature, using gloves when handling food, and policies that discourage employees with colds and other infectious diseases from working with food products.

The website is also a bulletin board for informing publics of the organization's community relations projects and other activities that give back to the public. The website can afford your organization the opportunity to be a Model 4 two-way symmetric company (see Chapter 2). It can encourage feedback, comments, and questions from publics and provide publics with responses and explanations. Finally, the website can reveal how the company is making changes as a result of public comment.

Blogs and Social Media

Monitoring blogs and social media channels is crucial. Sometimes the monitoring can be a prodrome (warning sign) and help prevent a crisis. The crisis communications plan should have a list of all blogs and social media networks relevant to the business and relevant to the types of crises. This can be an excellent way of achieving Model 4, two-way symmetrical communications with publics (see "excellence theory" in Chapter 2, "Crisis Communications Theory," pp. 36–40).

It is advisable, if social media are used proactively in marketing and public relations campaigning, that they would also be used in the crisis communications plan. Facebook friends and other contacts with whom the organization has built a relationship will spread the news to a wider group of people. For Twitter, prepare key messages in advance when communicators have time to work with the 280 characters. Make this list of key messages separate from the key messages going to the traditional news media but with the same sentiment.

Do not drop traditional news media in order to spend time with social media unless the crisis relates only to online issues and online publics.

Crises originating on social media should indeed be battled on social media—and sometimes also via traditional media. Similarly, crises not related to social media networks might also be fought through social media, as well as traditional media.

For example, in 1993, the soft drink manufacturer PepsiCo experienced a crisis brought on by consumers who placed hypodermic syringes in cans and claimed they found them there when they purchased them. The fear supposedly was that the syringes would cause HIV/AIDS, but actually the greedy consumers were hoping to get payoffs from PepsiCo. PepsiCo ended the crisis when it showed on television newscasts the following: (a) surveillance camera "B-roll" of a grocery store patron placing a syringe in a can; and (b) the canning process that showed how virtually impossible it would be for the syringes to have been placed in the cans at the plant. Today, in addition to television news, the visual pictures could have been shown via YouTube.

An e-blast might be sent to publics who subscribe to the organization's email list. However, e-blasts are being used less than in previous years as communicators employ other methods.

Trick Questions

When a crisis occurs, what questions can you predict the news media will ask a spokesperson? Check Chapter 6 for types of trick questions. Reporters may not ask certain questions intentionally to trick the spokesperson, but the end result—if a question is not answered carefully—can make the spokesperson and his or her organization look bad.

A spokesperson for a restaurant, for example, might be asked the following trick questions.

1. Off the record, didn't you know this might happen?
2. If the fire happened during the lunch hour, how many people might have been killed?
3. Don't you buy your ground beef from the meatpacker who sold bad meat to the other restaurant?
4. As at most popular restaurants, the work here is very fast-paced and stressful, right?

List of Prodromes

Prodromes are the warning signs that a crisis may occur. List these in the crisis communications plan. If any of the prodromes have actually happened, log into the plan what the company did in response and when. This helps the spokesperson answer the media question, "Did you have any warning that this might happen?"

As an example of a prodrome, consider the normally good employee who is unusually tardy and seems stressed out and irritable. Management notices the problem and gets help for the employee. Or take as another example several near-accidents in the organization's parking lot. Management takes notice, determines that the parking lot has confusing directional signs, and has the signs redone.

Heeding prodromes carefully can often prevent a crisis and help show that the organization is concerned with resolving problems. The prodromes section of the crisis communications plan should be regularly updated.

List of Related Internet URLs

List the URLs of organizations and companies that may have information you need during a crisis. Also include brief descriptions of the data available at the URLs. For example, a restaurant might list the URLs for the National Center for Infectious Diseases, the state department of health, the FDA, and the CDC.

Evaluation Form

Evaluation is a crucial step in preparing an effective crisis communications plan. As assessment, it is helpful in determining what did and did not work. It also helps plan for, prevent, and cope with future crises by pointing out what needs to be revised in the crisis communications plan. An evaluation form should be developed and placed at the end of the plan for later distribution to the team for input.

Appendix A

Generic Crisis Communications Plan for a Company

Contents

Definitions

    Crisis
    Minor Crisis
    Major Crisis

Communication Objectives

    Crisis Communications Team
    Roles and Responsibilities

Notification of a Crisis

    Notification Process in Brief

Communications Procedure for Handling a Minor Crisis

    Minor Crisis

Communications Procedure for Handling a Major Crisis

    Major Crisis

Emergency Operations Center (EOC) Activation
Identification of a Spokesperson
Guidelines for Spokespeople
Format for Briefing Someone Identified as a Spokesperson for Interviews/
    News Briefings
News Release

    Circumstances That May Require a News Release
    Writing an Initial Statement for Release
    Information Appropriate for Release
    Information That Is Not Appropriate for Release
    Writing a News Release

Definitions

Crisis

A *crisis* is an unplanned event that directly or potentially threatens our company's reputation; the environment; the health, safety, or welfare of employees; and the health, safety, or welfare of citizens in communities surrounding our plants. Events that fall into this category include: fires, explosions, bomb threats, civil disturbances, equipment malfunctions, environmental impacts, widespread illness, hazardous material spills, and other types of incidents.

Minor Crisis

A *minor crisis* is confined to a limited area of a building; results in minimal, if any, disruption of operations; is quickly brought under control; does not require evacuation other than of a few employees in the immediate vicinity; and causes minor injuries or none at all. Media inquiry is possible with events in this category, but they are apt to be minimal.

Major Crisis

A *major crisis* may involve significant injury or loss of life, prolonged disruption of normal operations, substantial property damage, or a significant environmental impact—and it holds potential for any of these. Media inquiry is more likely to occur with events in this category, especially if other municipal emergency response groups have been called in for assistance.

Communication Objectives

In the event of a minor or major incident on any of our sites, every effort will be made to communicate as appropriate to employees, management, surrounding communities, other target publics, and the news media promptly and accurately. The appropriate division of communications staff will be the primary information source available to the news media.

When a crisis occurs, it is necessary for communications personnel to gather facts and data quickly, including the nature of our response to the crisis. The following communication efforts will strive to alleviate employees' concerns, minimize speculation by the media, and ensure that our position is presented.

It should be noted, though, that many incidents occur that are relatively minor in nature and are consequently not covered by the media. Nevertheless, it is essential to gather facts about the incidents and have them available to communicate, if necessary, to appropriate audiences.

The nature of that communication is outlined in the following plan.

Crisis Communications Team Roles and Responsibilities

Each site's Crisis Team (at the various sites) is responsible for the following: identifying, confirming, and investigating crises; developing strategies for managing crises; and developing strategies for recovering from crisis incidents.

As members of the Crisis Team, communications personnel will perform the following duties.

- provide a representative at the Emergency Operations Center (EOC) if activated;
- control the release of information to employees, to surrounding communities, and to the news media;
- maintain contact with media representatives;
- establish and maintain a news conference center, if necessary;
- decide what content to release on the organization's social media platforms, update that content as needed, and monitor external social media sites for inaccurate or misleading information.

Two, and in some cases, three communicators may be required for adequate crisis communications response. Those communicators will function in the following roles: Public Relations (PR) Lead, Incident Command (IC) Interface, and PR Backup.

The responsibilities for each communication role are outlined as follows.

PR Lead

- receives initial notification;
- designates staff member as IC Interface;
- designates staff member as PR Backup (if necessary);
- receives initial facts and updates from IC Interface;
- prepares initial statement for release;
- fields media inquiries to office;
- briefs executive identified as spokesperson;
- joins EOC team, if activated;
- provides updates to senior executives;
- determines the appropriate use of the organization's social media platforms as an internal and/or external communication tool with publics.

IC Interface

- joins IC team;
- gathers and documents facts as they become known;
- shares initial facts and updates with PR Lead in main office;
- prepares initial statement for release (if necessary);
- briefs affected organization management and employees;
- fields media inquiries (if necessary);
- prepares potential content for the organization's social media platforms for PR Lead's review and approval.

PR Backup

- updates corporate personnel as necessary;
- fields additional media inquiries to office;
- fields employee inquiries to office;
- conducts in-field interviews with media (if necessary);
- sets up media conference room (if necessary);
- helps monitor external social media platforms for inaccurate or misleading information.

Notification of a Crisis

Notification is an extremely important process in managing crises and sending the right messages to all audiences. When notification goes well, it makes the rest of the crisis communications job more streamlined and effective than when it does not.

Notification of incidents and crises (both major and minor) have been examined by an Ad Hoc Committee to the Corporate Crisis Committee for the past year. Members of this Ad Hoc Committee included PR/Communications, Fire and Security, Facilities, and Emergency Response Coordinators.

This committee has reviewed the entire notification process from the moment a crisis begins to the point that a crisis warrants informing senior corporate executives, including the CEO. This committee has endeavored to determine the most reliable notification process for each site Crisis Committee to use.

Notification Process in Brief

Notification is initiated from the area where a crisis has occurred or been identified. The person who discovers the crisis or incident calls the site emergency number, which is connected to the site Fire Station Dispatch office. A senior Fire Officer is then dispatched to the incident site who evaluates the magnitude of the crisis and then contacts Fire Dispatch to notify additional emergency response organizations. From that point on, notification occurs according to defined call lists and through chain-of-command channels.

Site Communications personnel are now notified directly by the respective site Fire Dispatchers. Once that initial notification occurs, the Communications representative receiving the call should, in turn, notify Corporate PR offices and the company switchboard operators as soon as he/she obtains information about the incident, and then follow the procedure noted.

Communications Procedure for Handling a Minor Crisis

Minor Crisis

1. Division Communications receives notification from the Fire Dispatcher and compiles the basic facts and chronology of the event (possibly using an Incident Information Sheet).
2. Division Communications representative becomes the PR Lead and informs other communications team members.
3. PR Lead determines if more information is necessary and if a communicator should be dispatched to incident site (IC Interface).
4. PR Lead calls Incident Commander (this is usually the senior Fire Officer at the incident site).
5. PR Lead notes more details about the incident (type of incident, when and where the incident occurred, chemical involved and potential chemical reactions, emergency response personnel on site, number of employees evacuated, any injuries, work performed in the building, what is being done to mitigate the incident, and who the appropriate contacts are and how to reach them).

6. On-hours, PR Lead notifies and confers with PR Manager (or backup). Off-hours or on weekends, PR Lead notifies and confers with PR Manager and PR Duty Officer when practical. If the PR Lead determines that the off-hour incident is likely to generate media inquiries, such notification must be made immediately. The PR Duty Officer should notify the Switchboard Operators (555–1000) and tell them to direct media inquiries to the person serving as PR Lead.
7. PR Lead and PR Manager agree to key messages and response to query statement.
8. PR Lead or PR Manager notifies Corporate PR Manager.
9. PR Lead prepares response to query statement, confers with division management, and obtains approval on statement.
10. PR Lead sends statement via fax or other secure and agreed-upon mode of transmission to PR Manager and to Corporate PR Manager.
11. PR Lead serves as prime contact for media. PR Manager and Corporate PR Manager serve as backups.
12. PR Lead fields media inquiries and makes follow-up calls to media if necessary.

Communications Procedure for Handling a Major Crisis

Major Crisis

1. Division Communications receives notification from the Fire Dispatcher and compiles the basic facts and chronology of the event (possibly using an Incident Information Sheet).
2. Division Communications representative becomes the PR Lead and informs other communications team members.
3. PR Lead determines if more information is necessary and if a communicator (IC Interface) should be dispatched to incident site to obtain firsthand information. PR Lead also designates another person as PR Backup, if necessary.
4. IC Interface goes to site and obtains details from Incident Commander (type of incident, when and where the incident occurred, chemical involved and potential chemical reactions, emergency response personnel on site, number of employees evacuated, any injuries, work performed in the building, what is being done to mitigate the incident, and who the appropriate contacts are and how to reach them).
5. IC Interface calls PR Lead via cellular phone with details of incident. IC Interface should also continue to provide updates to PR Lead every 15–30 minutes or as circumstances change.
6. On-hours, PR Lead immediately notifies and confers with PR Manager (or backup). Off-hours or on weekends, PR Lead immediately notifies

and confers with PR Manager and also notifies the PR Duty Officer. The PR Duty Officer should notify the Switchboard Operators (555–1000) and tell them to direct media inquiries to the person serving as PR Lead.

7. PR Lead and PR Manager agree to key messages and response to query statement.
8. PR Lead or PR Manager notifies Corporate PR Manager.
9. PR Lead prepares response to query statement, confers with division management, and obtains approval of statement.
10. PR Lead sends statement via fax to PR Manager and to Corporate PR Manager.
11. PR Manager informs PR Operations Manager and PR-VP (or acting PR chief) to review the incident, determine the need for additional on-site support, and decide whether the PR news bureau should be opened if it is after working hours. PR-VP decides at this point if executives need to be notified.
12. PR Lead or PR Manager informs Internal Communications Manager who ensures that appropriate internal communications staff will work closely with Division Communications personnel in collecting data for a timely report to employees.
13. PR Lead and PR Backup serve as prime contacts for media. PR Manager and Corporate PR Manager serve as backups.
14. PR Lead determines if on-site media center is needed and designates PR Backup to set one up.
15. PR Lead continues to receive information from IC Interface and updates statements accordingly.
16. PR Lead, in turn, provides updates to PR Manager and PR Corporate Manager.
17. PR Lead, PR Manager, and PR Operations Manager confer on whether a press release is needed. If so, PR Lead writes the release and clears it with division management and PR Manager. PR Manager clears release with PR Operations Manager, PR-VP, and other senior officials as required.
18. PR Manager and/or Division PR Lead develop report analyzing communications aspects of the incident and lessons learned. Report is distributed to PR Operations Manager and PR-VP, Division Communications staff, and Corporate PR Manager.

Emergency Operations Center (EOC) Activation

An Emergency Operations Center (EOC) is a centralized location from which emergency response during a very severe crisis is coordinated and directed. A crisis that would force the site EOC to be engaged would be an earthquake or other incident (such as an act of terrorism) that causes multiple crises at once. Senior emergency preparedness personnel in the company contend that site EOCs along with the Corporate EOC would not be fully activated for a minimum of 2–3 hours after the devastating event (i.e., first tremors during an earthquake).

If the site EOC is engaged, all crisis communications would be directed from that point. For adequate communication response, it is recommended that two communicators should be assigned to the center. One communicator would serve as the Communications Manager responsible for coordinating external and internal communications, which may include the use of a runner system, in the event all electronic means of communications are out. The other communicator would serve as the Information Officer, responsible for documenting the sequence of events in support of communications and then generating any statements for release, either internally or externally.

Each site EOC will be equipped with maps, stationery supplies, white boards, flip charts, viewfoil machines (transparency projectors), telephones, and numerous other supplies. It is recommended that communicators make sure the following items are either stored in the EOC or are available nearby.

- pads and pencils;
- laptop computer(s);
- portable printer(s) or some other printing device, with paper;
- fax machine;
- cellular phone(s);
- radio(s);
- Division Crisis Communications Plan.

The procedure for communications response should be consistent with the procedure for handling a major crisis, the only difference being that all communications would be directed from the EOC itself.

The best and most effective means of communication may depend on the nature of the crisis. For example, if a crisis has destroyed or destabilized more conventional channels of communication, then alternative means of communication—including text messaging, an organization's intranet, or social media—may be a primary channel of communication. In extreme situations where most lines of communication are down or overloaded, volunteer amateur (ham) radio operators may be called upon to aid in long-distance communication.

Identification of a Spokesperson

After an initial assessment of an emergency, the Division General Manager (or designee, such as an outplant general manager) will identify the appropriate spokesperson for the division.

Appropriate spokespeople for most divisions are as follows.

- Division Vice President/General Manager;
- Plant General Manager (for other sites under division jurisdiction);
- Division Health Manager;
- Division Environmental Manager;
- Division Safety Manager;
- Director of Facilities;
- Division Communications Manager;
- Public Relations Manager;
- Corporate Public Relations Manager.

All releases of information outside the division and company shall be by or through the coordinated efforts of Division Communications, Group, and/or Corporate public relations personnel (as noted in the Communications Procedure for Handling Minor or Major Crises). Whenever possible, encourage the various inquiring publics to consult your organization's website for the most up-to-date and accurate content. Decisions must be made by the crisis communications team about the appropriate use of social media as channels of communication with publics.

All releases of information within the division will be coordinated by Division Communications personnel.

Guidelines for Spokespeople

1. *Do not speculate.* Always stick to the facts. A more in-depth investigation is required to determine cause.
2. *Focus on two or three key messages to communicate, and repeat them during the interview.* Keep answers short and to the point. TV reporters want "sound bites" of no more than 10–15 seconds. Try to bridge to your key messages throughout the interview.
3. *Use a technical expert.* There is no substitute for knowledge. If the questions are outside your area of expertise, find an appropriate technical spokesperson within the company.
4. *Speak in simple, common terms.* Avoid jargon.
5. *Remain calm.* Do not be intimidated into answering questions prematurely. You may tell a reporter that you need to clarify an important matter before you can answer questions.
6. *Do not use negative language.* Do not let reporters put words in your mouth.
7. *Consider human safety first.* When human safety or other serious concerns are involved, deal with those considerations first. You can admit concern without admitting culpability.
8. *Do not answer questions you do not understand.* Ask for clarification. Occasionally, this can be used to buy time to think.

9. *Ignore cameras and microphones.* Face the reporter. Don't look away or up at the sky. During videotaped interviews, it is acceptable to stop your statement and start over.
10. *Make only "on the record" statements.* There are no "off the record" statements.
11. *Avoid saying, "No comment."* If you don't know an answer, say so, then bridge to your messages.

Format for Briefing Someone Identified as a Spokesperson for Interviews/News Briefings

Executives scheduled to talk to the media should be provided a background briefing in advance of the interview. This policy should be followed even if the interview is only to be a brief telephone call.

The briefing should include the following 11 items.

- date, time, and location of the interview;
- name of the reporter;
- name of the publication, wire service, station, and so on;
- our experience with the reporter or publication—to help the executive understand the degree of caution needed in this interview and to prepare for the specific reporter's approach;
- subjects/issues/questions to be covered as requested by the reporter;
- our position or recommended response and the data needed to discuss these subjects;
- top 3–5 messages we wish to make in the interview (not necessarily based on the reporter's suggested topics);
- list of other executives to be interviewed during this visit, including key topics and messages you suggest the other executives cover;
- issues, if any, that the executive(s) should avoid, and recommendations on how to sidestep them;
- background information/statistics that would be useful in preparing for the interview;
- proposed length of interview.

If possible, this background material should be conveyed in writing so the executive(s) have a chance to review it carefully. Only under exceptional circumstances should you rely on an oral briefing.

In critical situations, it is also useful to prepare a thorough set of questions and answers to define the organization's positions and to use in rehearsing with the executive.

News Release

During an emergency situation, it may be determined that a news release should be distributed to the media. The purpose of the news release is to convey written information on the incident and to avoid misinterpretation. News releases are increasingly also made available on an organization's website and social media platforms.

Circumstances That May Require a News Release

- an accident, fire, or explosion that results in serious injury, death, or considerable property damage;
- a health or environmental incident, or discovery of a health or environmental hazard that may affect employees, the surrounding community, or the environment;
- a serious traffic or air accident involving company vehicles, products, and/or personnel;
- sabotage, abduction or extortion, bomb threats, or acts of terrorism involving company personnel, products, or property;
- news of an incident that is likely to be known by employees or circulated in the community and create misleading impressions;
- news of an event that is unusual enough to cause concern to employees, nearby residents, or community officials;
- consistently misleading news reports.

Writing an Initial Statement for Release

Often, reporters will call before all the facts have been gathered. In such an instance, a simple statement acknowledging the situation is useful. The short statement avoids "no comment" and acknowledges that our company recognizes the need to cooperate with the media.

Examples follow.

Our company is responding to the situation [or name the emergency]. We have trained and experienced people on site working on the situation.

Our first priority is the safety of our employees and the public. We are gathering information, and as soon as details become available, we will inform the media through regular news conferences and updates to our organization's website.

Information Appropriate for Release

During an emergency situation, there will be information that is appropriate to release to employees and to the media. Communications personnel should do the following.

- *Tell what happened*: give a description of the emergency situation.
- *Tell who is involved*: Report how many employees were evacuated and if any have been taken to the hospital for observation or due to injury.

Report when emergency team members and/or the various city or county fire departments and police arrived on the scene (if applicable).

- *Indicate where it occurred*: give the street address of the scene of the emergency.
- *Identify when it happened*: Give the time the incident began.

Information That Is Not Appropriate for Release

Obviously, there will be a lot of information that is not appropriate for release until more is known about the nature of the crisis response and the extent of the impact.

- *Do not speculate on why the emergency occurred or what type of hazardous materials are involved.* Likewise, don't make any statement that blames any individual for the accident. (Although the cause of the incident may appear obvious, it cannot be accurately determined without an extensive investigation, nor can the blame be placed on an individual without a thorough investigation.)
- *Do not include "off the record" information* because there is no such information.
- *Do not overreact to or exaggerate the situation.* For instance, during a hazardous material spill, a reporter may ask for the "worst-case scenario" of what could happen with the chemicals involved in the accident. It is impossible to determine this until you have specific data regarding the hazardous chemicals involved. Bridge back to facts and messages.
- *Do not minimize the situation.* Never regard an emergency as a minor incident.
- *Do not release the names of injured individuals,* unless the Human Resources department has authorized it following confirmation that the family or families of victim(s) have been notified.
- *Do not release dollar estimates concerning the extent of property damage.* Normally, there is no way to accurately determine this until extensive studies have been conducted.
- *Avoid the "no comment" response because it often leads the reporter to speculate.* If you don't know the answer to a reporter's question, or if you can't discuss something, explain why in simple terms.

Writing a News Release

By following a few basic principles when writing news releases, our company stands a better chance of having reporters use the information with only minor changes. Remember to consult the legal department as needed.

1. *Tell the most important information in your lead paragraph.* Your "story" competes with other news and information, so the most important point should be stated clearly in the first paragraph.
2. *Answer four of the "Five Ws"—who, what, where, and when.* Explain *what* the emergency is. Identify *who* is involved in the emergency, as well as the material and equipment involved. Tell *where* and *when* the emergency occurred. Explain *what* action we are taking to mitigate or respond to the emergency. Do not explain *why* the event occurred unless complete information is available.
3. *Attribute information to a qualified source.* A news release is useful only if it conveys credible information.
4. *Write remaining information in descending order of importance.* If the media cuts off the bottom of your story, they will cut information that is least important to the public.
5. *Explain technical points in simple language.* A direct quote can add the human element to otherwise technical information and help explain a situation or event in layman's terms. Tell the real story. Avoid using language that is overly bureaucratic.
6. *Be concise.* A good news release is judged by the quality of information it communicates, not by its length. Stop writing when you've said all you need to say.

Messages for the News Media During Environmental Crises

Mention of the following points during interviews may help the company communicate its position on environmental issues.

- Our primary concern is for the safety of our employees, the communities in which we operate, and the public.
- We operate state-of-the-art safety monitoring and control systems in our factories and laboratories.
- We are prepared at all times to mitigate a chemical spill or leak.
- We work continuously to reduce our use of toxic chemicals in manufacturing processes and to minimize waste.
- Our standards for "worker hazardous materials safety exposure" meet or exceed standards required by the U.S. Occupational Safety and Health Administration (OSHA).

- Our employees who work directly with hazardous materials receive special training in handling the materials safely. It is a mandatory requirement that employees attend such training.
- The company conducts periodic audits of its hazardous materials and hazardous waste installations, equipment, and operating procedures to ensure they comply with environmental regulations and permits during normal and emergency conditions.
- As in the past, the company will continue to work closely with state and federal agencies to meet or exceed environmental regulations, comply with test procedures, and report results to the Environmental Protection Agency (EPA) and the Department of Ecology (DoE).

Publics During a Crisis

To effectively communicate your message, it is essential to understand who your public or audience is and how you want your publics to react.

There are two key types of audiences during an emergency:

1. people directly affected by the emergency;
2. people whose attitudes about the company might be influenced by information about the emergency.

These two types of publics are broken into seven categories. Public Relations objectives in dealing with each of these publics are listed in what follows.

- *Employees*: We want employees to know that their safety is the No. 1 priority during an emergency. Employees need information regarding the emergency as soon as possible. This must be accomplished in a manner that assures employees that the company has their best interests at heart and that it can effectively handle emergencies.
- *Community Residents*: We want to quell any unnecessary fears. We want the surrounding community residents to know that we take quick, effective steps to protect the health and welfare of community residents and the environment. This can be best accomplished by responding quickly to community concerns and need for information.
- *Top Management*: This group needs to be kept informed in the event of an emergency, as well as to be accessible as a resource if necessary.
- *Government Officials*: Key members of this audience need to be kept apprised of the emergency situation, as determined appropriate by the Government Affairs Department.
- *Customers*: Customers need to know that the company is concerned about crises that affect its operating divisions and that may affect production.

- *News Media*: We want the news media to know that the company is credible, concerned, and effective at dealing with emergencies, and that we understand and meet the unique needs of each type of media.
- *Vendors, Contractors, and Suppliers*: We want these audiences to know that we operate state-of-the-art safety monitoring and control systems in our factories and laboratories, and that the company takes quick, effective steps to protect the health and welfare of its employees, vendors, and suppliers.

How People Receive Information During a Crisis

In order to determine the most effective ways of communicating during an emergency, it is important to consider how each key audience potentially can receive information. The following sources of information for each audience must be considered in communications strategy for each emergency.

Employees

- direct knowledge of the event;
- other employees;
- intercom and phone systems;
- managers;
- electronic mail;
- news media reports;
- fire department/police/hospital spokesperson;
- social media;
- intranet.

Community Residents

- direct knowledge of the event;
- neighbors;
- news media reports;
- website;
- social media.

Top Management

- Company Security, Communications/PR Manager;
- personal call(s) from concerned employee(s);
- news media reports;
- social media;
- intranet.

Government Officials

- Government Affairs;
- news media reports;
- concerned or scared citizen(s);
- social media.

News Media

- Public Relations representative;
- police and/or fire scanners;
- other news media;
- fire department/police/hospital spokesperson;
- eyewitnesses, including employees;
- bystanders with knowledge or hearsay;
- firsthand view of the situation;
- outside "experts";
- social media.

Vendors, Contractors, and Suppliers

- direct knowledge of the event;
- employees and/or management;
- news media reports;
- social media.

Tools to Use During a Crisis

The following documents are recommended tools that each communications group can use or adapt to specific requirements. Note that a few of the tools will definitely have to be adapted, such as site map(s), building facts and figures, and phone lists for key emergency response contacts.

These tools can prove very useful for documenting information related to incidents and for keeping track of media inquiries.

- emergency response contacts;
- key division directors/managers;
- key communications/PR contacts;
- incident information sheet;
- telephone log sheet;
- initial release;
- checklist for establishing a news conference center;
- maps of division plants;
- building facts and figures.

INCIDENT INFORMATION SHEET

Complete using ink pen

Date: _____ Time: _____ Initial Report: _____
Update: _____

Describe the incident (i.e., hazardous material spill, equipment malfunction, serious injury, bomb threat, fire, etc.):

Indicate when the incident occurred and when crisis personnel first responded:

Describe which crisis groups are responding:

Indicate where the incident occurred (building number, column number, east or west side of building, etc.):

Describe the work performed in the building(s) where incident occurred (i.e., machining, office functions, mix of factory and office functions):

Estimate the number of employees evacuated:

Estimate the number of employees injured, nature of their injuries (to clarify misleading reports), and where they are being examined/treated (i.e., on-site medical, local hospital):

Describe what is being done to mitigate the emergency:

TELEPHONE LOG SHEET

Priority: _____ Date: _____ Time: _____

Call received from:

Name _____

Organization _____

Location _____

Message:

_____

_____

_____

_____

_____

Call back by:

Date: _____ Time: _____

Notes:

_____

_____

_____

_____

_____

_____

EXAMPLE OF INITIAL STATEMENT FOR RELEASE

At approximately _____ (time) today _____ (date), a _____ (fire, explosion, etc.) occurred on the _____ site of the _____ Division.

Crisis Response personnel are now responding as well as _____ _____ (other support response groups or local municipalities). Our company's response groups include (list appropriate groups such as fire and security officers, medical doctors and nurses, safety personnel, industrial hygienists, environmental engineers, etc.).

_____

_____

_____

_____

Our major concerns are for the safety of our employees and the public and to minimize environmental impact.

We are now involved in determining what has happened and what is being done to mitigate the situation. As more details become available, we will pass them on to the media.

CHECKLIST FOR ESTABLISHING A NEWS CONFERENCE CENTER

In a major emergency, it may be necessary to establish a news conference center. This will be where the company can conduct briefings or news conferences, grant interviews, and issue official statements.

Because time is of the essence during a crisis, communications teams should designate certain locations as potential news conference centers and be prepared to carry out the checklist before an incident occurs.

Increasingly, news conferences can be streamed live on social media platforms like YouTube and Facebook. They can also be conducted on Zoom—exclusively or in hybrid form (simultaneously on Zoom and in person).

Preliminaries

1. Check for the best time with company spokesperson.
2. Notify media of time and location.
3. Compile list of names of reporters and editors who indicate they will attend.
4. Compile background information of interest to reporters.
5. Invite outside officials as appropriate.
6. Assign someone to handle the physical arrangements for the news conference.

   - Video services to record event?
   - Junction box for TV and radio mics?
   - Chairs, tables, podiums as required?

7. Brief staff on the subject, speaker(s), and schedule of events.
8. Prepare opening statement and review with lead speaker.
9. Review anticipated questions and answers with the speaker.
10. Check all sound equipment and voice recorders prior to the conference.
11. Place log sheet in conference room to obtain names and affiliations of attendees.
12. Place all news information and handout materials in conference room.

    - New releases.
    - Background information, such as fact sheets, maps, statistics, histories, and biographical information.
    - Copy of opening statement and other briefing materials.

13. Escort the media to the conference room.
14. Use sign-in sheet.
15. Distribute background materials.
16. Have assigned staff member open the conference and establish the ground rules.
17. Monitor questions and answers closely. Make any necessary clarifications before the end of the event.

Afterward/Follow-Up

18. Handle requests for follow-up information.
19. Monitor coverage received; contact any news organization that has an error in its report.
20. At an appropriate time, when the crisis atmosphere has cleared, contact reporters who attended and ask them what went well in terms of our handling the event and what could have been improved.

The news conference center is synonymous with the crisis command center.

Crisis Contacts

	Office	Cellular	Fax	Home
Key Division Directors				
Jennifer Jones (South)	555-0001	C: 555-4892	555-8101	555-9801
Kourtney Johnson (North)	555-0121	C: 555-4241	555-8294	555-9123
Rebecca Arnold (East)	555-2127	C: 555-4101	555-8711	555-9777
Jeremy Kahlil (West)	555-3122	C: 555-4801	555-8222	555-9554
Key Division Managers				
Mary Bland (South)	555-0092	C:555-1121	555-8111	555-9682
John Jackson (South)	555-0013	C: 555-6101	555-8221	555-9319
Sarah Yerima (North)	555-1764	N/A	555-8811	555-9276
Jonathan Kyle (East)	555-2809	N/A	555-8611	555-9211
Allison Millet (East)	555-2684	N/A	555-8314	555-9013
Nicholas Michael (West)	555-3093	N/A	555-8781	555-9901
Telephone Operators				
Mary Jackson (Supervisor)	555-2999	N/A	555-8722	555-3994
Fire Dispatch				
Adam Yerima	555-8894	C: 555-8676	555-9467	555-9276
Duane Troy	555-9075	C: 555-0328	555-5541	555-0101
Safety Manager				
Ron Nelson	555-1112	C: 555-3434	555-6875	555-0841
Julius Jones, Jr.	555-3756	C: 555-4441	555-1954	555-2395
Medical				
Ethan Floyd	555-7864	C: 555-3321	555-7764	555-1346
Allyson Bernardino	555-9090	C: 555-8341	555-5603	555-7651
Demetria Rudy	555-5642	C: 555-2390	555-6678	555-6431
Public Relations				
Nelson Johnson II	555-7490	C: 555-4431	555-5505	555-6490
Jerry Brown	555-7456	C: 555-2210	555-9898	555-7069
Corporate Public Relations				
Gina Arnold	555-8754	C: 555-7890	555-2479	555-0956
South				
Regina Arnold	555-8754	C: 555-7890	555-2479	555-0956
Blair Liggins	555-0293	C: 555-7902	555-2478	555-9154
North				
Kourtney Johnson	555-0121	C: 555-4241	555-8294	555-9123
Myrtle Jenkins	555-2123	C: 555-4545	555-9045	555-8456
East				
Beleria Fulks	555-2345	C: 555-7690	555-3147	555-9067
Anthony Hill	555-0789	C: 555-4680	555-4896	555-3558
West				
Anne Burford	555-1212	C: 555-0097	555-7847	555-0321
O. M. Thornton	555-9557	C: 555-4502	555-5575	555-3498
Katie Marsh (Backup)	555-9057	N/A	555-0092	555-2664

These are fictional contacts. When area codes are needed, they should be listed, also email addresses and text messaging when appropriate.

Appendix B

Sample Crisis Communications Plan for a Non-Profit (Originally for Seattle's Union Gospel Mission)

What Is a Crisis?

A crisis is a significant event that threatens the Mission's reputation, credibility, or financial situation and one that triggers the news media to investigate and report on.

Often, a crisis will be defined in the way that staff respond and react to media. Accurate and relevant information is the key to resolving any public relations crisis. Impressions are locked in an hour after the crisis hits. First impressions are important! It is critical that you demonstrate your caring about the people involved in the crisis and that you are responsive to questions. Keep to the facts but try to humanize those facts with story.

Examples follow.

Felonies/Misdemeanors

- sexual assault/molestation by a volunteer, staff, or resident;
- physical abuse allegations;
- assault or murder;
- any incidents dealing with a weapon;
- criminal activity by guest, resident, or staff;
- criminal activity by someone outside the Mission but affecting the Mission;
- issues surrounding domestic violence.

Disease/Sickness

- spread of disease (e.g. Ebola, SARS, TB, swine flu);
- food poisoning/E. coli on a mass scale;
- infestation of insects (bed bugs; cockroaches, etc.).

Complaints

- lawsuits that go public;
- inquiries regarding mandatory chapel and Bible studies;
- denial of services to an individual (who goes to the media);
- child abandonment during a field trip;
- fundraising abuse allegations.

Other

- fire/natural disaster;
- suicide;
- disgruntled employees or residents;
- malicious, harmful, false rumors that go viral on social media.

Notification Procedure

In the event of an emergency/crisis, the employee in charge *must notify* their *program director* and *the Mission's Public Relations Manager* immediately with all the details of the situation.

Step 1

- Notify Program Directors and Public Relations Manager. If Public Relations Manager is not available, then contact Chief Program Officer who will act as Public Relations Manager.
- Public Relations Manager will gather facts from Mission staff about the incident and inform human resources director to alert internal audiences.
- A media Spokesperson will be identified by the Public Relations Manager in consultation with senior staff if needed.

Step 2

Program Directors Call and Instruct Their Front Desk Personnel

Program directors call and instruct their front desk personnel on procedures to handle incoming calls about the crisis. The Public Relations Manager will distribute talking points and contact information to Program Directors.

Front Desks

Administration: 206.723.0767
Men's Shelter: 206.622.5177

Hope Place: 206.628.2008
Serve Seattle: 206.322.6801
Riverton Place: 206.242.5585

Public Relations Manager Notifies Mission's Executive Team

Responsibilities of Crisis Communications Team

- Investigate and examine the crisis situation and disseminate information to the Public Relations Manager.
- Answer phone calls from targeted audiences and take messages from reporters who are calling so that the spokesperson can get back to them in a timely manner.
- Work with Public Relations Manager and Director of Marketing on the development of messaging as information is obtained.
- Monitor communication channels about incident, including social media platforms. This will make sure messaging is being perceived accurately to the crisis and minimize rumors.

Crisis Procedure

1. Spokesperson is designated by President or Public Relations Manager.
2. Message development is determined by Public Relations Manager and Director of Marketing. Messages will be deployed by marketing team in all appropriate communication channels.
3. Public Relations Manager or the designated person will research and obtain all pertinent information; distribute to their spokesperson, executive staff, and reporters; and work with marketing department to add it to all Mission channels (Mission website, social media, e-blasts, YouTube, and all other communications to target audiences). The purpose is to keep all target audiences updated on current information so that accurate information is available to the public and to help dispel rumors.
4. Public Relations Manager and/or Director of Marketing will prepare a statement/news release and get approval for its release.
5. The Mission's Video Specialist will record a public statement by the spokesperson. This video will be uploaded to Mission website, Facebook, and YouTube platforms.
6. Determine accessibility vs. news conference route to inform media. If accessibility is chosen, the Public Relations Manager or a designated Mission staffer will make sure that media personnel are escorted at all times.
7. Public Relations Manager and Mission marketing staff will continually update target audiences and media on all new developments.

8. Public Relations Manager and Mission marketing staff will decide the appropriate use of social media for communication with both internal and external audiences, and will monitor social media channels (internal and external) for inaccurate, misleading, or false information.

Targeted Audiences

INTERNAL

1. staff members;
2. board members;
3. volunteers;
4. residents/participants in programs.

EXTERNAL

5. donors;
6. media (including bloggers);
7. Facebook fans;
8. general public;
9. vendors..

Guidelines for Handling Reporters

1. Refer all news inquiries to spokesperson(s) designated by Public Relations Manager.
2. Do *not* volunteer an opinion or make a statement to any media inquiries. "Off the top of my head," "they told me that," etc., answers are detrimental. State only factual information.
3. Make sure someone is monitoring the situation and escorting people away from the incident and reporters. Reporters tend to want to talk to people unofficially, and this is unadvisable.
4. Spokesperson obligations:

   - Respond immediately to media requests (helps prevent rumors from starting).
   - Be factual—only offer factual information you have at that time. If the media asks a question and you do not know the answer, tell them you will get back to them.
   - Offer empathy (if applicable) when speaking to the media, especially when something tragic affects another individual.
   - Take responsibility on behalf of the Mission, if applicable. Do not say "no comment" or "off the record"—say instead that the Mission

is looking into that matter and as soon as we can get an answer, we will get back to you.

- If you can't answer the questions, explain why.
- Don't be evasive or misleading—make short factual statements.
- Never speculate—just state the facts that are known at that moment.
- Don't make light of incidents or accidents.
- Don't place blame—just state the facts that are known at that moment.
- Eliminate jargon—use simple words that everyone can understand.
- Don't make promises you can't keep.
- Provide evidence, if applicable.
- Don't give names of dead or injured until the family is notified.
- Don't offer any humor or off-the-cuff impressions.

After the Immediate Crisis Communications, Consider the Following

- Running a full-age ad with a simple, heartfelt apology from the president with his photo and his promise to make things work.
- Having Mission president contact people affected immediately.
- Putting apology, explanations in receipt stuffers, website, social media, blogs, emails, and/or editorials.

Follow-Up

1. Issue a final statement regarding resolutions to prevent a reoccurrence (if appropriate) to the media.
2. Public Relations Manager conducts a de-brief meeting to include senior leadership, program staff affected, marketing, and Mission spokesperson.
3. Compile a record of crisis and the Mission's response (i.e. include newspaper clippings, radio/TV reports, and online accounts).
4. Determine if and how the situation could have been dealt with in a better fashion. *Any personnel changes/actions need to be made immediately.*

Appendix C

Crisis Communications Plan for a Cyberattack

ICTs Are Part of Everyday Life in Businesses

Most companies these days rely on information and communication technologies (ICTs) in some capacity for their day-to-day operations. For example, employees routinely use email for both internal and external communications on desktop computers, laptops, or hand-held devices like smart phones.

Company databases usually contain personal and confidential information about customers, including their financial information, as well as on employees and contractors.

Thousands—if not millions—of documents on a wide variety of topics are created, stored, and retrieved on a continuing basis either on company hard drives or in data "clouds" in remote locations.

Websites and social media are used to engage with publics and facilitate or increase business transactions and have become an essential part of business marketing and strategic communications.

Budgets, spreadsheets, inventories, orders, invoices, accounts payable, sales data, balances, shipping information, customer feedback, company policies, and so on, are typically saved, processed, and retrieved using computer software and hardware and transmitted over both wired and wireless computer networks.

Company executives, managers, and other employees rely on ICT to make and communicate decisions at all levels of the organization's operations. A substantial part of a company's success rests on its information and communication technology infrastructure.

No doubt, ICTs have made it easier to digitize and automate a lot of the work that was at one time the domain of hard copy materials like ledgers, paper documents, envelopes, stamps, and writing instruments. A company's heavy reliance on ICTs, however, can also make it vulnerable to cybercrime, an umbrella term that encompasses a wide range of illegal actions that have the potential to seriously harm customers, employees, and brand reputations—and by extension erode public trust in the safety and security of ICTs in business settings and electronic commerce.

Types of Cybercrimes

Examples of cybercrimes include hacking—or gaining unauthorized access to a company's secure computer system—and stealing personal, confidential information such as customers' or employees' contact information, credit card or bank account numbers, Social Security numbers, passwords, birthdates, private health information, and whatever else is maintained in a company's databases.

Another cybercrime is the installation of malicious software—or "malware"—in some part of a company's computer system. This malware has the potential to damage or compromise the security of a company's computers and its computer system through the use of things you have likely heard or read about in the news: ransomware, computer viruses like a Trojan horse virus, spyware, adware, worms, and so forth. These attacks on computer systems are harmful to different degrees and are done by different entities for different reasons, but they are all malicious and potentially very destructive, not only to computer systems but also to a sense of safety and security of those who use those systems.

For better or worse, people put a tremendous amount of confidence in the ability of a company to protect information that they do not want to fall into the wrong hands. The reality is that even the most advanced and sophisticated security protections on a computer system can become victim to cybersecurity attacks. It has happened to highly secure federal government computers in the United States, to international organizations, to small retail outlets, and to major multinational corporations. The goal of building more robust and effective cybersecurity programs has been undertaken by numerous companies and organizations, but the ability of malicious programmers to break through those protections has also evolved alongside those efforts.

While it is expected that companies will do everything in their power to protect the personal, confidential information that they collect and store, customers who provide that information can do their part by following in earnest the recommendations about creating difficult-to-guess passwords, or "passphrases," and never sharing them with others, changing passwords at appropriate intervals or as needed, using multifactor authentication when available (some systems now require this) to require more than one form of verification, not using the same password for different accounts, and keeping security protection and other software updated to benefit from the latest protections.

Be Careful What You Share Online

Of course, there are many ways today to share information about oneself and one's contacts on the Internet, especially through social media like Facebook, Twitter, Instagram, and so forth. Be judicious in what personal information—including photos—you put out into the world through cyberspace.

Be suspicious of any inquiries for personal information by email, phone, private messaging, etc. Don't click on suspicious or unknown links and attachments. Learn about how to identify phishing scams, which are prevalent, as cybercriminals attempt to use deception to gain personal, confidential information. Some scams are easier to identify than others because the messages or graphics they use do not appear professionally done, and the sender's email does not appear to be who the sender claims to be. But some phishing scams are sophisticated and even careful computer users may be fooled by them.

Most company and personal computers already have anti-virus software on them, but some personal computers need to have them installed. Use trusted anti-virus software to avoid fakes that could themselves cause problems on the systems they purport to help. Back up data regularly in case of accidental or intentional damage or disablement. The "cloud" refers to digital content that is stored and accessed using computer networks and is one form of backing up data, but there are other methods such as external hard drives and company-based servers. There are advantages and disadvantages to any form of digital storage. What they share in common is the need for strong protection against hacking.

WannaCry

In 2017, a ransomware threat called WannaCry spread globally. Users unknowingly downloaded ransomware onto their computers by clicking on an attachment, for example, or were attacked in other ways due to their computer's vulnerabilities. This kind of malicious software infects a computer system, locking up files on it. Cybercriminals then demand payment in some form to unlock the files. WannaCry was widespread and dangerous. It affected many different computer systems around the world, including hospitals, disrupting services. News reports everywhere helped educate the public about ransomware at the time and about how to avoid falling victim to this particularly malicious one. The solution involved updating software that contained patches to the software's flaws and vulnerabilities.

Update: IT Protections

Most companies large and small have someone—or an entire department—dedicated to managing the information technology (IT) infrastructure, including keeping that infrastructure safe from cyberattacks. These IT professionals should remain current about the latest threats and solutions, but employees also need to be vigilant and adhere to the IT professionals' guidance about cybersecurity. Employees should also immediately report any abnormalities with the computer system. Just like in a neighborhood in the real world, residents are often the first ones to notice suspicious behavior and are asked by neighborhood security watch groups to report these observations to the police immediately. The same can be said for the online workplace. If a suspicious email is sent to an employee, for example, that email should be reported to the organization's IT contact without clicking on any links or attachments. If an employee has already clicked on a link or attachment, the necessity to contact IT becomes even more urgent.

Preparing a Cyberattack Crisis Communication Plan

Despite all the efforts that companies and customers do to protect personal, confidential information, those efforts may not be enough to stop cyberattacks from occurring. In preparing a crisis communication plan, companies should always include a cyberattack scenario that seriously compromises the company's cybersecurity, causing widespread problems such as exposing customer or employee information to unknown adversaries and triggering a public relations crisis. Keep in mind that cybercriminals could be adversarial individuals, groups, and/or even governments. They are often not easy to identify because of their ability to disguise their origins, locations, and identities.

Exercise: Three Scenarios

Cybersecurity breaches are varied in their manifestations. To practice crisis response to a cyberattack, try to recall or search for news stories that refer to actual cybersecurity breaches and how they were handled. As an exercise here, imagine these three scenarios, filling in details as needed in your mind.

1. You are the director of marketing and public relations at a major metropolitan hospital. The head of the IT department at the hospital informs you and senior administration that a cyberattack occurred three hours ago but was just detected. It appears that the names and personal

clinical information of past and current patients in the hospital's psychiatric center were accessed for unknown reasons.

2. You are the principal at a local high school. An unknown person or persons hacked into the school's website and left a threatening message on the school's home page indicating that a violent crime may be in the planning stages and cryptically warns readers of the website to "BEWARE."

3. You are the communications director for a city government. You learn that about 200 city employees were sent a phishing message that appeared legitimate and asked employees to click a link and then enter their login and password to view time-sensitive salary information from the city's Human Resources department. About 75 employees clicked on the link and entered the information requested, only to learn that they were victims of a phishing scam and were tricked into providing login and password information to an entity or entities unrelated to the city government.

In all of these cases, the hospital, school, and city government must immediately go into crisis communication mode. Fortunately, all three organizations anticipated computer hacking as a possible crisis when they were developing their crisis management and communication plans. All three also believed their computer systems were secure, although the school admits that it may not have been completely up to date on its software. It is clear that the school ranked computer hacking of its website as having a low probability and so was lax on its timely updating of its website and other software, and did not rehearse for such a scenario, which made its website unnecessarily vulnerable to hacking. In each case, the news media were alerted to the security breaches and reporters are calling and appearing on site wanting their questions answered. The reality is that at this point in the investigation, there is not much to report except to state the facts. The implications of the cyberattacks have yet to be seen.

All three organizations understand that it should convey to the media that they care about its (a) patients; (b) students; and (c) employees, respectively. They identify a spokesperson to speak on behalf of the organization to convey this message, but the spokesperson and the crisis communication team—whose names are contained in a previously created directory—will together reach consensus about what information should be shared at this time and make sure that it is accurate, as well as anticipate any additional information and topics that the reporters may ask about.

Each case will have some different specifics, but there are some commonalities as well that can be shared here as recommendations.

Recommendations

1. Be sure that your crisis communication plan is printed out on paper. Cyberattacks to the organization's computer system may disable that system, either voluntarily (to avoid further breaches) by the IT department or involuntarily (as the result of malicious software). Plans solely kept in the computer system may not be accessible after a cyberattack.
2. Be sure that all the information the spokesperson(s) release to the public is authorized and accurate. Avoid speculating off the cuff, as reporters may ask—or pressure—you to do. You may misspeak and provide misinformation if forced to speculate under pressure. If you do not know the answer to a question, let reporters know that you will try to find out the information and get back to them. Alternatively, let reporters know that you are not able to discuss certain details at this time due to the ongoing investigation.
3. Acknowledge to reporters that you are providing information that is currently available so they can do their news stories. It is likely that more information will be available later, and you will share it at that time.
4. State the facts as you know them and as have been approved by the crisis management team. Reporters want to know the who, what, when, where, why, and how. You may not be able to answer all of these questions, but you can provide them with a fact-based lead such as:

   This morning at approximately 9:30 a.m., we detected a security breach in one part of our computer system. The names and clinical information of some of our patients may have been exposed during this breach. At this time we do not know the reason that this information was accessed by an unauthorized person or persons.

5. Then explain, "However, this is what we have done and what we are currently doing." Then state in simple, clear terms the procedures put in place to deal with this breach. Explain how you are helping those affected by the breach. In the city's case, for example, all logins and passwords were immediately changed upon learning of the phishing scam. In the school's case, the website was taken offline and relevant local school and law enforcement authorities immediately contacted to report the threat and seek guidance. In the hospital's case, strict protocols were followed regarding the unauthorized access of protected patient information.
6. Identify the relevant local, state, and/or federal law enforcement or regulatory bodies the organization is working in cooperation with.

Within the organization, there may be certain individuals who need to be on speed dial, such the hospital's HIPAA privacy officer or chief privacy officer, an individual responsible for overseeing adherence to the institution's privacy policies and procedures in regard to protected health information in compliance with federal and state laws. HIPAA stands for the Health Insurance Portability and Accountability Act, a 1996 U.S. federal law intended to protect sensitive patient health information.

7. Identify any other relevant person or organization you are working with regarding this matter, if appropriate. For example, in the school scenario, working with the parent–teacher organization and school counselors may be sensible. Developing appropriate messaging to parents and a means to deliver that message should be considered ahead of a crisis.

8. What measures are being taken to ensure that the organization's computer system is secured against future attacks? Avoid speaking in absolute terms. Don't say, "We resolve that this kind of breach never happens again in this organization." It is not a promise you can keep with absolute certainty.

9. Express concern and invite open communication with the parties affected, including family members who understandably want answers, too. Open communication does not necessarily mean revealing everything you know. For example, law enforcement may request that certain information be withheld as its investigation gets under way. A spokesperson can refer questions to the appropriate lead in another organization.

10. "This is an ongoing and evolving situation. Our priority is the safety and security of our [patients, employees, students] and to cooperate with the investigation." These are key talking points. Reassuring the public that more information will be released as it becomes available can also be helpful in implementing a thoughtful, careful, and incremental release of information.

11. Anticipate a question from reporters about when the next update may be forthcoming and try to answer realistically. If you don't know, say you don't know but will inform them ahead of the next press conference (and be sure to do it), working off a media contact list that you already have prepared.

As Always, Be Prepared

Breaches of an organization's cybersecurity are not uncommon. Sometimes the consequences of the breach are minimal or unknown; other times, it might be catastrophic. As with other types of crises identified in this text, a well–thought-out crisis management and communication plans must be prepared well ahead of the crisis. Expect cyberattacks as a modern-day threat to businesses and organizations. Preparation and planning will enable the organization to hopefully recover quickly after an attack, reassuring the organization's publics of the its resilience and ability to control and contain the crisis, react competently to public concerns, mitigate risk of adverse consequences, communicate to key stakeholders, and protect the company's or organization's brand and reputation from irreparable harm and public scorn.

The COVID-19 pandemic that began in 2020 ushered in an era of teleworking and teleconferencing at a level unprecedented in world history. Many employees, students, and friends connected to each other via audio/video/phone chat platforms like Zoom. A phenomenon known as "Zoom bombing" emerged when an unauthorized person or persons intrude on Zoom meetings with the intention to disrupt those meetings through inappropriate behavior and sometimes content. These acts may appear to be more immature pranks than cyberattacks, but these disruptive intrusions are both technical and social violations that can have harmful consequences, including interruptions to workflow. Participants in teleconferences should be aware of the potential for unauthorized entry of uninvited individuals and take steps to safeguard information in Zoom invites. The Zoom meeting host can also impose technical restrictions that help ensure that only those invited to a meeting will be allowed into the meeting.

Use the information in this textbook to envision a wide variety of scenarios that result in an organizational crisis due to a cyberattack. As pointed out earlier in this section, cybersecurity is not just the responsibility of the company or organization that owns and operates the computer system. People on the user-end also contribute to cybersecurity through sensible practices that enhance privacy and account security. All members of an organization play a role in cybersecurity by doing all they can to minimize risk of a cyberattack, but once that security is breached, they also play a role in helping the company recover and resume operations through effective crisis management and communication plans.

Index